Retrench, Defend, Compete

A VOLUME IN THE SERIES

Cornell Studies in Security Affairs

Edited by Austin Carson, Alexander B. Downes, Elizabeth N. Saunders, Paul Staniland, and Caitlin Talmadge

Founding Series Editors: Robert J. Art, Robert Jervis, and Stephen M. Walt

A list of titles in this series is available at www.cornellpress.cornell.edu.

Retrench, Defend, Compete

Securing America's Future Against a Rising China

CHARLES L. GLASER

Cornell University Press

Ithaca and London

Copyright © 2025 by Charles L. Glaser

All rights reserved. Except for brief quotations in a review, this book, or parts thereof, must not be reproduced in any form without permission in writing from the publisher. For information, address Cornell University Press, Sage House, 512 East State Street, Ithaca, New York 14850. Visit our website at cornellpress.cornell.edu.

First published 2025 by Cornell University Press

Librarians: A CIP catalog record for this book is available from the Library of Congress.

ISBN 9781501784842 (hardcover)
ISBN 9781501784859 (paperback)
ISBN 9781501784866 (pdf)
ISBN 9781501784873 (epub)

GPSR EU contact: Sam Thornton, Mare Nostrum Group B.V., Mauritskade 21D, 1091 GC, Amsterdam, NL, gpsr@mare-nostrum.co.uk.

Contents

Preface and Acknowledgments vii

Introduction 1

PART I. INTERNATIONAL RELATIONS THEORY AND CHINA'S RISE

1. Realism and China's Rise 31
2. State-Level Theories and China's Rise 74

PART II. US GEOPOLITICAL COMMITMENTS

3. Grand Strategy: Should the United States Retain Its Security Commitments in East Asia? 101
4. Taiwan: Should the United States Maintain Its Commitment? 139
5. South China Sea: How Much Risk Should the United States Run? 183

PART III. US MILITARY STRATEGY

6. Nuclear Strategy: Should the United States Pursue a Damage-limitation Capability? 227

CONTENTS

7. Conventional Strategy: How Much Offense Does the United States Need?   275

   Conclusion   311

   Index   *317*

Preface and Acknowledgments

I spent much of the 2000s writing a book that analyzed the impact of international structure on major powers. Working in the structural-realist tradition, the book's theory explored the conditions under which the system should drive states into competition and conflict and when instead states should be better able to increase their security through restraint and cooperation. The book focused on states that were acting to increase their security and strove to advance the development of what is commonly termed *defensive realism*. In addition, the book explained how states that were motivated to achieve more than security—greedy states—should act given the constraints imposed by the international system and how a security-seeking state should attempt to protect itself against the greedy state. This book was *Rational Theory of International Politics* (RTIP), and the overall argument I developed in it was a rational, strategic choice theory that reaches beyond defensive realism while retaining much of its focus on the dangers of insecurity and the importance of the security dilemma.

By the end of that decade, China's rise was getting a great deal of attention from the national security community, and with good reason. China's economy was growing rapidly, which supported the modernization of its military forces, which in turn were reducing US military dominance in East Asia. China appeared to be on its way to becoming a superpower, if not a truly global peer of the United States. Many international relations theorists and national security experts were pessimistic about China's rise, anticipating intense competition and a growing probability of war. Power transitions and a rising power's desire for regional hegemony were often-cited paths to a major-power conflict.

RTIP offered a more optimistic assessment of the structural pressures that were being generated by China's rise and of the equilibrium that would eventually be reached. The United States would be able to maintain the ability to protect its homeland from invasion and coercion because distance, the Pacific Ocean, and nuclear weapons strongly favored deterrence. Both the United States and China could be highly secure, which would essentially eliminate the international structural pressures that could drive the two countries into conflict.

RTIP's concluding chapter makes this basic point and explains that the dangers created by China's rise would be regional issues, not structure-driven issues. The extent of these dangers would depend on US grand strategy. If the United States retained its security commitments in East Asia, the greatest danger would be over Taiwan, which involved a fundamental disagreement about the status quo. This issue had the potential to strain US-China relations, leading both countries to see the other as quite threatening and fueling conventional and nuclear arms competitions. In addition, the competition itself might cause misperceptions that would make the situation still more precarious.

During the 2010s, the national security challenges posed by China only continued to grow. Following *RTIP*'s publication, I therefore analyzed in much greater length and depth some of the issues that the book's concluding chapter had raised, publishing articles on US nuclear strategy toward China and on an approach for avoiding the dangers posed by the Taiwan issue. I then set out to provide a broader, integrated analysis of how the United States should respond to China in a new book—this book. *Retrench, Defend, Compete* addresses all the key national security issues facing the United States that have been generated by China's rise, provides the theoretical foundation for analyzing them, and explores the interactions between them. It offers a full assessment of US policy options and prescribes a set of policies that have the best prospects for achieving America's national security objectives.

As the 2010s proceeded, I became less optimistic that China would rise peacefully. This was not because I had misevaluated the structural pressures. Instead, I believe that the growing tensions have been fueled primarily by China's increasingly assertive policies, especially in the South China Sea, as well as over Taiwan and Hong Kong, that largely reflect its greedy ambitions. And I believe China has misplayed its hand, as these policies are poorly matched to achieving the country's most important goals. The United States has also contributed to some of the decline in the US-China relationship, most importantly by watering down its "One China" policy during the first Trump and Biden administrations. All this said, even if both countries had pursued more measured policies, Taiwan would have remained a policy problem without any easy solutions. My hope is that *Retrench, Defend, Compete* will advance the debate over China by analyzing policy options that receive too little attention and thereby steer the United States toward improved policies.

Many have contributed to my understanding and the arguments presented in this book over the course of its evolution. I would like first to thank two coauthors who have generously agreed to let me use revised versions of our articles here: Steve Fetter, with whom I wrote on US nuclear strategy toward China, and Taylor Fravel, with whom I wrote on US policy toward the South China Sea. Their knowledge, insights, and analyses play a central role in this book's chapters on those subjects.

For unusually thorough and helpful comments on the entire manuscript, I thank Eric Heginbotham and Stephen Brooks. Both went far beyond reasonable expectations in providing thoughtful, detailed suggestions for how to improve my manuscript. I also thank John Schuessler for very helpful comments, especially on my grand strategy chapter. For valuable feedback on various chapters, I thank Steve Fetter, Taylor Fravel, David Glaser, Lloyd Gruber, and Caitlin Talmadge.

I would also like to thank members of the China and East Asia expert community who, beginning in the early 2010s, were willing to engage with an interloping international relations theorist who needed their help in understanding China and US policy toward East Asia. Among many, I especially thank Fiona Cunningham, Robert Daly, Taylor Fravel, Bonnie Glaser, Avery Goldstein, Eric Heginbotham, Mike Mochizuki, Richard Samuels, David Shambaugh, Robert Sutter, and Michael Swaine.

I thank my former colleagues at the Institute for Security and Conflict Studies and the George Washington University Political Science Department for providing a stimulating and supportive research environment that helped propel my project forward. Following my retirement from GWU, I was especially lucky to have the opportunity to join the Security Studies Program (SSP) at MIT. SSP provided an ideal setting for completing chapters, revising my entire manuscript, and pushing it to publication. I thank Jackie Teoh, my editor at Cornell University Press, for providing truly superb guidance throughout the process of turning my manuscript into this book.

I had the opportunity to present book chapters to numerous audiences and workshops that provided valuable feedback, including the Security Studies Program at MIT, the International Security Center at Notre Dame, the Albritton Center for Grand Strategy at the Bush School at Texas A&M, the Dickey Center for International Understanding at Dartmouth, and the Institute for Security and Conflict Studies at the Elliott School at George Washington.

For comments on articles that I revised for this book, I would like to thank James Acton, Stephen Brooks, Robert Daly, Alex Downes, Amitai Etzioni, David Firestein, Bonnie Glaser, Avery Goldstein, Eric Heginbotham, Daniel Jacobs, Michael Joseph, Austin Long, Michael McDevitt, Evan

PREFACE AND ACKNOWLEDGMENTS

Medeiros, Jim Miller, Mike Mochizuki, Brad Roberts, Ambassador Stapleton Roy, Richard Samuels, David Shambaugh, Walter Slocombe, Robert Sutter, Michael Swaine, Caitlin Talmadge, Chris Twomey, Hugh White, and William Wohlforth. Participants at numerous workshops also provided valuable feedback on these articles, including at the DC International Relations Workshop, the MacMillan International Relations Seminar at Yale University, the Research Program in International Security at Princeton University, the Institute for Security and Conflict Studies workshop at the Elliott School of International Affairs, the Kissinger Institute at the Woodrow Wilson International Center for Scholars, and the MIT Security Studies Asian Security Working Group. For excellent research assistance on these articles, I thank Daniel Jacobs, Cindy Liu, and Shahryar Pasandideh.

I thank MIT Press for giving me permission to publish revised versions of three articles that were originally published in *International Security*: Charles L. Glaser, "A U.S.-China Grand Bargain? The Hard Choice Between Military Competition and Accommodation" *International Security* 39, no. 4 (spring 2015): 49–90; Charles L. Glaser and Steve Fetter, "Should the United States Reject MAD? Damage Limitation and U.S. Nuclear Strategy Toward China," *International Security* 41, no. 1 (summer 2016): 49–98; and M. Taylor Fravel and Charles L. Glaser, "How Much Risk Should the United States Run in the South China Sea?," *International Security* 47, no. 2 (fall 2022): 88–134.

While writing this book, I had the opportunity to spend time away from my regular teaching and administrative capabilities as a fellow at the Kissinger Institute at the Woodrow Wilson International Center for Scholars and as the Roth Family Distinguished Visiting Scholar at Dartmouth. Both provided the invaluable opportunity to immerse myself in research while providing welcoming scholarly environments. In addition to the support provided by these institutions, research funding for a couple of my articles on China was provided by the Carnegie Corporation of New York.

As with my first book, published in 1990, I thank my wife, Carol Carter, for being a loving companion throughout this project and for being patient through many years without weekends. Now that I am retired, I plan not to be working on weekends! And, as with my first book, I dedicate this one to my parents, whose memory continues to keep me centered and cheerful.

Introduction

China's rise presents the United States with difficult foreign policy and defense policy choices. This is not evident, however, in the overwhelming majority of US discussions and analysis. Although the challenges created by China's rise are receiving enormous attention,[1] analysis and debate are taking place largely within strict policy boundaries: The implicit assumption is that the United States should continue to protect all of its interests in East Asia.[2] And, increasingly, the near-consensus approach for protecting these interests is to deepen US commitments and adopt increasingly competitive US military and diplomatic policies. Disagreements tend to be at the margins of these policies.

The challenges that China's rise pose to the United States deserve the enormous attention they are receiving from the US government, international policy experts, and the interested public. Since it began to transform its economy in the 1980s, China has grown to become the world's second-largest economy, greatly expanded and modernized its military forces, and become a manufacturing powerhouse and many countries'

---

1. Among the many important books on this topic, see Avery Goldstein, *Rising to the Challenge: China's Grand Strategy and International Security* (Stanford University Press, 2005); M. Taylor Fravel, *Strong Borders, Secure Nation: Cooperation and Conflict in China's Territorial Disputes* (Princeton University Press, 2008); Aaron L. Friedberg, *A Contest for Supremacy: China, America, and the Struggle for Mastery in Asia* (W. W. Norton, 2011); Andrew J. Nathan and Andrew Scobell, *China's Search for Security* (Columbia University Press, 2012); Thomas J. Christensen, *The China Challenge: Shaping the Choices of a Rising Power* (W. W. Norton, 2015); Elizabeth C. Economy, *The Third Revolution: Xi Jinping and the New Chinese State* (Oxford University Press, 2018); Rush Doshi, *The Long Game: China's Grand Strategy to Displace American Order* (Oxford University Press, 2021); and Susan L. Shirk, *Overreach: How China Derailed Its Peaceful Rise* (Oxford University Press, 2023).

2. This claim glosses over arguments that some academics have made in the debate over grand strategy—as explored in chapter 3, there are analysts who have called for ending the US alliance commitments in Asia. However, their arguments have not focused on the implications of China's rise and are largely separate from the debate over US policy toward China.

largest trading partner.³ There is some debate about how China's power—economic, technological, and human capital—compares with US power and about the future trajectory of China's growth.⁴ But there is no doubt that China has eliminated US military dominance in East Asia by significantly reducing the United States' ability to successfully fight a large war close to China's coast.⁵ Experts now frequently question whether the United States would be able to defend Taiwan.⁶ US prospects for defending its treaty allies—most importantly Japan and South Korea—are significantly better, yet these missions, too, have become more difficult.

Fundamental Reevaluation of US Policy Toward China Is Required

Given the fundamental shift in regional military capabilities and China's growing global capabilities, the United States needs to reevaluate its interests and commitments to protect them, starting from first principles. No state, especially a superpower, wants to contemplate being less influential or less able to pursue its interests. Nevertheless, we should definitely not assume that the United States should retain all of its international commitments. Nor should we assume that the best way for the United States to adapt to China's growing military forces is to adopt more competitive policies, even though China has become more assertive. Yet, both assumptions—preservation of the status quo and competition—pervade current US policy and its foreign policy discourse. A first-principles evaluation does not presuppose that the United States should trim its commitments or

---

3. If measured in purchasing power parity, China is the world's largest economy; see https://data.worldbank.org/indicator/NY.GDP.MKTP.PP.CD?name_desc=false. US gross domestic product per capita still greatly exceeds China's.

4. For works that challenge the argument that China's power is becoming comparable to US power, see Michael Beckley, *Unrivaled: Why America Will Remain the World's Superpower* (Cornell University Press, 2018), and Stephen G. Brooks and William C. Wohlforth, *America Abroad: The United States Global Role in the 21st Century* (Oxford University Press, 2016). More specifically on China's prospects for economic growth, see Michael Pettis, "What Will It Take for China's GDP to Grow at 4–5 Percent Over the Next Decade?," China Financial Markets, Carnegie Endowment (December 4, 2023), https://carnegieendowment.org/china-financial-markets/2023/12/what-will-it-take-for-chinas-gdp-to-grow-at-4-5-percent-over-the-next-decade?lang=en; and Arthur R. Kroeber, "Unleashing 'New Quality Productive Forces': China's Strategy for Technology-led Growth," Brookings (June 4, 2024), https://www.brookings.edu/articles/unleashing-new-quality-productive-forces-chinas-strategy-for-technology-led-growth/. More generally, see Arthur R. Kroeber, *China's Economy: What Everyone Needs to Know*, 2nd ed. (Oxford University Press, 2020).

5. However, on exaggerations of China's military capability in the American debate, see Michael Swaine, *Threat Inflation and the Chinese Military*, Quincy Paper No. 7 (June 2022), https://quincyinst.org/report/threat-inflation-and-the-chinese-military/.

6. See, for example, Demetri Sevastopulo, "US Navy Chief Warns China Could Invade Taiwan Before 2024," *Financial Times*, October 20, 2022. A fuller review is provided in chapter 5.

radically change its grand strategy. But whether the United States should make these changes needs to be put squarely on the analytic table.

US resistance to seriously considering reducing its international goals and commitments is not surprising. A dominant power's first inclination will often be to protect a geopolitical status quo that it helped establish, believes serves its interests, and even imagines is the "proper" international order.[7] Reducing commitments could require curtailing the pursuit of valued interests—for example, in the case of the United States, spreading and protecting democracy via the use of force. Scholars have proffered a variety of arguments to explain why states are unwilling or unable to change their grand strategies or reduce specific commitments.[8] Psychological biases, domestic and bureaucratic politics, and political culture may prevent leaders and analysts from adequately addressing the full array of reasonable policy alternatives. Resistance to changing US grand strategy has been explained as the result of deeply held ideas, shared across the foreign policy establishment, that unduly bound the range of options that can receive serious consideration within the government.[9]

There is an obvious exception to this characterization—President Trump—that requires comment. In his first term and to a still greater degree at the beginning of his second term, Trump has called virtually all of the United States' international commitments into question, including prominently security commitments to US allies. He may be the exception that proves the rule: To severely rattle the basics of US foreign and security policy required a president with tremendous domestic power and strong views but little apparent inclination to analyze them, who is an outsider to the US foreign-policy community. In keeping with his style, Trump has not offered consistent or coherent rationales for changing US international policies. What the broad contours of US foreign and defense policy will look like at the end of his term remains strikingly unclear. Thus, the basic analytic work required by China's rise remains to be done.

---

7. I explore problems with the international-order concept in Charles L. Glaser, "A Flawed Framework: Why the Liberal International Order Concept Is Misguided," *International Security* 43, no. 4 (spring 2019): 51–87.

8. For an overview, see William D. James, "Grand Strategy and the Challenges of Change," in *The Oxford Handbook of Grand Strategy*, ed. Thierry Balzacq and Ronald R. Krebs (Oxford University Press, 2021). Arguing that states have adjusted more frequently and effectively than these arguments suggest are Paul M. Montgomery and Joseph M. Parent, *Twilight of the Titans: Great Power Decline and Retrenchment* (Cornell University Press, 2018), esp. 16–20.

9. Patrick Porter, "Why America's Grand Strategy Has Not Changed: Power, Habit, and the US Foreign Policy Establishment," *International Security* 42, no. 4 (spring 2018): 9–46. See also Ronald R. Krebs, *Narrative and the Making of National Security* (Cambridge University Press, 2015).

INTRODUCTION

STRUCTURE OF THE ANALYSIS

To do this analysis, we need to widen the aperture on US options for responding to China's rise. A state that fails to reevaluate its new international situation may maintain commitments that are too risky—they generate a probability of a large war that is incommensurate with the state's interests. Maybe less important, but still significant, diverting resources to compete effectively against a newly capable adversary could reduce the state's ability to meet its domestic goals. These domestic costs in economic prosperity, health, environmental quality, and social cohesion could exceed the benefits of protecting all of a state's existing international commitments.

In principle, a major power's broad geopolitical options for dealing with a rising power or new peer competitor can span a wide spectrum, ranging from full retrenchment[10]—ending all alliances and partnerships and adopting an isolationist grand strategy—to partial retrenchment and appeasement,[11] to leaving current policies unchanged, to increasing defense spending and seeking allies to preserve the geopolitical status quo, and, finally, to territorial expansion and preventive war.[12] The declining state could also pursue a variety of options for slowing or ending its decline, including investments designed to spur its economic growth and trade policies designed to slow the rising power's growth relative to its own. Some of these options could be combined; for example, a state could reduce some of its commitments—partially retrench—while at the same time increasing defense spending to better protect its remaining commitments, increasing its investments in economic growth, or both.

The declining state's policy should depend partly on the type of adversary it faces. Appeasement is intended to satisfy an adversary that has limited aims, in the hope and expectation that it will thereafter not pursue further expansion. In contrast, retrenchment can be intended simply to avoid

---

10. On retrenchment, see MacDonald and Parent, *Twilight of the Titans*. They use a broader definition of what retrenchment can entail, including cutting defense spending; I focus more narrowly on territorial concessions and allow for an overall policy that involves retrenchment to also include increases in defense spending and alliance commitments.

11. On the range of definitions of appeasement and the logics by which it could work, see Stephen R. Rock, *Appeasement in International Politics* (University Press of Kentucky, 2000), 10–14, and Daniel Treisman, "Rational Appeasement," *International Organization* 58, no. 2 (spring 2004): 345–51. See also Norris M. Ripsman and Jack S. Levy, "Wishful Thinking or Buying Time?: The Logic of British Appeasement in the 1930s," *International Security* 33, no. 2 (fall 2008): 148–81, who use appeasement to cover aspects of retrenchment and explain that it can complement balancing.

12. On the range of options, see Paul K. Macdonald and Joseph M. Parent, "Grand Strategies of Decline," in *The Oxford Handbook of Grand Strategy*, ed. Balzacq and Krebs; Randall L. Schweller, "Managing the Rise of Great Powers: History and Theory," in *Engaging China: The Management of Emerging Powers*, ed. Alastair Iain Johnston and Robert S. Ross (Routledge, 1999); and Robert Gilpin, *War & Change in World Politics* (Cambridge University Press, 1981), chap. 5.

conflict with an adversary, including one that may have unlimited aims, and possibly to redirect resources to protecting interests that are more important and/or easier to protect than the abandoned commitment. Preventive war is intended to enable the state to avoid a future war or concessions when facing a rising power that the state believes is likely to use its growing capabilities to conquer or compel it.

Not all of these options will be available or plausibly reasonable for all declining powers. A declining power may not have the resources to increase defense spending over an extended period while at the same time meeting the essential needs and expectations of its own population. The risks and costs of preventive war may be clearly out of proportion to the threat posed by the rising power, as was certainly the case for the United States facing a rising China. If an adversary is known to have unlimited aims, the state should reject appeasement; partial retrenchment might, however, remain a reasonable option.

The state's best option will depend on a wide range of factors, including the extent of its interests, its current and future power relative to the rising power, the need for resources to meet domestic needs, the difficulty of protecting its own and allies' territory, the extent to which its credibility is connected across issues (can the state reduce some commitments while preserving its credibility for protecting others?), and the state's estimate of the rising state's motives and objectives. In the case of the United States and China, experts disagree about many of these factors. As already noted, there is disagreement about China's growth trajectory. Analysts who believe China's growth is slowing, or even stalling, may be inclined to favor more competitive options or at least to oppose US concessions if they believe advances in China's military capabilities will slow significantly. Analysts who believe China has great ambitions and unlimited aims will be inclined to oppose concessions, while analysts who believe China has limited aims will be more inclined toward concessions and diplomacy.

This book's first analytic task is to assess these options for the United States as it adjusts to China's rise in the face of important uncertainties. To foreshadow my conclusions, I argue that the United States should engage in partial retrenchment. The United States should retain the central features of its grand strategy, including its East Asian treaty alliances. In addition, the United States should continue to broaden and deepen its alliances and partnerships to balance against the growing threat from China, as it is with AUKUS and the QUAD.[13]

---

13. AUKUS is a trilateral security partnership involving Australia, the United Kingdom, and the United States that was established in 2021; see https://www.defense.gov/Spotlights/AUKUS/. The QUAD is a diplomatic partnership involving Australia, India, Japan, and the United States; it dates to the early 2000s but was reinvigorated and transformed beginning in the late 2010s; see https://asiasociety.org/policy-institute/quad-backgrounder.

The United States, however, should end its commitment to defend Taiwan, shifting from its ambiguous commitment to use force to come to Taiwan's defense to making clear that it will not fight to defend Taiwan. The risks of maintaining this commitment, which include some significant probability of major-power conventional war and, in turn, some probability of escalation to nuclear war, have simply become too large. China places great value on unification with Taiwan, seeing it as essential to its national rejuvenation. It has significantly increased its ability to blockade and invade Taiwan, although whether it could succeed in either mission remains far from certain. It has also modernized and enlarged its nuclear force, thereby eliminating a potential US bargaining advantage in an all-out conventional war. The risks are unwarranted because, although Taiwan is an important US interest, it is not a vital one.

So long as China does not become more assertive, the United States should retain its current policies in the South China Sea, which include freedom of navigation operations, ambiguous commitments to protect countries' territorial claims, and military exercises. If, however, China were to adopt significantly more assertive policies toward littoral states and their maritime rights, the United States should reduce its opposition to China's efforts to achieve peacetime dominance of the South China Sea. A more assertive Chinese policy would increase the probability of war, creating risks the United States should be unwilling to run, given its quite limited interests. The United States should, however, retain the capability to deny China wartime freedom of movement in the South China Sea because it enhances the ability of the US to defend its allies.

Overall, then, while its commitments in East Asia would be reduced, the United States would continue to pursue its core security purposes in the region—protecting its treaty allies and reducing the probability of a major-power war in East Asia. Adjustments to US commitments, which would constitute a carefully calibrated form of partial retrenchment, would bring them into better alignment with its interests, given the challenges and risks posed by an increasingly capable and determined China.

Before proceeding, I want to make clear that I would strongly prefer that partial retrenchment was not the United States' best option. I certainly take no satisfaction in reaching this conclusion, far from it, and I am sensitive to its costs. But the combination of China's ambition and growing power has created a situation in which some concessions are now the United States' best option. China's rise could have gone much more smoothly, and China is largely responsible for the decline in US-China relations.[14] If China had been more restrained in challenging its neighbors' claims in the South China and East China Seas over issues of little material importance, the

---

14. Charles Glaser, "Will China's Rise Lead to War? Why Realism Does Not Mean Pessimism," *Foreign Affairs* 90, no. 2: 80–91.

past couple of decades would likely have played out very differently. Instead, China chose to be uncompromising for seemingly little gain. Taiwan is more complicated, but here, too, China could have been less assertive without compromising its long-term goals. With good reason, the United States now sees China as far more dangerous than just a few decades ago. Unfortunately, this is the situation the United States now faces. Undesirable and unlikeable as it is, the case for partial retrenchment should not be given short shrift.

Although concessions and retrenchment are often envisioned as highly risky, which they can be, we need to fully appreciate that maintaining all of the United States' current commitments is also risky. In fact, maintaining all of the United States' commitments is now the far riskier route. Current policy might well succeed, as the probability of a major war with China over Taiwan or the South China Sea, while increasing, is not large. But staying the course is not the United States' best bet: While not large, the probability of war is also not very small, either; given the limited US interests at stake in Taiwan, the expected costs—the probability of war multiplied by its costs—are unwarranted.

The standard objection to this conclusion is that China is a highly revisionist state—determined to achieve at least regional hegemony, if not global dominance—and that making any concessions to this type of state is misguided and extremely dangerous. This objection is overstated for a few important reasons. To start, China's ambitions may well be far more limited than this characterization suggests. True, China is determined to achieve unification with Taiwan and has explicitly reserved the option of using military force if necessary. Beyond Taiwan, however, the extent of China's ambitions is far less clear. China would likely prefer to have a sphere of influence in East Asia—which would require the departure of US military forces and the end of its alliances—but is probably unwilling to pay a high price to achieve it. China does have global ambitions, including increasing its international influence and status, enhancing the security of its authoritarian regime, and reducing the international standing of liberal norms. However, as a wide range of US experts on China and US foreign policy argued in 2019, Beijing is not "an existential national security threat that must be confronted in every sphere."[15] These experts were writing to challenge the appearance of a growing Washington consensus on China's extreme ambitions and the need for highly competitive US policies. Although US experts' beliefs about China's ambitions have changed significantly since the mid-2000s—with the distribution of views shifting toward more malign Chinese ambitions—significant disagreements continue and should be factored into US policy.

---

15. M. Taylor Fravel et al., "China Is Not an Enemy," *Washington Post*, July 3, 2019.

Given the range of expert assessments, the United States should search for and, if possible, pursue a policy that is robust in the face of uncertainties about the nature and extent of China's expansionist ambitions, and is cognizant of China's own insecurity. A robust US policy would take into account the distribution of judgments about China's ambitions, ensure that the United States is adequately protected against plausible worst outcomes, avoid policies that would be self-defeating if designed for the wrong type of China, maintain the potential to adjust as the United States gains new information about China's ambitions, and not unduly drain US resources.

In addition, the standard objection conflates the purposes of appeasement and retrenchment. Successful appeasement hinges on satisfying the goals of a revisionist state that has limited aims. If the adversary, in fact, has much more expansive aims, appeasement can leave the state worse off—for example, less militarily capable of deterring a still highly revisionist state and/or less able of credibly threatening to defend its remaining interests, thereby resulting in an increased probability of war. In contrast, successful retrenchment depends less on correctly assessing the limits of the adversary's goals. For example, if the state's concessions eliminate a major point of conflict, and if the state's remaining commitments are easier to defend than the conceded territory, then retrenchment would reduce the probability of war, albeit at the cost of the concessions. Thus, even if one believes China is extremely ambitious, retrenchment deserves consideration. In the case of East Asia, defending US allies—for example, Japan—would be significantly easier than defending Taiwan.[16] This by itself does not mean the United States should end the commitment, but it does suggest that retrenchment deserves careful analysis.

The book's second task is to analyze the military strategy, missions, and forces—conventional and nuclear—that the United States requires to best protect its interests and meet its commitments. For this portion of the analysis, I assume that the United States retains its current political commitments. Although I favor some significant changes, the United States is not planning them now and may not make them for the foreseeable future. Therefore, focusing primarily on the military strategy required to meet current US commitments in East Asia provides insights that are immediately relevant to current US policy.

The most basic criterion for judging a strategy is its potential to deter a Chinese attack. China's increasing power and large investments in its military forces are reducing US military capabilities in East Asia and making key military missions more difficult to accomplish. Strategies the United

---

16. In addition, ending the US commitment to Taiwan would not significantly reduce the US ability to defend its allies, which makes retrenchment more attractive. This claim is contentious, however, as there is debate over the military implications of Chinese control of Taiwan; chapter 4 addresses the debate.

States has relied on may no longer be feasible, requiring the United States to adapt and shift to new ones. Military forces that were once adequate may need to be restructured, modernized, and/or enlarged.

Beyond the feasibility and deterrent effectiveness of various missions, the United States must also consider the threat that its military forces could pose to China and the pressures they could create for escalation in a severe crisis or war. A strategy and forces that decrease China's security could fuel an arms race and be self-defeating because a more insecure adversary can be more difficult to deter. This trade-off is captured in the well-known concept of the security dilemma, which explains that a state's efforts to increase its own security by improving its military capabilities can fuel reactions that leave the state less capable of defending itself and convince both states that the opposing state is more dangerous. The net result can be an increase in the probability of war.[17] Achieving the balance required by the security dilemma can be easy and straightforward under certain conditions but difficult or impossible under other conditions. Given the growing American support for competitive approaches to dealing with China, attention to the potential downsides of military competition is especially important.

The United States must also consider the escalatory pressures and incentives created by its strategy and forces. Under some conditions, a state can minimize escalatory pressures without forgoing valuable military capabilities. Under other conditions, however, the state faces a trade-off between increasing the capability of its forces and decreasing pressures for escalation.

Maybe the best-known example of this tension concerns nuclear forces—analysts have cautioned that adversaries that can effectively target each other's nuclear forces will generate crisis instability, resulting from interlocking preemptive incentives to escalate to all-out nuclear attacks early in a major crisis or war.[18] This type of danger is not limited to nuclear forces, however. Consequently, the United States must also consider the incentives created by both the vulnerability of its conventional forces and its ability to attack China's conventional forces early in a conflict.

Another type of escalation can result from crossing thresholds/saliencies.[19] One way to keep a war limited is for both countries to agree, tacitly, to fight within certain boundaries—including territorial borders, the types of weapons employed, and/or the types of targets attacked. A state could intentionally cross a threshold to signal its willingness to fight a larger, more costly war. But undesired escalation can result if a state crosses a

17. Robert Jervis, "Cooperation Under the Security Dilemma," *World Politics* 30, no. 1 (January 1978): 167–214; Charles L. Glaser, "The Security Dilemma Revisited," *World Politics* 50, no. 1 (October 1997): 171–201.

18. Thomas C. Schelling, *The Strategy of Conflict* (Harvard University Press, 1960), chap. 9; Thomas C. Schelling, *Arms and Influence* (Yale University Press, 1966), chap. 6.

19. Schelling, *Arms and Influence*; Richard Smoke, *War: Controlling Escalation* (Harvard University Press, 1978).

threshold without considering or appreciating its significance or because the state was unwilling to forgo the military advantages of crossing the threshold. The limits that the United States has set on its involvement in the war between Ukraine and Russia—including the types of weapons it would provide and the goals that it would support—reflect evolving US beliefs and uncertainties about Russian escalation saliences.[20]

I conclude that the United States should adopt relatively defensive military strategies to deter Chinese attacks. These would enable the United States to minimize political and escalatory pressures while meeting its deterrence requirements. In the nuclear realm, this requires a strategy that forgoes efforts to regain a damage-limitation capability—the ability to deny China the ability to essentially destroy the United States in a nuclear retaliatory attack.[21] In the conventional realm, this requires a strategy that gives priority to the survivability and resilience of US forces deployed in East Asia and avoids operations that depend on early deep attacks into China's mainland. The nuclear strategy is reasonably straightforward; the conventional strategy is far more complicated.

IMPLICATIONS OF THE TRUMP ADMINISTRATION

As I noted at the outset, President Trump has reshaped the discourse on US foreign and security policy. Before Trump, the possibility of the United States engaging in retrenchment was not taken seriously by the US government. Although not well spelled out or carefully explained, the possibility of the United States reducing its international commitments is now part of the US foreign-policy zeitgeist. Nevertheless, Trump's handling of US international policy has damaged US interests, not advanced them. He views US allies through a very narrow lens—focusing on their dollar cost to the United States—while seemingly overlooking their value to US security and prosperity. The result is merely a policy inclination supported by a weak and flawed foundation.

The partial retrenchment that I prescribe depends on the United States being able to preserve its credibility both with its treaty allies, most importantly Japan and South Korea, and with China. Trump has undermined this credibility. His administration has given the most public attention to reducing the United States' security involvement in Europe, possibly even ending the NATO alliance. Trump's policy toward East Asia is less clear, although confronting China is frequently identified as a top priority. Yet Trump has greatly increased doubts among the United States' East Asian allies about

---

20. Dan Altman, "The West Worries Too Much About Escalation in Ukraine: NATO Can Do More Without Provoking Moscow," *Foreign Affairs*, July 12, 2022.
21. Chapter 6 provides a more precise definition of a damage-limitation capability.

the reliability and longevity of US security commitments.[22] This fits poorly with the purported focus on confronting China because these US allies would play a central role in opposing China's expansion.

My analysis in this book looks beyond the chaos and uncertainty created by Trump, focusing instead on the United States' *potential* to effectively pursue partial retrenchment and the military strategies that can best support it. A central question is whether the United States can engage in partial retrenchment while, at the same time, preserving its credibility for coming to its allies' defense. It makes sense to ask this question only if the United States values its alliances and wants to preserve them. My analysis finds that this should be possible, but that success will require dedicated, sustained policies that make clear the United States' interests and intentions. There can be no doubt that Trump's negative perspective on US allies, and the lack of pushback from the Republican party, will cast a shadow over future US efforts to accomplish the complicated mix of policies required for success.

Finally, I want to highlight that the partial retrenchment that I call for—most importantly, making clear that the United States will not use force to defend Taiwan—shares nothing with Trump's disdain for US allies and partners. The United States should end its commitment to Taiwan because the risks of a major war are too large, not because the commitment is too expensive for the United States, some sort of a bad financial deal. In fact, in combination with terminating the US commitment, I favor contributing substantially to Taiwan's ability to defend itself, because the United States has political and ideological interests in Taiwan.[23] Partial retrenchment has the potential to increase US security and advance US interests, but only if implemented with a steady foreign-policy hand.

Policy Questions

To reach the conclusions sketched above, this book analyzes the key national security policy questions facing the United States. In combination, an analysis of three key questions—about US grand strategy, Taiwan, and the South China Sea—identifies the extent and nature of US interests in East Asia, evaluates the risks and costs of the commitments required to protect them, and recommends which interests the United States should continue to defend. The analysis of two additional questions—about US nuclear strategy and US conventional strategy—explains how the United States can

---

22. For example, see Kenji Kushida, "Japan Is Trying to Be a Model Partner. Trump Is Pushing It Away," Carnegie Endowment for International Peace (April 18, 2025), https://carnegieendowment.org/emissary/2025/04/japan-trump-tariffs-negotiation-security-trade?lang=en.

23. Charles L. Glaser, "Considering a US-Supported Self-Defense Option for Taiwan," *Washington Quarterly* 48, no. 1 (spring 2025): 187–204.

INTRODUCTION

best protect these commitments. Answers to these questions determine the broad outlines and overall character of US security policy toward China.

Although the debate over US policy toward China is continually changing, the analysis of these questions will provide enduring insights. Most of the day-to-day and month-to-month debate is about the narrow specifics of US policy. These debates take place within the boundaries set by the answers to the questions this book addresses.

My evaluation of these questions follows a standard policy-analysis approach: identify and assess US interests and threats to those interests; specify the range of relevant options for protecting these interests; examine the feasibility, benefits, and costs of these options; and reach a policy conclusion by comparing the benefits, costs, and risks.[24] International relations (IR) theory plays a central role in many steps of the analysis. It identifies which features of a state's international environment are important; sheds light on the nature and extent of threats a state may face; and characterizes the options a state has for achieving its goals. Theories also provide the causal link between a state's policy options and the outcomes those options are intended to achieve. Disagreements about IR theory can therefore lead to disagreements about threats and how best to confront them. I place my analyses within the context of current US policy and scholarly debates and highlight how disagreements about theories generate policy disagreements. Throughout, I attempt to make transparent the structure of my analysis, the uncertainties about facts and theories that necessarily complicate a thorough analysis, and the trade-offs between options' costs and benefits. In some cases, these trade-offs involve apples and oranges that are especially difficult to compare—for example, ideological values, such as protecting democracies, and avoiding war. In these cases, I try especially hard to make my judgments as explicit as possible.

The first and most basic question: What grand strategy can best achieve US security interests vis-à-vis China? More specifically, should the United States maintain its alliance commitments in East Asia? Grand strategy matches ends with means, reflecting a state's assessment of its interests, threats to those interests, and its capabilities—actualized and potential—for protecting those interests. For a major power facing a rising power, whether it needs its alliances and whether it can protect them are key grand-strategic questions. The United States established enduring alliances in Europe and Asia following World War II to balance against the Soviet Union, and it retained those alliances following the dissolution of the Soviet threat.

China's increased and increasing military and economic capabilities, and the growing adversarial relations between the United States and China, re-

---

24. For a more extensive discussion in the context of grand strategy, see Charles L. Glaser, "Rational Analysis of Grand Strategy," in *The Oxford Handbook of Grand Strategy*, ed. Balzacq and Krebs.

quire that we ask the most basic questions about the United States' East Asian alliances: What purposes do they serve? Are they necessary to protect the US homeland and US prosperity? Do they reduce the probability of major-power war? Can the United States still protect them? China's capabilities, combined with its possibly growing ambitions, could make these alliances both more valuable and riskier. An overall assessment needs to consider both effects.

Second: Should the United States retain its security commitment to Taiwan? Taiwan is widely believed to be the most dangerous source of conflict between the United States and China. China considers Taiwan to be an integral part of its homeland—therefore a truly vital interest—and is determined to bring Taiwan under its full sovereign control. The United States has an ambiguous commitment to come to Taiwan's defense if Taiwan is attacked by China; it continues to leave uncertain whether it will respond and what factors might influence its decision. Recent debate has focused on whether the United States should make a more certain commitment to come to Taiwan's defense and on ways to enhance Taiwan's ability to defend itself. While important, these debates skip over the more fundamental question of whether the United States should retain a commitment to use force to defend Taiwan or instead end this commitment entirely.

The United States needs to reevaluate its commitment because the risks have grown dramatically. Whereas a few decades ago China had virtually no chance of effectively blockading or invading Taiwan, China's military buildup has greatly improved its prospects for achieving these missions. In addition to being more capable, China may also be less willing to wait for peaceful unification, among other reasons because Taiwan appears increasingly unlikely to accept peaceful unification and because President Xi Jinping has created a sense of urgency by connecting Taiwan to his goals of national rejuvenation and restoration of China's international status. Coming to Taiwan's defense would likely result in a major conventional war between the United States and China, which is an increasingly capable nuclear power.

Third: How strenuously should the United States oppose China in the South China Sea? The South China Sea reaches from the southern tip of Taiwan and the Taiwan Strait to Malaysia, is a major commercial sea-lane that connects the Indian Ocean to East Asia, and is home to numerous maritime territorial disputes between China and other littoral states. China became more assertive in the South China Sea starting in the late 2000s, with behaviors that included building and militarizing artificial islands in the Spratly Islands, gaining control of Scarborough Shoal, rejecting an international tribunal ruling that decided against China's claims to historic rights within the so-called nine-dash line (which includes the vast majority of the South China Sea), and using maritime forces to harass states that were exploring hydrocarbon reserves in their own waters. Many foreign policy experts place great importance on the South China Sea, worrying that Chinese control of it would significantly reduce US influence in the region, possibly enabling China to dominate East Asia.[25]

As with Taiwan, the risks of strenuously opposing China in the South China Sea have grown. China's maritime forces can now maintain a forward presence throughout the South China Sea. If China were to forcibly take control of a feature in the Spratly Islands, US efforts to regain control could result in a large war, which could include attacks against the Chinese mainland. Although this is unlikely to escalate to the scale of a war over Taiwan, the probability of a conflict in the South China Sea may be greater.

Having explored the United States' key interests and commitments in East Asia, the next set of questions concern US military strategy and forces. The fourth question is: What nuclear strategy can best protect US interests and commitments in East Asia? The United States relies on its nuclear forces to deter not only nuclear attacks against its homeland but also nuclear and conventional attacks against its allies. For decades, China's nuclear force was small and highly vulnerable to US nuclear attack. The US ability to destroy most or all of the Chinese force likely enhanced deterrence and might have provided a bargaining advantage in severe crises. Starting in the mid-2000s, China began increasing the size and survivability of its nuclear force, which now or soon will provide an assured destruction capability. The United States can no longer significantly reduce the costs of Chinese nuclear retaliation in politically relevant scenarios. The pivotal US decision regarding nuclear strategy is whether to compete to regain its damage-limitation capability. This would require the United States to invest in improved surveillance, targeting, and missile defense capabilities and, down the road, improved antisubmarine warfare capabilities. The United States would also likely have to increase the size of its nuclear force. Nuclear competition, however, might not be successful—China might be able to offset US efforts, thereby maintaining the ability to inflict essentially unlimited retaliatory damage against the United States. And competition might be self-defeating, generating incentives to escalate early in a crisis and further straining US-China relations.

Finally: What conventional military strategy can best protect US interests and commitments in East Asia? The United States relies on its conventional forces to protect its treaty allies in East Asia—including Japan, South Korea, and the Philippines—as well as Taiwan from Chinese invasion, blockade, and coercion. In addition, US conventional forces can contribute to the US ability to prevent Chinese intimidation of countries throughout East Asia.

---

25. See, for example, Ely Ratner, "Course Correction: How to Stop China's Maritime Advance," *Foreign Affairs* 96, no. 4 (July/August 2017): 64. See also Patrick M. Cronin and Ryan Neuhard, *Total Competition: China's Challenge in the South China Sea* (Center for a New American Security, January 2020): 1, and Hal Brands and Zack Cooper, "Getting Serious About Strategy in the South China Sea," *Naval War College Review* 71, no. 1 (winter 2018): 16.

The key US decision concerns how offensive its conventional strategy and forces should be. Attacking forces deployed deep in the Chinese mainland early in a conflict might enable the United States to greatly reduce the size and effectiveness of the forces that China could bring to the battle. This approach, however, likely increases the probability that a crisis will escalate to a limited conventional war and that this conventional war will escalate to an all-out conventional war and possibly a nuclear war. The more defensive alternative would forgo attacks against the entire Chinese force and focus instead on the forces China is using to launching an invasion, thereby taking advantage of the ability of US forces to destroy ships crossing water.

The book addresses these questions in a layered fashion. The grand-strategy debate can dominate the Taiwan and South China Sea questions—that is, if the United States terminates its defense commitments to East Asia, the other two questions are answered. Therefore, I analyze the Taiwan and South China Sea questions starting from the assumption that US grand strategy remains unchanged. This is productive analytically because it is useful to delink these questions, and it is practical because there are currently no plans for making such a large change in US grand strategy. The book takes a similar approach to the military strategy questions, although I do also consider the implications of ending the US commitment to Taiwan for US military requirements.

Analysis and Findings

To lay the foundation for addressing these questions, part 1 of this book—"International Relations Theory and China's Rise"—reviews, extends, and applies international relations theories that shed light on how dangerous China's rise is for the United States. Applying these theories to China requires placing them in the context of China's power, geographic position, history and political culture, and governance structure.

Chapter 1 applies two complementary strands of realism to China's rise. These are strategic-choice theories that make assumptions about a state's goals and analyze which strategy/policy can best achieve them, given the constraints and opportunities the state faces. Much of the chapter employs defensive realism—a version of structural realism—to understand the pressures generated by the structure of the international system as China's power grows and plateaus. To isolate the impact of structure, the theory assumes that states are driven only by their desire for security, not by non-security (greedy) motives. Opposing states, however, do not know that they face a security seeker and consequently must make decisions under uncertainty. International structure is constituted by the distribution of power and other material factors that influence states' potential military capabilities as well as states' initial understandings of the opposing state's motives. Defensive realism highlights the security dilemma, explaining both its essential role in generating competition and its policy guidance, which warns of the dangers that can result when a state's efforts to defend itself also decrease its adversary's security. A state that is insecure because it believes it might face a greedy state and is at least somewhat vulnerable to attack might decide to start a war to increase its security by acquiring strategically valuable territory and/or by weakening the opposing state. Arms competition can lead both states to conclude that the other is more likely to be a dangerous/greedy type, which can in turn make war more attractive.

Defensive realism shows that, contrary to the common fear that conflict is likely between a rising power and a (relatively) declining power, international-structural pressures should not push the United States and China into intense military competition and war. Their separation by vast distance and the Pacific Ocean, and the deterrent value of their nuclear weapons, combine to make it possible for both countries to be highly secure, thereby making security competition unnecessary. These defensive advantages also greatly reduce US security incentives for preventive war and China's security incentives for pursuing regional hegemony. Geography and the nature of military capabilities essentially eliminate the security dilemma. If international structure were all that mattered, China could rise peacefully without generating intense competition with the United States.

Chapter 1 next applies motivational realism, which focuses on greedy states and helps explain both the dangers they pose and the policies a defender should choose when facing one.[26] Unlike defensive realism, motivational realism sees international structure as constraining greedy states but not causing their interest in expansion. Considering greedy states is important because much of the US concern about China's rise reflects beliefs about its greed. Experts agree that China is committed to achieving unification with Taiwan, but they disagree about China's goals beyond Taiwan. Chapter 1 briefly reviews the US expert debate: Some experts believe China is deeply determined to achieve regional hegemony, global dominance, and the disintegration of the West. In sharp contrast, others believe China would pay little to achieve regional hegemony in East Asia and is not dedicated to spreading its authoritarian model of governance.

It is the combination of China's greed and America's commitments in East Asia that result in the danger posed by China's rise. Taiwan is especially dangerous because China places great value on unification and Taiwan is close to China, which makes it harder for the United States and Taiwan to defend. Protecting US allies is becoming increasingly difficult, but it poses a

---

26. I use *motivational realism* to cover some of what is typically termed *classical* and *neoclassical realism*. The latter, however, includes a wide mix of additional state features and does not focus primarily on greedy states.

much smaller danger. In large part, this is because China likely does not place great value on achieving regional hegemony—which would require the end of US alliances. In addition, US allies are further from China, which makes them easier to defend. Nevertheless, the challenge is not negligible, among other reasons because US threats to come to its allies' defense, including by employing nuclear weapons, are less credible than US threats to defend its own homeland. In the parlance of deterrence theory, extended deterrence is more difficult than homeland deterrence. In addition, the allies' proximity to China makes them much harder to defend than the US homeland. Following chapters explore the policy implications.

Chapter 1 next briefly considers mixed-type states—states that are both insecure and greedy. Dealing with this type of adversary can be especially difficult because the defender can require highly capable forces to deter expansion, but the more capable these forces, the greater the insecurity they tend to create. Unfortunately, China is a complicated mixed type: For it, unification with Taiwan is a security goal, and US capabilities for defending Taiwan therefore make it insecure. For the United States, however, China's unwillingness to reject the use of force to achieve its goals regarding Taiwan makes it a greedy state. Even purely defensive US military capabilities would appear threatening to China; thus, if the United States maintains the capability to come to Taiwan's aid, it will generate Chinese insecurity.

Chapter 1 also briefly presents the realist perspective on a liberal-structural theory that has played an influential role in US debates over China's rise. This theory holds that economic interdependence creates peaceful relations between countries that have large trade flows and engage extensively in other types of financial interactions. Contrary to this argument's expectations, the chapter finds that US-China economic interdependence has likely done little to make peace more likely and is now adding significantly to strains in US-China relations.

Chapter 2 draws on a variety of unit-level/state-level theories to gain additional insights into the dangers posed by China's rise. Whereas strategic-choice theories assume states' motives, unit-level theories focus on specific state features—including a state's national identity, its desire for status and prestige, and its regime type—that help to explain states' motives and decisions. These theories can provide a theoretical unpinning to the views held by US experts on China and American foreign policy and complement motivation realism by providing explanations for the motives that the theory simply posits. These state-level theories explain why rising powers have typically wanted to fulfill goals inherent to their national identity that were previously beyond reach and to achieve the international status consistent with their new power position. Applied to China, these theories help explain the great value that China places on unification with Taiwan and, to a lesser extent, controlling the South China Sea, and in turn why China is determined to revise the geopolitical status quo in East Asia. Central to

INTRODUCTION

China's national identity are memories of its historical glory and its century of humiliation. China believes that fully restoring its standing and status requires gaining control of Taiwan. These theories also show that certain types of authoritarian regimes—personalist dictatorships—are more likely to initiate conflict than are democracies and other types of authoritarian regimes. President Xi's consolidation of domestic power has pushed China toward this type of regime, making China more dangerous.

Whether China's identity and status goals will make China highly determined to achieve regional hegemony in East Asia is less clear. These state-level theories do suggest that China is likely to desire regional hegemony—rising powers have often desired a sphere of influence for reasons of status. However, they say little about the magnitude of the value China is likely to place on achieving it. As noted above, China experts continue to disagree on this issue. The question is complicated by Taiwan because US alliances play a central role in supporting US capabilities for defending Taiwan, thus creating a strong security reason for China to want the alliances dissolved. The harder question is, if China gained control of Taiwan, which would greatly reduce the security value of regional hegemony, would China still place great value on regional hegemony for reasons of status and identity? If it would, then we should expect intense competition in East Asia, unless the United States is willing to accept full retrenchment by radically changing its grand strategy, which is unlikely. There is, however, little evidence that supports this most worrisome characterization of China.

The next three chapters compose part 2 of this book—"US Geopolitical Commitments." Chapter 3 tackles the question of US grand strategy. Since the end of the Cold War, there has been an extensive and evolving debate over US grand strategy. The key schools in this debate—including Neoisolation (which includes certain versions of the strategy of Restraint[27]), Offshore Balancing (which also includes certain versions of Restraint), Deep Engagement, Liberal Hegemony, and Primacy—provide a foundation from which to assess the impact of China's rise. Very briefly, Neoisolation argues that the United States does not require allies because the United States is so capable of defending its homeland without them. In addition, these alliances could draw the United States into crises and war with China, thereby generating unnecessary costs and risks. And, although ending these alliance commitments would increase the probability of some former treaty allies—Japan and South Korea—acquiring nuclear weapons, Neoisolation does not see this as a prohibitive risk because these countries would be highly capable and responsible nuclear powers.

---

27. On the spectrum of views within the Restraint school and the overlap with isolation, see Miranda Priebe et al., *The Limits of Restraint: The Military Implications of a Restrained US Grand Strategy in the Asia-Pacific* (RAND, 2022), 6–8, https://www.rand.org/pubs/research_reports/RRA739-4.html.

In sharp contrast, Deep Engagement holds that US alliances are necessary for both US security and prosperity. These alliances reduce the probability of major-power wars that could draw the United States into a massive conflict in East Asia and help to preserve the open international economy. In addition, ending US alliances could lead to nuclear proliferation by former US allies, which would increase the probability of nuclear war, including one that involves the United States. Offshore Balancing, like Deep Engagement, holds that US security can require alliances and forward-deployed forces, but only in regions where the threat to US interests is large and imminent. Thus, Deep Engagement and Offshore Balancing can converge regarding East Asia—US alliances need to be preserved and strengthened—while diverging regarding the North Atlantic Treaty Organization (NATO), with Offshore Balancing holding that NATO can be diminished or dissolved.[28] Liberal Hegemony adds a dimension to Deep Engagement, arguing that the United States should support the spread and preservation of democracy and human rights abroad, in addition to its security and prosperity interests. Primacy argues that the United States needs to be the globe's dominant military and economic power to adequately protect its international interests.

Although the US grand strategy has been intensely debated for decades, my overall assessment is that there is not a clear winner between Neoisolation and Deep Engagement. In their best presentations, they are based upon sound arguments and involve complex trade-offs. Liberal Hegemony suffers a variety of weaknesses, including leading the United States into costly unnecessary wars and running inappropriate risks when its vital interests are not at stake. Primacy is not feasible because, even if the United States continues to be far more wealthy and militarily powerful than China, it will be unable to regain military dominance of China in East Asia, which is where the countries' military capabilities will be most important.

The question, then, is how China's rise influences the relative strength of the Neoisolationist and Deep Engagement arguments and whether this breaks the deadlock. The result is somewhat counterintuitive—in broad terms, China's rise increases the strength of the arguments for both preserving US alliances and terminating them. In support of Neoisolation, China's rise is increasing the probability of war in East Asia, possibly quite significantly, which increases the risks of maintaining US alliances, thus strengthening the case for terminating them. In addition, China's growing military forces increase the economic costs of adequate US military capabilities, thereby reinforcing the case for Neoisolation, which worries that excessive defense spending robs other national needs. In contrast, Deep Engagement finds that the benefits of retaining US alliances in East Asia have increased

---

28. This articulation of the strategy preceded the 2022 Russian invasion of Ukraine.

because the probability of war has increased: Thus, if the United States ends its alliances in East Asia, the probability of getting drawn back into a major-power regional war has increased. In addition, the threat posed by China has increased the probability that ending US alliances would result in Japan and South Korea acquiring nuclear weapons and the global economy suffering from both war and a breakdown of the established economic order.

A closer look suggests, however, that the case for Neoisolation comes out stronger. This is because the US commitment to Taiwan and US regional forces committed to its defense do not sufficiently reduce the probability of war to make Deep Engagement/Offshore Balancing the United States' best bet. If, however, the United States ended its commitment to Taiwan while retaining its alliance commitments, creating a subcategory within the standard grand-strategy categories, the choice becomes quite different. I would then favor retaining US treaty alliances in East Asia—Deep Engagement minus Taiwan. The United States would have much better prospects for defending its remaining commitments and would avoid the large uncertainties that ending its security involvement in East Asia would generate, many of which could play out badly for the United States.

Chapter 4 analyzes US policy toward Taiwan, focusing on whether the United States should terminate its ambiguous security commitment to the island. The key argument in favor of ending the US commitment is straightforward—it has become too risky, given the limited US interests. The combination of China's increased capability and immense determination suggests that the probability of a war over Taiwan has increased significantly. If the United States comes to Taiwan's defense, the war will be a large conventional war involving massive US attacks against China's air and naval forces. In addition, it could quite possibly include attacks against forces deployed on the Chinese mainland, Chinese attacks against US bases in the region, most importantly in Japan, and Chinese attacks against US regional allies that are supporting the US war effort. In a range of unlikely but plausible scenarios, this large conventional war could escalate to nuclear war. Ending the US commitment and staying out of a war between China and Taiwan would enable the United States to avoid these risks. In addition, although hard to envision now during the current downward trajectory of US-China relations, ending the US commitment might at some point contribute to improving US-China relations: Taiwan is arguably by far the most important issue that divides the two countries and, as explained in chapter 1, the international structural pressures for competition are mild.

Against these risks of the US commitment, we must weigh the cost of ending the US commitment. The most direct and clear cost would be to US political and ideological values of protecting freedom and democracy and to the people of Taiwan. Taiwan is a vibrant democracy of over twenty-three million people; China would almost certainly not respect Taiwan's democracy or its people's political freedoms. In addition, ending the US commitment to Taiwan might reduce US credibility with China for protecting the United States' regional allies and might reduce US credibility with US allies for protecting them against China, thereby damaging the alliances. Finally, China's possession of Taiwan might increase its ability to prevent US forces from operating near its periphery and increase its ability to move strategic submarines into the Pacific Ocean.

An overall assessment requires comparing apples and oranges—ideological and human rights concerns versus national security concerns. Giving reasonable weight to US security results in concluding in favor of ending the US commitment, based primarily on the logic of retrenchment. The United States should be able to keep the credibility costs quite small by pursuing a variety of policies that make clear that it remains deeply committed to the defense of its East Asian treaty allies. Of course, if the Trump administration continues not to give priority to preserving US alliances, then the credibility cost of ending the United States' commitment to Taiwan would be much larger. But this risk then would be generated by a reevaluation of US interests and an overall revision of its alliance policies, not its Taiwan policy. The United States might lose some military capability if China controls Taiwan, but these reductions would likely not be large. More importantly, because China is much less determined to conquer US allies than to control Taiwan, and because the United States would retain the capabilities required to deter attacks on its allies, the reductions would be acceptable—they would not significantly increase the probability of China attacking US allies.

I argued in previous research for a grand bargain—China would make concessions in the South China Sea and publicly accept the US military presence in East Asia in return for the United States ending its commitment to Taiwan.[29] This bargain now appears infeasible, as China's shift to more assertive policies indicates it would be unwilling to make those concessions. The less satisfactory option of ending the US commitment unilaterally is now the United States' best option. Ending the US commitment to Taiwan might not satisfy all of China's goals in the region, but it would remove the issue that is by far most likely to lead to a large war while leaving the United States capable of protecting its allies.

Chapter 5 explores US policy toward the South China Sea. The first step in this analysis is to identify US interests. Based on the current US grand strategy (Deep Engagement/Liberal Hegemony), US security depends on the security of its East Asian allies, and US prosperity depends on the region's open trade and prosperity. The question then is how China's policies

---

29. Charles L. Glaser, "A US-China Grand Bargain? The Hard Choice Between Military Competition and Accommodation," *International Security* 39, no. 4 (spring 2015): 49–90.

in the South China Sea affect these interests. Maybe surprisingly, US security interests turn out to be quite limited. The United States does not need to pass through the South China Sea to protect Japan or South Korea—or, likely, Taiwan; protection of the Philippines would, however, benefit from access to the South China Sea. At least as important, China's actions in the South China Sea have added little to its ability to prevent the United States from operating naval and air forces in the South China Sea. Instead, the key challenges come from China's land-based forces—its antiaccess/area-denial forces. In addition, China's Spratly bases are vulnerable to early destruction in a war with the United States and therefore would not contribute significantly to Chinese capabilities. The threat that China's South China Sea policies pose to US prosperity is also exaggerated. While it is true that a large volume of trade passes through the South China Sea, China would be quite unlikely to interrupt trade during peacetime; during a war, most trade could be rerouted to avoid the South China Sea.

Other threats to US interests are more subtle. Paralleling the credibility arguments about Taiwan, if the United States decided not to resist China's assertive behaviors in the South China Sea, US credibility with allies and partners for protecting their interests, and with China for opposing it elsewhere, might be reduced. This might occur, for example, if the United States made clear that it would not protect contested features (almost all of which are too small to qualify as islands) if China used force to gain control of one or more of them. But the United States should be able to minimize reductions in its credibility by deepening its core alliance commitments and distinguishing them from issues of little material or security importance. There are no guarantees, but the risks should be small.

Some experts see a threat to the "rules-based international order," including the rules established by the United Nations Convention on the Law of the Sea, which address states' rights within their Exclusive Economic Zone (EEZ) and "high sea freedoms." However, while there is value in the "rules-based order," proponents have exaggerated its benefits and the urgency of protecting all the rules from Chinese transgression. For example, if China were to prevent US military exercises within its EEZ—which it has not done so far—little would be lost because the United States would likely not want to fight from there in an actual war.

In broad terms, the United States has three options along a continuum—increased resistance to China's assertive policies, current US policy, and partial South China Sea retrenchment. Because US security interests are quite limited, a significantly firmer US policy, which would generate an increased risk of war with China, is unwarranted. Especially with the growing consensus for competing more intensively against China, the United States will require a clear understanding of its limited interests to avoid shifting to this option. In contrast, given the caution China has demonstrated, the risks of current US policy appear to be relatively small and consistent with its interests, most importantly preserving its regional credibility.

If, however, future Chinese actions indicate that its determination to control these waters has significantly increased, the United States should, reluctantly, shift to a policy of partial South China Sea retrenchment. Given quite limited US security interests, China's growing military capabilities, and this greater determination, the risks of war would no longer be warranted. The United States would scale back its goals—for example, making clear that it would not defend its allies' claims to small, disputed maritime features—while reassuring allies that it was fully prepared to defend their mainlands. Although not a happy outcome, a partial Chinese sphere of influence in the South China Sea may well be a "natural" outcome of China's rise.

Part 3 of this book—"US Military Strategy"—analyzes the broad military policies the United States should adopt to protect its commitments in East Asia. Chapter 6 addresses US nuclear policy toward China. The key question is whether the United States should pursue a damage-limitation capability—the ability to significantly reduce the costs that China can inflict in all-out nuclear retaliation—or instead accept China's maintenance of an assured destruction capability. The US decision about a damage-limitation strategy will determine the overall character of its nuclear strategy. A damage-limitation strategy is inherently competitive, requiring the United States to thwart China's efforts to make its nuclear forces highly survivable. In contrast, if the United States forgoes a damage-limitation requirement, US and Chinese force requirements would be largely compatible. Both states would be able to satisfy their most important deterrence requirement—maintenance of the capability required to deter massive nuclear attacks against their homeland—and competition between them should taper off. This is why nuclear weapons are said to essentially eliminate the security dilemma.

A damage-limitation capability could provide the United States with three types of benefits. Most directly, it could reduce the deaths and destruction that the United States would suffer in an all-out nuclear war. In addition, a damage-limitation capability might provide the United States with bargaining advantages in a severe crisis or war, because the United States would suffer less than China in an all-out war, which could enable the United States to press harder—generate a larger probability of escalation—to convince China to make concessions. Finally, Chinese awareness of this US bargaining advantage and the pressures for escalation created by the US damage-limitation capability could contribute to the deterrence of Chinese aggression, thereby reducing the probability of crises and conventional war. The size of these benefits would depend on the effectiveness of the US damage-limitation capability.

A disqualifying barrier to gaining these benefits is the difficulty of achieving a significant damage-limitation capability. The United States has poor prospects for regaining and maintaining a significant damage-limitation capability. Although China deployed a relatively small and highly vulnerable nuclear force until the mid-2000s, it has increased the size, diversity, and survivability of its nuclear forces and is continuing to do so. Given the damage that can be inflicted by a single thermonuclear weapon and the increasing size and quality of China's force, US counterforce systems—including its intercontinental ballistic missiles (ICBMs), ballistic missile defenses, antisubmarine warfare forces, and intelligence and reconnaissance capabilities—would have to be extremely effective to provide the United States with significant protection. However, China is deploying mobile ICBMs that the United States cannot target effectively with currently deployed systems and Chinese countermeasures should be able to defeat future US technologies, including space-based radar satellites and improved national ballistic missile defenses.

Beyond its likely infeasibility, the pursuit of damage limitation would bring a variety of costs and risks. It would fuel an arms race that would further strain US-China relations; although the relationship is already bad, an intense arms race could contribute to making it still worse. Probably more important, a US damage-limitation strategy would create incentives for early escalation in a conventional war. For example, China would face pressures to mobilize its nuclear forces earlier in a crisis, and the United States would have incentives to destroy them before they became impossible to target. In addition, the vulnerability of China's fixed land-based forces and possibly of its ballistic missile submarines could increase the probability of escalation based upon flawed information by creating time pressures for China to launch its force on warning of a US attack. Interestingly, these escalation risks could also produce the benefit noted above—China's appreciation of them could deter a crisis or war. Chapter 6 argues that these risks exceed the deterrence benefit. Combined with the poor prospects for regaining a significant damage-limitation capability, the case against such a competitive nuclear strategy is strong.

The possible exception concerns Taiwan. Deterring a Chinese attack against Taiwan is harder than deterring attacks against US treaty allies, because it is harder to defend and because China places great value on controlling Taiwan. In addition, in a crisis or war, China would have a bargaining advantage because it values Taiwan far more than the United States does. Competing for a damage-limitation capability might help offset some of these disadvantages by communicating US determination to defend Taiwan. It might even create some doubt among China's leaders about whether the United States believes it has acquired a damage-limitation capability, even if it has not. Of course, if the United States ended its commitment to defend Taiwan, then these arguments would become irrelevant. But I conclude that even if the United States maintains its commitment, the risks of pursuing damage limitation are too large.

Chapter 7 analyzes the United States' conventional strategy for protecting its interests in East Asia. It focuses on deterring an attack against Taiwan and defeating a Chinese invasion if deterrence fails. There are other conventional missions that the United States needs to be able to perform in East Asia, including protecting Japan from blockade and invasion and protecting Taiwan from a blockade. I focus on the Taiwan invasion scenario because a major war would be most likely over Taiwan and because a conventional invasion would stress US forces and generate the largest risks of escalation. If the United States were to end its commitment to Taiwan, many of the same arguments and conclusions would hold for protecting Japan, but the challenges and risks facing the United States would be much smaller.

This chapter begins with a basic political point—there is no way to defend Taiwan without creating Chinese insecurity. Unlike situations that are driven by a security dilemma, even purely defensive US forces would appear threatening to China. The root of the problem is that the United States and China disagree about the political status quo. This observation does not mean the United States should end its commitment to defend Taiwan—defense policy involves complicated trade-offs. However, the United States needs to appreciate how China is likely to interpret and respond to its conventional capabilities. Failing to do so will support unnecessarily provocative US reactions to China's responses.

In broad terms, the United States' choice is between two approaches. Offensive Denial is designed to destroy China's forces early in a war and thereby achieve victory quickly. In contrast, Defensive Denial is designed to defeat China's ability to invade Taiwan by focusing on destroying ships crossing the Taiwan Strait, thereby ensuring that China does not win quickly. A couple of key factors favor the latter approach. To start, a longer war would allow time for the United States to swing substantial military capabilities into the region; the majority of US conventional forces are based outside of East Asia. In addition, the offense-defense balance for an invasion favors defense because crossing water with large invasion forces and then resupplying them is inherently difficult. Improvements in antiship missiles and reconnaissance capabilities are making this still more difficult. The United States can increase the survivability of its antiship missiles by deploying them on mobile launchers and dispersing its tactical aircraft to a larger number of smaller bases in the region. The United States can also deploy antiship missiles on long-range bombers that are based far beyond the reach of China's conventional missiles.

In addition, Defensive Denial would avoid or at least reduce some pressures for escalation that would be created by Offensive Denial, including from a crisis into a large conventional war and from a conventional war into a nuclear war. These include pressures for early massive US conventional strikes against the Chinese mainland and pressures for escalation to nuclear use that could be created by US attacks against

Chinese command and control and surveillance systems. However, neither strategy would avoid the most basic source of nuclear escalation—the country losing the conventional war could escalate to limited nuclear attacks to compel the other to concede. China's looming loss of a vital interest would make it the state more likely to escalate.

Chapter 7 ends by identifying several choices that would significantly shape how the United States implements Defensive Denial and that deserve extensive military-technical analysis. These choices include deciding on the mix of platforms on which to deploy antiship missiles; whether, when, and how intensively to attack the Chinese mainland, which many analysts believe is a Chinese redline; whether to launch kinetic attacks against Chinese satellites that provide targeting information on the location of US aircraft carriers, which would increase the probability of Chinese attacks against satellites the United States uses to locate ships in the Taiwan Strait; and whether to deploy US ground troops to Taiwan.

The conclusion reiterates the book's call for partial US retrenchment, reviewing how it flows from the detailed analysis in the preceding chapters.

The book fills two gaps in the already large literature on China. It draws on a wide range of IR theories to understand the dangers posed by China's rise and to support analysis of the broad national security policy questions facing the United States. Explicitly applying IR theory both increases the transparency of the analysis—exposing the logic of arguments and potential disagreements—and places the policy analysis within the context of more general debates. In addition, few book-length treatments identify the full set of major security policy choices facing the United States and provide an integrated assessment of their strengths and weaknesses.[30]

By adopting the policies analyzed and prescribed in this book, the United States can greatly reduce the dangers generated by China's rise, while achieving its most important goals. The United States will have preserved the core of its security involvement in East Asia—its alliances—and its ability to influence the trajectory of East Asian politics and economics, including deterring a major-power war while greatly decreasing the probability a major war with China. Given current fears about the dangers of China's rise, this should be considered an excellent outcome.

The United States could strive to achieve even more—to preserve the current status quo, including its commitment to protect Taiwan's de facto independence. However, although the United States might well succeed, the risks—a not unlikely large conventional war with China, which could quite plausibly escalate to nuclear war—would be unwarranted. If a few

---

30. Important policy-focused books include James Steinberg and Michael E. O'Hanlon, *Strategic Reassurance and Resolve: US-China Relations in the Twenty-First Century* (Princeton University Press, 2014), and Lyle J. Goldstein, *Meeting China Halfway: How to Defuse the Emerging US-China Rivalry* (Georgetown University Press, 2015).

decades from now, the new status quo created by partial US retrenchment is well established, albeit competitive and contested, and a major war has been avoided, the United States will have achieved as much as it can reasonably expect. A major shift in the global balance of power will have occurred peacefully, and the United States will have protected its most important international interests. Certainly, China's rise will have been much less dangerous than the prevailing US mood is anticipating and the US expert commentary has been predicting.

PART I. INTERNATIONAL RELATIONS THEORY AND CHINA'S RISE

CHAPTER 1

Realism and China's Rise

How dangerous is China's rise? This is a surprisingly complicated question, partly because the answer does not depend entirely upon China. US interests and the policies that the United States adopts to protect them will also matter, influencing the intensity of competition and the probability of a major war. US policy, in turn, should depend partly on assessments of China: What are China's international goals, why does China have these goals, what value does it place on them, and how capable is China of achieving them? This chapter and chapter 2 focus on the China piece of the puzzle; they apply a variety of international relations theories to shed light on the implications of China's rise for US national security. The following chapters analyze the key broad security-policy choices facing the United States.

The question of the impact of China's rise is theoretical because we need to predict how China will respond to emerging pressures and opportunities and to US actions—whether cooperative or competitive—that are designed to influence China's behavior. We are asking a cause-and-effect question: What conditions and policies will cause China to act in certain ways? The question of China's rise is also theoretical because theories can provide insights into what China wants—is it primarily interested in security, or does it have nonsecurity (greedy)—motives as well?

China's rise could be dangerous for a variety of reasons. One set of arguments emphasizes the implications of international structure, including changes in the balance of power. Maybe most prominent in the ongoing foreign policy discourse is the belief that the power transition created by China's explosive economic and military growth greatly increases the probability of war. Related dangers include the challenges of facing a peer competitor—an adversary with capabilities comparable to the United States'—and the political and military strains that are being generated by the intensified arms race between the United States and China. A different set of arguments emphasizes China's ambitions—including unification with Taiwan, the dominance of the South China Sea, and possibly the achievement of regional hegemony—and the dangers that flow from its increasingly authoritarian regime.

Naturally, these two types of arguments can be combined, as China's increased capabilities are central to making its ambitious goals more feasible. In contrast, still other arguments hold that China's rise will be far less dangerous because extensive economic interdependence between China and the United States and many US allies greatly moderates incentives for war.

To assess these dangers, this chapter and chapter 2 summarize, extend, and apply an array of international relations theories. This chapter uses theories that focus on the international situation a state faces and on the implications of variation in states' motives and goals. Chapter 2 turns to theories that explore the sources of states' motives—including their regime type, national identity, and desire for status and prestige—to provide insights into the nature and extent of China's expansionist motives.[1] Both chapters briefly present the empirical information that is required to apply these theories to China.

This chapter begins with a brief overview of defensive realism, which it then applies to the question of China's rise. Defensive realism is a member of the structural realist family, a set of theories that focus on states that are pursuing security under international anarchy, in the face of the incentives and pressures created by international structure. It explains competition and conflict as the result of states' efforts to achieve security and the insecurity that these efforts can generate. The intensity of competition, and the possibility of avoiding it, depend on the intensity of the security dilemma. There are deep divides within structural realism. Defensive realism is substantially stronger, both theoretically and empirically, than the alternative structural realist strands, which is why I employ it in the following analysis. At some key points, I address why other strands of structural realism reach divergent predictions.[2]

The chapter then moves beyond purely structural theories to address the implications of greedy states—states that want to expand for reasons other than security, including possibly in pursuit of wealth, fulfillment of their national identity, and achievement of international status or ideological dominance. Greedy states are the focus of motivational realism.[3] The moti-

---

1. There are a variety of narrower theories that are also required to analyze US policy that are not explored in these chapters but are addressed in the following chapters. For example, theories about how tightly a state's credibility is connected across issues are very important to US policy toward Taiwan and the South China Sea and are discussed and employed in chapters 4 and 5.

2. Charles L. Glaser, *Rational Theory of International Politics: The Logic of Competition and Cooperation* (Princeton University Press, 2010), includes qualifications and elaborations of many of the arguments presented in this chapter and extensive citations.

3. As noted in the Introduction, I use *motivational realism* to cover some of what is typically termed *classical* and *neoclassical* realism. The latter, however, includes a wide mix of additional state features and does not focus primarily on greedy states. See Charles L. Glaser, "Realism," in *Contemporary Security Studies*, 7th ed., ed. Alan Collins (Oxford University Press, 2025). Also on motivational realism, see Andrew Kydd, "Sheep in Sheep's Clothing: Why Security Seekers Do Not Fight Each Other," *Security Studies* 7, no. 1 (autumn 1997): 114–54.

vational realist argument sees international structure as constraining states, but, unlike defensive realism, structure does not cause states to desire expansion. Considering greedy states is important because there are conditions under which a greedy state should adopt competitive and expansionist policies, but a security seeker should choose cooperative ones. On the flip side, the policies a state should choose to deal with a greedy state can be different from those it should pursue to deal with a security-seeking adversary. These two theories—defensive realism and motivational realism—are complementary and can be combined into a single, more comprehensive theory that address states that are simultaneously greedy and security-seeking.[4]

The United States views China primarily as a greedy state. Experts agree that China places great value on unification with Taiwan; China's retention of the option to use force to achieve this goal means China is a greedy state. Experts disagree, however, over the value that China places on achieving regional hegemony and global dominance. Some believe China's goals are limited to regaining lost territory; others believe China is determined to push the United States out of East Asia, to become the world's dominant military and economic power, and to export its authoritarian governance model across the globe. US policy should take into account these uncertainties about China's greed. But China is also a security-seeking state—at a minimum, it sees unification with Taiwan as necessary to achieve the integrity, and therefore the security, of its homeland. The United States should therefore factor in the possibility that overly competitive policies can create unnecessary insecurity and thereby be self-defeating.

The dangers posed by China's rise depend on US security commitments in East Asia. The United States has important allies in East Asia, with the most important being Japan and South Korea. Whether to maintain these alliances is the key grand strategy choice facing the United States; these alliances are not clearly required by the United States' structural/international situation. In addition, the United States has an ambiguous political commitment to defend Taiwan if it is attacked by China. Further, the United States is committed to maintaining freedom of navigation and preserving the "rules-based order" in East Asia, including in the South China and East China Seas and the Taiwan Strait. For the discussion here, I assume that the United States maintains its current long-standing commitments to the region. Chapter 3 evaluates US grand strategy and whether to end US alliance commitments to East Asia; chapter 4 assesses the US commitment to Taiwan, and chapter 5 evaluates US commitments in the South China Sea.

---

4. Glaser, *Rational Theory of International Politics*, and Andrew H. Kydd, *Trust and Mistrust in International Relations* (Princeton University Press, 2005).

CHAPTER 1

The final section of this chapter briefly explores the realist assessment of the liberal argument that economic interdependence reduces the probability of war. This is a structural theory that focuses on the political implications of states' trade relations, and economic activity more generally, and has played an influential role in the debate over China's rise.

This chapter produces three key findings. First, defensive realism shows that the structural pressures pushing the United States and China toward military competition and war are weak. In broad terms, both countries can be highly secure due to the distance that separates them, the difficulty of crossing the Pacific Ocean, and the highly effective deterrent capabilities provided by nuclear weapons. The dangers created by a power transition, including preventive war, are small or nonexistent. Contrary to the dire warnings that have been highlighted by offensive realism, defensive realism finds that, although some rising powers should desire regional hegemony, China should not; it can be secure without fully dominating its region. Finding a lack of structural pressures for competition and conflict opens the door for cooperative US policies. If intense competition were essentially inevitable, there could be no benefit to US restraint and concessions, only costs and risks. Contrary to prominent arguments, however, this is not the situation the United States faces.

Second, the key dangers generated by China's rise come from other sources, specifically China's regional ambitions, with the unification of Taiwan being the most important. The nature of these dangers is consistent with motivational realism's emphasis on greedy states, although regional issues tend to fall below the radar of theories cast at the global level. In addition, as explored in chapter 4, Taiwan is an especially complicated issue that should not be understood entirely in terms of China's greed: As noted above, for China, Taiwan is a security issue because it believes Taiwan is part of China, which in turn makes unification of Taiwan a truly vital security interest. Beyond Taiwan, however, the dangers posed by China's greed are far smaller, partly because China appears to be much less committed to pushing the United States out of East Asia and achieving regional hegemony, and partly because the United States and its allies are far more capable of preventing China from succeeding. Third, US and Chinese economic interdependence does little to support peace and can generate dynamics that intensify economic and military competition and strain US-China political relations.

Defensive Realism: Security Seekers Under Uncertainty

THE REALIST FAMILY

Realist theories attempt to understand states' choices and international outcomes by employing a general framework that abstracts away from the details of specific states and the international system. The international system is characterized in terms of states' potential to achieve their objectives, including importantly their power. States are typically characterized in terms of their basic motives and interests—security and greed. Realism gives little or no weight to individual states' political systems, their leaders, or other specific attributes of their domestic political systems. Its most direct competitor is liberalism.[5]

Realism, however, is a broad family of theories and arguments, not a single well-defined theory.[6] The deepest divide is between structural realism—which emphasizes the impact of international anarchy and states' need for security—and motivational realism—which emphasizes the expansionist/greedy (nonsecurity) motives and goals of the states in the international system. A key strand of structural realism—defensive realism—finds that the international system does not generate a general tendency toward competitive behavior. Under certain international conditions, states can be highly secure and cooperative policies will be their best option. It is the other key strands of structural realism—Kenneth Waltz's realism and especially offensive realism—that predict much more dangerous competition.[7] This divergence reflects some key assumptions about how to characterize states' military potential and how states should respond to uncertainty about opposing states' motives and intentions.[8]

Much of the discussion of China's rise is cast in essentially realist terms. A wide range of realist dangers is commonly believed to flow from the tendency of the international system to force major powers to compete intensely for security, which in turn pushes them toward war. Maybe most prominent is the concern that power transitions—situations in which a rising major power becomes more powerful than the (relatively) declining power—tend to generate war. This danger has recently been dubbed the "Thucydides's Trap."[9]

---

5. For comparisons of the two, see Michael W. Doyle, *Ways of War and Peace: Realism, Liberalism, and Socialism* (Norton, 1997), and John J. Mearsheimer, *The Great Delusion: Liberal Dreams and International Realities* (Yale University Press, 2018).

6. Glaser, "Realism"; William C. Wohlforth, "Realism," in *The Oxford Handbook of International Relations*, ed. Christian Reus-Smit and Duncan Snidal (Oxford University Press, 2008).

7. Kenneth N. Waltz, *Theory of International Politics* (Random House, 1979), and John J. Mearsheimer, *The Tragedy of Great Power Politics* (Norton, 2001).

8. On assuming the worst about a state's motives, see Sebastian Rosato, "The Inscrutable Intensions of Great Powers," *International Security* 39, no. 3 (winter 2014/15): 48–88; disagreeing are Charles L. Glaser and Andrew H. Kydd, "Correspondence: Can Great Powers Discern Intentions?," *International Security* 40, no. 3 (winter 2015/16): 197–202.

9. Graham Allison, *Destined for War: Can America and China Escape Thucydides's Trap?* (Houghton Mifflin Harcourt, 2017). Arguments about power transitions run parallel to the defensive realist arguments and can be integrated with them. See the discussion of preventive war later in this chapter.

CHAPTER 1

DEFENSIVE REALISM'S KEY ASSUMPTIONS AND VARIABLES

Defensive realism attempts to understand states' actions in terms of the pressures and opportunities created by the international system. It emphasizes that the international system is anarchic—there is no international authority that can enforce agreements and prevent the use of force between major powers.

In line with structural realism more generally, defensive realism makes several simplifying assumptions. First, states are motivated by security.[10] Security reflects a state's prospects for preserving control of its territory, avoiding war to protect its territory, and preventing coercion that would undermine its international interests. This is a simplifying assumption because a state can also have greedy motives for expansion. This simplification is analytically useful because if states that are interested only in security end up in competition and war, we then know that the pressures created by the international system are very important indeed, and states' abilities to escape them may be quite limited.

Second, states are envisioned as unitary actors. Although states are made up of leaders, governing institutions, interest groups, and populations, realist theories make this assumption because it is analytically productive—helpful for focusing on key features of the choices any state would face in a given international situation. Third, states act rationally—states make decisions that are well matched to the achievement of their interests, given the constraints imposed by their capabilities and the uncertainties they face about other states' capabilities and motives. States are strategic when making these decisions—that is, they take into consideration how other states will react to their policies. Assuming rationality is appropriate for assessing what a state *should* do; that is, for prescribing policy. Fourth, related to the unitary-actor assumption, defensive realism "black-boxes" opposing states—that is, states assess each other in terms of their power, capabilities, and international actions, not in terms of the variation that exists within states, including such domestic characteristics as regime type, the nature of leadership, ideology, and so on.

The strategies available to a security-seeking state and its prospects for success depend on the constraints and opportunities created by its international environment, which depends on both material and information variables. A state's ability to achieve its objectives depends on its ability to perform military missions. Protecting territory depends on the state's ability to deter attacks and to defend if deterrence fails. Taking territory requires the

---

10. Even states that internationally want only security do, of course, have domestic motives, most obviously consumption. On the security versus consumption trade-off, see Robert Powell, *In the Shadow of Power: States and Strategies in International Politics* (Princeton University Press, 1999), chap. 2.

ability to coerce an opposing state to make territorial concessions or to attack, conquer, and control territory if coercion fails.

A state's power—its resources that can be converted into military assets compared to the adversary's resources—plays a central role in determining its ability to acquire military capabilities. The factors that can contribute to a state's power include its wealth, population, human capital, and level of technological development.[11]

Power, however, does not by itself determine a state's potential military capability—that is, its ability to perform military missions. A state needs to convert its power into military forces, and those forces then confront the adversary's forces. Consequently, the theory requires a variable that captures the relative difficulty of offensive and defensive missions—the offense-defense balance.[12] The offense-defense balance depends on a variety of factors, including geography and the nature of military technology. For example, distance and terrain that is difficult to cross—for example, water and mountains—tend to favor defense. Nuclear weapons can create a large advantage for deterrence via the threat of retaliation. In offense-defense terms, deterrence can be understood as the functional equivalent of defense. Thus, nuclear weapons favor defense because maintaining retaliatory capabilities for deterrence is typically less costly than the forces required to destroy these retaliatory capabilities.[13] The combination of a state's power and the offense-defense balance determines a state's potential mission capability. When defense has the advantage, a state requires less power to be secure; a weaker state may be able to protect itself from a much stronger (more powerful) state.

In addition to these material variables, a state's strategy should depend on its information about the opposing state—specifically about the opposing state's motives and goals. Although defensive realism assumes all states are security seekers, the states in the system do not know this; states are uncertain about opposing states' motives. As discussed in the following section, although states would like others to know that they desire only se-

---

11. On the distinction between latent power and actual military power, see Mearsheimer, *The Tragedy of Great Power Politics*, chap. 3.
12. Charles L. Glaser and Chaim Kaufmann, "What Is the Offense-Defense Balance and Can We Measure It?," *International Security* 22, no. 4 (spring 1988): 44–82. Scholars have challenged the analytic value of the offense-defense balance; see Keir A. Lieber, *War and the Engineers: The Primacy of Politics over Technology* (Cornell University Press, 2008), and Mearsheimer, *The Tragedy of Great Power Politics*, 427, even though he emphasizes the stopping power of water and recognizes the difficulty major powers have in gaining nuclear superiority, which reflects the deterrent (defense) dominance of nuclear weapons.
13. This does not mean, however, that in a competition between two unevenly matched states, a wealthier and technologically more capable state cannot somewhat reduce its vulnerability to retaliation via offense—counterforce and missile defense. This is because power advantages can offset offense-defense balance advantages.

curity, under certain international conditions, communicating this information is too risky.

Information about the opposing state's motives can influence the policy a state should choose. For example, a state that believes it likely faces a greedy state might require greater military capabilities because a greedy state could be harder to deter; the state therefore might need to compete more intensely to meet its military requirements. On the flip side, a state that believes it likely faces a security-seeking state should be more inclined to moderate its military competition and possibly make concessions because reducing the opposing state's insecurity could increase the state's own security. The state, however, will usually face uncertainty about the opposing state's motives; its information about the adversary will then be an estimate of the probability that it faces a security-seeking state. Whether the state should adopt policies recommended by the spiral model, the deterrence model, or a combination of the two depends on this estimate.[14]

SECURITY DILEMMA

If a security-seeking state knew that all others were security seekers, the state would be able to cooperate, avoiding military competition and war, and ending up highly secure.[15] However, opposing states may be unable, at acceptable risk, to convince the state that they are, in fact, security seekers. To convey—signal—this information, a state would need to reduce its ability to attack. If doing so, however, would also reduce the state's ability to defend, then signaling could be too risky.

When in this situation, the state faces a security dilemma: It cannot increase an opposing state's security without decreasing its own. This occurs when the forces it relies on for offense are also necessary for defense—that is, when offense and defense are at least partially indistinguishable. The flip side of the security dilemma is that actions the state takes to increase its security will reduce the adversary's security; the adversary's reactions can, in turn, reduce the state's own security.

The intensity of the security dilemma depends on both material and information variables. Two material variables are key. As just mentioned, of-

---

14. Robert Jervis, *Perception and Misperception in International Politics* (Princeton University Press, 1976), chap. 3; Charles L. Glaser, "Political Consequence of Military Strategy: Expanding and Refining the Spiral and Deterrence Models," *World Politics* 44, no. 4 (July 1992): 497–538.

15. This would also require that the other states knew the state was a security seeker and that the state knew this—and that the state had confidence that others' motives would not change. On the security dilemma, see Robert Jervis, "Cooperation Under the Security Dilemma," *World Politics* 30, no. 1 (January 1978): 167–214, Charles L. Glaser, "The Security Dilemma Revisited," *World Politics* 50, no. 1 (October 1997): 171–201, and Kydd, *Trust and Mistrust in International Relations*, chap. 2.

fense-defense distinguishability captures whether a state can acquire the military capability required to defend itself without simultaneously increasing its ability to attack an adversary. When it can, offense and defense are distinguishable, which reduces or even eliminates the severity of the security dilemma. The second variable—the offense-defense balance—influences the severity of the security dilemma via a different logic. When defense has the advantage, the adversary needs to invest less to defend than the state spent building up its forces; in an action-reaction arms competition, the state's buildup thereby generates less insecurity.

As a result, when defense has the advantage, two equally powerful states can both be highly secure; they will rely on defensive doctrines and have little potential to undermine each other's defense. Action-reaction cycles of arming and arms races should peter out, thereby avoiding the negative political spirals that arms competition can generate. All of these outcomes are reversed when offense has the advantage. War can become more likely for a variety of reasons, including that offense advantage results in states being more insecure, which can increase the value of territorial expansion, and offensive advantage increases the advantages of striking first, which can increase the probability of crises escalating via preemptive attacks and accidents.[16]

The intensity of the security dilemma also depends on states' information about other's motives. A high probability that the adversary is a security seeker results in a less severe security dilemma. Cooperation with a security-seeking adversary is less risky than with a greedy adversary. Thus, a high probability that the opposing state is a security seeker enables the state to cooperate even when offense-defense conditions make this risky. Similarly, when the opposing state is likely to be a security seeker, increases in its offensive capability pose a smaller increased threat. This in turn allows the state to adopt a smaller response to the adversary's buildup, which reduces the negative security impact of the state's reaction.

When facing a security dilemma, the state needs to consider options for reducing the adversary's insecurity as a means of increasing its own security. Acceptable options may not be available—the security dilemma can render them too risky. But under certain conditions, cooperative policies or unilateral restraint can be the state's best option.

A state can increase its adversary's security in two reinforcing ways. First, the state can adopt policies that reduce its ability to defeat the adversary's defenses. This might be achieved by forgoing offensive forces or limiting the size of its forces that challenge the adversary's ability to defend. The state may also be able to increase its adversary's security by giving up

---

16. Stephen Van Evera, *Causes of War: Power and the Roots of Conflict* (Cornell University Press, 1999).

territory that is strategically valuable and by agreeing not to deploy forces in certain areas.

Second, a state can signal that it is a security seeker, which, as described above, can increase the adversary's security. To signal benign motives, the state must send a "costly signal"—take an action that is more likely to be taken by a security seeker than a greedy state (because it would be more costly for the greedy state to forgo the capabilities). For example, a greedy state is less likely to forgo offensive capabilities than a security seeker; thus, forgoing offensive capacities sends a costly signal.

DEFENSIVE REALISM AND CHINA

While there is agreement that China's power has greatly increased—reflected in its gross domestic product (GDP), advances in scientific and technological capabilities, and human capital—there is debate over whether China will become more powerful than the United States and whether China's economic growth will continue.[17] Nevertheless, for our purposes, a precise estimate of relative US and Chinese power is not essential. For analyzing US policy toward China, we can work with the estimate that China and the United States will have roughly comparable power for at least the next couple of decades.

Among the reasons that a more precise comparison is not essential is that the offense-defense balance between the two countries strongly favors defense, which reduces the significance of differences in power and enables both countries to be highly secure. Nuclear weapons make it relatively easy for major powers to maintain highly effective deterrent forces, which is a form of defense advantage. Even if China becomes far more powerful than the United States, the United States would still be able to maintain nuclear forces that could inflict massive damage following a Chinese attack. The same will be true of China once it completes the modernization and expansion of its nuclear force.[18] In addition, China and the United States are separated by the Pacific Ocean, which also significantly favors defense due to the difficulty of attacking across distance and water.[19] Consequently, neither country will be able to acquire conventional forces that are sufficiently capable to pose a significant threat of homeland invasion.[20] This defense

---

17. For citations, see introduction, n. 4.

18. Some analyses reach a different conclusion; chapter 6 provides a full analysis of China's ability to acquire and maintain a large retaliatory force.

19. For qualifications, see John M. Schuessler, Joshua Shifrinson, and David Blagden, "Revisiting Insularity and Expansion: A Theory Note," *Perspectives on Politics* 21, no. 4 (December 2023): 1304–18, who explore the implications of separation by oceans for non-territorial expansion, especially spheres of influence.

20. The United States does have the ability to interrupt most trade to China, which could provide some coercive capability in a long war.

advantage greatly reduces the intensity of the security dilemma facing the United States and China.

In addition to defense advantage, nuclear weapons systems make offense and defense partially distinguishable. Consequently, the United States could choose a nuclear strategy and forces that pose little threat to China's retaliatory capabilities. This would signal benign US motives. More importantly, choosing a more offensive strategy—the pursuit of a damage-limitation capability—would clearly signal malign motives because the United States would be working against the offense-defense balance to achieve a significant military advantage. As explained in chapter 6, the United States has chosen nuclear competition over restraint, which has unnecessarily reduced China's security and strained the US-China relationship.

US estimates of China's motives and goals have changed significantly since the mid-2000s, shifting toward a greater likelihood that China is a greedy state, possibly a very greedy one that is determined to achieve regional hegemony. Although there is still disagreement among experts,[21] the distribution of views has clearly shifted, and this more malign view of China has been integrated into US policy. A more malign view of China tends to increase the severity of the security dilemma, somewhat offsetting the impact of defense advantage. The United States should be somewhat more reluctant to adopt restrained, cooperative policies because they risk reducing China's assessment of US credibility for protecting its regional interests. As a result, China may end up being somewhat more insecure.

Nevertheless, from a structural perspective, the overall picture remains quite positive: the advantage of defense between the countries' homelands is so large that both can be highly secure, even if political relations are severely strained. From this perspective, international structure should not push the United States and China into intense security competition and should not generate a significant probability of large war.

In sum, defensive realism finds that the pressures for competition created by the international system are weak; if these were the only factors that mattered, the probability of war between the United States and China should be quite small.

Defensive Realism and Dangers Generated by a Rising Power

The previous discussion considered a static picture in which China has already achieved power comparable to the United States. In contrast, many

---

21. As an indication of disagreement, see the public letter organized by M. Taylor Fravel, J. Stapleton Roy, Michael D. Swaine, Susan A. Thornton, and Ezra Vogel, "China Is Not an Enemy," *Washington Post*, July 3, 2019.

discussions of the danger posed by China focus on a more dynamic picture, looking specifically at the implications of China rising and how it would act differently from when it was less powerful. We can draw on and extend the preceding defensive realist arguments to evaluate some of the dangers that a rising power is commonly believed to pose to a declining power.[22] Although defensive realism emphasizes how variation in the offense-defense variables and information about motives should influence states' behavior, the theory also sheds light on the implications of changing power. Defensive realism finds that a declining state can face a variety of dangers, many of which have been explored by other structural theories, but it holds that the magnitude of these dangers is contingent on other variables. The declining state may have a spectrum of options for responding to the rising state, ranging from preventive war to retrenchment, with arming and allying in between.[23]

POWER TRANSITIONS AND PREVENTIVE WAR

Likely the most frequently identified dangers generated by a rising power are power transitions and incentives for preventive war.[24] A declining power has an incentive to launch a preventive war if fighting now, while it is still relatively stronger, is better than fighting later and better than making the larger concessions it could be required to make to avoid war, when it would be relatively (and possibly absolutely) weaker.[25]

To more fully characterize the declining state's decision, a number of variables should be included. First, the size of the shift in power would matter. For example, declining from a large power advantage to parity would often have different implications than declining to a large power disadvantage. Second, in addition to overall power, the offense-defense

---

22. Joshua R. Itzkowitz Shifrinson, *Falling Giants: How Great Powers Exploit Power Shifts* (Cornell University Press, 2018), presents a theory of when a rising power will adopt a predatory policy and how intense it will be. I develop my arguments rather differently and reach many similar—but some divergent—predictions.

23. On the range of options, see Randall L. Schweller, "Managing the Rise of Great Powers: History and Theory," in *Engaging China: The Management of Emerging Powers*, ed. Alastair Iain Johnston and Robert S. Ross (Routledge, 1999).

24. Key works include Dale C. Copeland, *The Origins of Major War* (Cornell University Press, 2000); Van Evera, *Causes of War*, chap. 4; and Robert Gilpin, *War and Change in World Politics* (Cambridge University Press, 1981).

25. Although frequently stated this way, rational bargaining theory explains that the declining power should actually only be comparing the cost of war now to the costs of concessions it would have to make later since, in the later stage, it would lack incentives for war. See James D. Fearon, "Rationalist Explanations for War," *International Organization* 49, no. 3 (summer 1995): 379–414; also see Powell, *In the Shadow of Power*, chap. 4, who explains that, during a power transition, war is not more likely during the period when states' power crosses—becomes roughly equal—than at other stages of the transition.

balance must be included to adequately capture the impact of decline on the state's security. Defense advantage reduces the impact of power shifts by making the state's ability to defend less sensitive to reductions in its power. For a state that has extended deterrence or other distant geopolitical commitments, there may be more than a single relevant offense-defense balance. For example, considering the United States facing China, in addition to offense-defense balances for nuclear and conventional weapons involved in securing the US homeland, the offense-defense balances for missions required to protect allies could also be relevant.

Third, the probability that the rising power, once power has shifted in its favor, would attack or coerce the declining power is also important. A key factor will be the state's assessment of the rising power's motives and goals, including the extent of any expansionist goals. If the rising power is believed to lack expansionist goals and has good political relations with the declining state, then the declining power will have less to fear and preventive war would be less appealing. A rising adversary that the state believes has a limited desire to expand its territory and/or revise the rules of the international system would be less likely to launch a large war than one determined to achieve global hegemonic ambitions, which would reduce the relative attractiveness of preventive war.[26] Of course, the rising power could become more expansionist/greedy and the declining state should include this risk in its assessment. But this could still leave preventive war an unattractive option.

The declining state's decision about preventive war should also depend on its alternative options, of which there are a few key possibilities.[27] The declining state could attempt to reduce its decline by slowing its adversary's growth relative to its own—possibly by limiting trade—and/or by increasing its own rate of growth. Alternatively, it could make territorial or political concessions that it hopes will satisfy the rising power at a reasonable cost; that is, the declining state could appease the rising state. Appeasement—making concessions to satisfy a state that is likely to have limited aims—comes with the cost of the concession, plus possible costs to the state's reputation for protecting its interests, plus the risk that the rising power will not be satisfied and instead will demand more. Concessions could be in a variety

---

26. The state's own motives and goals would also matter—a greedy state with unsatisfied ambitions would have incentives to launch a war to achieve its goals before being constrained by decline.

27. The possibility of other options is often not included in the assessment of preventive war, which results in an exaggeration of its attractiveness and probability. On this point and other weaknesses in common preventive war arguments, see Paul A. MacDonald and Joseph M. Parent, *Twilight of the Titans: Great Power Decline and Retrenchment* (Cornell University Press, 2018), 14–16. On these possibilities and others—including adopting policies to reverse its power decline—see Gilpin, *War and Change in World Politics*, 186–97, who arguably underestimates their potential to avoid preventive war.

CHAPTER 1

of different issue areas, including ending commitments to allies, giving up territory, accepting changes in the international economic system or the "international order" more generally (which the declining state had shaped to its advantage), and taking measures to increase the rising power's status. Finally, a declining state could retrench to align its commitments with its reduced power. Unlike concessions designed to satisfy the rising power, retrenchment is intended to reduce the power the declining state requires to meet its commitments, enabling it to shift resources toward defending against the rising power, and/or to simply avoid conflict over an existing commitment.[28] And, in contrast to appeasement, retrenchment can be the declining state's best option even when the rising power has unlimited aims.

In sum, defensive realism identifies conditions under which preventive war would be a state's best option. Under a wide range of conditions, other options—including preserving the status quo via deterrence, appeasement, and retrenchment—would be preferable.

Rising China and Preventive War. Although China's power has surged relative to the United States, US incentives for preventive war have been small and are now virtually nonexistent. Much of the explanation is captured in the preceding discussion of China as a superpower—the United States will be able to maintain a high degree of security even if facing a China that is more powerful than it is because the offense-defense balance between the countries' homelands strongly favors defense. Moreover, the prospects for defending US allies would remain favorable. The greatest geopolitical risk is over Taiwan, but few analysts identify this danger when describing the broad dangers of China's rise, and still fewer argue that protecting Taiwan would warrant a preventive war. That said, if trying to make the best case for preventive war, it would focus on the dangers posed by war over Taiwan as China's power and military capability have improved.

Although the case for preventive war was always weak, it was stronger a few decades ago than it is now. Since the 1990s, China has been improving its nuclear capabilities; while it is hard to seriously contemplate a preventive war that involves launching a major nuclear attack to destroy China's nuclear force, the mission has become increasingly risky and difficult.[29] And China's conventional capabilities are greatly improved. The window has essentially closed.

At least in retrospect, the option that the United States should have considered more thoroughly was whether to oppose China's economic and technological growth instead of supporting it. Although pretty much a lone

---

28. On retrenchment, see MacDonald and Parent, *Twilight of the Titans*. For a more nuanced comparison of retrenchment and appeasement, see chapter 4.
29. It is true, however, that a surprise attack that caught China's nuclear force on day-to-day alert would have had a good chance of being highly successful.

voice at the time, writing in 2001, John Mearsheimer, argued that "the United States has a profound interest in seeing Chinese economic growth slow considerably in the years ahead."[30] This recommendation was based on offensive realist arguments that predicted that China's rise would be quite dangerous, with war between the United States and China not unlikely. Although defensive realism sees smaller structural dangers, it could support a similar recommendation because China's increased power would foreseeably create regional dangers that pose some threat to US security and potential conflict over Taiwan that would pose a grave danger. However, seeing smaller structural dangers, defensive realism could argue against this type of containment, among other reasons because it would signal malign US motives. In retrospect, the decline in US-China relations weakens this argument.

Instead, the United States supported China's full integration into the international economic system—most importantly supporting its inclusion into the World Trade Organization (WTO)—which contributed to China's economic growth, helping to lay the foundation for the multiple challenges it now poses. Whether a US-led multilateral effort to slow China's growth would have been successful—in either the near term or the long term—is an open question. But at the time, US policy was guided by the hope that China would not only rise peacefully but also join the established major powers in sustaining a desirable international order. Underpinning US policy was the bet—for some, even the expectation—that economic growth would lead to democratization, or at least liberalization, in China and that participation in key international institutions would produce socialization and political convergence.[31]

RISING POWER'S SECURITY-DRIVEN PURSUIT
OF REGIONAL HEGEMONY

A rising power might need regional hegemony—a situation in which it is the only major power in its region—to achieve sufficient security. Then, if it also believed its increased power made achieving regional hegemony feasible, the state would pursue competitive policies, make coercive threats, and/or use force to push the other major powers out of its region.

Offensive realism argues that all major powers strongly desire regional hegemony to ensure their survival. Consequently, a major power that has a reasonable shot at achieving hegemony will pursue it. Moreover, if a regional hegemon exists, it will compete to prevent other major powers from

---

30. Mearsheimer, *The Tragedy of Great Power Politics*, 402.
31. For a nuanced discussion of these expectations, see Alastair Iain Johnston, "The Failures of the 'Failure of Engagement' with China," *Washington Quarterly* 42, no. 2 (summer 2019): 99–114.

achieving hegemony in their own regions. This is because a regional hegemon is "essentially free to cause trouble in the fearful great power's backyard."[32]

In contrast, defensive realism offers a more conditional argument about the desirability of achieving and maintaining regional hegemony: A major power's security requirement for regional hegemony depends on the offense-defense balance as well as power. Defense advantage reduces the value of regional hegemony because power advantages are unnecessary, or at least less valuable, for deterrence, and therefore reduces the risks major powers should run to achieve it. For example, a rising power that is separated by water from other major powers in its region could well conclude that regional hegemony was unnecessary. Similarly, nuclear weapons might provide sufficient security that regional hegemony was not required even by major powers that share a land border; at a minimum, regional hegemony would contribute less to the state's security.

Defensive realism also diverges from offensive realism on whether a regional hegemon should fear and, therefore, devote extensive resources to opposing the achievement of regional hegemony by a major power in a different region. The key question is whether this regional hegemon would have the resources to pose a security threat by acquiring the military capabilities required to coerce or conquer. During the Cold War, a common concern was that Soviet conquest of Western Europe would provide the resource required to directly threaten the United States; containment of the Soviet Union was designed in part to prevent this danger. In contrast, opposing the achievement of regional hegemony for the purpose of keeping an opposing power pinned down in its own region would usually be unnecessary. A regional hegemon should find that directly opposing encroachment in its own region is much easier, less risky, and more efficient than forming distant alliances and preparing to fight a major war to prevent an aspiring rising regional hegemon from succeeding.[33]

China and Security-Driven Regional Hegemony. For China to achieve regional hegemony, the United States would have to withdraw its forces from East Asia and likely end its alliance commitments altogether. The first question is whether this is necessary for China to be adequately/highly secure. In broad terms, the answer is no. As elaborated above, a number of factors work together to make China's homeland highly secure, even with the United States deployed in its region: China's size, separation from the United States by the Pacific Ocean, its greatly improved nuclear arsenal, and features of its cut-

---

32. Mearsheimer, *The Tragedy of Great Power Politics*, 40–42.
33. These arguments are explored more thoroughly in chapter 3, which analyzes US grand strategy.

ting-edge conventional capabilities all favor defense and make China extremely hard to attack and conquer.[34] In addition, China's power—wealth and technological sophistication—is likely to continue to grow, which would enable China to continue along this path for decades. Consequently, US alliances and forward-deployed forces pose little threat to China's security.

There is, however, an important qualification to this conclusion: The forward deployment of US forces in East Asia and the support the United States may get from its regional allies greatly reduce China's ability to coerce and invade Taiwan. China considers Taiwan to be part of its homeland; unification is therefore a security goal for China. The United States' alliance with Japan—which provides the United States with military bases on its territory and includes understandings to support US military operations in defense of Taiwan—therefore poses a security threat to China. US alliances with the Philippines, and to a lesser extent South Korea, could also be valuable in a Taiwan scenario. China might well, therefore, want regional hegemony—specifically, US withdrawal from East Asia—because it believes this would greatly improve its prospects for achieving unification with Taiwan.

China's efforts to gain control of Taiwan would almost certainly begin as a direct attack against Taiwan, not as a military bid for regional hegemony. However, if China chose a different approach—trying to undermine US alliances or actually using force to push the United States out of the region—the United States would have excellent prospects for undermining and deterring these efforts. Although much harder than protecting the US homeland, the United States has good prospects for defending its treaty allies. The conventional offense-defense in the region favors defense. Japan's separation from China by two hundred miles of water makes invasion very difficult. In addition, the technologies for defeating an invasion across water—including antiship missiles—have an advantage over those required for invasion.[35] This advantage, however, may not be so clear or large that it will greatly suppress conventional military competition. Nevertheless, facing the US-Japan alliance, China should have little chance of winning a quick victory, which meets the requirements for deterring China from starting a war to conquer Japan.[36]

---

34. Stephen Biddle and Ivan Oelrich, "Future Warfare in the Western Pacific: Chinese Antiaccess/Area Denial, the US AirSea Battle, and Command of the Commons in East Asia," *International Security* 41, no. 1 (summer 2016): 7–48; Eugene Gholz, Benjamin Friedman, and Enea Gjoza, "Defensive Defense: A Better Way to Protect US Allies in Asia," *Washington Quarterly*, 42, no. 4 (winter 2020): 171–89.

35. Assessments of these technologies are discussed in chapter 7.

36. On the requirements for conventional deterrence, see John J. Mearsheimer, *Conventional Deterrence* (Cornell University Press, 1983). If China contemplates a long conventional war, assessing its prospects becomes more complicated; its import vulnerabilities and the overall power advantages of the United States and its allies should result in pessimistic assessments.

In addition to military capabilities, the United States will need to maintain its credibility for defending its allies, both to deter China and to preserve its alliances. This could be challenging because the United States does not value its allies as much as its homeland, which creates a potential credibility problem.[37] This credibility problem is even greater when the adversary is capable of inflicting high costs on the United States in a war. China has acquired this capability—it has deployed an increasingly large and survivable nuclear force. Under these combined conditions, protecting one's allies requires the deterrer to run large risks that may exceed its interests. As a result, China might doubt the United States would run these risks, which would weaken the US deterrent.

There are clear parallels to the challenge the United States faced in extending deterrence to Western Europe during the Cold War. Most experts believed that deterrence of nuclear attacks against the US homeland was relatively easy; the weight of US concern and effort focused on extending deterrence of a conventional attack to the United States' North Atlantic Treaty Organization (NATO) allies. Conventional deterrence of a Chinese attempt to conquer Japan should be easier than deterring a Soviet invasion across the inter-German border because a couple hundred miles of water makes conquest harder. Because NATO was commonly viewed as suffering conventional inferiority, it relied on the doctrine of nuclear first use and deployed thousands of theater nuclear weapons in Europe.

The United States does pursue a variety of policies to increase the credibility of its commitments to its East Asian allies, including making clear treaty commitments, forward-deploying conventional forces, and including its allies under the US nuclear umbrella.[38] The United States does not, however, currently deploy nuclear weapons on its allies' territory, as it did in South Korea during the Cold War. Overall, although concern about the adequacy of the US extended deterrent is likely to continue increasing as China's forces become larger and more capable, the prospects for successfully deterring China from starting a war to conquer a US ally appear to be quite good.[39] Consequently, even if China wants to become the regional hegemon in East Asia, its prospects are poor and the probability of war resulting from this desire is extremely low.

---

37. Structural realism does little to address the effectiveness of deterrence beyond its impact on states' capabilities. In contrast, deterrence theory explores these issues in depth, and I draw on it here. Foundational works include Thomas C. Schelling, *Arms and Influence* (Yale University Press, 1966), and Glenn H. Snyder, *Deterrence and Defense: Toward a Theory of National Security* (Princeton University Press, 1961).

38. The Trump administration's hostility toward and disregard for US allies has damaged US credibility. My points here focus on the options the United States has for maintaining its credibility, if it wants to. Although I highlighted in the introduction the analytic issues raised by the policies of the Trump administration, I mention this again as a reminder.

39. The possibility that China would attack Japan in a Taiwan scenario is a quite different issue and is addressed in chapter 4.

RISING POWER'S INTENSIFIED PURSUIT OF LIMITED GOALS

A rising power may acquire the capability to pursue previously infeasible goals—motivated by security, greed, or both—that run contrary to the declining power's interests.[40] The result can be increased possibilities for war over limited goals and the intensification of competition. In addition, war over limited goals often comes with some probability of escalation to larger and unlimited war. Although defensive realism can shed some light on the probability of these conflicts, shifting to deterrence theory and bargaining theory provides greater analytic leverage.

The declining power that faces a rising power that has acquired, or will acquire, the capability to pursue previously infeasible goals faces a range of options. As discussed above, preventive war is one possibility—especially if the declining power finds these limited changes unacceptable or is concerned that the rising power's goals may be unlimited. However, under most conditions, a preventive war would be far riskier than the value of the issues at stake. A range of other options may be more attractive when the rising power's goals are likely limited. The declining power could decide to oppose the rising power's achievement of its new goals, engaging in military competition and employing deterrence policies. The declining power could also try to build or deepen a balancing coalition to reinforce its own capabilities for opposing the rising power. The prospects for success and the probability of war will depend on the standard factors that influence deterrence and bargaining, including the states' military capabilities, the extent of their interests, the states' information about the other's capabilities and interests, the divisibility of disputed territory, and the probability of escalation to a larger war.[41]

A declining power could also consider conceding one or more goals to the rising power to avoid conflict over the territory that the rising power values most. Depending on the rising power's objectives, the logics of appeasement and or retrenchment could support making concessions. A declining power's choice between these options will depend on numerous factors, including the state's information about the nature and extent of the opposing state's goals, as well as the balance of interests, states' military capabilities, and beliefs/theories about the extent that a state's credibility is connected across issues.

China's Limited Goals. In contrast to structure-driven conflict, limited goals create an especially clear and important challenge for the United

---

40. A rising power could also adopt new goals; structural/rationalist theories typically do not capture this type of change.
41. Classics on bargaining theory include Powell, *In the Shadow of Power*, chap. 3, and Fearon, "Rationalist Explanations for War," which emphasize the role of states' incentives to misrepresent their interests and of commitment problems as the deep causes of bargaining failure and war.

CHAPTER 1

States in dealing with China's rise. China has long-standing disputes in its region. The most important is Taiwan. In addition, China has disputes with several countries in the South China Sea and with Japan in the East China Sea. From China's perspective, these are security issues because it believes that these disputed territories and maritime spaces are parts of China that it needs to regain control of.[42] (In contrast, the United States sees these ambitions as a result of China's greed, as discussed in the following section.) The dramatic growth in China's military capabilities has significantly increased its ability to assertively pursue these limited goals and prevail if war occurs.

China places great importance on the unification of Taiwan and has been unwilling to renounce the use of force to achieve unification. President Xi Jinping has increased the urgency by upping the intensity of Chinese military harassment of Taiwan and by stating that the Taiwan issue "should not be passed down from generation to generation."[43] The value that China places on unification makes war over Taiwan much more likely than war between China and the United States' East Asian treaty allies. In addition, China's ability to invade or blockade Taiwan has greatly increased since the 1990s. Invasion would be difficult, but it would be significantly easier than an invasion of Japan because Taiwan is closer to the mainland, militarily less capable, and has a much smaller population and GDP. Some recent evaluations suggest China would win a war over Taiwan, although the best available assessments find that if the United States joins the war, Taiwan would prevail under most conditions.

Although Taiwan is not a US treaty ally, the United States has an ambiguous commitment to come to Taiwan's defense. The United States has long opposed the use of force to change the political status quo between China and Taiwan. If China does attack Taiwan, the United States would probably come to its defense, although experts do disagree about how likely this is. A war over Taiwan involving the United States would be a large conventional war that could escalate. This is the possibility that makes China's rise very dangerous.

The South China Sea and East China Sea disputes are striking because, unlike with Taiwan, there is little material at stake. Chapter 2 explains that China's national identity and desire for international status fuel China's interests in these disputes. They have roiled the US-China relationship, and

---

42. This insecurity does not result from international structure and therefore does not fit neatly within structural realist explanations. However, these issues share many of the features that the security dilemma and defensive realism address. A key difference, however, is that nonthreatening forces will not reduce China's desire to gain control of these territories.

43. Richard C. Bush, "8 Key Things to Notice from Xi Jinping's New Year Speech on Taiwan," Brookings, January 7, 2019, https://www.brookings.edu/blog/order-from-chaos/2019/01/07/8-key-things-to-notice-from-xi-jinpings-new-year-speech-on-taiwan/.

the United States believes it must present a firm response to China's assertive policies in the South China Sea to protect its interests in East Asia

The South China Sea disputes are widely considered the most likely locus of US-China conflict. This assessment largely reflects the lower risks of China's provocations—a conflict in the South China Sea is unlikely to escalate to a large conventional war, and China is therefore more willing to make these challenges. There are, however, paths via which a confrontation could escalate—including due to accidents or, more likely, pressures that China and/or the United States feel to preserve their credibility or to act quickly in a changing military situation—that would lead to a larger war than either country initially anticipated. The South China Sea is therefore also a locus of serious danger.

RISING POWERS AND ARMS COMPETITION

As a weaker power rises, it has the potential to build up its military, which it could need to increase its security and/or to increase its ability to pursue nonsecurity changes to the status quo. Even if only for security, when the rising power faces a security dilemma, its buildup is likely to threaten the declining power. Moreover, an arms competition is likely even if offense-defense variables moderate the security dilemma because a declining power that wants to preserve its military capabilities will need to build up its forces simply to offset the growth in the rising state's increasingly large and/or sophisticated military forces. In addition to reducing the declining state's ability to protect its interests, the arms competition could communicate malign motives, even if the rising power is interested only in security. The result can be an action-reaction process/arms race that reduces the declining power's ability to protect its interests and strains the states' political relationship. One or both states can come to believe that the opposing state is more likely to be greedy (or to be greedier) than previously estimated.[44]

This negative political spiral can fuel more competitive foreign policies because compromises and concessions to greedy states are more dangerous and competition can communicate resolve. These policies can in turn contribute to or generate crises and increase the probability of war. All of this can be exacerbated by misperceptions and by flawed analysis that fails to appreciate that the opposing state has reasonable security needs and faces a security dilemma and that one's own military forces threaten the opposing state's security. Flawed analysis may be especially common during power

---

44. This shift could occur via a rational process or misperceptions. On rational spiraling, see Glaser, "Political Consequence of Military Strategy"; on the likelihood and implications of misperceptions for spirals, see Jervis, *Perception and Misperception in International Politics*, chap. 3.

CHAPTER 1

transitions: The declining power will tend to see the status quo as legitimate, thereby overlooking the rising power's grounds for trying to increase its security by changing the status quo; on the flip side, the rising power can see itself as simply trying to achieve security that was previously unavailable.

To minimize these dangers, both states should search for arms programs and policies that pose as little threat as possible, while achieving their required missions. As described above, under certain conditions, a state might even forgo some military capability to reduce the threat it poses, thereby moderating the arms competition and the negative political spiral. However, when an arms buildup is driven by greedy motives, offensive capabilities will be required, which greatly reduces the possibilities for a state to moderate the threat that it poses. And, when the forces required for offensive and defense missions are similar, the possibilities for restraint will be quite limited.

China and Arms Competition. As would be expected by a rising power in China's situation, China's conventional and nuclear arms buildups are well underway. In simple military spending terms, China's defense budget has grown rapidly since 1990, roughly doubling during the 2010s.[45] China has greatly expanded its conventional capabilities, including forces designed to prevent the United States from operating military forces near its maritime periphery—antiaccess/area-denial (A2/AD) capabilities that combine an array of missile, naval, and intelligence, surveillance, and reconnaissance assets; forces to attack, invade, and blockade Taiwan; and forces that extend China's capability to project power to the southern reaches of the South China Sea. China is also modernizing its nuclear force, increasing its size, diversity, and ability to survive a US attack.

If the United States were committed simply to protecting its homeland, but not its East Asian allies and partners, China's buildup would require little, if any, US response, for the reasons laid out above.[46] However, given US commitments in East Asia, China's buildup is reducing the United States' ability to perform necessary military missions, with the most significant shift being over Taiwan. In addition, the United States' ability to protect Japan is being reduced or at least is facing new challenges that require significant adjustments to US force structure. The impact of China's buildup

---

45. Congressional Research Service, *China's Military: The People's Liberation Army (PLA)*, R46808 (Congressional Research Service, June 4, 2021), 47–48, https://crsreports.congress.gov/product/pdf/R/R46808. Growth in China's defense budget has tracked growth in its GDP.

46. This counterfactual is more complicated than it might first appear because the Chinese buildup would be very different if the United States did not have these commitments. Nevertheless, the basic points remain sound.

is creating still larger challenges to the United States' ability to defend South Korea.[47] The United States has responded by increasing the proportion of its forces allocated to East Asia (the "rebalance" to the Asia Pacific) and developing military plans for countering China's A2/AD, including initially the Air-Sea Battle concept.[48]

The US and Chinese militaries now focus primarily on each other in assessing the missions they must be able to perform and the forces they should procure.[49] China views US military capabilities and alliance policies as a threat to its security and interprets US reactions to its buildup as reinforcing this threat because they signal malign US motives and reduce China's military advances. For example, the 1996 revision of the US-Japan defense guidelines—which allowed Japan to support the United States in a conflict over Taiwan—"alarmed the Chinese," who saw the United States asserting itself aggressively; the Obama administration's "rebalance" to the Asia Pacific accelerated tensions in the South China Sea,[50] and US national ballistic missile defenses have increased concerns about US intentions.[51] Similarly, although US perceptions of China are being strained by many sources—including underlying geopolitical disputes and competitive economic policies—China's military buildup has also contributed significantly to negative American views of China's objectives.[52] Having surveyed the decades-long interaction between Chinese and American military policies, Philip Saunders concludes, "Military competition is likely to have a negative impact on the overall bilateral relationship. . . . It is too early to tell whether this will produce a US-Soviet-style cold war, but the relationship is headed in this direction."[53]

As the United States tries to maintain capabilities it judges necessary for deterrence and defense, the political/spiral implications of competition should be included in analyses of US policies for responding. Chapter 6 argues that the United States has a stark choice between a highly competitive nuclear policy and a restrained one. The chapter explains that defense (nuclear retaliation) likely holds an advantage over damage limitation, which

---

47. Eric Heginbotham and Richard J. Samuels, "Vulnerable US Alliances in Northeast Asia: The Nuclear Implications," *Washington Quarterly* 44, no. 1 (spring 2021): 158–59.

48. Air-Sea Battle was replaced by a somewhat less offensive concept—Joint Concept for Access and Maneuver in the Global Commons (JAM-GC).

49. Phillip C. Saunders, "The Military Factor in US-China Strategic Competition," in *Cold Rivals: The New Era of US-China Strategic Competition*, ed. Evan S. Medeiros (Georgetown University Press, 2023).

50. On these examples, as well as China's generally threatening view of the United States, see Wang Jisi, "From Reluctant Cooperation to Assertive Competition: China's Reaction to US Strategic Pressure, 1979–2020," in Medeiros, *Cold Rivals*.

51. Henrik Stalhane Hiim, M. Taylor Fravel, and Magnus Langset Troan, "The Dynamics of an Entangled Security Dilemma: China's Changing Nuclear Posture," *International Security* 47, no. 4 (spring 2023): 147–87, esp. 161–64.

52. Hiim, Fravel, and Troan, "Dynamics of an Entangled Security Dilemma," 152.

53. Saunders, "The Military Factor in US-China Strategic Competition," 224.

greatly reduces the United States' prospects for maintaining a significant damage-limitation capability. This defense advantage provides the United States with the opportunity to significantly moderate the US-China nuclear competition, while forgoing little if any deterrent capability. Chapter 7 explains that US efforts to protect Taiwan and Japan will unavoidably appear threatening to China because China needs the ability to conquer Taiwan. In addition, however, certain US and allied approaches will appear still more threatening than others, partly because of the indistinguishability of offense and defense and partly because of their escalatory risks.

Motivational Realism: Greedy States

The preceding discussion focused, albeit not exclusively, on states that are driven by the insecurity generated by international structure. A fundamentally different motive for expansion is greed—a state's desire to expand for nonsecurity reasons, including increasing its wealth and prosperity, enhancing its international status, spreading its political ideology or religion, or achieving its leader's narrow interests. Motivational realism focuses on greedy states and envisions the international situation as constraining a greedy state's actions, but not generating its motives. The theory typically focuses on how variation in the extent of the great powers' motives and power influences their behavior, not on explaining the sources of states' greed itself.[54] Expansion and war are explained primarily in terms of the extent of the adversary's greed and the power and military capability that the defender can rely on to deter and defeat the greedy state, including by forming alliances.

In contrast to a security-seeking state, a greedy state's desire for expansion cannot be eliminated by defensive strategies and military forces that pose no threat. A greedy state, even if unthreatened, will continue to be dissatisfied with the geopolitical status quo. Under a wide range of conditions, deterrence will be the defender's best strategy. Under certain conditions, appeasement or retrenchment may also be viable options.

Policies for dealing with a greedy state are often captured by the deterrence model (to be distinguished from deterrence theory), which holds that the defender need not avoid military capabilities that could appear threatening to the greedy state. For this to be the case, the adversary must be confident that the state will not use its offensive capabilities against it, if the adversary does not start a war. Proponents of the deterrence model hold

---

54. There are exceptions, however. For example, Hans Morgenthau, a preeminent classical realist, emphasized the role of human nature in leading great powers to be greedy. See Jack Donnelly, *Realism and International Relations* (Cambridge University Press, 2000), chap. 2.

that this is possible because the greedy adversary is confident that the defender seeks only security and understands the defender's military capabilities accordingly, which renders its offensive capabilities unthreatening.[55] Consequently, according to the deterrence model there is no downside to competitive policies against a greedy state.

Greed can vary in both depth and breadth.[56] Depth refers to the nonsecurity value that a greedy state places on acquiring territory or achieving other types of changes to the status quo. Some greedy states may be willing to pay only a small amount to expand, while others may place great value on expansion and thus be willing to run grave risks to achieve it. Breadth refers to the extent of a greedy state's aims. A greedy state can have limited aims, which can range from the desire to acquire a small amount of adjacent territory or a nearby uninhabited island to much more extensive regional expansion. A greedy state with unlimited aims would desire global hegemony or at least regional hegemony.

A defending state's strategy for dealing with a greedy state should depend on both these dimensions. For example, making concessions to a limited-aims adversary may be a state's best option via the logic of appeasement or retrenchment. Among other considerations, this would depend on the value of the territory to the defender, the defender's ability to deter the greedy state, and the risks if deterrence fails. The state's prospects for deterrence would depend on the states' power, the offense-defense balance regarding the territory in question, the state's other military commitments, and the relative value that the state places on the territory in question. The defending state's prospects are better when its power is greater, the balance favors defense, it does not have other military commitments and can therefore concentrate its forces in the region, and it values the territory more than the greedy state and therefore has credibility and bargaining advantages. The state's ability to defend either itself or other states will also depend on its ability to form a balancing alliance, which could be especially important if the greedy state is able to form an offensive bandwagoning alliance.[57]

The state's strategy should also depend on its assessment of whether a greedy state's aims were actually limited. States will almost always face some uncertainty about the true extent of an adversary's aims. Making concessions would be more attractive if the state were reasonably confident that the greedy state's aims were limited, not unlimited. A key barrier to

---

55. See Glaser, "Political Consequence of Military Strategy."
56. On the variety of types of states, see Randall L. Schweller, *Deadly Imbalances: Tripolarity and Hitler's Strategy of World Conquest* (Columbia University Press, 1998).
57. On greedy states and bandwagoning, see Randall L. Schweller, "Bandwagoning for Profit: Bringing the Revisionist State Back In," *International Security* 19, no. 2 (summer 1994): 72–107.

CHAPTER 1

concessions is the possibility that an adversary's aims are actually unlimited, especially if concessions would increase the adversary's wealth or military capabilities, or if they would undermine the state's credibility for protecting its other interests.

CHINA AS A GREEDY STATE

To evaluate the danger of war generated by China's greedy motives, we need an assessment of how determined it is to take territory and achieve other international goals. One source of this information is IR theories that explain the sources of states' motives, especially theories that focus on rising powers. The following chapter employs this approach. A second source is country experts who have deep knowledge of a country's history, domestic politics and structure, and political culture. This section employs that approach.

Experts disagree about the breadth and depth of China's greedy goals both in East Asia and across the globe. There is a consensus that China places great value on unification with Taiwan—which China sees as a security goal, but the United States sees as reflecting greed—although there is disagreement about the risks China would be willing to run to achieve unification.[58] Beyond this, however, there is a range of expert beliefs. Since the late 2000s, the distribution of American expert views has been shifting significantly toward views of China that are more threatening, but a wide spectrum remains.[59] The discussion in this section can only capture the basic contours of that debate, but it is sufficient to support an assessment of the dangers posed by China's rise and to clarify the policy choices the United States faces. Chapter 2 sheds additional light on China's goals by reviewing and applying theories about the sources of expansionist greed.

For our purposes, the most important divide is over whether China desires regional hegemony. A second divide concerns China's global ambitions—whether and to what extent it wants to overturn the liberal/rules-based international order and become the world's dominant military, economic, and political power. The question of regional hegemony is the more important one for the focus of this book—US national security—because East Asia is where the continuing Chinese military buildup poses a

---

58. The United States does not take a position on unification but holds that change should not be achieved by the use of force. Experts tend to see China as greedy because China is unwilling to reject the possibility of using force to achieve unification and because it employs coercive tactics during peacetime.

59. Jessica Chen Weiss, "The Case Against the China Consensus: Why the Next American President Must Steer Toward a Better Future," *Foreign Affairs*, September 16, 2024, observes that "the apparent hardening of a US consensus on China is shallower and wobblier than it appears." Although the US debate has shifted since 2019, see also Fravel et al., "China Is Not an Enemy."

potential threat to US allies, where US policy on Taiwan is most tightly connected with its credibility for protecting its allies, and where war is most likely. In contrast, although global ambitions may sound more worrisome because their scope is grander, China's global ambitions pose a smaller danger. They include challenges to a variety of US interests—including economic, ideological, and normative interests—but none of these pose a major direct threat to US security.

Oversimplifying a bit, we can divide the debate over regional hegemony into two positions. The first holds that China is determined to protect the territory it currently controls and to acquire the territory it claims, but not more. Writing in 2012, scholars Andrew Nathan and Andrew Scobell argued that on the military front, "there is no sign that China intends to use military force to seize territory beyond what it already claims, to drive the US out of Asia, or to compete with Western military influence in the Fourth Ring."[60] They anticipate the possibility that China would build a navy capable of projecting power beyond East Asia but see it as primarily defensive—designed to protect China's growing overseas investments and imports. Paul Heer, who served as national intelligence officer for East Asia in the Office of National Intelligence, in assessing China's goals in East Asia, argues that "China is not trying to extrude the United States from the region or deny American access there. . . . China is not trying to impose its political or economic systems on its neighbors, and it does not seek to obstruct commercial freedom of navigation in the region."[61] He warns that exaggerating China's goals in East Asia unnecessarily narrows the search for ways of managing or resolving the sovereignty dispute over Taiwan. Having reviewed the evolution of China's view of US alliances and its desire to see them terminated, Adam Liff concludes, despite China's "frustration" and "even outright opposition to US alliances . . . it is not clear that Beijing possesses the will, much less the ability, to actively seek to fundamentally undermine the alliance system."[62]

The alternative view holds that China is determined to gain a sphere of influence in East Asia, which would require the United States to withdraw its forces from Northeast Asia and end its alliances there. This is essentially the official position of the US government. The 2022 National Defense Strategy states that "the PRC seeks to undermine U.S. alliances and security partnerships in the Indo-Pacific region, and leverage its growing capabilities, includ-

---

60. Andrew J. Nathan and Andrew Scobell, *China's Search for Security* (Columbia University Press, 2012), 347. The "Fourth Ring" refers to disparate regions beyond East Asia, including Europe, the Middle East, Africa, Latin America, and Canada (171).

61. Paul Heer, "Rethinking US Primacy in East Asia," *The National Interest*, January 9, 2019, https://nationalinterest.org/blog/skeptics/rethinking-us-primacy-east-asia-40972.

62. Adam P. Liff, "China and the US Alliance System," *The China Quarterly* 233 (March 2018): 157–58.

CHAPTER 1

ing its economic influence and the People's Liberation Army's (PLA) growing strength and military footprint to coerce its neighbors and threaten their interests."[63] The 2022 US *National Security Strategy* holds that "Beijing has ambitions to create an enhanced sphere of influence in the Indo-Pacific and to become the world's leading power."[64] Both of these statements contain some ambiguity—arguably, undermining alliances and gaining an enhanced sphere of influence might not require forcing the United States out of East Asia. Nevertheless, these statements point strongly in the direction of regional hegemony: China is unlikely to succeed in seriously threatening US allies' interests and gaining the key features of a sphere of influence if the United States retains its alliance commitments and forward-deployed forces.

China's desire for regional hegemony has perhaps been most fully developed by Rush Doshi, who served as deputy senior director for China and Taiwan on the National Security Council (NSC) from 2021 to 2024. He argued before joining the government that "a fully realized Chinese order might eventually involve the withdrawal of US forces from Japan and Korea, the end of American regional alliances, the effective removal of the US Navy from the Western Pacific, deference from China's regional neighbors, unification with Taiwan, and the resolution of territorial disputes in the East and South China Seas." Doshi argues further that China has pursued its regional strategy more assertively since 2008, laying the foundation for achieving regional dominance, and may pursue it "if the United States acquiesces or is defeated in a regional conflict."[65] Doshi attributes this more assertive behavior to China's conclusion following the 2008 financial crisis that American power had significantly declined. Along the same lines, Ryan Hass, who served as director for China, Taiwan, and Mongolia on the NSC from 2013 to 2017, argues that "Chinese leaders also wish to weaken and ultimately abolish America's alliance structure in Asia . . . China would like to be seen now as a leader in Asia on par with the United States, and eventually as the uncontested power in the region."[66]

Elbridge Colby, who became the under secretary of defense for policy in 2025, argued before returning to the government that China will pursue regional hegemony to gain the benefits of establishing an economic bloc in

---

63. Secretary of Defense, *National Defense Strategy 2022*, Department of Defense, October 27, 2022, 4, https://media.defense.gov/2022/Oct/27/2003103845/-1/-1/1/2022-NATIONAL-DEFENSE-STRATEGY-NPR-MDR.pdf.

64. *National Security Strategy 2022* (White House, October 2022), 23, https://www.whitehouse.gov/wp-content/uploads/2022/10/Biden-Harris-Administrations-National-Security-Strategy-10.2022.pdf.

65. Rush Doshi, *The Long Game: China's Grand Strategy to Displace American Order* (Oxford University Press, 2021), 4, 24.

66. Ryan Hass, *Stronger: Adapting America's China Strategy in an Age of Competitive Interdependence* (Yale University Press, 2021), 56.

East Asia. An economic bloc would advance China's economy, increase its ability to "shape its own social and political future," weaken the United States relative to China, and provide China with the status that flows from its economic preeminence. Colby emphasizes that his argument is primarily structural—any state in China's position would be inclined to pursue regional hegemony and would be a threat to the United States. China is a still larger threat because it is controlled by the Chinese Communist Party (CCP). Colby acknowledges that there is debate over whether China is pursuing regional hegemony. But given China's incentives for pursuing regional hegemony and the greater difficulty of reversing hegemony once attained, the United States needs to make sure that China cannot succeed.[67]

Some of the disagreement over China's pursuit of regional hegemony likely reflects disagreement about the depth of China's desire. Many analysts who believe China is not actively pursuing regional hegemony nevertheless believe that China would prefer it. But they also judge that China does not place great value on regional hegemony. Thus, given the established US security commitments in East Asia, China sees the costs and risks of trying to be too high. In contrast, other experts believe that China places great value on regional hegemony. For the most part, however, even these experts have not argued that China would be willing to fight a large war against the US-Japan alliance to force the United States out of East Asia. If China is unwilling, then its chances for achieving regional hegemony are much poorer, and the dangers it poses are much smaller. Economic coercion is unlikely to undermine US alliances when the allies have truly vital interests at stake.

Regarding China's global ambitions, experts agree that China wants to significantly increase its international influence, especially its economic influence and overall international standing. There is substantial disagreement, however, over whether China wants to overturn the international order and how much changes to the order would negatively affect the United States.[68] Elizabeth Economy, who served as a senior advisor on China in the Department of Commerce from 2021 to 2023, argues that China's leaders want to "reorder the world order." They are "not satisfied with their country's position within the international system, the values and

---

67. Elbridge A. Colby, *The Strategy of Denial: American Defense in an Age of Great Power Conflict* (Yale University Press, 2021), 11–15, quote at 11. He served as deputy assistant secretary of defense from 2017 through 2018.

68. For an analysis of China's views of the international order and disagreements in the United States, see Michael J. Mazarr, Timothy R. Heath, and Astrid Stuth Cevallos, *China and the International Order* (RAND, 2018). Alastair Iain Johnston, "China in a World of Orders: Rethinking Compliance and Challenge in Beijing's International Relations," *International Security* 44, no. 2 (fall 2019): 9–60, argues that instead of a single order, there are different orders in different domains, and the extent of China's compliance and/or challenge depends on the specific order.

CHAPTER 1

policy preferences that the system embodies, how power is distributed, and how decisions are made." This reordering will include regional dominance—both gaining control over contested territories in Northeast Asia and the retreat of the United States from the region—but it will go well beyond it, with China acquiring global influence along many dimensions. Among its goals, China will become the world's dominant economy, demonstrate the superiority of its governance model, and transform the "institutions, norms, and values that govern relations among international actors, as well as China's place within that system."[69] Doshi's characterization is similar. Emphasizing that China's goals are directly related to achieving national rejuvenation by 2049, he argues that China "seeks to displace the current order led by the United States and its allies and partners, first at the regional level and now at the global level."[70]

A harsher, albeit largely consistent, view of China's global goals is presented by Matt Pottinger, who was US deputy national security advisor during the first Trump administration, and Mike Gallagher, who chaired the House Select Committee on the Chinese Communist Party. Pottinger and Gallagher believe China "is pursuing a raft of global initiatives designed to disintegrate the West and usher in an antidemocratic order," "the CCP has no desire to coexist indefinitely with great powers that promote liberal values and thus represent a fundamental threat to its rule," and Xi is "an agent of chaos."[71] They argue that Xi is determined to prevail in a global struggle between capitalism and socialism and is trying to dissolve Western alliances, use international institutions to achieve autocratic aims, and undermine the Westphalian system of nation-states.[72]

To deal with these challenges, Pottinger and Gallagher call for an especially competitive US strategy: The United States should pursue peaceful victory in its competition with China; the Chinese people will then find the inspiration "to explore new models of development and governance that don't rely on repression at home." They are essentially calling for the end of the CCP's authoritarian rule, which they make clear should not be achieved via

---

69. Elizabeth C. Economy, *The World According to China* (Polity, 2022), quotes on 5, 8.
70. Rush Doshi, "No Exit from Rivalry: How Steady States Can Guide Strategy," in Jude Blanchette and Lily McElwee, *Defining Success: Does the United States Need an "End State" for Its China Policy?* (Center for Strategic and International Studies, October 2024), 16, https://www.csis.org/analysis/defining-success-does-united-states-need-end-state-its-china-policy. The term *displace* leaves Doshi's claim unclear, because it leaves open the possibility of an order shaped by both countries; this would be quite different than replacing the United States.
71. Matt Pottinger and Mike Gallagher, "No Substitute for Victory: America's Competition with China Must Be Won, Not Managed," *Foreign Affairs* 103, no. 3, (May/June 2024) 26, 39, 39.
72. Matt Pottinger and Mike Gallagher, "What Does America Want From China? Debating Washington's Strategy—and the Endgame of Competition," *Foreign Affairs* 103, no. 4, (July/August 2024) 183–87.

force.[73] Pottinger and Gallagher also call for "a generational effort directed by the president to restore US primacy in Asia."[74] A number of experts disagreed with these policy prescriptions, focusing on the dangers of such an intense challenge to China, the low probability of US policies resulting in the collapse of the CCP, and the infeasibility of regaining primacy in the Pacific.[75]

More important for our discussion here, many experts believe that China's global ambitions are far more limited. Iain Johnston argues that "there is less to the liberal international order than many believe, and that at present China's challenge to order is less deep and/or wide than the current narrative suggests."[76] Heer argues that "China is focusing on maximizing its wealth, power, and influence in a multipolar world rather than on making a bid for global supremacy and legitimizing its governance and development model rather than expecting other states to adopt it."[77] Michael Swaine and Andrew Bacevich, while acknowledging that China wants to reduce the influence of Western liberal values in global regimes, hold that "despite some American rhetoric to the contrary, Beijing is not energetically engaged in a deliberate effort to duplicate its system across the world." They go on to argue that, unlike many modern imperialist powers, "China has not espoused an ideology or mindset that views . . . the coercive expansion of its system to other countries as essential to its continued national vitality."[78] Jessica Weiss, having explored the nature of the ideological contest between the United States and China, concludes that "a strategy that makes the world safer for authoritarianism is distinct from a messianic effort to spread autocracy or defeat democracy. There is scant evidence that the CCP has pursued a deliberate strategy to export autocracy and undermine democracy . . . the corrosive effects of China's influence on liberal democracy reflect collateral damage rather than a deliberate strategy to subvert democracy."[79]

---

73. This would not be an entirely new type of policy; on US efforts to destabilize the CCP and China's concern about these efforts, see David Shambaugh, "Parsing and Managing US-China Competition," in *Cold Rivals: The New Era of US-China Strategic Competition*, ed. Evan S. Medeiros (Georgetown University Press, 2023): 364–67.

74. Pottinger and Gallagher, "No Substitute for Victory," 26.

75. See the responses by Rush Doshi, "The Biden Plan"; Jessica Chen Weiss and James B. Steinberg, "The Perils of Estrangement"; and Paul Heer in "A Possible Partner," in "What Does America Want From China?" 174–83.

76. Johnston, "China in a World of Orders," 12.

77. Paul Heer, "The Diminishing Prospects for US-China Détente," *The National Interest*, October 24, 2024, https://nationalinterest.org/feature/diminishing-prospects-us-china-détente-213361.

78. Michael Swaine and Andrew Bacevich, *A Restraint Approach to US-China Relations: Reversing the Slide Toward Crisis and Conflict*, Quincy Paper No. 11, April 2023, 30–31.

79. Jessica Chen Weiss, "An Ideological Contest in US-China Relations? Assessing China's Defense of Autocracy," in *After Engagement: Dilemmas in US-China Security Relations*, ed. Jacques deLisle and Avery Goldstein, Brookings Institution, 2021, 144.

CHAPTER 1

Assuming for the sake of analysis that China holds the more ambitious set of global ambitions, how large a danger would they pose to the United States? These dangers are harder to assess succinctly because these goals are diverse, spanning political, economic, military/security, and ideological objectives. Many of these dangers are not national security dangers; while this does not make them unimportant, it does suggest that the threat to US interests is smaller than much of the American debate suggests. It also means that addressing these issues lies largely outside the focus of this book.

An obvious point that is nevertheless worth noting is that China does not pose an expansionist threat to the US homeland. Even experts who see China as having extremely ambitious global goals do not believe China wants to militarily conquer the United States. Moreover, no matter how much China's economy and capabilities grow, it will lack the ability required to do this.

The dangers posed by many of the other purported global challenges are rarely analyzed and often likely exaggerated. The United States might not like having China's economy become larger than its own (which increasingly looks to be a long way off), but US status concerns aside, the costs would not be large. Unless China's economy far outpaces that of the United States, the security dangers it would pose to US allies would not significantly increase. But even the economic costs need to be carefully evaluated. For example, if the renminbi joined the US dollar as the world's leading reserve currency, damage to the US economy might well not be large.[80] The impact of revisions to the international order would depend on the specifics. So long as the United States retains its alliances, the costs could be quite limited. On trade, US preferences are changing, which could reduce the economic costs posed by China's unfair trade and intellectual property practices. The United States increasingly prefers reductions in free trade and at the beginning of the second Trump administration the United States became the global leader in instituting tariffs. Regarding governance models, the United States would certainly prefer that more countries in the developing world become democracies instead of adopting or deepening their authoritarian regimes—the people of these countries will likely suffer under nondemocratic rule. But undesirable as autocracy would be, US security would not be threatened, and its economic interests might not be damaged either.

Two broader points deserve highlighting. First, while the United States would dislike that increases in China's power enable it to bring about certain global changes, this does not mean these changes are necessarily very bad for the United States. The possible future changes need to be specified and evaluated to avoid exaggerating (as well as possibly underestimating) the threat to US interests. Especially when these changes do not signifi-

---

80. Anshu Siripurapu and Noah Berman, "The Dollar: The World's Reserve Currency," CFR Backgrounder, updated July 19, 2023, https://www.cfr.org/backgrounder/dollar-worlds-reserve-currency.

cantly reduce US security, the United States will need to be clear-eyed about the nature of the challenge and adapt, as well as compete, to protect its interests. Second, the most important US responses to many of China's purported global ambitions will be domestic policies, not international ones. For example, the United States' ability to maintain prosperity and international competitiveness will depend most heavily on policies that invest in and support economic, technological, and human capital development at home. And, if the danger is the disintegration of the West, then the challenges lie primarily in the West itself—strengthening the foundations of its democracies, demonstrating the ability of capitalist systems to both grow and distribute wealth, and, for the United States, continuing to be a politically and ideologically attractive, reliable, and capable ally.

My own assessment of China's ambitions lies close to the less ambitious end of the regional and global spectrums. Chapter 2 identifies theoretical reasons that China might well want a sphere of influence in Northeast Asia, even though China's security does not require it. However, there is little to suggest that China is willing to run large risks to achieve this outcome. The military capabilities that China would require to coerce and invade Taiwan overlap quite extensively with the capabilities it would require to forcibly achieve regional hegemony. Consequently, China's extensive military buildup provides little information about the value it places on regional hegemony. China's effort to change some aspects of the international order will run contrary to US interests, but the United States needs to be careful not to misattribute the motives that fuel these challenges. Virtually any country that has achieved tremendous economic and technological growth, especially if its economy is approaching the size and sophistication of the world's leading economy, should be expected to want greater influence over the international economic regime and international institutions.[81] Because the post–World War II liberal international order largely reflects US interests and power, China's rise would almost inevitably result in challenges to norms and institutions that were designed to favor the United States.

But adjudicating the debate over China's aims is beyond my expertise. Even some China experts, while holding their own conclusions, recognize the difficulty of reaching definitive conclusions about the dangers of China's rise.[82] In addition to this unavoidable uncertainty, there is always the possibility that China's ambitions could change for the worse.

---

81. For example, Harry Harding, "The United States and China: From Partners to Competitors in America's Eyes," in Medeiros, *Cold Rivals*, 72, argues that once China joined the international order, "it understandably want[ed] to be a rule maker rather than simply the rule taker that the United States envisioned."

82. For example, Evan Medeiros, having noted a variety of explanations for the downturn in US-China relations, observes, "Most of these forecasts are equally logical (i.e., the causal links are clear and often historically grounded) and have a reasonable probability of materializing." Evan S. Medeiros, "Introduction: A New Strategic Reality," in Medeiros, *Cold Rivals*, 3.

US policy should therefore be cognizant of the entire spectrum of possible Chinese ambitions, instead of choosing and focusing exclusively on one. If the United States had unlimited resources, it could strive to deploy overwhelming military capabilities to deter China from pursuing each of its ambitions. This could involve highly competitive policies and offensive doctrines designed to win the military competition, to increase the costs and risks to China of pursuing provocative policies, and to demonstrate the United States' resolve to contain China.

Such a competitive policies, however, suffers two potentially serious shortcomings. First, the United States does not have unlimited resources. Consequently, the United States should give greater weight to the more likely and dangerous possibilities while hedging against the less likely ones. Second, in addition to having greedy motives, China also has security motives that drive its ambitions. The fact that China is a mixed state—greedy and insecure—requires the United States to adopt a more nuanced set of policies.

CHINA AS A MIXED-MOTIVE STATE

The debate over how to deal with a major-power adversary is often cast as depending on whether the adversary is motivated by security or greed. The spiral model and the deterrence model capture how these different types of adversaries will respond to a defender's policies and the dynamics of these interactions. In the end, however, this is a false choice because an adversary could be motivated both by insecurity created by international structure and by greed that reflects a state's internally driven ambitions.[83] Combining defensive and motivational realism to form a more general strategic choice theory enables us to analyze mixed states, especially when states face uncertainty about each other's motives.

The value a mixed-motive state places on expansion will be the combination of its security value and greed value, which makes this type of state more difficult to deter. The defending state, however, should not simply increase its deterrent capability because posing an increased threat can decrease the security of the mixed-motive state, which would make it still harder to deter. In other words, security-dilemma logic applies to mixed-motive states as well as pure security seekers. When facing a mixed-motive state, the defender may have to strike a somewhat more competitive balance between enhancing its deterrent capabilities and decreasing the threat that it poses to the adversary's security. This is because deterring the mixed state requires more capable deterrent forces than deterring a comparable pure security-seeking state.

---

83. Charles L. Glaser, "Fear Factor: How to Know When You're in a Security Dilemma," *Foreign Affairs* 103, no. 4, July/August 2024, 122–28.

The preceding sections make clear that the United States should view China as an especially complicated mixed type. China sees itself as insecure because it does not control some territory that it believes is part of its homeland and because it lacks the political and military capabilities to gain control. The military challenges China faces are not limited to the Taiwan Strait or even East Asia because the vulnerability of its sea lines of communication could enable the United States to weaken it in a long war over Taiwan.

In addition to its insecurity, China is also a greedy state. In part this reflects the countries' divergent perspectives on Taiwan. Whereas Taiwan is a security issue for China, the United States sees China's drive to control Taiwan as reflecting greedy motives, at a minimum because China refuses to reject the use of force as a legitimate means for resolving the dispute. Moreover, China's goals may reach beyond control of Taiwan. As reviewed above, experts disagree on the extent and nature of China's aims for both regional hegemony and global hegemony. Consequently, if possible, the United States should pursue a policy that is robust in the face of these uncertainties—one that does well against the greatest dangers and the most likely ones, does reasonably well against the less likely dangers, and can be adjusted in a timely fashion as the United States gains more information about China. A robust policy must account for the risks that can be generated by competitive policies that increase China's insecurity, as well as the risks of posing an inadequate deterrent to the China's drive for expansion that is driven by its combination of insecurity and greed.

In broad terms, a robust US policy should now give priority to Taiwan and hedge against the possibility that China is or will become highly determined to achieve regional hegemony. The Taiwan problem poses the greatest danger because China's desire to achieve regional hegemony is smaller than its desire to unify with Taiwan—likely much smaller; China's political prospects for undermining US alliances are poor, if the United States acts as a steady-handed committed ally; and China's military prospects for winning a regional war that would force the United States out of East Asia are quite poor. US policy toward Taiwan is explored thoroughly in chapter 4. Whether the United States should hedge against China's pursuit of regional hegemony depends on a prior set of question about the extent of US interests in preserving its allies' security, which are evaluated in the analysis of US grand strategy in chapter 3. I conclude the United States should pursue policies designed to preserve its security alliances in East Asia. However, the key reason for preserving US alliances is not to prevent China from achieving regional hegemony but instead to prevent a regional war that could involve the United States.

The conventional and nuclear military policies that support this type of hedged policy should give priority to defensive strategies, if military technology and geography enable the United States to maintain high-quality deterrent capabilities while doing so. These strategies should generate little Chinese insecurity while posing potent deterrent threats. Chapters 6 and 7 argue that highly effective defensive strategies are possible, most easily for US nuclear forces but also for the conventional forces the United States requires to defend Taiwan and its Northeast Asian allies.

Most important to US success in preserving its alliances will be demonstrating that the United States continues to have large/vital interests in protecting its allies' security. President Trump's negative attitude toward and lack of respect for the United States' most important allies has created deep doubts in East Asia about the United States' future role in the region. If the United States decides once again that it is committed to its allies' security, it has a variety of options for preserving them, although rebuilding US allies' confidence will require time. The tightening, deepening, and extending of US alliances and partnerships in the region starting in the mid-2010s, which the United States pursued in response to China's more assertive policies, clearly indicate these countries are inclined to balance against the threat posed by China. And the United States has the potential to make outsized contributions to its allies' security. Restoring confidence in the United States as a reliable ally is the key to successful hedging.

Realism's Take on Economic Interdependence

Before turning, in chapter 2, to a variety of theoretical arguments that focus on the features of individual states that influence their greediness, a key liberal argument—economic interdependence as a source of peace—should be included in our discussion of structural theories.[84] The argument is structural in that it focuses on the states' economic relationship, not on their unit-level characteristics, for example, regime type and economic system.[85] The argument has played an important role in the US debate over China's rise, offering an optimistic prediction about the implications of China's growing power—the increasing benefits of trade decrease the probability of war and could enable China to rise peacefully. In addition, economic openness—

---

84. There are two other key liberal arguments. The democratic peace is not a structural argument and is addressed in the following chapter. International institutions as a source of peace are structural but suffer from endogeneity problems; see Glaser, *Rational Theory of International Politics*, 161–66. These institutions have played a far less prominent role in the debate over China's rise. But see G. John Ikenberry, "The Rise of China and the Future of the West: Can the Liberal System Survive?," *Foreign Affairs* 87, no. 1, (January/February 2009), 23–37, who emphasizes the importance of the openness of the international order and its institutions for accommodating China's rise.

85. However, unlike power and the offense-defense balance, a state can choose to change its trade relationship relatively quickly.

including the interdependence it creates and the benefits it provides—is a central component of the liberal international order, which its proponents believe can make the US-China power transition a peaceful one. The study of the relationship between the global economy and conflict has reached beyond trade to include international finance and the globalization of production, among many dimensions. Space limitations prevent a thorough discussion, but given the importance of the interdependence argument, a short summary, application to China, and brief review of the realist objections are worthwhile.

The standard liberal argument is that trade—and economic interdependence more generally—reduces the probability of war: States give priority to increasing their prosperity; trade, foreign investment, and efficient international financial systems can play a central role in producing prosperity; war between trading partners would eliminate these economic benefits; and, because states do not want to lose these benefits, trade reduces the probability of war. In effect, war is deterred by the anticipated economic losses it would produce. The higher the level of economic interdependence, the larger its benefits, and, therefore, the larger the economic costs of war. Implicitly, the argument assumes that trade would continue unless war occurs and that trade ends once war occurs; states are considering the future value of trade that would be interrupted by war.[86]

The potential costs of economic disruptions will not always follow from the direct value of lost trade. Globalization now requires that states participate in the international economy to remain competitive in leading commercial sectors and maybe especially in cutting-edge defense systems. Losing access to global supply chains can therefore have disproportionate effects on an advanced state's economy. A state that could be isolated from the global economy by a war and in its aftermath should be especially concerned about the economic costs of war, which should increase the deterrent value of globalized interdependence.[87]

States may not be equally vulnerable to the economic disruptions that could flow from war. This asymmetry could reflect many factors, including different contributions of trade to the states' GDPs, different degrees of dependence on

---

86. For a succinct review of these arguments, and numerous qualifications and debates, see Dale C. Copeland, *Economic Interdependence and War* (Princeton University Press, 2014), 16–50. Copeland's argument emphasizes the importance of focusing on future trade expectations, not current trade; he diverges from the standard liberal argument by focusing on the security implications of trade, not the prosperity implications. See also Waltz, *Theory of International Politics*, 129–60 and Daniel W. Dresner, "The Dangers of Misunderstanding Economic Interdependence," CATO Institute (September 12, 2023), https://www.cato.org/publications/dangers-misunderstanding-economic-interdependence.

87. Stephen G. Brooks, *Producing Security: Multinational Corporations, Globalization, and the Changing Calculus of Conflict* (Princeton University Press, 2005), 76–78.

international supply chains, the greater ability of one state to use its military forces to prevent the other state from trading, and a state's dominant control of critical hubs in global financial and information markets.[88] Asymmetric vulnerability should influence the deterrent effect of economic interdependence: The less vulnerable state would suffer smaller economic costs in war and, therefore, should be less deterred from starting one. In addition, during peacetime the less vulnerable state may be able to use its advantage to compel the more vulnerable state to make economic or geopolitical concessions. It could also use trade restrictions on military equipment and components to limit its adversary's military capability. The United States and its allies used this type of policy against the Soviet Union during the Cold War.[89]

A key realist argument challenges the assertion that economic interdependence causes peace by bringing the value that states place on their security back into the discussion: When a state's security is at stake, the security value of war will usually greatly exceed the economic value of interdependence. Consequently, although the state values prosperity, it will risk war, and fight if necessary, to preserve or increase its security, even though it will suffer the lost trade. In addition, a greedy state might fight a war of nonsecurity expansion for similar reasons. The point is not that the logic of the liberal argument is fully wrong but rather that it exaggerates the constraining effect of economic interdependence when the security stakes are large.[90]

Another line of argument questions the size of the interdependence costs of war and, therefore, the potential of economic dependence to deter. There are theoretical reasons to expect states to trade extensively during war, and historically, states have done so. Consequently, the trade costs of war can be much smaller than they might at first appear.[91] In addition, the costs of interrupted trade would be reduced when a state can reasonably quickly replace trade with domestic production or a new international supplier. The costs of disrupted trade will also depend on the length of the war, with shorter wars tending to result in lower overall costs; however, this will also depend on whether trade is restored following the war.

A state facing economic vulnerabilities may not feel threatened when its relationship with the opposing state is good and war is considered quite unlikely. However, if war seems more likely, economic vulnerabilities can be a source of insecurity, leading a state to reduce its dependence, which

---

88. On the latter phenomenon, see Henry Farrell and Abraham L. Newman, "Weaponized Interdependence: How Global Economic Networks Shape State Coercion," *International Security* 44, no. 1 (summer 2019): 42–79.

89. Michael Mastanduno, *Economic Containment: Cocom and the Politics of East-West Trade* (Cornell University Press, 1992).

90. Mearsheimer, *The Great Delusion*, 207–9.

91. Mariya Grinberg, "Wartime Commercial Policy and Trade Between Enemies," *International Security* 46, no. 1 (summer 2021): 9–52.

reduces the deterrent value of the remaining dependence. Moreover, policies designed to reduce a state's economic dependence can fuel policies that make war more probable. For example, a state with vulnerable import supply lines may choose to build up forces and/or establish alliances and partnerships that help protect the resources. These policies can in turn fuel military and territorial competition with a state's adversary, which can then strain the states' political relationship. For example, during the Cold War, US commitments in the Persian Gulf region reflected the country's desire to protect the flow of oil; these commitments, however, contributed to US competition with the Soviet Union for influence in the region.[92]

Once an opposing state is judged to be a serious security threat, the state could restrict trade to reduce the adversary's overall power relative to the state's. Because power is the foundation of military capability, this relative weakening could over time reduce the adversary's military capability and possibly its international ambitions. To be successful, this economic containment would have to be more damaging to the adversary's economy than to the state's own economy. These trade restrictions and the trade war they would likely generate would further stress the states' political relationship, possibly increasing the probability of war.

Because there are many different types of trading situations and a variety of cross-cutting incentives within them, we might expect that the influence of economic interdependence on the probability of war varies quite substantially. Possibly reflecting this complexity, a recent review of empirical studies of trade finds that some support a positive effective of trade on war, some identify mixed effects, and others find no effect. At least as important, their results are "unwieldy, and sometimes contradictory."[93] Nevertheless, the impact of economic interdependence on a specific pair of countries might be clearer. With this in mind, we turn to the United States and China.

US-CHINA ECONOMIC INTERDEPENDENCE

Since China's economic opening under Deng Xiaoping in the late 1970s, the country's economy and international trade have grown enormously, making China the world's second-largest economy and largest trading state.[94] US

---

92. Rosemary A. Kelanic, *Black Gold and Blackmail: Oil and Great Power Politics* (Cornell University Press, 2020), chap. 6.

93. For a succinct summary of the state of knowledge, see Stephen G. Brooks, "The Trade Truce: When Economic Interdependence Does—and Doesn't—Promote Peace," *Foreign Affairs* 103, no. 4 (July/August 2024), 143. For earlier assessments, see Edward D. Mansfield and Brian M. Pollins, eds., *Economic Interdependence and International Conflict: New Perspectives on an Enduring Debate* (University of Michigan Press, 2008).

94. Wayne M. Morrison, *China's Economic Rise: History, Trends, Challenges, and Implications for the United States*, Congressional Research Service, updated June 25, 2019, https://crsreports.congress.gov/product/pdf/RL/RL33534.

CHAPTER 1

policies supported China's growth, including, perhaps most importantly, backing its entry to the WTO in 2001. However, as US-China relations have soured and the United States has come to see China as a strategic competitor, the US view of trade with China has changed quite dramatically. Under the Biden administration, the United States decided to "de-risk" its economic interdependence with China, which was intended to protect US national security by slowing China's ability to improve its military forces and preserving US advantages in artificial intelligence (AI). De-risking involves limiting or banning the sale of advanced technologies to China and limiting US investments in China's development of technologies that are critical for military, AI, and cyber capabilities.[95] In addition to trade restrictions, to reduce China's ability to coerce the United States or damage the US economy, the United States is investing in the ability to produce advanced semiconductors at home—the vast majority of which are currently manufactured in Taiwan—and to reduce its dependence on potentially critical supply chains that run through China, including for rare earth metals and components of the transition to a carbon-free economy.

During the Biden administration, the United States held that its goal was to protect US security, not to slow China's development and economic growth. The shift in terminology from *decoupling* to *de-risking* was intended to emphasize this distinction. Chinese leaders, however, appeared to see little difference between the two and believed that the United States was trying to contain China.[96] Even before the United States implemented these de-risking policies, China had pursued policies to enhance its development of advanced technologies and to become more self-sufficient in their production, which have generated a range of economic and security concerns in the United States.[97] And, while deteriorating US-China relations have increased China's concerns about its economic dependence, China has long viewed the vulnerability of its imports, especially oil, as a key source of insecurity. It has pursued policies to reduce this vulnerability, which have fueled military competition with the United States.[98]

Some experts believe that China has been constrained by its economic dependence. The United States and China have passed through a power

95. Sarah Bauerle Danzman and Emily Weinstein, "A New White House Order Is Taking Aim at Investment in Chinese Tech. How Will It Actually Work?, *Atlantic Council*, August 10, 2023, https://www.atlanticcouncil.org/blogs/new-atlanticist/a-new-white-house-order-is-taking-aim-at-investment-in-chinese-tech-how-will-it-actually-work/.

96. Lily McElwee, "Beijing's Emerging Assessment of De-risking," CSIS, October 17, 2023, https://www.csis.org/analysis/beijings-emerging-assessment-de-risking.

97. Institute for Security & Development Policy, *Made in China 2025*, Backgrounder, June 2018, https://isdp.eu/content/uploads/2018/06/Made-in-China-Backgrounder.pdf.

98. Charles L. Glaser, "How Oil Influences US National Security," *International Security* 38, no. 2 (fall 2013): 112–46; Michael A. McDevitt, *China as a Twenty-First-Century Naval Power: Theory, Practice, and Implications* (Naval Institute, 2020).

transition, yet war has not broken out. Maybe economic interdependence contributed to this peaceful transition.[99] At the same time, the possibility of greater losses of trade and investment during the Biden administration did not deter China from pursuing more assertive policies—including with respect to Taiwan and the South China Sea—that have seriously strained US-China relations and, in turn, contributed to US support for additional sanctions and de-risking.[100] These costs, however, are much smaller than the likely interdependence costs of a major war and therefore may tell us little about their contribution to deterring war.

Early in the second Trump administration, the United States imposed high wide-ranging tariffs on China. However, the United States also imposed tariffs on allies and other adversaries at varying levels and has failed to offer a consistent message explaining the tariffs on China. As of this writing, these US tariffs are too recent to assess whether and how they will influence China's assertive policies, but because the United States did not link them to China's foreign policy, the tariffs do not provide a good test of the coercive potential of China's economic dependence.

China's leaders could anticipate numerous ways that a major war with the United States over Taiwan could result in economic-interdependence costs: sanctions during the war; the intentional military disruption of ocean-borne trade; the unintentional disruptive effect of the war itself, which would result from intense fighting in the South China and East China Seas and the Taiwan Strait; and trade restrictions that the United States and its allies could impose after the war, either to punish China for the war, to weaken it, or both.

These resulting economic costs would be large but would involve some important uncertainties. For example, China's leaders might doubt the United States and its allies would impose sanctions that could trigger severe damage to their own economies, and China might believe the war would be short, which could greatly reduce the economic costs.[101] In addition, China has pursued some measures to reduce its vulnerability, including building a large strategic

---

99. Dresner, "The Dangers of Misunderstanding Economic Interdependence."

100. This claim may be overstated, however, as some analysts believe that China has limited its military exercises in the hope of not discouraging international investors while still sending a strong signal to Taiwan. David Pierson and Amy Chang Chien, "China Holds War Games Encircling Taiwan in Warning to Islands Leader," *New York Times*, October 12, 2024.

101. "Could the West Punish China the Way It Punished Ukraine?," *Economist*, April 22, 2022. The Western ability to coordinate and maintain sanctions against Russia could, however, convince China's leaders that severe sanctions would be imposed. M. Taylor Fravel, "China's Potential Lessons from Ukraine for Conflict over Taiwan," *Washington Quarterly* 46, no. 3 (fall 2023), 19. A blockade of Taiwan would interrupt supply chains, disrupt global banking and financial markets, and put foreign investments in China at risk. A 2022 study estimated that over two trillion dollars of economic activity would be at risk; this estimate did not include the cost of international responses and second-order effects. Charles Vest, Agatha Kratz, and Reva Goujon, "The Global Economic Disruptions of a Taiwan Conflict," Rhodium Group, December 14, 2022, https://rhg.com/research/taiwan-economic-disruptions/.

petroleum reserve and developing an alternative to the US-dominated system for processing international financial transactions. Nevertheless, China's leaders would almost certainly anticipate large economic costs from a major war.

In addition, the United States and its allies may have the potential to inflict larger and more asymmetric costs than is generally appreciated. Recent analysis argues that, contrary to the conventional wisdom, the damage inflicted by cutting off trade would inflict much greater economic damage on China than on the United States. Both the magnitude of the costs and the asymmetry reflect China's dependence on high technologies developed and supplied by the United States and its allies. In contrast, the United States could much more readily replace the goods it imports from China; rare-earth metals may be the key exception. The United States cannot inflict truly massive damage, however, unless its allies participate in the trade cutoff against China.[102]

Whether these economic costs would play a significant role in deterring China from starting a war over Taiwan is a largely different question, however. The military and political risks and costs of war with Taiwan would be enormous. China's leaders should anticipate losing thousands, likely tens of thousands of military personnel and much of their navy and air force. If the United States comes to Taiwan's defense, which China's leaders appear to believe it will, then China would also be risking large attacks against military targets in its homeland and the possibility of escalation to nuclear war. And, maybe most important, China would be risking losing the war over Taiwan, which could jeopardize the CCP's hold on power. Still, China's leaders might be willing to incur these costs if they became convinced that unification could not be achieved by other means and especially if Taiwan moved significantly toward independence. If China were willing to run these risks, then the economic-interdependence costs would likely be dwarfed and would therefore be unlikely to tip the balance.

To briefly summarize, this chapter has shown that the structural pressures that exist during China's rise, as well the pressures that will exist once China reaches its full power potential, should not push the United States and China toward war or even intense competition. According to defensive realism, the international situation that China and the United States face is quite promising—distance, oceans, and nuclear weapons ensure their homeland security, essentially eliminating pressures for preventive war, drives for regional hegemony, and incentive for a politically unsettling arms race.

---

102. Stephen G. Brooks and Ben A. Vagle, "The Real China Trump Card: The Hawk's Case Against Decoupling," *Foreign Affairs* 104, no. 2 (March/April 2025): 76–89.

Instead, the key dangers generated by China's rise stem from China's desire for greedy/nonsecurity expansion. Because the United States has security commitments in East Asia, China's goals create the potential for conflict. War over Taiwan is by far the most dangerous possibility. For a variety of reasons, China's interests in regional hegemony and global dominance pose much smaller dangers.

CHAPTER 2

State-Level Theories and China's Rise

This chapter explores state/unit-level theories—theories that focus on specific features of states—to understand China's motives and to more fully appreciate the implications of China's rise. Chapter 1 employed defensive realism to explain the international-structural pressures created by China's rise and to provide a broad foundation from which to analyze major-power security interactions. In addition, it used motivational realism to explore how greedy states, constrained by the international system, would act as their power increased. To provide estimates of China's greed, chapter 1 turned to the judgements of China experts. Some of this analysis employed basic deterrence theory and bargaining arguments to explore the regional implications of China's rise.

Supplementing these realist/strategic-choice theories with unit-level theories enhances our ability to analyze specific cases. Defensive realism assumes that states are uncertain about others' motives but does not theorize a state's initial estimates of opposing states' motives, specifically the probability that they are greedy. Greedy states play a more prominent role in motivational realism, but this theory too does not explore the sources of states' motives. This is how strategic-choice theories work; they identify key variables and explore the implications of different values of those variables. This approach gives them much of their analytic leverage but leaves them incomplete. Put differently, state-level theories complement strategic-choice theories by theorizing the value of key variables.[1] State-level theories also complement the assessments of country experts, both providing a different set of perspectives on the state's motives and exposing the theoretical underpinnings of the experts' assessments.

In addition, and less abstract, state-level theories can guide our thinking about the sources, depth, and breadth of an opposing state's goals as well as its propensity to use force to achieve these goals. Particularly relevant to

---

1. On the complementary nature of rational theories, including defensive realism, with other types of theories, see Charles L. Glaser, *Rational Theory of International Politics: The Logic of Competition and Cooperation* (Princeton University Press, 2010), 23–27.

China are theories of nationalism and national identity, international status and prestige, and regime type—most broadly, autocracy versus democracy.

My motivation for considering state-level theories is not driven solely by the analytic value of complementarity, however. Some of China's policies since around 2008 are hard to understand primarily as security-driven, which raises the question of what else China might be trying to achieve. Most glaringly, its assertive policies in the South China Sea have done little if anything to increase China's ability to defend itself, but they have played a central role in negatively shifting the United States'—and many other states'—assessments of China's goals and ambitions.[2] The net effect has been a tightening of US alliances in the region, an increase in US defense spending with a focus on East Asia, a growth in the number of incidents that could generate crises, and an increase in China's sense of encirclement.

Unit-level theories identify a variety of sources of China's greed. China's national identity is often captured in terms of its need to overcome the indignities of its century of humiliation and to return to its former regional preeminence. Consideration of China's national identity provides a deeper understanding of the significance that China places on Taiwan and the depth of its determination to achieve unification. In addition to the narrow importance of gaining sovereign control, China understands Taiwan as central to its rejuvenation and the successful achievement of major/superpower status. Similar arguments and narratives are used to explain its policies in the South China Sea.

China's desire for status likely further increases its incentives to pursue changes to the geopolitical status quo. Not achieving the changes pictured by its identity is not only unsatisfactory on its own terms; it also fuels the belief that the United States is disrespecting China and failing to acknowledge its achievements. A key question and uncertainty is whether national identity and status desires will drive China to demand a sphere of influence, as rising powers often have in the past. A full sphere in East Asia would require the United States to withdraw from the region and result in regional hegemony; the implications would be much more far-reaching than ending the United States' commitment to Taiwan because US alliances lie at the core of US grand strategy. Status is also believed to be influencing China's nuclear buildup and may be a factor in influencing the size of China's strategic nuclear force.

China's regime type—which increasingly under President Xi Jinping is a personalist dictatorship—is further cause for concern. Xi has largely eliminated collective decision-making and reduced elite opposition to his poli-

---

2. A potential source of greed is the desire to acquire resources to increase a country's prosperity. Although frequently mentioned as a rationale for China's South China Sea policy, resources are likely of only secondary importance; see chapter 5.

cies, thereby giving himself greater leeway to pursue his ambitious international agenda and possibly preventing himself from receiving adequate assessments of China's military capabilities.

Nationalism and National Identity

Nationalism is a complex concept that captures a state's beliefs about itself and can include both domestic and international dimensions.[3] For our purposes, the international dimension of national identity—which typically makes claims "to historical uniqueness, to the territory that the nation-state ought to occupy, and to the kinds of relations that should prevail between one's nation and others"—is key.[4] Historical memory, which governments influence by what they teach and celebrate, can play a central role in the formation of national identity.[5] Understanding an opposing state's national identity can provide information about its motives and goals, its assessments of other states' motives, and, more generally, its worldview. Each of these, in turn, can influence how competitive the state's own policy should be, where it is most likely to face territorial challenges, and whether war is likely.

Maybe most basic, national identity influences the territory that a state believes is its own or should be part of its country. A state may place great value on territory that lacks significant material value simply because its national identity includes possession of this territory. An important feature of these beliefs can be that the national territory is indivisible, which makes compromise over the territory difficult or impossible. A state has a variety of tools that can generate beliefs about what territory belongs to it, including its portrayal of its history, education, symbols, maps, and national myths.[6] Among the possible results is that modern states infused with nationalism will usually fight very hard to protect their homelands and acquire territory they believe is part of their national territory.

---

3. Although commonly used, the term *nationalism* does not have an agreed-upon meaning. This partly reflects the different questions that analysts are studying and the complexity of the phenomena of interest; for discussion of this point, see Ernst B. Haas, "What Is Nationalism and Why Should We Study It?," *International Organization* 40, no. 3 (summer 1986): 707–44, and Harris Mylonas and Maya Tudor, "Nationalism: What We Know and What We Still Need to Know," *Annual Review of Political Science* 24 (2021): 109–32.

4. Haas, "What Is Nationalism and Why Should We Study It?," 727–28. For discussion of nationalism as social identity, different types of nationalisms, and their implications for conflict, see Kathleen E. Powers, *Nationalisms in International Politics* (Princeton University Press, 2022).

5. Zheng Wang, *Never Forget National Humiliation: Historical Memory in Chinese Politics and Foreign Relations* (Columbia University Press, 2012), 2–7.

6. C. Barak Kadercan, "Politics of Survival, Nationalism, and War for Territory," PhD diss., University of Chicago, August 2011, 31–32.

National identity can be a source of disagreement and fuel conflict between states for a variety of reasons, including because control of territory resulted from political events, including wars and the dissolution of a larger state, which a state views as illegitimate; because two or more states' identities define the same territory as part of their state; and because states' depiction of the histories that define their state paint contrasting and inconsistent pictures of their past behavior.[7]

Nationalism and national identity can also include beliefs about a state's proper or necessary international role (which can create overlaps with its desired status, which I address in the following section). For example, a state could believe that it should be the leader of its region or the regional hegemon because it is the region's most powerful state. This, in turn, could cause the state to believe it deserves a sphere of influence in which other major powers do not interfere and in which it influences and constrains the other regional states' foreign policies. This belief could reflect true security concerns but could also be largely separate from them.

A state could also believe that among its defining purposes is to spread its political ideology or religion, or to protect the international order. These beliefs may be partially based in logics that connect these roles to the state's material interests, but they could also be partly or entirely separate from these interests. In the latter case, explaining and anticipating a state's actions and reactions will require considering its national identity.

Although Americans usually consider nationalism when thinking about other countries, the United States in fact has a strong national identity that significantly influences its international policy. For example, the United States typically understands itself as special among nations, a rule follower, and an order builder and maintainer. Some of this is captured in then–Secretary of State Madeleine Albright's famous statement: "If we have to use force, it is because we are America; we are the indispensable nation. We stand tall and we see further than other countries into the future."[8] The United States also believes the world should mirror its systems and preferences by embracing democracy and (at least until recently) free markets and accepting the international order that it established following World War II.[9] Even its frequently stated goal of maintaining military preeminence and dominance may reflect its worldview as much as the United States'

---

7. On ways in which nationalism can lead to war, see Stephen Van Evera, "Hypotheses on Nationalism and War," *International Security* 18, no. 4 (spring 1994): 5–39.

8. Secretary of State Madeleine K. Albright, interview with Matt Lauer, *The Today Show*, NBC-TV, Columbus, OH, February 19, 1998, https://1997-2001.state.gov/statements/1998/980219a.html.

9. Colin Dueck, *Reluctant Crusaders: Power, Culture, and Change in American Grand Strategy* (Princeton University Press, 2006).

actual need for these capabilities, as the military need is rarely demonstrated or carefully analyzed.[10]

National identity can also include a country's beliefs about specific other countries—whether they are friends or enemies, liked or disliked. Here history tends to play a central role. Countries that suffered under invasion or imperial rule tend to have negative, even hateful, views of their oppressors, as do countries that have fought major wars. These views are not written in stone, however. Change is often possible, as the past fades and new relationships become more salient, especially if a state takes actions designed to support this transformation. Positive beliefs among western European countries and US relationships with former adversaries attest to the possibilities for change along this dimension of national identity.

CHINA'S NATIONAL IDENTITY

China's more assertive foreign policy has generated recent debate about whether China's nationalism has been rising.[11] However, for our purposes, this question is less important than understanding the content of China's national identity. As China becomes more powerful, whatever nationalism exists becomes more important because China will have greater capability to pursue goals identified by or integral to this national identity.

China's modern national identity is frequently characterized in terms of two defining strands—historical glory and a century of humiliation—that fuel its drive for national rejuvenation.[12] Key elements of its historical glory include China's millennia-long civilization, its leadership of great empires, and its cultural advances and great scientific inventions. The century of humiliation refers to the period from the Opium War in 1839 to the conclusion of China's civil war in 1949. During this period, China was invaded by foreigners (mostly Western countries and Japan), forced to sign unequal treaties, faced independence movements in Tibet and Mongolia, and fell into civil war. China lost control of roughly a third of the territory it had controlled.[13]

---

10. See, for example, *The National Security Strategy of the United States of America*, White House, December 2017, 4, https://trumpwhitehouse.archives.gov/wp-content/uploads/2017/12/NSS-Final-12–18–2017–0905.pdf, and *National Security Strategy*, White House, 2015, 8 https://obamawhitehouse.archives.gov/sites/default/files/docs/2015_national_security_strategy_2.pdf.

11. Alastair Iain Johnston, "Is Chinese Nationalism Rising?: Evidence from Beijing," *International Security* 41, no. 3 (winter 2016/17): 7–43, argues that popular nationalism is not rising.

12. On China as a responsible great power, see Hoo Tiang Boon, *China's Global Identity: Considering the Responsibilities of a Great Power* (Georgetown University Press, 2018), who also notes other identities, including socialist, third-world, and developing nation, xx–xxii.

13. Alison Adcock Kaufman, "The 'Century of Humiliation,' Then and Now: Chinese Perceptions of the International Order," *Pacific Focus* 25, no. 1 (April 2010): 5.

The century of humiliation plays an important role in how China views itself and the world.[14] The Chinese Communist Party (CCP), having shed its commitment to standard communist economic principles, now bases its legitimacy and the case for one-party rule on its success in enabling China to leave behind its past humiliation.[15] China's official curriculum has included "'national humiliation education' that teaches students that the PRC needs to defend itself against a hostile world."[16] And memory of the past stands as a warning that China could once again fail and be victimized by outsiders. Nevertheless, the memory of China's past does not generate agreement among Chinese elites about the basic nature of the international system—whether intense competition is inevitable and what role China should play as its power continues to increase.[17]

There is broad agreement, however, that recovering territory that was lost when the Qing dynasty collapsed is central to overcoming China's past humiliation and regaining its lost glory. When Hong Kong was returned to Chinese control in 1997, China's president Jiang Zemin said, "The occupation of Hong Kong was the epitome of the humiliation China suffered in modern history."[18] Central to this view of its territory in China's national identity is Taiwan, which China sees as an issue that was left unresolved by its civil war, which ended in 1949.[19] China's claims in the South China Sea are also cast within this framework. Andrew Chubb explains that "even though none of its Southeast Asian rivals were imperialist powers, the party-state's official positions on the South China Sea disputes place the issue with a near-identical narrative of past and present victimization."[20] Compromise on these issues is difficult not only because of the value that

---

14. William A. Callahan, *China: The Pessoptimist Nation* (Oxford University Press, 2012); Tianbiao Zhu, "Nationalism and Chinese Foreign Policy," *China Review* 1, no. 1 (fall 2001): 1–27.

15. Callahan, *China*, 3; Wang, *Never Forget National Humiliation*, 126–29; Kaufman, "The 'Century of Humiliation,'" 3.

16. Callahan, *China*, 12 (see also 194 for a similar point).

17. Kaufman, "The 'Century of Humiliation'"; David Shambaugh, *China Goes Global: The Partial Power* (Oxford University Press), 2013, chap. 2, which presents a spectrum of views among Chinese analysts about the role nationalism should play in China's foreign policy.

18. William A. Callahan, "National Insecurities: Humiliation, Salvation, and Chinese Nationalism," *Alternatives* 29 (2004): 212.

19. The issue has an even longer lineage, however; in his diary in 1928, Chiang Kai-shek wrote, "Recover Taiwan and Korea. Recover the land that was originally part of the Han and Tang dynasty. Then, as descendants of the Yellow Emperor, we will have no shame." Howard W. French, *Everything Under the Heavens: How the Past Helps Shape China's Push for Global Power* (Alfred A. Knopf, 2017), 249.

20. Andrew Chubb, "Chinese Popular Nationalism and the PRC Policy in the South China Sea," PhD diss., University of Western Australia, 2016, 52–55, quote at 52. He also holds that "the realization of these disputed maritime claims [in the SCS] has long been portrayed as a matter of national survival" (47).

Chinese nationalism creates for these territories but also because concessions will be interpreted through the lens of China's national identity as signs of weakness in confronting foreign powers.[21] Bill Hayton argues that Chinese discussions of the South China Sea "now take place within a discourse that begins by assuming that the islands are naturally 'ours' . . . [this] creates a national narrative that, in effect, stakes the legitimacy of the ruling elite upon their performance over these tiny islands."[22]

The importance of China's past is also captured in its goal of national rejuvenation, which emphasizes not only that China is rising but also that it is returning to its former position of major-power standing. The combination of past glory and the century of humiliation provides the foundation for China's understanding of its current success as a right and inevitable, and "'the restoration' of China's natural status as a great power at the center of global politics."[23] Rejuvenation has been an important theme starting, at the latest, with China's past leader Jiang Zemin.[24] China's next leader, Hu Jintao, emphasized that "the two sides of the Strait are bound to be unified in the course of the great rejuvenation of the Chinese nation."[25] And rejuvenation stands at the center of President Xi's vision for China. He has described China's rejuvenation as "the greatest dream of the Chinese nation in modern history."[26]

While China has not spelled out exactly what rejuvenation would entail for the region beyond unification with Taiwan, analysts have tried to sort this out. Timothy Heath, drawing on the Chinese Constitution and official interpretations, finds that although Chinese leaders do not explicitly link rejuvenation with calls for achieving preeminence in Asia, they do hint at regional hegemony as a desirable outcome. For example, Dai Bingguo, who was a high-ranking foreign policy official under Hu Jintao, rejected "hege-

---

21. China has, however, compromised on many of its territorial disputes, but these have been frontier disputes, not homeland or offshore island disputes, which largely reflects the different value that China places on them; see M. Taylor Fravel, *Strong Borders, Secure Nation: Cooperation and Conflict in China's Territorial Disputes* (Princeton University Press, 2008).

22. Bill Hayton, *The South China Sea: The Struggle for Power in Asia* (Yale University Press, 2014), 178. He also holds that the situation is quite different from the late 1990s, when the Spratly conflict played a much weaker role in the nationalism discourse.

23. Callahan, *China*, 196–97.

24. Elizabeth C. Economy, *The Third Revolution: Xi Jinping and the New Chinese State* (Oxford University Press, 2018), 4–5. See also Andrew Scobell et al., *China's Grand Strategy: Trends, Trajectories, and Long-Term Competition* (RAND, 2020), who categorize China's grand strategy since 2004 in terms of rejuvenation, https://www.rand.org/content/dam/rand/pubs/research_reports/RR2700/RR2798/RAND_RR2798.pdf, and Avery Goldstein, "China's Grand Strategy Under Xi Jinping: Reassurance, Reform, and Resistance," *International Security* 45, no. 1 (summer 2020): 164–201, who argues that China's grand strategy has been guided by rejuvenation since 1992.

25. Wang, *Never Forget National Humiliation*, 129–33, quote on 131.

26. Economy, *The Third Revolution*, 2–5, quote on 3.

monism," but "pointed instead to China's tradition of 'harmony and neighborly benevolence' drawing from 'thousands of years of political and cultural traditions.' Although not spelled out, such traditions have been largely predicated on a political order centered on China."[27] Howard French finds that without ending US primacy in the Western Pacific, "China will not feel it has restored its place in the world."[28] Xi's call for a new Asian security concept, one without treaty alliances and with a limited role for non-Asian countries, helps to flesh out what form this would take.[29]

A different but largely complementary strand of China's national identity is reflected in its evolving understanding of World War II. Over the past few decades, China has been reinterpreting its role, highlighting its substantial contribution to the Allied victory. This narrative has the benefit of casting China in a positive light with moral content, in contrast to the humiliation narrative. It is also valuable because it implies that China deserves a greater say in shaping the regional order, given that the order was shaped by the victorious powers, and that Japan's standing is unwarranted.[30] Exactly what China believes it deserves is unclear, but the thrust parallels the humiliation narrative, supporting China's discontent with its still-limited ability to determine alliances and geographical boundaries in East Asia.

In contrast to these features of China's national identity, which are supported and reinforced by China's policies and broadly shared by its population, popular nationalism—nationalist public opinion—appears to play only a limited role in driving China's policy. Studies of China's provocative actions find little support for the proposition that China's leaders would have chosen less assertive policies if not facing mobilized publics.[31] China's leaders can manipulate protests to communicate resolve, allowing them to demonstrate the costs of China's backing down, but they are rarely driven into assertive policies by protests.[32] According to a study of how China deals with nationalist protests focused on Japan, "The repeated eruption and temporary influence of popular protests in China in response to perceived slights of national pride signal not

---

27. Timothy R. Heath, "What Does China Want? Discerning the PRC's National Strategy," *Asian Security* 8, no. 1 (2012): 60.

28. French, *Everything Under the Heavens*, 253. He also argues that Xi's ambition "involves supplanting American power and influence in the region as an irreplaceable stepping-stone along the way to becoming a true global power" (11).

29. Lindsay W. Ford, "Network Power: China's Effort to Reshape Asia's Regional Security Architecture," Brookings, September 2020, https://www.brookings.edu/research/network-power-chinas-effort-to-reshape-asias-regional-security-architecture/.

30. These arguments are developed in Rana Mitter, *China's Good War: How World War II Is Shaping a New Nationalism* (Harvard University Press, 2020).

31. Andrew Chubb, "Assessing Public Opinion's Influence on Foreign Policy: The Case of China's Assertive Maritime Behavior," *Asian Security* 15, no. 2 (2019): 159–79.

32. Jessica Chen Weiss, *Powerful Patriots: Nationalist Protest in China's Foreign Relations* (Oxford University Press, 2014).

CHAPTER 2

the emergence of an uncontrollable populace, but rather the outward manifestation of policymakers' strategic and nuanced response to social pressures."[33] While Chinese leaders are sensitive to their public, they can manage protests without making major changes in foreign policy.

Status and Prestige

Status is a collective belief about a state's membership in a group or a ranking within a group. It is a collective belief because it requires recognition by other states and recognition by other states of others' recognition.[34] In contrast, national identity is developed by a state and does not depend upon recognition.[35] For our purposes, the relevant groups could be major powers or regional powers, and superpowers among major powers. A state's achievement of a certain status will be reflected by other states acting in ways that demonstrate they recognize its status.

The literature argues that a state could desire status for a variety of reasons.[36] The first is essentially instrumental; that is, a state values status because it can provide material benefits.[37] Higher status, for example, could increase a state's ability to change the geopolitical status quo, shape international institutions, or increase its credibility. Second, a state could value status because higher status increases the self-esteem of individuals living in that state. This argument builds on social psychological research that explores the relationship between group status and individual self-esteem.[38]

---

33. James Reilly, *Strong Society, Smart State: The Rise of Public Opinion in China's Japan Policy* (Columbia University Press, 2012), 9. Reilly does, however, conclude that under certain domestic conditions—specifically when the leadership is divided on policy—that public opinion does have some influence on China's foreign policy (208–13).

34. On various definitions, see Deborah Welch Larson, T. V. Paul, and William C. Wohlforth, "Introduction," in *Status in World Politics*, ed. T. V. Paul, Deborah Welch Larson, and William C. Wohlforth (Cambridge University Press, 2014), 7–13; Jonathan Renshon, *Fighting for Status: Hierarchy and Conflict in World Politics* (Princeton University Press, 2017), 33–44; and Allan Dafoe, Jonathan Renshon, and Paul Huth, "Reputation and Status as Motives for War," *Annual Review of Political Science*, 17 (2014): 374–76.

35. There is, however, an understanding of identity that depends on recognition by other states; see Michelle Murray, *The Struggle for Recognition in International Relations: Status, Revisionism, and Rising Powers* (Oxford University Press, 2019), on role identity and the intertwining of identity and recognition, esp. 40–46.

36. Steven Ward, *Status and the Challenge of Rising Powers* (Cambridge University Press, 2017), 35–40.

37. Robert Gilpin, *War and Change in World Politics* (Cambridge University Press, 1981), 30–33, on the hierarchy of prestige.

38. Deborah Welch Larson and Alexei Shevchenko, "Status Seekers: Chinese and Russian Response to US Primacy," *International Security* 34, no. 4 (spring 2010): 63–95; William C. Wohlforth, "Unipolarity, Status Competition, and Great Power War," *World Politics* 61, no. 1 (January 2009): 34–38.

Third, status could be important to a state's leader because it increases the leader's domestic legitimacy; when nationalists care about the state's status and have domestic influence, the state's leader will also tend to be concerned about it. Finally, and maybe especially important in the case of China, a state could desire status because it confirms its own identity. Identity and status become linked in this way when a state's identity includes a certain standing among states or expectations due to this standing. Although a state forms its identity on its own, if other states do not act in ways consistent with that identity—that is, if they do not recognize it—then the state will conclude that others are rejecting its identity, which it can find deeply unacceptable and insulting.

Historically, rising powers have believed they have not been accorded the status that their increased power warrants; a rising power facing a unipolar power is especially likely to engage in status competition.[39] A rising power can pursue a variety of approaches to indicate it has achieved major-power or superpower status. These indicators will depend on the specific historical context. For example, if major powers have built certain types of weapons systems, then a state that believes it has achieved major-power status might build that type of weapon, even if doing so does not increase its national security. Germany's building of battleships in the decades before the First World War and some countries' acquisition of nuclear weapons have been explained by this logic.[40] A state may join or aspire to join an international institution because belonging indicates its status is comparable to that of the other members. A state might desire colonies because the other major powers have them, even though colonies themselves may be of little value. A rising power/superpower might desire a sphere of influence not only due to the political value of subordinating other states in its sphere but also because other major powers are expected to refrain from using their military capabilities within this region. A sphere of influence indicates status not only because the state has the power to deter others from intervening but also because the restraint/deference exercised by other major powers reflects the rights and expectations that come with being a major power.

A growing literature argues that the desire for status by a rising power can be a cause of competition and war via a variety of distinct logics. What might be termed the standard model holds that a state's drive to achieve status leads to competition and conflict when this status is denied by other powers; arms

---

39. Ward, *Status and the Challenge of Rising Powers*; Murray, *The Struggle for Recognition in International Relations*; Wohlforth, "Unipolarity, Status Competition, and Great Power War."

40. Murray, *The Struggle for Recognition in International Relations*, chap. 5; Scott D. Sagan, "Why Do States Build Nuclear Weapons," *International Security* 21, no. 3 (winter 1996/97): 54–86.

races that strain relations and wars over a sphere of influence or territory are possible. Other paths by which status concerns can lead to war include "status dilemmas"—in which a state's uncertainty about its status drives competition, and "status immobility"—in which a state believes its appropriate status cannot be achieved within the status quo order and therefore adopts policies that reject the existing order.[41] Conflict could also occur when states agree on status but disagree about what flows from major-power status.

While the status literature has developed extensively over the past couple of decades, challenges to its findings, of course, remain. Among the most important continuing concerns is whether the desire for status is actually just a rhetorical device for pursuing interests via power.[42] Nevertheless, the case made by this overall body of work is sufficiently compelling that its findings should be factored into our analysis of China.

CHINA AND STATUS

China's economic and military rise has clearly established it as the materially dominant state in East Asia. Separating the material and security rationales for its policies—foreign policy, security policy and statements—from its status-driven rationales is challenging because they often run in parallel. Nevertheless, there are reasons for concluding that status plays an important role in driving China's policies. Most generally, as noted above, rising powers have a track record of desiring status, and we have little reason to expect that China is an exception.

Studies of China's status concerns find that China—its leaders and populace—place great importance on international status.[43] Zheng Wang finds that for the CCP by the late 1990s, "some nonmaterial interests that have been defined by historical memory, such as national dignity, face, and respect from other countries, have become equally important or even more important than China's material interests such as trade, security, and territory." In a similar

---

41. William C. Wohlforth, "Status Dilemmas in Interstate Conflict," in *Status in World Politics*, ed. T. V. Paul, Deborah Welch Larson, and William C. Wohlforth (Cambridge University Press, 2014); Ward, *Status and the Challenge of Rising Powers*; and Murray, *The Struggle for Recognition in International Relations*.

42. For an assessment of the literature, see Paul K. MacDonald and Joseph M. Parent, "The Status of Status in World Politics," *World Politics* 73, no. 2 (April 2021): 358–91. For a skeptical perspective on the instrumental value of status, see Jonathan Mercer, "The Illusion of International Prestige," *International Security* 41, no. 4 (spring 2017): 133–68.

43. Yong Deng, *China's Struggle for Status: The Realignment of International Relations* (Cambridge University Press, 2008), finds that "the PRC may very well be the most status-conscious in the world," (8) but he uses a very broad definition of status (21), which leaves his analysis unclear on the functional and material aspects of status versus its intrinsic value to China. Xiaoyu Pu, *Rebranding China: Contested Status Signaling in the Changing Global Order* (Stanford University Press, 2019), also uses a broad understanding and holds that "with its own version of exceptionalism, China is striving for a unique and respected status in the world" (35).

vein, he finds that "important indications of China's national rejuvenation, such as Taiwan and *international respect and recognition*, have become top objectives of Beijing's foreign policy."[44] Consistent with this analysis, Yan Xuetong, a prominent Chinese scholar writing as China was beginning its rise, held that "the Chinese regard their rise as regaining China's lost international status rather than as obtaining something new. This psychological feeling results in the Chinese being continuously dissatisfied with their economic achievements until China resumes its superpower status."[45] David Shambaugh, in summarizing key traditions that have influenced China's foreign policy, finds that "over time, there has been an obsession with maintaining China's status, ritualistic practices, and saving 'face' in dealing with foreigners."[46]

Analyses of specific Chinese policies have argued that status has been a key factor. However, separating the material value of these policies from their status value has been difficult. Analysts have argued that China's deployment of aircraft carriers and pursuit of a blue-water navy partly reflects its desire to signal its status.[47] This is a natural place to look because, among other reasons, the role of status in Germany's decision to pursue a battle fleet at the turn of the nineteenth century has been well demonstrated. However, because China's carriers also have security and foreign policy value for China—including providing a "limited power-projection capability that increase[s] China's ability to defend regional interests in contingencies not involving the United States"—the contribution of status may not be large.[48] Status may also play a role in China's expansion and modernization of its nuclear force. Unlike earlier leaders, President Xi Jinping has connected China's nuclear forces to its great power status.[49] He has claimed that the Strategic Rocket Force is "the 'strategic pillar' of

---

44. Wang, *Never Forget National Humiliation*, 135–36; emphasis added. In this context, *face* combines ideas of respectability and deference, as in "to lose face."
45. Yan Xuetong, "The Rise of China in Chinese Eyes," *Journal of Contemporary China* 10, no. 26 (2001): 34.
46. Shambaugh, *China Goes Global*, 54; see his chapter 3 for a variety of specific examples involving dignity, legitimacy, and nationalism.
47. Xiaoyu Pu and Randall L. Schweller, "Status Signaling, Multiple Audiences, and China's Blue-Water Naval Ambitions," in *Status in World Politics*. For different but related arguments, see Robert S. Ross, "China's Naval Nationalism: Sources, Prospects, and the US Response," *International Security* 34, no. 2 (fall 2009): 46–81.
48. Michael A. Glosny, Phillip C. Saunders, and Robert Ross, "Correspondence: Debating China's Naval Nationalism," *International Security* 35, no. 2 (fall 2010): 161–75, quote from Glosny and Saunders at 166; Michael A. McDevitt, *China as a Twenty-First Century Naval Power: Theory, Practice, and Implications* (Naval Institute, 2020); Andrew Scobell, Michael McMahon, and Cortez A. Cooper III, "China's Aircraft Carrier Program: Drivers, Developments, Implications," *Naval War College Review* 68, no. 4 (autumn 2015): 65–80.
49. Henrik Stalhane Him, M. Taylor Fravel, and Magnus Langset Troan, "The Dynamics of an Entangled Security Dilemma: China's Changing Nuclear Forces," *International Security* 47, no. 4 (spring 2023), 168.

China's 'great power status.'"⁵⁰ There are, however, as discussed in chapter 6, other important and complementary reasons for China's nuclear policy, with increasing the survivability and retaliatory capability of its nuclear force likely the most important.⁵¹

The influence of status appears to play a clearer role in China's policies in the South China Sea, including its insistence on rights within the nine-dash line, its infringement on littoral countries' Exclusive Economic Zones, and its building of military bases. Although often explained in terms of resources, the amounts of oil and gas are too small to warrant the political costs that China has incurred for its assertive policies. There is also no strong military rationale for China's policies—its building and militarization of islands in the South China Sea will be of virtually no value in protecting China's interests in a large war, including protecting sea-lanes that are vital for trade.⁵² Instead, China's need to have its identity recognized—which includes the South China Sea as largely under China's control—offers a more compelling explanation. In this vein, Howard French, after describing China's increasingly assertive policies in the South China Sea, observes that the ideological foundations of China's policy were grounded in the belief "that it was China's manifest destiny to once again reign preponderant over a wide sphere of Asia. . . . Only by doing so could the country realize its dreams; only in this way could its dignity be restored."⁵³

This conclusion is supported by research that extends the scope of status arguments, explaining that states that care about their ranking in a hierarchy should be expected to value and insist on status recognition from smaller states as well as from major powers, and demonstrates that this is true for China.⁵⁴ This need for status recognition deepens China's determination to achieve its territorial claims in the South China Sea, where the countries with

---

50. Tong Zhao, *Political Drivers of China's Changing Nuclear Policy: Implications for US-China Nuclear Relations and International Security* (Carnegie Endowment for International Peace, 2024), 10, who argues, contrary to Stalhane, Fravel, and Troan, that status concern about nuclear weapons were held by China's previous leaders; see https://carnegieendowment.org/research/2024/07/china-nuclear-buildup-political-drivers-united-states-relationship-international-security?lang=en.

51. David C. Logan and Philip C. Saunders, *Discerning the Drivers of China's Nuclear Force Development: Models, Indicators, and Data* (Center for the Study of Chinese Military Affairs, National Defense University, July 26, 2023), explore a variety of different explanations and find support for both strategic and status models.

52. These arguments are developed in chapter 5.

53. French, *Everything Under the Heavens*, 248–49.

54. Alex Yu-Ting Lin, "When David Challenges Goliath: Insubordination from Smaller States and Rising Power Status Dissatisfaction," PhD diss., University of Southern California, 2021; "Contestation from Below: Status and Revisionism in Hierarchy," *International Studies Quarterly* 68, no. 3 (2024). For a different mechanism that can lead a more powerful state to challenge or attack a weaker one in pursuit of status, see Joslyn Trager Barnhart, *The Consequences of Humiliation: Anger and Status in World Politics* (Cornell University Press, 2020).

competing claims—for example, the Philippines and Vietnam—are smaller states. In line with these arguments, Chubb argues that "The characterization of China's rivals as 'small countries' also invokes the Confucian moral imperative to act in accordance with one's place in a hierarchy, which in this case would mean recognizing, and perhaps deferring to, the PRC as a 'major country' and regional great power."[55]

Status also plays a role in China's desire for unification of Taiwan. Alan Wachman argues that instead of a single causal explanation for why China places such great value on Taiwan, a multicausal explanation is required. He thoroughly develops the argument that in addition to the dominant national identity argument, geopolitical rationales—including Taiwan's importance for China's economic, political, and especially security objectives—should be one of the explanations. Wachman also comments on the status concerns that China attaches to Taiwan, however, observing that as China's power has increased, "Beijing seeks respect and to a degree deference. Where Taiwan and other maritime territorial claims are concerned, the urge for greater international stature has lowered the PRC's threshold of tolerance for conditions that seem incommensurate with its greatness."[56] More generally, since Taiwan is central to China's rejuvenation—which it not only wants to achieve, but also wants to have recognized—we should expect that status is among the reasons China is so determined to achieve unification with Taiwan.

China also likely has status interests in achieving a sphere of influence in East Asia, which would include the ending of US regional alliances and withdrawal of its military forces. For starters, as reviewed above, theories of rising powers and status both predict and find that rising powers' drive for status has led them to pursue spheres of influence. We might reasonably expect the same from China. However, separating status motives from security motives is particularly difficult for regional hegemony and a full sphere of influence. Until China gains control of Taiwan, China will see substantial security value in the United States leaving East Asia, because US withdrawal would greatly improve China's ability to invade and/or coerce Taiwan. Interestingly, this was not always the case because, among other reasons, China valued the US-Japan alliance because it reduced Japan's military requirements. However, the tightening of the alliance in the 1990s and 2000s and the growing

---

55. Chubb, "Chinese Popular Nationalism and the PRC Policy in the South China Sea," 54.
56. Alan M. Wachman, *Why Taiwan: Geostrategic Rationales for China's Territorial Integrity* (Stanford University Press, 2007), 124. Wachman also argues that for Beijing "the inability to frame and set the terms for resolving the dispute over Taiwan exposes the PRC as impotent in a critical contest at a moment when it is, otherwise, determined to be viewed as ever-more powerful" (23).

CHAPTER 2

role that it would play in Taiwan scenarios led China to see the alliance in a much more negative light.[57]

With this important caveat, China's call for reordering East Asian security arrangements is worth considering. Over the past two decades, high-level Chinese leadership statements have indicated that China opposes US-led alliances in the region and thus, by implication, that it desires regional hegemony. China began in the late 1990s to propose an alternative to US-led alliances in the region with its introduction of a "new security concept," which held that "the old security concept based on military alliances and build-up of armaments will not help ensure global security."[58] In 2002, CCP General Secretary Jiang Zemin declared that Asia should rely on itself rather than other powers for security.[59] A 2003 PRC Ministry of Foreign Affairs position paper identified the new security concept as part of an effort to "discard the mentality of the Cold War," with the aim to "rise above one-sided security and seek common security through mutually beneficial cooperation."[60]

Discussions of Asian security with no role for US alliances accelerated under Xi Jinping.[61] In a 2014 speech, Xi built on Jiang's idea to introduce a "new Asian security concept for new progress in security cooperation," stating that "to beef

---

57. Xinbo Wu, "The End of the Silver Lining: A Chinese View of the US-Japan Alliance," *Washington Quarterly* 29, no. 1 (winter 2005/6): 119–30.

58. Jiang Zemin, "Jiang Zemin's Speech at the Conference on Disarmament (March 26, 1999, Geneva)," Ministry of Foreign Affairs of the People's Republic of China, March 26, 1999, https://www.mfa.gov.cn/ce/ceno//eng/wjzc/cjjk/jhwx/t110973.htm. For an excellent overview of China's views of US alliances, see Adam P. Liff, "China and the US Alliance System," *China Quarterly* 233 (March 2018): 137–65, https://doi.org/10.1017/S0305741017000601.

59. "Statement by H. E. Mr. Jiang Zemin, President of the People's Republic of China," Conference on Interaction and Confidence Building Measures in Asia (CICA), Internet Archive, last modified May 12, 2020, https://web.archive.org/web/20201205112855/https://www.s-cica.org/page/china/. These views were restated by Dai Bingguo, head of the CCP's foreign affairs office in 2010. "Statement by H. E. Mr. Dai Bingguo State Councilor of the People's Republic of China," CICA, Internet Archive, last modified April 12, 2020, https://web.archive.org/web/20201205055930/https://www.s-cica.org/page/china10/.

60. Ministry of Foreign Affairs of the People's Republic of China, "China's Position Paper on the New Security Concept," July 2002, https://www.fmprc.gov.cn/ce/ceun/eng/xw/t27742.htm.

61. Another of Xi's security concepts, "a new model of great power relations," launched in the early 2010s, did not call for ending alliances, but was arguably motivated primarily by the pursuit of status rather than material policy goals. As two Brookings scholars explained, "China wants to be viewed as an equal. By using the term 'Great Power' to primarily, if not solely, refer to China and the United States, China aims to elevate itself to a level playing field. Obtaining U.S. support of the concept would imply Uncle Sam's recognition of China's strength and power. This is what China's official media sought to show when it suggested Obama's support of the concept: parity and respect between the two countries." Cheng Li and Lucy Xu, "Chinese Enthusiasm and American Cynicism Over the 'New Type of Great Power Relations,'" *China-US Focus* (December 4, 2014), https://www.chinausfocus.com/foreign-policy/chinese-enthusiasm-and-american-cynicism-over-the-new-type-of-great-power-relations/.

up and entrench a military alliance targeted at a third party is not conducive to maintaining common security" and that "it is for the people of Asia to run the affairs of Asia, solve the problems of Asia and uphold the security of Asia."[62] At around the same time, China introduced the slogan "community of common destiny," which envisions alliances as a source of insecurity.[63]

IMPLICATIONS OF NATIONAL IDENTITY AND STATUS FOR US-CHINA COMPETITION AND CONFLICT

Considering China's national identity and desire for international status provides a richer understanding of the importance that China places on key disputes. While China's territorial claim to Taiwan is well known, understanding Taiwan in the context of China's past humiliation, current progress toward rejuvenation, and desire for international status further clarifies the central importance and great value that China places on unification. Taiwan is not only a territorial/sovereignty dispute over a truly vital, core interest, but it is also central to China's national identity and its interpretation of its international standing. Similar insights apply to the South China Sea disputes. China sees far more at risk than the material stakes can suggest. The South China Sea is far less important than Taiwan, and China's historical-nationalist narrative may be more malleable than its Taiwan narrative, but the South China Sea's linkage to this identity narrative nevertheless does much to explain China's unwillingness to compromise on these disputes.

Especially if China continues to advance economically and technologically, thereby further establishing itself as the globe's second superpower, China will increasingly believe that its achievements warrant international standing and respect equal to that enjoyed by the United States. China would then increasingly see US barriers to its claims in the South China Sea and Taiwan as indicating a rejection of China's superpower status and of the regional influence and deference that should flow from this status. These beliefs would increase China's determination to resolve these disputes and possibly increase time pressures for doing so.

The preceding discussion also indicates that China would prefer the end of US alliances in East Asia. China, drawing on long historical traditions, views itself as the preeminent country in its region. US security involvement

---

62. Xi Jinping, "New Asian Security Concept for New Progress in Security Cooperation," remarks at the Fourth Summit of the Conference on Interaction and Confidence Building Measures in Asia, Shanghai Expo Center, May 21, 2014, https://www.mfa.gov.cn/ce/cenz//eng/ztbd/yxhfh/t1159951.htm.

63. Xi Jinping, "Working Together to Forge a New Partnership of Win-Win Cooperation and Create a Community of Shared Future for Mankind," United Nations, September 28, 2015, https://gadebate.un.org/sites/default/files/gastatements/70/70_ZH_en.pdf.

CHAPTER 2

in East Asia is inconsistent with this self-image and will likely become more so as China continues to grow economically, militarily, and technologically. Status concerns could reinforce these national identity arguments. On this issue China's national identity and status concerns interact—being the preeminent power in its region is required for China to achieve the international standing and recognition that it desires. Moreover, the United States has long maintained a sphere of influence in the Western Hemisphere. China could easily believe that its status as one of the two superpowers can only be fully recognized by achieving comparable regional dominance.

What remains uncertain, however, is how *much* China values achieving regional hegemony due to its national identity and status motives. Among other reasons, this is difficult to discern because China has such clear security motivations for regional hegemony due to the implications for Taiwan. In addition, identifying the existence of identity and status desires is inherently easier than assessing their likely influence on China's foreign policy.

Consequently, considering these ideational factors helps only a little in sorting out the debate among China experts over the value China places on regional hegemony. Recall that the spectrum of views ranged from great value to little or none at all. China clearly places some ideational value on achieving regional hegemony. At the same time, however, there is little to indicate that China would risk huge costs to push or fight the United States out of East Asia simply for these status and identity goals. The value seems likely to be dwarfed by the value that China places on achieving unification with Taiwan.

From a policy perspective, therefore, the key insights offered by appreciation of China's identity and status goals for regional hegemony apply only once the Taiwan issue is resolved. Until then, the difficulty and risks of maintaining the United States' current alliances and partnerships and, in turn, its current grand strategy, will be defined by Taiwan. If, however, the United States ends its commitment to protect Taiwan, then China's national identity and international status goals would play a far more important role in shaping China's determination to push the United States out of East Asia. Given the uncertainty about the value China places on these goals, the United States should be prepared for the possibility that it might continue to face significant pressure from China to leave the region even if the United States terminates its Taiwan commitment.

Regime Type

Different types of regimes—for example, democracies versus autocracies—could have different motives and goals, and their leaders could face different domestic constraints. In addition, a state's beliefs about an opposing state's motives and goals could depend upon the opposing state's regime type. Each of these differences could influence the degree of competition between states and the probability of war.

Democratic peace theory, which holds that democracies do not go to war with each other, is the most prominent strand of research on regime type.[64] The question for the United States, however, is not whether the democratic peace conclusion is correct but is instead the related question of whether autocracies are more likely to start wars against democracies and, more generally, whether they are more likely to pursue policies that make war more likely.[65] If democracies are less likely to go to war than are democratic-autocratic dyads, a democracy facing an autocracy has greater reason to fear for its security (if autocracies are the ones that start the conflicts) and larger incentives to adopt competitive policies.

Theorists have developed a variety of arguments about why autocracies are more likely to have greedy motives. According to one line of argument, an expansionist foreign policy enables an autocratic leader to extract greater resources from its society by increasing the size of the state, and therefore its total resources, and by inflating the external threat, which increases the willingness of society to support the state.[66] A different material argument holds that cartelized systems—those "dominated by a number of interest groups or 'cartels,' each with concentrated interests different from those of other such groups"—are more likely in authoritarian systems and are inclined toward overexpansion, that is, expansion beyond the country's interests.[67] An identity-based argument sees autocracies as committed to promoting their ideology internationally due to a shared transnational identity. As a result, they will support other illiberal states and adopt confrontational policies toward and be fearful of liberal democratic states.[68]

A different set of arguments addresses how regime type influences states' understandings of others' goals. Liberal democracies tend to see other democracies as peaceful and illiberal authoritarian states as interested in ex-

---

64. See, for example, Michael W. Doyle, *Ways of War and Peace: Realism, Liberalism, and Socialism* (W. W. Norton, 1997), 205–311, Bruce Russett, *Grasping the Democratic Peace: Principles for a Post–Cold War World* (Princeton University Press, 1993), and John M. Owen, "How Liberalism Produces Democratic Peace," *International Security* 19, no. 2 (fall 1994): 87–125.

65. Showing that there are important exceptions to the claim that democracies have not fought each other is sufficient to create uncertainty between democracies and thereby restore some of the pressure for competition generated by a security dilemma. However, simply finding exceptions does not show that there is no difference between the war-launching propensities of autocracies and democracies, which is more directly relevant here.

66. David A. Lake, "Powerful Pacifists: Democratic States and War," *American Political Science Review* 86, no. 1 (March 1992): 24–37.

67. Jack Snyder, *Myths of Empire: Domestic Politics and International Ambition* (Cornell University Press, 1991), quote at 44.

68. John M. Owen, "Transnational Liberalism and US Primacy," *International Security* 26, no. 3 (winter 2001/2): 117–52.

pansion and untrustworthy.[69] This information about the opposing state can, on the one hand, reduce or eliminate the security dilemma between democracies, while it can, on the other hand, fuel competitive policies by democracies against autocracies. If these judgments are wrong, then democracies will be inclined to adopt overly competitive policies when facing autocracies, increasing the probability of conflict.

These arguments about autocracies' motives are complemented by arguments that hold that autocratic leaders face weaker constraints to pursuing expansionist policies. According to this logic, democratic leaders are constrained by domestic publics that will oppose costly wars especially because they will incur the direct costs of fighting.[70] In contrast, authoritarian leaders, because they are less vulnerable to public disapproval, have a freer hand to pursue their expansionist objectives. A related argument explains that authoritarian regimes do less well in crisis bargaining because their leaders are less able to signal their resolve via their willingness to incur these audience costs, which are assumed to be greater in democracies.[71] In combination, the motives arguments and constraints arguments envision autocracies as doubly dangerous—more motivated to expand and less constrained domestically from pursuing these expansionist policies.

Subsequent research has challenged these arguments about constraints, explaining that certain authoritarian leaders are constrained by elite audiences and therefore are not so different from democratic leaders. Autocracies can vary depending on whether there are government insiders who can hold the leader accountable for foreign policy failures and whether the leader and insiders are military officials or civilians. Civilian leaders who are accountable to civilian insiders are the least likely to initiate military conflicts and are no more likely to do so than democratic leaders. Personalist leaders—those who face little domestic accountability—are more likely to initiate conflict than either accountable civilian autocrats or democratic leaders. Military personalist leaders are the most likely to initiate conflicts, but not much more so than personalist civilians. Among the features that can make personalist leaders more willing to use force are a history of using force to rise to domestic power and possession of grand international ambi-

---

69. See, for example, Owen, "How Liberalism Produces Democratic Peace," Emanuel Adler and Michael Barnett, "A Framework for the Study of Security Communities," in *Security Communities*, edited by Emanuel Adler and Michael Barnett (Cambridge University Press, 1998), 40–41, and Thomas Risse-Kappen, "Collective Identity in a Democratic Community," in *The Culture of National Security: Norms and Identity in World Politics*, ed. Peter J. Katzenstein (Columbia University Press, 1996).

70. For an opposing view, see Jonathan D. Caverley, *Democratic Militarism: Voting, Wealth, and War* (Cambridge University Press, 2014).

71. James D. Fearon, "Domestic Political Audiences and the Escalation of International Disputes," *American Political Science Review* 88, no. 3 (September 1994): 577–92.

tions.⁷² Other research further narrows the democracy-autocracy gap, arguing that authoritarian leaders can be constrained by popular uprisings because these protests can undermine the government's legitimacy, maybe especially for leaders who rely on nationalist myths to maintain power.⁷³ Of course, a sufficiently repressive regime may be able to avoid these costs by quashing protests. Finally, on the democracy side of the equation, critics have found little evidence that audience costs play a significant role in democratic leaders' decisions.⁷⁴

In sum, while debate about the dangers posed by authoritarian regimes continues along multiple dimensions, there are grounds for expecting that certain authoritarian regimes are more likely to challenge and get into conflict with democracies than are democracies. Personalist leaders, the ability of authoritarian leaders to prevent protests, and the material benefits that accrue disproportionately to leaders can each increase the probability of authoritarian expansion. When confronting this type of regime, policies designed to deter the adversary become more important, and policies designed to decrease the adversary's insecurity become relatively less important. However, all else equal, against other types of autocracies, this balance should be struck differently.

CHINA AND REGIME TYPE

The dangers and challenges posed by China's authoritarian regime are a common theme in US arguments about the dangers posed by China's rise. For example, Aaron Friedberg argues, "The yawning ideological chasm that separates the two nations is both an obstacle to measures that might reduce uncertainty and dampen competition, and a source of mutual hostility and mistrust . . . democracies also tend to regard non-democracies as inherently untrustworthy and dangerously prone to external aggression."⁷⁵ Whether or not this characterization is warranted, this understanding of China has contributed significantly to the US tilt toward more competitive policies. Analysts fear that not opposing China's rise will result in a challenge to the democratic model that the United States has historically supported and to the liberal world order that it has championed since the end

---

72. Jessica L. Weeks, "Strongmen and Straw Men: Authoritarian Regimes and the Initiation of International Conflict," *International Organization* 106, no. 2 (May 2012): 326–47; Jessica L. Weeks, *Dictators at War and Peace* (Cornell University Press, 2014).

73. Jessica Chen Weiss, *Powerful Patriots: Nationalist Protests in China's Foreign Relations* (Oxford University Press, 2014), 19–20.

74. Following the early audience cost arguments, a large literature developed exploring, among other things, how they work and whether they actually constrain democratic leaders. See, for example, Jack Snyder and Erica Borghard, "The Cost of Empty Threats: A Penny, Not a Pound," *American Political Science Review* 105, no. 3 (August 2011): 437–56.

75. Aaron L. Friedberg, *A Contest for Supremacy: China, America, and the Struggle for Mastery in Asia* (W. W. Norton, 2011), 42.

of the Second World War. For example, Hal Brands argues that "different models of order at home produce different visions of order abroad: Russia and China want to weaken, fragment, and replace the existing international system because its foundational liberal principles are antithetical to their illiberal domestic practices."[76] In March of 2021, President Joe Biden claimed, "It is clear, absolutely clear . . . that this is a battle between the utility of democracies in the 21st century and autocracies."[77]

China has parallel regime-based/ideological fears of the United States. China's concern that the United States wants to transform it into a democracy is long-standing. US policy following the Cold War was explicit about this goal, and the United States did not see its policy as hostile. Economic engagement was intended partly to bring about changes that would make China democratic; this was clearly unacceptable to the CCP. China's ideological focus took a sharper turn under Xi. In 2013, an official party document warned against seven false ideological views and activities, including the promotion of Western constitutional democracy in "an attempt to undermine the current leadership and the socialism with Chinese characteristics of governance" and promoting universal values, civil society, and neo-liberalism.[78] During his first term, in speeches to People's Liberation Army (PLA) and CCP officials, Xi argued that the United States would not accept a Communist-led China that was growing quickly and might eventually surpass the United States.[79] A broad analysis of China's grand strategy finds that starting in the 2000s, "the threat from the United States was perceived as twofold—stemming from US hard and soft power. Not only was the CCP-PLA-PRC at risk from America's military might and economic sway, but the regime was endangered by US-promoted ideals of democracy and human rights. While the hard power threat was very visible and physical, the soft power threat was less tangible but more insidious."[80]

---

76. Hal Brands, "The Emerging Biden Doctrine: Democracy, Autocracy, and the Defining Clash of Our Times," *Foreign Affairs*, June 29, 2021.

77. "Remarks by President Biden in Press Conference," March 25, 2021, at https://www.whitehouse.gov/briefing-room/speeches-remarks/2021/03/25/remarks-by-president-biden-in-press-conference/.

78. "Document 9: A ChinaFile Translation," https://www.chinafile.com/document-9-chinafile-translation; Susan L. Shirk, *Overreach: How China Derailed Its Peaceful Rise* (Oxford University Press, 2023), 263–64; Nathan Levine, "A Clash of Worldviews: The United States and China Have Reached an Ideological Impasse," *Foreign Affairs*, August 30, 2023, https://www.foreignaffairs.com/china/clash-worldviews-united-states-ideological-impasse. Levine holds that the shift toward ideological struggle began under Xi's predecessor, Hu Jintao.

79. Christopher Buckley, "Behind Public Assurances, Xi Jinping Has Spread Grim Views of the US," *New York Times*, November 13, 2023, https://www.nytimes.com/2023/11/13/world/asia/china-xi-asia-pacific-summit.html.

80. Scobell et al., *China's Grand Strategy*, 17–18.

A key question here is whether China's authoritarian regime is accurately characterized by these statements by American analysts and leaders: How much more dangerous is China because it is an authoritarian regime? Part of the answer depends on a rather circular argument—China is more dangerous because US leaders believe it is, and vice versa: Whether or not autocracies actually pose a larger threat, if the United States believes they do and acts accordingly, it will pursue competitive policies that generate Chinese reactions that are dangerous. The same holds on the flip side: If China views the United States as threatening because it is a democracy, it will adopt policies that generate US reactions that increase the probability of confrontation. The regime-type identity argument predicts this type of interaction and negative spirals, which appears to be occurring between the United States and China.

This still leaves the question of whether China is actually pursuing policies designed to spread its authoritarian model and weaken democracies. The support for this claim is weak. As discussed throughout this chapter and chapter 1, there are other, much stronger explanations for most or all of China's assertive behavior.[81] Nevertheless, so long as US and Chinese leaders adopt these beliefs about the other's regime type, a competitive spiral will be fueled.

The potential material sources of authoritarian greed do not appear to be especially worrisome in the case of China. Assuming that Chinese leaders are motivated by the desire to increase their own wealth via extraction from a larger and/or more prosperous state, territorial expansion is not an attractive strategy because the prosperity benefits of expansion are much smaller in the current postindustrial era than in previous times.[82] In addition, China has so much potential to continue growing economically that an extraction-oriented leader would have large incentives to focus on domestic growth, supported by open trade, instead of territorial expansion.

The lack of material incentives for expansion might, however, be partially offset by the dangers of cartelization. In important ways, the structure of China's domestic political system seems well designed to avoid these dangers. The processes and structure of the CCP—including the importance of merit in promotion and the paths available for joining the party's inner circle, which require rising through the ranks of local and then regional government—could make unlikely the collaboration of narrow interests to significantly shift China's foreign policy toward international ex-

---

81. On a related point, see Wang Jisi, "America and China Are Not Yet in a Cold War, But They Must Not Wind Up in Something Even Worse," *Foreign Affairs*, November 23, 2023.

82. Carl Kaysen, "Is War Obsolete: A Review Essay," *International Security* 14, no. 4 (spring 1990): 42–64; Stephen G. Brooks, *Producing Security: Multinational Corporations, Globalization, and the Changing Calculus of Conflict* (Princeton University Press, 2005).

pansion.⁸³ This may not have been the case: Susan Shirk traces China's increased assertiveness to a combination of narrow-interest logrolling and decision-making fragmentation during former President Hu Jintao's collective leadership, with China's policies in the South China Sea being the prime example of its changed policies. Civilian maritime law enforcement agencies, state energy companies, and the PLA Navy, among others, combined their interests to increase China's reach and activities in the South China Sea: "Hu was dragged into a more assertive foreign policy."⁸⁴

At the same time that China's authoritarian motives may have become somewhat more dangerous, the constraints that China's authoritarian regime imposes on its leader appear to be weakening. Specifically, China has transitioned from being a civilian-elite-constrained regime to a personalist regime, which is a more dangerous type.⁸⁵ Reacting to the errors made by former chairman of the CCP Mao Zedong, China put into place a variety of measures to limit the power of its leader, including institutionalizing collective leadership, delegating power from the CCP to government agencies, and instituting term limits. Xi Jinping has reversed many of these changes—the constitution has been revised to allow him to serve more than two terms, and Xi has gained direct control of much of the government, purged many of his rivals, and censored critics.⁸⁶ Jude Blanchette argues that "Xi's increasingly singular position within China's political system will forestall policy alternatives and course corrections. . . . An environment in which an all-powerful leader with a single-minded focus cannot hear uncomfortable truths is a recipe for disaster."⁸⁷

In sum, although not all authoritarian regimes are especially dangerous, China appears to have become a more dangerous type. In light of the ambitious international goals that Xi has laid out, which, as described above, have roots in national identity and status desires, this further increases the probability of highly assertive and potentially misguided Chinese policies.

A variety of state-level arguments contribute to estimating the scope and depth of China's expansionist ambitions—which are simply variables in motivational realism—and provide at least partial theoretical underpinnings for China experts' assessments of China's motives and goals. Considering national identity and status suggests that the importance that China

---

83. Bruce J. Dickson, *The Party and the People: Chinese Politics in the 21st Century* (Princeton University Press, 2021), chaps. 1, 2.

84. Shirk, *Overreach*, esp. chap 5, quote at 124.

85. Weeks, *Dictators at War and Peace*, 40, classifies post-Mao China as the former.

86. See Susan Shirk, "China in Xi's 'New Era': The Return to Personalist Rule," *Journal of Democracy* 29, no. 2 (April 2018): 22–36.

87. Jude Blanchette, "Xi's Gamble: The Race to Consolidate Power and Stave Off Disaster, *Foreign Affairs* 100, no. 4, July/August 2021, 12.

places on Taiwan may be even greater than is generally believed. In addition, these considerations contribute to understanding the importance that China places on the South China Sea and possibly on achieving regional hegemony or a sphere of influence. Adding to these worries are China's regime type and overall governance structure. China's transition to personalist rule creates greater leeway for Xi to follow his own inclinations, which include substantial international ambition. In addition, and possibly more importantly, Xi may be less likely to receive the information and analysis that is required to judge US policies and to enable him to make fully informed decisions about the use of military force.

The implications are increased challenges for US policy. The possible importance of China's goals beyond unification with Taiwan raises the possibility that the incompatibility of US and Chinese regional goals may be still greater. US regional alliances, which the United States considers vital to the preservation of its national security, are entirely incompatible with a full Chinese sphere of influence. Thus, the concessions required to eliminate the key sources of conflict between China and the United States may be more radical than "simply" ending the US commitment to Taiwan and are still more likely to be unacceptable to US leaders and publics. The good news—to the extent that there is any—is that there is little evidence that China places great value on having the United States end its alliance security commitments to East Asia. Most likely, China sees this outcome as desirable but not essential. Nevertheless, given the United States' current grand strategy, US policies that involve concessions to China on Taiwan and possibly the South China Sea will need to hedge against the possibility that China is determined to push the United States out of East Asia. This could require the United States to maintain highly capable conventional forces designed to deter China and to pursue a variety of military and diplomatic policies designed to reassure US allies.

PART II. US GEOPOLITICAL COMMITMENTS

CHAPTER 3

Grand Strategy

Should the United States Retain Its Security Commitments in East Asia?

What are the implications of China's rise for US grand strategy? Given the tremendous growth of China's economy and military capabilities, the United States needs to ask the most basic questions about its national security and economic policies. Should it retain and deepen its alliances in East Asia or instead terminate these commitments and withdraw from the region? If retaining its commitments, how should the United States stay in Northeast Asia? Should it pursue military dominance and an overall competitive approach or should it take a more moderate military and political approach? Should it give priority to limiting defense spending and solving alliance burden-sharing problems?

The United States' key treaty allies in East Asia are Japan and South Korea. The Philippines and Thailand are also treaty allies; in recent years, the Philippines has increased coordination of its defense capability with the United States. Australia, too, is a treaty partner, and although not in East Asia, Australia is becoming increasingly important for the US projection of power into the region.[1] Singapore is a US security partner, but not a treaty ally.[2] As already discussed, the United States has an important ambiguous political commitment to come to Taiwan's defense. More broadly, and vaguely, the United States strives to preserve the "rule-based order" in East Asia, as well as globally, which it understands to include the protection of freedom of navigation in the South China Sea and elsewhere. The United States has forward-deployed forces in Japan and South Korea and has ac-

---

1. Kristy Needham, "US Military, Seeking Strategic Advantages, Builds Up Australia's Northern Bases Amid China Tensions, *Reuters*, July 26, 2024.
2. US Department of State, "U.S. Security Cooperation with Singapore," April 12, 2023, https://www.state.gov/u-s-security-cooperation-with-singapore/.

cess to military bases in the Philippines and Australia. In addition, the United States has major military bases in Guam.[3]

We do not need to start from scratch to begin to answer these questions about the impact of China's rise. The US grand-strategy debate that began with the end of the Cold War and is still evolving provides a template from which to analyze them.[4] Employing standard categories, I first divide the spectrum of grand strategies into four types: Neoisolation, which calls for terminating US alliances for at least the foreseeable future, and Deep Engagement, Offshore Balancing, and Primacy, each of which calls for preserving US alliances in Asia but for different reasons and/or via different means.

These four grand strategies give priority to US security interests and, maybe to a lesser extent, US prosperity. Many of their judgments about security are built on realist theories, but the schools differ on the arguments they emphasize, with some focusing on states' abilities to maintain adequate defensive capabilities and to avoid generating insecurity in opposing major powers, others on the propensity of states to balance against power or threats, and still others on the inclination of allies to free-ride when presented with the opportunity. Regarding economic interests, the grand strategies disagree about hegemonic stability theory and, in turn, about the importance of US alliances in supporting the international economic system and US prosperity. At the same time, however, many key arguments are built on more specific, midlevel theories and complicated assessments of risks and benefits.

In addition, there is a third set of interests at play in the US grand-strategy debate: liberal political and ideological goals, including, most importantly, spreading and preserving democracy and, to a lesser extent, protecting human rights. In principle, each of the four security-focused grand strategies could vary along this dimension. In practice, the combination of Neoisolation with a high priority on spreading democracy is rare.[5] To keep the categories relatively simple, while staying close to the existing debate, I identify only one additional grand strategy—Liberal Hegemony, which combines Deep Engagement with a high priority for spreading democracy, including

---

3. Congressional Research Service, *Guam: Defense Infrastructure and Readiness*, August 3, 2023, https://crsreports.congress.gov/product/pdf/R/R47643.

4. For an analytic review of the grand-strategy debate in the 1990s, see Barry R. Posen and Andrew L. Ross, "Competing Visions for U.S. Grand Strategy, *International Security* 21, no. 3 (winter 1996/97): 5–53. More recent reviews include Paul. C. Avey, Jonathan N. Markowitz, and Robert J. Reardon, "Disentangling Grand Strategy: International Relations Theory and U.S. Grand Strategy," *Texas National Security Review* 2, no. 1 (November 2018): 29–51, and Rebecca Friedman Lissner, "What Is Grand Strategy? A Conceptual Minefield," *Texas National Security Review* 2, no. 1 (November 2018): 53–73. Benjamin Miller and Ziv Rubinovitz, *Grand Strategy from Truman to Trump* (Chicago University Press, 2020) provide a theory-driven explanation of change in US grand strategy.

5. But see Van Jackson, "Left of Liberal Internationalism: Grand Strategies Within Progressive Foreign Policy Thought," *Security Studies* 31, no. 4 (August–September 2022): 553–92.

possibly through the use of force if necessary, and protecting human rights; this school has received extensive attention in the ongoing debate. All told, then, I explore five different grand strategies.

Neoisolation has received relatively little attention in the recent round of the grand-strategy debate, but it deserves consideration because its arguments are clear and its conclusions provide a sharp alternative to those offered by the other grand strategies.[6] Moreover, a variant of the grand strategy of Restraint, which has been increasingly prominent in the grand-strategy debate since the 2010s, comes close to Neoisolation.[7] Other variants of Restraint can be adequately captured by variants of Deep Engagement, thus I do not address Restraint as a distinct grand strategy.[8]

At some risk of oversimplification, the various grand strategies reflect divergent answers to several largely independent questions:

- Would a regional hegemon threaten the security of the US homeland?
- Would a major-power war (that did not initially involve the United States) threaten US security because the United States might get drawn in?
- How large a threat does nuclear proliferation pose to the United States?
- Is military primacy feasible—can the United States decisively out-compete China in East Asia?
- Do US alliances contribute to US prosperity by supporting the international economic regime, including globalization and economic interdependence?
- How important is reducing/limiting US defense spending?
- How important is spreading and preserving democracy abroad?

---

6. President Donald Trump's criticism of US alliances shares something with Neoisolation, but less than initial appearances suggest. For example, his emphasis on burden sharing does not imply that allies are not necessary for protecting US security, only that they are not paying their fair share. In contrast to Neoisolation, Trump favors a large US military, although for what purposes is unclear.

7. On the varieties of Restraint, see Miranda Priebe, John Schuessler, Bryan Rooney, and Jasen Castillo, "Competing Visions of Restraint," *International Security* 49, no. 2 (fall 2024): 135–69; Miranda Priebe, Kristen Gunness, Karl P. Mueller, and Zachary Burdette, *The Limits of Restraint: The Military Implications of a Restrained U.S. Grand Strategy in the Asia Pacific* (RAND, 2022), esp. 6–8, which terms the variant that is close to Neoisolation "Defensive Restraint," and Emma Ashford, "Strategies of Restraint: Remaking America's Broken Foreign Policy," *Foreign Affairs* 100, no. 4 (September/October 2021): 128–41. Barry Posen, *Restraint: A New Foundation for U.S. Grand Strategy* (Cornell University Press, 2014) is the fullest statement of Restraint; unlike Neoisolation, Posen believes that the "United States has a strategic interest in preventing a single state from dominating Eurasia" (95); he favors a measured disengagement that shifts greater military responsibility to US allies.

8. Offshore Balancing is typically categorized as a type of Restraint. However, as I explain below, it is in important ways better understood as a variant of Deep Engagement. This argument actually requires two moves: First, we need to understand Deep Engagement as combining a grand strategy focused on security with hegemonic stability arguments that address the economic implications of US grand strategy; Second, Offshore Balancing is a conditional variant of the security portion of Deep Engagement.

CHAPTER 3

The grand strategies I have identified do not reflect the full potential variation produced by this range of issues. Instead, the grand strategies tend to hold bundles of positions on these questions that support their overall conclusion. Moreover, not all scholars who are typically identified as proponents of a given grand strategy fully agree on all these issues. The following discussion explores ideal types—defined by central positions on key issues—instead of attempting to fully describe the ongoing US grand-strategy debate. This labeling/categorization results in some variation within schools. Because the purpose of this chapter is to identify the implications of China's rise for US grand strategy, my analysis will gloss over most of this within-school variation.

In addition to these issues, a new aspect of US economic and security policy deserves inclusion in assessments of US grand strategy—de-risking/ decoupling the US economy from China's.[9] Since the first Trump administration, US policy has included moves in this direction. The US decision to de-risk its economy is driven partly by concern about US strategic vulnerabilities, including in semiconductors and energy technologies, that could give China leverage over the US economy during a war or serious political dispute. De-risking is also driven by the US desire to deprive China of technologies that can contribute significantly to its military capabilities. *Decoupling* is a term that was used in earlier versions of US policy and was often interpreted as a less discriminating policy that could include the full separation of the US and Chinese economies. The shift in terminology partly reflected the US desire during the Biden administration to emphasize that it was not trying to damage the Chinese economy and partly reflected the infeasibility and economic costs of full decoupling. President Trump imposed very high tariffs on China at the outset of his second term; the purpose of these tariffs was unclear as was how long the United States would keep them in place. My assessments of the implications of China's rise for the various grand strategies briefly consider how their core arguments would judge de-risking and decoupling.

---

9. On the basic logic of decoupling, see Charles W. Boustany and Aaron L. Friedberg, *Partial Disengagement: A New U.S. Strategy for Economic Competition with China*, NBR Special Report #82, November 2019, https://www.nbr.org/wp-content/uploads/pdfs/publications/sr82_china-task-force-report-final.pdf. On de-risking, see Jon Bateman, *U.S.-China Technological "Decoupling": A Strategy and Policy Framework* (Carnegie Endowment for International Peace, 2022), https://carnegieendowment.org/2022/04/25/u.s.-china-technological-decoupling-strategy-and-policy-framework-pub-86897, "Remarks by National Security Advisor Jake Sullivan on the Biden-Harris Administration's National Security Strategy" (October 12, 2022), https://www.whitehouse.gov/briefing-room/speeches-remarks/2022/10/13/remarks-by-national-security-advisor-jake-sullivan-on-the-biden-harris-administrations-national-security-strategy/, and Cameron F. Kerry et al., *Is US Security Dependent on Limiting China's Economic Growth?* Brookings (October 3, 2023), https://www.brookings.edu/articles/is-us-security-dependent-on-limiting-chinas-economic-growth/.

The deepest divide among the security-focused grand strategies is between Neoisolation, which calls for ending US major-power alliances, and the spectrum of other security-focused grand strategies that call for retaining them, at least under certain conditions. The weight of recent debate has been between these latter strategies, including most versions of Restraint. These grand strategies disagree on when and how the United States should retain its alliances and/or on what is required to meet the security demands of these alliances, but they do not disagree over preserving them. The other deep divide in the debate is between Liberal Hegemony and the security-focused strategies, which place less relative weight on achieving US political and ideological values. To the extent that there has been a shift in the US grand-strategy debate since the end of the Cold War, Liberal Hegemony has been somewhat discredited by the failures of US interventions in Afghanistan, Iraq, and Libya, which were fueled partly by democratic and humanitarian objectives. That said, liberal values continue to play an influential role in current US grand strategy, including in East Asia.

My assessment of the impact of China's rise is counterintuitive—China's rise increases the strength of arguments for both preserving US alliances and terminating them. Although intense debate has continued over decades, my assessment is that the case between staying and leaving—that is, between maintaining US alliances and terminating them, especially between Deep Engagement and Neoisolation—has been a close call. The best arguments, if not all the arguments, in these schools are logically sound, their assumptions are reasonable, their overall case is internally consistent, and the trade-offs they call for are well explained. At least in broad gauge, China's rise strengthens both sets of arguments and does little to strengthen one relative to the other, leaving the choice between them a close call.

In contrast, China's rise weakens the case for Primacy and for Liberal Hegemony. China's rise makes Primacy, at least its military requirements, infeasible. Although China may struggle to match the United States' global military capabilities, its military capabilities in East Asia have already greatly reduced US regional military dominance and the United States' prospects for regaining dominance are exceedingly poor. Fortunately, the United States has excellent prospects for defending its allies without the capabilities implied by Primacy. The case against Liberal Hegemony is quite different. When a state's vital interests are not at risk, it has the leeway to pursue the spread and preservation of democracy through the use of force. This was arguably the situation from the end of the Cold War until China's growing power began to shift the balance of power and redefine the military situation in Northeast Asia; that is, during what is often termed the period of US unipolarity. Now the United States has far less leeway. Fighting a large war outside of Asia would weaken the military capabilities the United States had available to deter and fight China. Much more important, fighting a war in East Asia to preserve democracy in Taiwan would put US security and possibly even its survival at serious risk.

The following sections summarize the arguments offered by the schools of thought in the US grand-strategy debate and then evaluate how China's rise influences their strength. The concluding section offers two arguments. First, a more nuanced and controversial assessment suggests that China's rise makes terminating the United States' alliances in and commitments to East Asia its best option. The risks of war are too high, which makes Neoisolation the United States' best option. Second, ending US alliances may not, however, be the United States' best option because the spectrum of grand strategies fails to identify the possibility of retaining some of the United States' East Asian commitments while ending others. We should consider this possibility because there is significant variation in the nature, importance, and risks of US commitments in East Asia, ranging from alliance commitments to Japan, to complicated commitments to Taiwan, to still less clear commitments in the South China Sea. My conclusion is that the United States' best option is to end its commitment to Taiwan (which is explored fully in chapter 4) while retaining its alliance commitments to Japan, South Korea, and the Philippines. I dub this *Deep Engagement Minus*.

Neoisolation

SUMMARY

Neoisolation believes that the United States can be highly secure without security alliances.[10] According to this view, two key features enable the United States to be highly secure. First, large oceans on the east and west protect the United States from all direct threats of invasion. The combination of distance and water make invasion extremely difficult, if not entirely impossible. Second, nuclear weapons are highly effective at deterring attacks against a country's homeland, and the United States would be able to maintain extensive retaliatory capabilities—an assured destruction capability and more—against even a wealthy and technologically capable competitor. In other words, the United States enjoys a large advantage of defense over offense. Water and distance favor defense, as do nuclear weapons, especially when combined with the wealth and technological skill of a major

---

10. The central arguments are presented in Eugene Gholz, Daryl G. Press, and Harvey M. Sapolsky, "Come Home, America: The Strategy of Restraint in the Face of Temptation," *International Security* 21, no. 4 (spring 1997): 5–48. For an earlier analysis along these lines, see Eric A. Nordlinger, *Isolation Reconfigured: American Foreign Policy in a New Century* (Princeton University Press, 1995).

power.[11] A country would have to be much wealthier, possibly an order of magnitude wealthier or more, than the United States to effectively undermine the capabilities it requires for deterrence or to win a war against the United States. Thus, a Eurasian hegemon—a state that was able to acquire and harness the majority of the continents' wealth—would be unable to deny the United States the capabilities it requires for deterrence.

In addition, during the 1990s, Neoisolation included a third argument—a regional hegemon was unlikely to arise. There was a rough balance of power in Europe, and geography (particularly separation by water) favored defense in Northeast Asia. In addition, the major powers that lacked nuclear weapons could acquire them if their security required it and would be responsible and capable nuclear powers. Eurasian wealth would therefore remain safely divided.

Consequently, the United States was triply secure. Oceans and nuclear weapons individually meant that a hegemon would be unable to undermine necessary US military capabilities. In addition, a hegemon was not going to arise anyway.

Neoisolation offers a range of additional arguments, many of which responded to or anticipated critiques from other grand strategies. Critics argued that because war in Europe or Asia could not be ruled out and the United States might then get drawn into it—that is, choose to join, as it had in the First and Second World Wars—the United States should maintain its alliances to prevent these major-power wars. According to Neoisolation, however, US security would not be threatened by these wars, so the United States should stay out of them. Although the United States might be tempted to join a major-power war, it should be able to exercise the judgment required to avoid doing so. Moreover, deterrence could fail even if the United States maintained its alliance commitments, in which case, its forward-deployed forces would guarantee US involvement in a war that it should have skipped.

Critics also fear that ending US alliances would lead to nuclear proliferation by major powers—prominently Germany, Japan, and South Korea—that have not acquired nuclear weapons because they are covered by US extended deterrence commitments and the country's nuclear umbrella. Neoisolation counters that these countries have the wealth, technological capability, political institutions, and political stability required for nuclear proliferation to be safe, possibly even desirable.

Neoisolation favors open international trade but believes that US security alliances are not necessary to preserve it. Because trade is in the inter-

---

11. On offense-defense theory, see Robert Jervis, "Cooperation Under the Security Dilemma," *World Politics* 3, no. 2 (January 1978): 167–214, and Charles L. Glaser and Chaim Kaufmann, "What Is the Offense-Defense Balance and Can We Measure It?," *International Security* 22, no. 4 (spring 1998): 44–82.

ests of all the major powers, a hegemonic power or a global security provider is not required to maintain the openness of the international economy. Although the termination of US alliances could result in some countries becoming less secure, this would not significantly reduce their willingness to trade because relative economic gains between powers of comparable size tend to be small and take a long time to accumulate. Furthermore, although a war between other major powers, which the United States did not join, would hurt the US economy, it would not be crippling.[12] Trade accounts for a relatively small share of the US economy, and not all, or even most, of this trade would be lost. In any event, the economic costs would be much smaller than the economic and personnel costs of preparing to fight and then fighting such a war; they would also be smaller than the risk that escalation of a major-power conventional war involving the United States would escalate to nuclear weapons being used against the US homeland.

Finally, Neoisolation aims to limit US defense spending, highlighting the inherent value of investing instead in US well-being and the instrumental value of maintaining and nurturing US economic growth and technological strengths.

CHINA AND NEOISOLATION

We can use this summary to evaluate the impact of China's rise on the strength of the Neoisolationist analysis. In the coming decades, China's economic growth may produce an economy on the scale of the Eurasian hegemon that the United States feared during the Cold War.[13] China's wealth and growing investment in its economy, combined with increasing knowledge of and experience with advanced technology, may enable it to become a global military power in the coming decades. Unlike the Cold War fear, China would achieve this imposing economic capability and its related military potential without war and conquest. Although there would be several militarily capable countries in its region, China would have the wherewithal to pursue global ambitions.

Nevertheless, the Neoisolationist argument remains strong—the United States will be able to maintain the military capabilities required to protect its homeland against attack and coercion, even if facing such an economically capable, technologically advanced China. The Pacific Ocean will continue to provide a highly effective buffer against an invasion of the US homeland.

---

12. Gholz and Press argue a step further, holding that the US economy might even benefit; see Eugene Gholz and Daryl G. Press, "The Effects of Wars on Neutral Countries: Why It Doesn't Pay to Preserve Peace," *Security Studies* 10, no. 4 (summer 2001): 1–57. For disagreements, see Stephen G. Brooks and William C. Wohlforth, *America Abroad: The United States' Global Role in the 21st Century* (Oxford University Press, 2016), 184–87.

13. On the debate over China's economic and technological trajectory, see note 4 in the introduction.

Advances in reconnaissance capabilities and conventional precision-guided weapons are increasing the advantage of the defender, thereby further increasing the difficulty of crossing the Pacific to launch an invasion and driving up the costs required by the forces to attack versus those required to defend.[14] In addition, the United States will be able to maintain highly effective nuclear deterrent forces against a determined China. Advances in reconnaissance are making certain types of nuclear-weapons delivery systems more vulnerable, but the competition between retaliation and damage limitation will almost certainly continue to favor the US ability to retaliate for the foreseeable future, at a minimum due to the survivability of US ballistic missile submarines.[15] In short, China's rise will not seriously challenge the United States' ability to keep its homeland abundantly secure.

The situation in East Asia has become rather different than that predicted by Neoisolation in the early post–Cold War period.[16] Although water favors defense, the size and sophistication of China's military capabilities are posing an increasingly serious threat to regional states. Even with the United States involved in the fight, China's air and naval capabilities may enable it to effectively blockade Taiwan.[17] The United States and Japan should be able to protect Japan from a blockade, but this will take a dedicated effort. Japan's prospects without the United States would be much reduced. Japan's concerns about China's growing military capabilities and assertive regional policies are reflected in its 2022 decision to roughly double its defense spending over five years.[18] South Korea faces a far more substantial threat than does Japan.[19] Moreover, the military competition in East Asia is straining political relations, as are China's more assertive regional policies. Consequently, in Northeast Asia, the probability of crises and escalation to war is increasing and will likely continue to increase in the coming decades.

---

14. On antiaccess capabilities, see Toshi Yoshihara, *Going Anti-Access at Sea: How Japan Can Turn the Tables on China* (Center for a New American Security, 2014), and Stephen Biddle and Ivan Oelrich, "Future Warfare in the Western Pacific: Chinese Antiaccess/Area Denial, U.S. AirSea Battle, and the Command of the Commons in East Asia," *International Security* 41, no. 1 (summer 2016): 7–48.

15. See chapter 7 for an analysis of this technology competition. On the survivability of US ballistic missile submarines, see Owen R. Cote Jr., "Invisible Nuclear-Armed Submarines, or Transparent Oceans? Are Ballistic Missile Submarines Still the Best Deterrent for the United States?," *Bulletin of the Atomic Scientists* 75, no. 1 (January 2019): 30–35, and Tom A. Stefanick "Undersea Nuclear Forces: Survivability of Chinese, Russian, and US SSBNs," *Journal of Strategic Studies* 48, no. 2 (2025): 334–406.

16. See Gholz, Press, and Sapolsky, "Come Home, America," 21–22, 31–32.

17. See chapter 4 for citations.

18. Jennifer Lind, "Japan Steps Up: How Asia's Rising Threats Convinced Tokyo to Abandon Its Defense Taboos," *Foreign Affairs* (December 23, 2022), https://www.foreignaffairs.com/japan/japan-steps.

19. Eric Heginbotham and Richard J. Samuels, "Vulnerable US Alliance in Northeast Asia: The Nuclear Implications," *Washington Quarterly* 44, no. 1 (spring 2021): 158–59.

Maybe counterintuitively, from the Neoisolationist perspective, this increased probability of war makes the case for leaving Northeast Asia more urgent. This increased probability means there will be more crises and wars that the United States could become involved in. This, in turn, strengthens the case for the United States to end its alliances and security commitments to the region, thereby enabling it to avoid these wars. The temptation will be for the United States to do exactly the opposite—to deepen its commitments to enhance its deterrent. However, according to Neoisolation, although the greater prospect of conflict is clearly bad for the countries of Northeast Asia, it need not be nearly as bad for the United States. US security will be largely unaffected by a war in which it is not involved. The real danger is that the United States retains its security commitments in East Asia; if deterrence fails, the United States will almost certainly be involved in the war, which, among other dangers, risks escalation to attacks against the US homeland.

Ending the US alliances with Japan and South Korea would increase the probability that they will acquire nuclear weapons. Although Neoisolation may not consider this nuclear proliferation desirable, it does not see it as very dangerous. Both countries meet the economic, technological, and political requirements for being capable nuclear powers. There might even be security benefits because these countries' nuclear forces would be more effective at deterring major attacks than are the United States' extended deterrence commitments because the states' threats to use nuclear weapons to protect their own security would be more credible.

Neoisolation believes that the economic risks of ending the US security commitment to Northeast Asia would be relatively small. To start, whether or not the United States stays, the global economy will shift toward bipolarity. The United States will be unable to fully maintain its leadership position in the international economy because this role reflects its economic power, not its security commitments. This will not greatly hurt US prosperity, however, because a hegemon is not required to preserve the open trading system. In addition, according to the Neoisolationist argument, trade does not depend on high degrees of security between trade partners. Consistent with this argument, the relative gains from trade between China and the United States, as well as between China and its other trading partners, are now small enough that relative-gains concerns should not inhibit open trade. This prediction is supported by recent history. Relative-gains concerns did virtually nothing to slow US trade with China when the relative gains were likely much larger—that is, during the period when China grew from a small economy to the world's second largest.[20] Moreover, withdrawing from Northeast

---

20. Whether the United States should have supported China's economic growth in earlier decades is a largely separate question; arguing that it should not have is John J. Mearsheimer, *The Tragedy of Great Power Politics* (Norton, 2001).

Asia could improve US-China relations, which if anything would support open trade. There is, however, the possibility that China, once not constrained by the US forward presence, would become more assertive in East Asia, which could further strain US-China political relations, even once the United States had ended its security commitments to the region. Either way, the insensitivity of trade to political relations should ensure that US trade and prosperity would not be significantly damaged.

Neoisolationists should be relatively unsympathetic to recent arguments for de-risking—reducing US economic dependence on the Chinese economy to reduce its strategic vulnerability to trade cutoffs and reducing US exports that could enhance Chinese military capabilities. Ending US security commitments to East Asia would greatly reduce US concern about the security threat posed by China, which could weaken the case for de-risking in two ways. First, the United States would be less likely to get into serious disputes in which China would want to wield its economic leverage. Second, given the robustness of US homeland deterrence and defense capabilities, the United States would care less about selling technology that would enhance China's military capability. Nevertheless, Neoisolation might want the United States to pursue some de-risking because it could still face serious foreign policy disputes in which China might use trade coercively. It might also want to reduce the military threat that China could pose to its neighbors, not because Neoisolation views this as a threat to US security but rather because the United States could value these countries' well-being.

In sum, China's rise strengthens the Neoisolationist case for ending US security commitments to Northeast Asia. The US homeland would remain highly secure whether or not the United States has allies in East Asia. The probability of conflict in East Asia is growing, however, thereby raising the probability of a war that the United States does not need to and should not fight. If the United States remains committed to Northeast Asian security, China's rise would therefore reduce its security. In contrast, if the United States ends these commitments, as Neoisolation calls for, then China's rise would leave US security essentially unchanged. Reinforcing the case for ending the US alliances is the fact that the costs of US forces required to maintain the military capabilities necessary to defend US allies will continue to grow. Cutting the US commitment will therefore provide larger financial savings, which could be used to strengthen the US economy. Trade with China should continue whether or not the US retains its alliances and might even be enhanced by terminating them. Some strategic de-risking might be appropriate, but it is not required to enhance US security. Finally, although the increased probability of regional war does somewhat increase the possibility of damage to the US economy and its prosperity, the risks of being directly involved in the war increasingly dwarf these costs.

CHAPTER 3

Deep Engagement

SUMMARY

Deep Engagement holds that US security is increased by preserving peace among the globe's major powers and by a lack of intense security competition among them.[21] In addition, US security alliances support features of the international economy that increase US prosperity. Both the security and the economic dimensions identify Europe and Asia as the key major-power regions in which US vital interests are at stake.[22] Preserving US alliances in Europe and Asia is essential for protecting these interests. In various forms and iterations, Deep Engagement has been the core of US grand strategy since the early days of the Cold War.

Deep Engagement identifies two key arguments linking US alliances and forward-deployed military forces with increased US security. First, reducing the probability of a major-power war in Europe or Asia will increase US security because the United States is likely to get drawn into such a war. Even if the United States was not allied with countries in the fight, it might choose to join the conflict once it starts.[23] The United States was in this situation before the twentieth century's two world wars and joined them. Therefore, a prudent grand strategy requires acknowledging that it might do so again. Moreover, getting drawn into a major-power war in Eurasia is now far more dangerous than before the Cold War because it could escalate to nuclear attacks against the US homeland. Consequently, the United States increases its security by maintaining alliances that reduce the probability of major-power war. The bet is that this is safer than ending US alliances and then planning and attempting not to join a war.

According to Deep Engagement, US alliances reduce the probability of a major-power war by contributing US military capabilities to the overall deterrent capability of its regional allies. In addition, US leadership of the alliance reduces cooperation and coordination problems among its regional

---

21. Deep Engagement is similar in many respects to what was earlier termed *Selective Engagement*. Robert J. Art uses the term in a series of articles and in Robert J. Art, *A Grand Strategy for America* (Cornell University Press, 2003). These strategies are sufficiently similar that I blend their arguments in the discussion that follows. That said, Selective Engagement includes goals that go beyond those included in Deep Engagement, including spreading and preserving democracy and preventing mass murder in civil wars; however, it also makes clear that these are important, not vital, interests and that the United States should use military force to achieve these goals only under quite narrow conditions.

22. Brooks and Wohlforth, *America Abroad*, chaps. 5 and 6 include extensive citations to the earlier literature.

23. Art, *A Grand Strategy for America*, 55–58.

allies, thereby enhancing their overall deterrent capability. Furthermore, in certain cases, the US alliances could reduce the probability of conflict among its alliance partners, thereby increasing their willingness to engage in security cooperation with each other. For example, reducing countries' fear of Germany was an important role for the North Atlantic Treaty Organization (NATO) during periods of the Cold War.

Second, Deep Engagement emphasizes that US security commitments are necessary to reduce countries' incentives to acquire nuclear weapons. Via its alliances, the United States extends deterrence to major powers that would likely otherwise acquire nuclear weapons. Japan and South Korea are among the most likely candidates in East Asia; Germany might also acquire nuclear weapons. Some proponents of Deep Engagement believe that nuclear proliferation increases the probability of nuclear use, even when the new nuclear states are technologically capable and politically stable.[24] Others worry less about the danger posed by these major powers and focus instead on the damage that their acquisition of nuclear weapons would inflict on the Nuclear Nonproliferation Treaty and the broader regime that it supports. This weakening would in turn result in an increased probability of nuclear acquisition by states that are less technologically and politically capable and/or more dangerous because they want to revise the geopolitical status quo, and possibly by nonstate actors.[25] For either or both reasons, Deep Engagement holds that a grand strategy that reduces the probability of nuclear proliferation increases US security.

It is worth noting that Deep Engagement tends not to rely on an argument that was long associated with the origins of US containment policy during the Cold War. The concern was that that a Eurasian hegemon would control resources sufficient to enable it to attack and invade the United States or to blockade and compel it. This argument, however, turns out to be weak, largely for the reasons emphasized by Neoisolation and now recognized by other grand strategies—ocean buffers and nuclear weapons provide the US homeland with an exceptionally high level of security, even against an equally powerful or more powerful (wealthy and capable) adversary.[26]

In addition to these security-focused arguments, Deep Engagement holds that US security commitments increase US prosperity. To start, a major-power war and intense security competition would be bad for trade

---

24. Brooks and Wohlforth, *America Abroad*, 107–10.
25. Art, *A Grand Strategy for America*, 53.
26. Robert Art, "A Defensible Defense: America's Grand Strategy After the Cold War," *International Security* 15, no. 4 (spring 1991): 10–23. See, however, Elbridge A. Colby, *The Strategy of Denial: American Defense in an Age of Great Power Conflict* (Yale University Press, 2021), 6–10, which discusses this logic while placing greater weight on economic rationales.

and would therefore damage US prosperity. Most basically, a large-scale war would disrupt the international economy, hurting the United States via lost trade. Stephen Brooks and William Wohlforth, who have provided the fullest statement of Deep Engagement, reject the argument made by some Neoisolationists who claim that a major-power war that did not involve the United States would not hurt the US economy. Although the United States may have been insulated in previous eras, modern globalization now leaves the US economy much more vulnerable to a major-power war.[27] In addition, the decreased international security that would be generated by the termination of US alliances would reduce states' willingness to preserve open trade because, among other reasons, "the security commitments of Deep Engagement support the global economic order by reducing the likelihood of security dilemmas, arms racing, instability, regional conflicts, and, in extremis, major power war."[28] Related, although international relations theorists have shown that the cooperation required to generate economic openness could be created and maintained without a hegemonic economic power and thus could continue without US leadership, Deep Engagement explains that economic openness is nevertheless more likely with US leadership because it can help reduce collective-action and relative-gains problems.[29] Thus, Deep Engagement calls for maintaining US security commitments to protect US prosperity via international openness.[30]

Moreover, Deep Engagement argues that US security commitments help sustain US leadership of the world economy and thereby help preserve features of the international economy that benefit the United States. For example, the United States benefits from having the dollar serve as the world's dominant currency, and US security commitments help in a variety of ways to preserve the dollar's standing.[31]

We should note that the security and prosperity arguments that are bundled by Deep Engagement are largely separable. The Deep Engagement arguments about the security value of alliances stand largely on their own; they need not be paired with the prosperity arguments. Consequently, we can identify another grand strategy—built on the combination of Deep Engagement's security rationales for US alliances with the Neoisolationist arguments about the independence of the open international economic sys-

---

27. Brooks and Wohlforth, *America Abroad*, 184–87.
28. Stephen G. Brooks, G. John Ikenberry, and William C. Wohlforth, "Don't Come Home, America: The Case Against Retrenchment," *International Security* 37, no. 3 (winter 2012): 41.
29. Duncan Snidal, "The Limits of Hegemonic Stability Theory," *International Organization* 39, no. 4 (autumn 1985): 579–614.
30. Brooks and Wohlforth, *America Abroad*, 159–61.
31. Brooks and Wohlforth, *America Abroad*, 176–81.

tem from US alliances and the US provision of global security more broadly. This possibility is valuable for understanding Offshore Balancing, which is discussed in the following section.

CHINA AND DEEP ENGAGEMENT

From the perspective of Deep Engagement, China's rise increases the importance of preserving US alliances in Northeast Asia. China's expanding and improving military capabilities, combined with its increasingly assertive regional foreign policies, increase the probability of a war. Therefore, given Deep Engagement's core argument—the risks of retaining US security commitments and forward-deployed troops are smaller than the risks of leaving the region and then getting drawn back into a large war—the importance of preserving US alliances in Northeast Asia increases.

The value of these alliances also increases because the United States is likely to incur greater costs when fighting against a more militarily capable China. Not only will the states' forces be more comparably matched; a US-China war would also likely be fought in ways that increase the probability of escalation to higher levels of conflict. Analyses of large conventional-force operations have highlighted the possibility that US plans for defeating China's area-denial capabilities could fuel pressures for escalation to a still-larger conventional war, including early attacks against US space-based assets, and even to nuclear war.[32]

A closer look, however, paints a more complicated picture. Although US alliance commitments likely reduce the probability of war, they also increase the probability of a larger regional war. The most likely scenario in which the United States and China get into a large war is over Taiwan. If a war occurred between China and Taiwan, and the United States came to Taiwan's defense, China would have large incentives to attack Japan. This is the scenario that most Japan experts envision when anticipating a large war involving Japan and China. China would have two complementary reasons for attacking Japan. First, it would want to destroy US forces that are forward-deployed in Japan. These forces would be essential to US efforts to defeat a Chinese campaign against Taiwan. Second, since the mid-1990s, Japan has become more likely to support US forces in a conflict over Taiwan, which creates incentives for China to attack Japanese bases and forces. Changes in the terms of the US-Japan alliance made during the 2010s—including a moderate expansion

---

32. Avery Goldstein, "First Things First: The Pressing Danger of Crisis Instability in U.S.-China Relations," *International Security* 37, no. 4 (spring 2013): 49–89; Caitlin Talmadge, "Would China Go Nuclear?: Assessing the Risk of Chinese Nuclear Escalation in a Conventional War with the United States," *International Security* 41, no. 4 (spring 2017): 50–92. For elaboration, see chapter 7.

of the conditions under which Japan could employ force in response to an attack on a third party, an increase in bilateral military exercises and intelligence operations, and a variety of institutional arrangements that deepen the US-Japan alliance—have moved Japan further in this direction. And large increases in Japan's defense spending, initiated in 2022, will increase its ability to play an important role in this scenario.[33]

In contrast, without the US security commitment to the region, a Chinese attack would be much more likely to be limited to Taiwan itself. Even if the United States had ended its commitment, it might consider joining this more limited conflict—that is, get drawn back in. Consequently, the key comparison is between retaining US alliances and risking a regional war and terminating the alliances and risking returning to engage in a war over Taiwan. Arguably, the probability of the United States returning to protect Taiwan is lower than the probability of retaining US alliances and then protecting them in a regional war. If this is the case, then China's rise does less to strengthen the case for Deep Engagement.

The impact of China's rise on nuclear proliferation seems clearer. China's growing conventional military capabilities pose an increased threat to Japan, which increases the probability that US withdrawal would lead Japan to acquire nuclear weapons. In fact, the combination of the growing Chinese threat and increasing doubts about the depth of the United States' commitment—fueled both by Donald Trump's criticism of alliances during and after his first term as president and by domestic US debates about its role in the world—have already increased Japanese discussions of this possibility.[34] South Korea faces a growing North Korean nuclear capability, which would be the immediate concern if the United States ended its alliance.[35] China's growing capabilities would add to these pressures. Thus, ending the US alliance commitment to South Korea would very likely result in South Korea acquiring nuclear weapons. Therefore, given Deep Engagement's beliefs about the dangers of nuclear proliferation, China's rise increases the value of continuing and deepening the Unites States' commitments to its Northeast Asian treaty allies.

Overall, Deep Engagement finds that China's rise reduces US security. Preserving US alliances can reduce the danger of China's rise but not elimi-

---

33. Adam P. Liff, "Japan's Security Policy in the 'Abe Era': Rational Transformation or Evolutionary Shift?" *Texas National Security Review* 1, no. 3 (May 2018): 13–21.

34. Heginbotham and Samuels, "Vulnerable US Alliance in Northeast Asia."

35. Seukhoon Paul Choi, "As World Order Shifts, So Does South Korean Security Policy," *Arms Control Today* 53, no. 6 (July/August 2023): 12–18, https://www.armscontrol.org/act/2023-07/features/world-order-shifts-does-south-korean-security-policy; Jennifer Ahn, "The Evolution of South Korea's Nuclear Weapons Policy Debate," Council on Foreign Relations, August 16, 2022, https://www.cfr.org/blog/evolution-south-koreas-nuclear-weapons-policy-debate.

nate it. This may seem obvious—facing a more powerful state reduces US security. But recall that Neoisolation concludes otherwise, if the United States adopts its preferred grand strategy. This is an important, often underappreciated, divide between these grand-strategy schools.

Turning to economic impacts, as summarized above, Deep Engagement holds that US alliances support US prosperity by reducing the probability of a major-power war, supporting open international trade, and preserving the benefits of US economic leadership. However, focusing on China's rise draws all of these claims into question.

First, the Deep Engagement arguments about economic openness are less compelling when applied to China. As argued above, the US security commitments reduce Chinese security. Thus, the calming and economically beneficial effects that alliances are supposed to generate are not being produced evenly across East Asia. This is because the impact of US alliances differs from their Cold War impact. NATO did reduce security concerns within Western Europe, that is, *within* the alliance, which supported trade among alliance members. It did not, of course, have this effect between NATO and the Soviet Union. However, unlike the Soviet Union, which was not economically important, China has a huge, technologically advanced economy that is deeply integrated into the global economy. Because US security commitments now reduce China's security and strain political relations via arms racing and political spirals, these alliances should, according to Deep Engagement, be bad for trade. And, since the mid-2010s, US shifts toward economic decoupling and de-risking have reflected this security competition. If the United States ended its security commitments to the region, arms competition between the United States and China would become far less intense and China's security would increase. Regional military competition would likely increase, Japan would become less secure, and relative gains concerns could result in reduced trade between Japan and China. However, if military competition driven by security dilemmas hurts the international economy, as Deep Engagement holds, then the net economic impact of US termination of its alliances could be positive for US prosperity because it would support increased trade between the massive US and Chinese economies.

There is, though, a countervailing set of considerations. Some proponents of preserving US alliances believe that if the United States withdraws from East Asia, China would likely use its dominant regional position to create a trading bloc that favors its economy and other regional economies, while limiting US trade access to the region. According to this argument, in a worst-case scenario, the result could open the United States to coercion and undermine its national security and domestic stability.[36]

---

36. Colby, *The Strategy of Denial*, 10–15.

Even in this case, though, the net effects on global power are unclear. The globe's other major economies would likely respond by limiting China's access to their markets. While the US economy would suffer, so would China's, as well as the overall global economy. China's relative share of the global economy could decrease, as would its ability to coerce the United States. US prosperity would be damaged, possibly significantly, but its security might not be because China's economy could be hurt as much or more than the US economy.

Second, if China's economy continues to grow faster than the US economy for the next couple of decades, China might provide a test of the importance of US security commitments in maintaining US economic leadership. Even if these commitments do support the United States' leading role in the global economy, it may well be that the dominant determinant is the size of the US economy. As China's economy comes to equal and then exceed the size of the US economy, China's global economic influence will almost certainly continue to grow. Security commitments or not, US leadership is likely to be whittled away. Here again, the beginning of this shift is already evident. China is now the leading trade partner of the countries of East Asia and has concluded a region-wide trade agreement. At the same time, specific US competitive advantages may turn out to be more important than sheer size for determining leadership. For example, US superiority in innovation and the underlying technologies for producing advanced semiconductors and in global financial networks may make US global economic influence more robust. In addition, comparing the US and Chinese economies may capture only part of the picture. Instead, it may be that the combined economic weight of the US and its allies' economies will limit China's growing influence.

Deep Engagement should be supportive of de-risking the US and Chinese economies because this will limit China's military capabilities and thereby help enhance US and allied deterrent capabilities. It might also support de-risking to reduce China's ability to use trade to coerce the United States over issues in East Asia. Deep Engagement does not have a clear position on a broader decoupling—if it could provide large relative economic gains (which remains something of an open question), then Deep Engagement might support decoupling. However, any advantages in power would need to be weighed against the absolute economic costs the United States would suffer. In addition, Deep Engagement could worry that the international political strains of all-out economic competition with China would more than offset the power advantages.

In sum, then, Deep Engagement sees the value of US alliances and forward deployments increasing with China's rise, primarily because, as a war in East Asia becomes more likely, the alliances' contribution to deterring it becomes more valuable. China's rise does, however, generate a number of tensions within Deep Engagement's collection of arguments. While reducing the probability of war in Northeast Asia, US commitments may at the same time be increasing the probability of US involvement in a war that involves its East Asian treaty allies. In addition, the jury remains out on whether China's economic growth, if it continues over the long term, will end US leadership of the international economy, even if the United States retains its security alliances.

Offshore Balancing

SUMMARY

Offshore Balancing holds that the United States should forward-deploy its military forces and even maintain alliances only under certain limited conditions: A regional hegemon is otherwise likely to arise, and this regional hegemon would threaten US security.[37] US forces might need to be forward-deployed during peacetime if a potential hegemon might succeed so quickly in conquering its region that US forces would be unable to return to the region before US allies were defeated. But if a war was expected to progress slowly, the United States could keep its forces deployed at home and then decide to join the war only after the fighting made clear that its potential allies could not defeat the aspiring hegemon. Among its advantages, Offshore Balancing would create incentives for other states to balance against a hegemonic threat, allowing the United States to invest less to achieve its own security. Arguably more important, Offshore Balancing could reduce the risks of achieving US security because if its allies are successful, the United States could stay out of the war entirely. Framed in terms of international relations theory, Offshore Balancing is a buck-passing strategy, designed to get other states to take responsibility for preventing the rise of a regional hegemon while preserving the option of balancing if those states fail to or are unable to balance.

Key examples of offshore balancing are the United States' decisions to join the First and Second World Wars only once Germany had reasonable

---

37. Key statements include Mearsheimer, *Tragedy of Great Power Politics*, Christopher Layne, "From Preponderance to Offshore Balancing: America's Future Grand Strategy," *International Security* 22, no. 1 (summer 1997): 86–124, and Christopher Layne, *The Peace of Illusions: American Grand Strategy from 1940 to Present* (Cornell University Press, 2006). Posen, *Restraint* favors preserving some presence in East Asia and having the ability to balance against an emerging hegemon. Thus, he fits into a version of Offshore Balancing.

prospects of winning.[38] The United States' deployment of troops in Europe during the Cold War has also been characterized as a form of Offshore Balancing—the United States preferred not to have its forces deployed in Europe, but the potential speed of a successful Soviet invasion of Western Europe required US forward deployment.[39]

Although Offshore Balancing focuses on US security, it does address its implications for open international trade, the global economy, and US prosperity. Offshore Balancing, like Neoisolation, holds that US alliances, or at least forward-deployed forces, are not necessary for preserving the open international economic system and the United States' ability to maintain valuable trade.[40] Offshore Balancing—again, like Neoisolation—stresses the value of reducing defense spending and redirecting those resources to domestic purposes. Proponents call for the United States to achieve this both by decreasing its alliance commitments when conditions allow and by demanding that its allies increase their own defense spending. Terminating or attenuating its alliance commitments will motivate the United States' current allies to spend more on defense and, more broadly, to take greater responsibility for their own behavior.

Offshore Balancers disagree among themselves about whether a regional hegemon would pose a threat to the United States. Some argue that a regional hegemon would threaten the United States only under narrow conditions, most importantly, if a revolution in military technology held out a serious possibility of undermining the defense dominance created by oceans and nuclear weapons.[41] Others, however, find that any regional hegemon would threaten US security.[42]

This creates quite a divide or spectrum within the set of positions that are typically included as Offshore Balancing. Analysts who hold the first position are quite close to the Neoisolationist argument about US security. Analysts who take the second position—any regional hegemon or major-power war that might produce a regional hegemon poses a serious threat—are sim-

---

38. Disputing this characterization of the US decision to enter WWI is Galen Jackson, "The Offshore Balancing Thesis Reconsidered: Realism, the Balance of Power in Europe, and America's Decision for War in 1917," *Security Studies* 21, no. 3 (2012): 455–89.

39. Mearsheimer, *Tragedy of Great Power Politics*, 256; however, Layne, *The Peace of Illusions*, 106, disputes this characterization.

40. Layne, *The Peace of Illusions*, 172–78; John J. Mearsheimer and Stephen M. Walt, "The Case for Offshore Balancing: A Superior U.S. Grand Strategy," *Foreign Affairs* 95, no. 4 (July/August 2016): 78–79.

41. Layne, "From Preponderance to Offshore Balancing," 117, identifies the possibility of changes in military technology that "greatly enhanced conventional warfighting capabilities," thereby weakening deterrence and partly offsetting the nuclear revolution. A key statement of Neoisolation identifies a similar set of conditions for reengaging, including a "potential aggressor must solve the 'nuclear problem.'" Gholz, Press, and Sapolsky, "Come Home, America," 47. These Offshore Balancers and Neoisolationists are strikingly similar.

42. Walt and Mearsheimer, "The Case for Offshore Balancing."

ilar in a key way to the Deep-Engagement argument about US security (although not necessarily economics).[43] This overlap between these Offshore Balancers and Deep Engagers is not complete, however, because the Offshore Balancers must decide whether a potential hegemon poses a sufficiently swift and potent threat to require deployment onshore. In contrast, Deep Engagers believe that the possibility of a hegemon or major-power war in Europe or Asia is sufficient to require US forward deployment in these regions.[44]

In theory, Offshore Balancing could be built on the same security logic as Deep Engagement—avoiding the risk of the United States getting drawn back into a regional hegemonic war and preventing nuclear proliferation. In practice, however, although present, these logics have been less prominent in the current debate. For example, some proponents of Offshore Balancing argue that if the major-power war would not produce a hegemon, then the war would not threaten US security and presumably the United States would stay out of it.[45] Moreover, the United States would know if a country was gaining the capability to become a hegemon and could redeploy forces before this danger was acute. However, other analysts who could be counted as Offshore Balancers do worry about the possibility of being drawn into a regional war under certain conditions.[46]

Instead of these arguments, a prominent version of Offshore Balancing emphasizes a different rationale for worrying about the rise of a regional hegemon. These Offshore Balancers emphasize the ability of a regional hegemon, drawing on its economic and technological resources, to project power globally. In contrast, a major power that has not achieved regional hegemony must focus on regional dangers, which makes global power projection riskier, if not impossible. John Mearsheimer and Stephen Walt argue that a regional hegemon might "ally with countries in the Western Hemisphere and interfere close to U.S. soil" and that the United States should attempt to "maintain the regional balance of power so the most powerful state in the region . . . remains too worried about its neighbors to roam into the Western hemisphere."[47]

As argued briefly in chapter 1, the security argument for maintaining distant alliances to prevent a potential regional hegemon from achieving hegemony and then "roaming" into one's own region is weak. Under most if not

---

43. Priebe, Gunness, Mueller, and Burdette, *The Limits of Restraint*, 7–8, term this position "counterhegemonic restraint."

44. Of course, it is possible that Deep Engagers have determined, without explicitly addressing the question, that the threats in the regions are sufficiently large to require onshore deployment. They may also require onshore deployment for a variety of other reasons, including providing peacetime security that supports the open international economy.

45. Mearsheimer and Walt, "The Case for Offshore Balancing," 73, 82; Layne, "From Preponderance to Offshore Balancing," 119–22, but see also 117.

46. Posen, *Restraint*, 131.

47. Mearsheimer and Walt, "The Case for Offshore Balancing," 73.

all conditions, a regional hegemon can better achieve security—that is, at lower cost and risk—by engaging with and policing its own neighborhood than by maintaining distant alliances to prevent the rise of a hegemony in a different region. In large part, this is because the costs and risks of preventing the rise of a regional hegemon will usually be large. By definition, the United States would be risking or actually becoming involved in a major-power war. In addition, given the regional hegemon's influence in its own region, the rival hegemon is unlikely to pursue alliances significant enough to provoke it.[48] These flaws may not be fatal to the overall case for Offshore Balancing, however, because the danger of getting drawn back into a large war could be added to its arguments or simply replace the roaming argument.

Offshore Balancing holds that the threat of a hegemon arising in Europe is sufficiently small that the United States could withdraw its troops from the continent.[49] This conclusion partly reflects the judgment that the European Union (EU) states have the potential to defend themselves. Either NATO would be disbanded—with the expectation that the EU would figure out how to replace it—or the nature of the US commitment would be renegotiated, removing the guarantee that the United States would definitely intervene if a current European member of NATO were attacked. Deep Engagement disagrees, questioning the EU's ability to defend itself for both political and material reasons.[50]

Offshore Balancing also differs from Deep Engagement in its assessment of the dangers of nuclear proliferation. Some Offshore Balancers believe that proliferation is undesirable but not necessarily very dangerous and largely beyond US control, while acknowledging that reducing US commitments could lead a few states to acquire nuclear weapons. Others conclude that certain nuclear proliferation may, in the more distant future, be desirable—for example, by Japan—but caution that this process would need to be carefully managed, both politically and militarily.[51] This set of arguments is closer to the Neoisolationist position on proliferation. (The diversity within Offshore Balancing and its overlap with both Neoisolation and Deep En-

---

48. On these points, see John M. Schuessler, "Ambivalent Offshore Balancer: America in the Middle East and Beyond," *Parameters* 53, no. 4 (winter 2023–24): 53–67.

49. Although these analysts might not change their conclusions, it is worth noting that their arguments were made before Russia's 2022 invasion of Ukraine. This should not change conclusions about the prospects for a hegemon, but it could, for other reasons, lead to revised conclusions about withdrawal of US forces from Europe.

50. Hugo Meijer and Stephen G. Brooks, "Illusions of Autonomy: Why Europe Cannot Provide for Its Security If the United States Pulls Back," *International Security* 45, no. 4 (spring 2021): 7–43. In contrast, see Barry Posen, "Europe Can Defend Itself," *Survival* 62, no. 6 (December 2020): 7–34.

51. On the former, see, for example, Mearsheimer and Walt, "The Case for Offshore Balancing," 79; on the latter, see Posen, *Restraint*, 101.

gagement illustrates the point made at the outset of this chapter—positions on a variety of key questions can be combined in numerous ways.)

CHINA AND OFFSHORE BALANCING

In contrast to their position on Europe, some Offshore Balancers have called for the United States to retain and deepen its commitments in Northeast Asia. According to these arguments, there is a reasonable probability that China's economic growth will continue, enabling China to build military capabilities that other states in the region will be unable to offset, thereby creating the potential for it to become the regional hegemon. However, other Offshore balancers conclude that the United States can withdraw its forces from Northeast Asia while possibly retaining its treaty alliances.

A key example of an Offshore Balancer who wants the United States to deepen its commitment to East Asia is John Mearsheimer, who has called for the United States to "lead the effort against China and focus much of its formidable power on that goal" and to coordinate an effective alliance among the region's far-flung states, including India, Japan, and Vietnam.[52] In contrast, other Offshore Balancers call for pulling US troops out of the region. Christopher Layne argues that if the United States continues to forward-deploy forces, "its alliance with Japan risks dragging it into a war with China in which American strategic interests would not be engaged."[53] In a sort of in-between position, Barry Posen concludes that the United States should limit US support of its alliance with Japan, at least for the time being. First, the United States enjoys a highly secure strategic position; China must overcome many obstacles before it would pose a threat to the United States, and it may not be successful. Second, because China is fearful of the United States, highly competitive offensive policies risk generating a negative political spiral that makes China's rise more dangerous. The continuing shift in the focus of US military planning toward East Asia and its military doctrine that plans to attack China's mainland are likely to generate these negative effects.[54] Third, the United States needs to work to reshape its alliance with Japan, both to reduce the amount the United States currently spends but also to ensure that Japan is ready, politically as well as militarily, to shoulder the burden and responsibility of balancing against China. This will require reducing US troop deployments and renegotiating

---

52. John J. Mearsheimer, *The Tragedy of Great Power Politics*, updated ed. (W. W. Norton, 2014), 385.

53. Christopher Layne, "China's Challenge to US Hegemony," *Current History* 107, no. 705 (January 2008): 18.

54. Robert S. Ross, "The Problem with the Pivot: Obama's New Asia Policy Is Unnecessary and Counterproductive," *Foreign Affairs* 91, no. 6 (November/December 2012): 70–82, argues that the US pivot to Asia has had this effect.

CHAPTER 3

the US-Japan treaty to shift primary responsibility for defending Japan from the United States to Japan.[55]

Considering China's rise further highlights the weakness of one of Offshore Balancing's key arguments—the "free to roam" argument: Does it really make sense for the United States to remain committed to East Asian security to prevent China from eventually posing a security threat in the Western Hemisphere? The risks generated by US commitments are clear and arguably large. Mearsheimer agrees, having argued that China's rise will bring "considerable potential for war."[56] In contrast, the possibility that China will pursue significant security alliances in the Western Hemisphere remains entirely theoretical. Moreover, the United States would have many advantages in countering any such Chinese military deployments, including the advantages of distance. In addition, in anticipation of this potential future danger, the United States could invest more economically and diplomatically throughout Central and South America to weaken China's ability to develop threatening inroads. However, even if we eliminate the free-to-roam argument, the security argument for Deep Engagement—the possibility of getting drawn into a regional war—can be used to preserve an overall argument for Offshore Balancing.

In addition, the Offshore Balancing proponents of deepening US–East Asian alliances have left a key question unanswered: Could China win a war quickly against Japan? If not, then Offshore Balancing should call for not keeping US troops forward-deployed but instead based in the United States and prepared to flow quickly into the East Asian theater if Japan is unable to blunt China's attack. Although China's military is much larger than Japan's, China might not be able to win quickly because of the difficulty of invading across water. If this is the case, then the United States should stay offshore.

In sum, from these grand-strategic prescriptions, we can sort out the impact of China's rise on the Offshore Balancing arguments. Excluding the flawed "free to roam" argument, China's rise strengthens both strands of Offshore Balancing—the one that finds any regional hegemon poses a serious threat and the one that finds regional hegemons pose a threat only under narrow military conditions. This should not be surprising since they build on logics of Neoisolation and Deep Engagement, both of which were strengthened by China's rise. Offshore Balancing, however, is more complicated because it requires more nuanced judgments about whether the threat posed by China is large enough—specifically, likely to succeed fast enough—to warrant onshore balancing.

---

55. Posen, *Restraint*, 91–102.
56. John J. Mearsheimer, "The Gathering Storm: China's Challenge to US Power in Asia," *The Chinese Journal of International Politics* 3, no. 4 (winter 2010): 282.

Primacy

SUMMARY

Primacy calls for the United States to maintain (or regain) its global military and economic dominance. Proponents of Primacy argue that states pursue primacy to "insure their security, promote their interests, and shape the international environment."[57] Like Deep Engagement, Primacy calls for maintaining the United States' key alliances. But it sets a higher standard for US military capabilities and broadly calls for more competitive military and economic policies.[58]

The United States became the globe's dominant military power at the end of the Cold War. This dominance was not required by its grand strategy during the Cold War and in large part was then infeasible. Although the Soviet economy was much smaller than the US economy, the Soviet Union spent a much larger percentage of its gross domestic product (GDP) on defense. Maybe more important, the defense advantage created by nuclear weapons and difficulties of fighting across distance and oceans would have prevented the United States from acquiring militarily dominant capabilities, and for the most part it did not try to.[59]

Following the end of the Cold War, interest emerged in preserving the United States' dominant position. Possibly the clearest statement was in a draft of the Defense Planning Guidance that was leaked in early 1992 during the George H. W. Bush administration. The document states, "Our first objective is to prevent the re-emergence of a new rival, either on the territory of the former Soviet Union or elsewhere, that poses a threat on the order of that posed by the former Soviet Union. This is a dominant consideration underlying the new regional defense strategy and requires that we endeavor to prevent any hostile power from dominating a region whose resources would, under consolidated control, be sufficient to generate global power." The document goes on to argue that "we must maintain the mechanisms for deterring potential competitors from even aspiring to a

---

57. Samuel P. Huntington, "Why International Primacy Matters," *International Security* 17, no. 4 (spring 1993): 70. For a skeptical view authored at the same time, see Robert Jervis, "International Primacy: Is the Game Worth the Candle?," *International Security* 17, no. 4 (spring 1993): 52–67.

58. For discussion of the various uses and meanings of *primacy*, see Van Jackson, "American Military Superiority and the Pacific-Primacy Myth," *Survival* 60, no. 2 (April/May 2018): 107–32.

59. This partial exception concerns US nuclear policy, which was dedicated to counterforce targeting for much of the Cold War and did see value in a damage-limitation capability; on US pursuit of a damage-limitation capability, see Austin Long and Brendan Rittenhouse Green, "Stalking the Secure Second Strike: Intelligence, Counterforce, and Nuclear Strategy," *Journal of Strategic Studies* 38, nos. 1–2 (2015): 38–73.

larger regional or global role. An effective reconstitution capability is important here, since it implies that a potential rival could not hope to quickly or easily gain a predominant military position in the world."[60]

Consistent with the importance it places on military advantages, Primacy strongly supports nonproliferation because the acquisition of nuclear weapons by additional states would reduce the United States' ability to employ its conventional military advantages against them. The document argued further that in addition to meeting these demanding military requirements, the United States should try to accommodate the interests of major powers to convince them that US dominance was not a threat to their interests.[61] Interestingly, this rendition of Primacy included this cooperative dimension as well as highly competitive ones. Whether accommodation would have been successful is far from clear because, among other reasons, potential competitors would face uncertainty about US goals, and the associated risks they faced would be increased by US military dominance.

Although the United States never fully adopted Primacy as its grand strategy, elements of its spirit and language have appeared in the national security documents of many administrations. For example, the George W. Bush administration's 2002 *National Security Strategy of the United States* held that "we must build and maintain our defenses beyond challenge," including the ability to "decisively defeat any adversary if deterrence fails." Echoing the 1992 leaked guidance, it goes on to claim that "our forces will be strong enough to dissuade potential adversaries from pursuing a military build-up in hopes of surpassing, or equaling, the power of the United States," which is a significantly higher standard than being able to deter and defeat an adversary. It also took an unusually assertive position on the proliferation of weapons of mass destruction, stating that "the United States can no longer solely rely on a reactive posture as we have in the past. The inability to deter a potential attacker, the immediacy of today's threats, and the magnitude of potential harm that could be caused by our adversaries' choice of weapons, do not permit that option."[62]

Significantly, however, the United States did not adopt two policies that were likely required to support a Primacy grand strategy over the long term. First, it did not attempt to prevent potential challengers from fully joining the international economy, which, if successfully coordinated with the other major economic powers, would have at least slowed the rise of

60. "Excerpts from the Pentagon's Plan: 'Prevent the Re-emergence of a New Rival,'" *New York Times*, March 8, 1992, 14, https://www.nytimes.com/1992/03/08/world/excerpts-from-pentagon-s-plan-prevent-the-re-emergence-of-a-new-rival.html.

61. For a fuller description of the 1990s version of Primacy, see Posen and Ross, "Competing Visions for U.S. Grand Strategy," 32–43.

62. George Bush, *The National Security Strategy of the United States of America*, White House, September 2002, 29, 30, 15.

the challengers. In fact, the United States led efforts to bring China into the World Trade Organization (WTO). Second, the United States did not attempt to restrict the flow of advanced technology and human expertise that would have hindered both the economic growth and military potential of a challenger. In addition, the United States did significantly decrease its defense spending and forces structure during the 1990s, although the 9/11 attacks generated a reversal.

There are three key questions we need to ask about Primacy.[63] First: Are its military requirements necessary to achieve US objectives? There is likely no general answer—different potential peer competitors, in different regions of the globe, will generate different deterrence requirements. Second: Is Primacy militarily feasible against the peer competitor? This question has two components: (1) Would a vast military advantage convince the rising power not to try to undermine US military capabilities? and (2) Does the United States have the economic and technological capability to win this competition if the rising power decides to compete? Third: Do the potential political costs of Primacy—the insecurity it could instill in the adversary, which could in turn fuel more aggressive policies—offset its benefits? The following subsection addresses these questions for the specific case of China.

CHINA AND PRIMACY

China's rise has generated renewed calls for Primacy. A 2014 version developed by Ashley Tellis holds that "the loss of primacy to China would fundamentally undermine the national security interests of the United States in the most comprehensive sense imaginable."[64] The loss of primacy would weaken US alliances, could well lead Japan and South Korea to acquire nuclear weapons, could undermine international institutions that support economic growth and advance US values and desirable norms, and could eventually even "allow Beijing to challenge Washington closer to U.S. shores."[65] The latter point suggests the Offshore-Balancing logic about the danger posed by a regional hegemon's ability to roam.

---

63. Another key question specific to China, related to the prior paragraph, is whether the United States could have mustered international support for preventing China's economic and technological rise.

64. Ashley J. Tellis, *Balancing Without Containment: An American Strategy for Managing China* (Carnegie Endowment for International Peace, 2014), 19. He also holds that "the loss of American hegemony would be dangerous to U.S. security because it would entail a diminution of strategic autonomy, the first and most important benefit of possessing greater power than others in a competitive environment" (14) and "The loss of American primacy to China, therefore, would put Washington at Beijing's mercy far more than is currently the case" (14). See also Robert D. Blackwill and Ashley J. Tellis, *Revising U.S. Grand Strategy Toward China*, Council Special Report No. 72, Council of Foreign Relations, March 2015.

65. Tellis, *Balancing Without Containment*, 18–19, 31.

Tellis argued that Cold War–style containment was not an option for a variety of reasons, including the dense economic ties between China and the United States and the low probability that other countries would join the United States in trying to isolate China economically. Consequently, this version of Primacy focuses on the military dimension—the United States should compete militarily to maintain its military superiority, including "the U.S. ability to operate freely along the Asian littorals." In addition, it calls for the United States to enjoy all of the benefits of nuclear deterrence, which would likely require preserving the damage-limitation capability the United States then had against China's nuclear forces.[66] Tellis argues that a distant blockade—from the Persian Gulf to the Strait of Malacca—would fail to meet basic US requirements because, among other reasons, it would not prevent China from succeeding in a relatively quick war. Thus, the United States needed to adopt an offensive conventional strategy—something along the lines of the Air-Sea Battle concept—to meet the military and political dimensions of its alliance commitments.[67] In addition, although economic containment is not possible, to preserve its economic dominance, the United States should pursue regional economic pacts that exclude China, place tighter constraints on the export of militarily valuable technology, and adopt a multipronged strategy for revitalizing the US economy.[68] Here Tellis's argument anticipates more recent calls for decoupling and de-risking: Although recognizing that full decoupling is infeasible, his Primacy calls not only for limits on militarily valuable trade but also for policies designed to improve the US economy relative to China's.

A 2021 paper authored for the Atlantic Council makes a related case for maintaining US military advantages, arguing that without them China's leadership will continue to pursue policies designed to overthrow the US-led international order. The military requirements include preventing "any unacceptable shift in the strategic nuclear balance," "maintaining US global conventional military dominance over any other adversary, in all theaters and in all current and emerging military technologies, platforms, and domains," and "maintaining regional conventional US military predominance in the Indo-Pacific region so that the United States can prevail in the event of armed conflict."[69]

Ironically, while China's rise has generated some calls for Primacy, it also almost certainly makes a US grand strategy of Primacy infeasible. China's

---

66. Tellis, *Balancing Without Containment*, 65–66; Ashley J. Tellis, "No Escape: Managing the Enduring Reality of Nuclear Weapons," in *Asia in the Second Nuclear Age*, ed. Ashley J. Tellis, Abraham M. Denmark, and Travis Tanner (National Bureau of Asian Research, 2013), 26–28.
67. Tellis, *Balancing Without Containment*, 64–65.
68. Tellis, *Balancing Without Containment*, 42–54.
69. Anonymous, *The Longer Telegram: Toward a New American China Strategy* (Atlantic Council, 2021), quotes from 9 and 57.

growing wealth and technological sophistication, combined with the nature of the military missions that Primacy calls for the United States to be able to perform in East Asia, make military dominance extremely difficult, almost certainly impossible for the United States to achieve.

The issue here is not whether the United States, at least for the next couple of decades, can spend more on its military than China. Although the gap has narrowed, the United States continues to outspend China by almost a factor of three (and spends roughly twice as large a percentage of its GDP) and will continue to outspend China for the foreseeable future.[70] Of course, the United States has military commitments across the globe, so adequately comparing spending dedicated to the Pacific Theater is more complicated.

Instead, the question is whether the United States would be able to maintain or achieve the ability to perform the missions required by Primacy: the ability to operate freely along the East Asian littorals and to limit damage to the United States in an all-out nuclear war. These capabilities are almost certainly beyond the United States' reach, especially going forward. As noted above, the technologies that support antiaccess/area-denial (A2/AD) missions relatively near a country's maritime periphery have an advantage over the technologies required to defeat them. Thus, competition between the United States and China over control of the South China Sea and the East China Sea along China's periphery is creating a no-go zone in which neither country will be able to operate freely or protect ships trying to transit this zone during a major war. Even a large and expensive US and allied military buildup has poor prospects for regaining the ability to operate freely near China's coast.[71]

The prospects for regaining a significant nuclear damage-limitation capability are as bleak. Although China's nuclear force was relatively small for decades, China is increasing both its size and survivability, most importantly by deploying mobile intercontinental ballistic missiles but also by deploying increasingly capable sea-based nuclear weapons. While future technologies promise to increase the prospects for finding and destroying

---

70. M. Taylor Fravel, George J. Gilboy, and Eric Heginbotham, "Estimating China's Defense Spending: How to Get It Wrong (and Right)," *Texas National Security Review* 7, no. 3 (summer 2024): 40–54, https://tnsr.org/2024/06/estimating-chinas-defense-spending-how-to-get-it-wrong-and-right/. This article explains that there are large uncertainties involved in estimating China's defense spending. See also China Power, "What Does China Really Spend on Its Military," last updated June 29, 2022, https://chinapower.csis.org/military-spending/.

71. Biddle and Oelrich, "Future Warfare in the Western Pacific"; for debate over their analysis, see Andrew S. Erikson et al., "Correspondence: How Good Are China's Antiaccess/Area-Denial Capabilities," *International Security* 41, no. 4 (spring 2017): 202–13; see also Eugene Gholz, Benjamin Friedman, and Enea Gjoza, "Defensive Defense: A Better Way to Protect US Allies in Asia," *Washington Quarterly* 42, no. 2 (winter 2020): 171–89.

these mobile missiles, a variety of countermeasures should enable China to win the competition between retaliatory and counterforce capabilities.[72]

Fortunately, the United States does not need the military capabilities specified by Primacy to meet its alliance commitments in East Asia. As discussed fully in chapter 6, the United States' nuclear forces will contribute substantially to extended deterrence even when China has an assured destruction capability. A significant US damage-limitation capability might contribute to deterrence, but it is not necessary. (The possible exception is the US commitment to Taiwan, which is analyzed in chapter 4.) Similarly, as explained in chapter 7, the United States does not need that ability to operate its conventional forces unimpeded in the South China and East China Seas. The United States will be able to defend its allies if it can prevent China from operating effectively in this space, which is both a less demanding and less offensive mission.

There is a political logic for competing to regain Primacy, even if the United States' prospects for success are poor. Pursuing military dominance could communicate US resolve—the extent of its interests in East Asia—to China. Consequently, China would better appreciate the futility of demanding concessions, and, if crises occur, deterrence would be more likely to succeed. The United States' willingness to invest vast resources and political capital might also contribute to convincing its allies that US commitments to come to their defense were highly credible. These political arguments are consistent with and reinforce Primacy's overall approach.

There is, however, a significant downside to such an offensive, competitive policy: It gives little weight to the possibility that highly competitive policies will fuel Chinese insecurity, thereby generating more competitive and risky Chinese policies instead of deterring them. Given that China is an insecure state as well as an ambitious/greedy one, Primacy prescribes overly competitive policies. Realist theories that address both the pressures created by international structure and possibility of greedy states highlight the existence of mixed-motive states, which require appreciating that a security dilemma can exist even when facing a greedy state. As a result, the United States needs to face the trade-off between the deterrent value of a policy and the insecurity it can generate.[73] Proponents of Primacy may disagree, holding that China is driven solely by its nonsecurity motivations for

---

72. Charles L. Glaser and Steve Fetter, "Should the United States Reject MAD? Damage Limitation and U.S. Nuclear Strategy Toward China," *International Security* 41, no. 1 (summer 2016): 49–98; Thomas MacDonald, "Tracking Mobile Missiles," *Journal of Strategic Studies* 48, no. 2 (2025): 297–333; chap. 6 of this book.

73. Put differently, a state must attempt to properly balance the prescriptions offered by the deterrence and spiral models; see Robert Jervis, *Perception and Misperception in International Politics* (Princeton University Press, 1976), chap. 3; and Charles L. Glaser, *Rational Theory of International Politics* (Princeton University Press, 2010).

revising the status quo—that China is a purely greedy state. But this characterization misreads China, failing to account for divergent US and Chinese understandings of the status quo with respect to Taiwan, for China's view of its import vulnerabilities, and for divergent beliefs about the legitimacy of the so-called rules-based international order.

In sum, Primacy holds that US security requires truly superior and militarily dominant capabilities: without them, the United States will be unable to meet its alliance commitments, risks losing the confidence of its allies, and may even suffer direct threats to its homeland. In part, the strength of the argument depends on its feasibility. On this dimension, it fails because China is well on its way to denying these capabilities to the United States, and its continuing investment in military capabilities will put them further out of reach. For proponents of Primacy, therefore, China's rise greatly reduces US security. Fortunately, Primacy's military requirements are inflated. Less capable US and allied forces should be able to deter China and preserve the allies' confidence in the US commitment to their defense, while at the same time avoiding unnecessarily increasing China's insecurity.

Liberal Hegemony

SUMMARY

US grand strategy could be designed to advance liberal values globally—including, most importantly, spreading and preserving democracy as well as protecting human rights and saving lives in civil wars—in addition to the security and prosperity values that guide the grand strategies discussed above. The United States could have a variety of reasons for advancing these values. Spreading democracy could generate peace via the logic of democratic peace theory, increase the number of countries inclined to ally and cooperate with the United States, reduce violations of individual rights in previously illiberal countries, and support liberalism in the United States. Most broadly, commitment to these liberal values combined with the United States' post-WWII security alliances provide the foundation for the liberal international order, which includes rules, norms, and institutions that the United States has developed and championed.[74]

In principle, each of the four security-focused grand strategies discussed above could be paired with this additional set of goals, producing still more grand strategies. In practice, however, only one additional grand strategy

---

74. G. John Ikenberry, *Liberal Leviathan: The Origins, Crisis and Transformation of the American World Order* (Princeton University Press, 2011).

plays a significant role in the ongoing debate over US grand strategy—Liberal Hegemony—which is essentially Deep Engagement combined with policies designed to pursue these liberal values.[75] It is important to note that there are significant differences among analysts who have argued for placing significant weight on advancing democracy and liberal values. Neoconservatives, who favored the use of force for regime change, and liberal institutionalists, who place greater weight on developing the preconditions for effective democracy and multilateral action, have both been included under the Liberal Hegemony label.[76] Nevertheless, this simplification is not problematic for the purpose of this chapter—assessing the implications of China's rise for US grand strategy.

Liberal Hegemony might at first appear to be a combination of Primacy with liberal values. This is partly because it is often associated with US grand strategy following the Cold War, when the United States became the only superpower, the unipolar power. However, although the unipolar power, the United States did not adopt Primacy as its grand strategy during this period, as explained in the previous section. Moreover, the United States pursued liberal values during the Cold War, when it was not a unipolar power, although it was the world's most powerful state.[77] In contrast to the Cold War, during the post–Cold War decades, the United States had the power and international leeway—because it did not face a major-power threat—to pursue a much more assertive set of policies guided by liberal values, including using large-scale military force to achieve liberal goals. It did this while essentially pursuing the alliance, security, and international economic policies prescribed by Deep Engagement.

During these post–Cold War decades, the United States did not directly challenge the other major powers—China and Russia. Instead, it used the leeway created by its power position to pursue a variety of policies that had liberal goals, including, among others, the Iraq and Afghan interventions, followed by counterinsurgency and state building, involvement in overthrowing the regime in Libya, NATO expansion, and support for "color revolutions" in former Soviet republics. Many of these policies were not driven entirely by liberal aims—for example, the US decision to invade Iraq was also motivated by US counterproliferation and counterterrorism goals, and NATO expansion was designed partly as a hedge against a resurgent Russia.

---

75. Brooks and Wohlforth, *America Abroad*, 7–8, term this "deep engagement plus."

76. See, for example, G. John Ikenberry and Anne-Marie Slaughter, dirs., *Forging a World of Liberty Under Law: U.S. National Security in the 21st Century*, Final Report of the Princeton Project on National Security, Woodrow Wilson School of Public and International Affairs, September 27, 2006, and William Kristol and Robert Kagan, "Toward a Neo-Reaganite Foreign Policy," *Foreign Affairs* 75, no. 4 (July/August 1996): 18–32.

77. Tony Smith, *America's Mission: The United States and the Worldwide Struggle for Democracy*, expanded ed. (Princeton University Press, 2012).

Further, analysts disagree about the relative contribution of liberal values and security interests to the formation of these policies.[78] Critics of Liberal Hegemony have argued that liberal goals underpinned these US policies, which they judge to be foreign policy errors that resulted in international failures, huge economic costs, and damage to US liberal values at home.[79]

An evaluation of a US policy that is guided by liberal values requires assessing its prospects for success, the benefits of achieving democracy and advancing human rights, and the costs and risks. Of course, if multiple types of goals are being pursued simultaneously with liberal goals, then these other goals should be factored into an overall assessment. Virtually all US analysts believe that liberal goals have value. Critics have focused on their low feasibility—for example, the poor prospects of bringing democracy or even stability to Afghanistan—the greater importance of US security, and the large potential costs of pursuing liberal values globally. Many question whether force should be used to advance democracy.[80]

CHINA AND LIBERAL HEGEMONY

The implications of American liberal values for US grand strategy in East Asia may not be immediately apparent—opportunities for the types of military interventions that defined the worst of Liberal Hegemony appear unlikely in the region. However, liberal values and ideas currently play important roles in the US policy toward China. Taking Liberal Hegemony as the combination of Deep Engagement with US liberal values, current US policy in East Asia is a form of Liberal Hegemony (Liberal Deep Engagement).[81]

First, the Biden administration framed the competition between China and the United States in terms of democracy versus autocracy. In a 2022 speech, President Joe Biden argued, "We're seeing the world align not in

---

78. Challenging the importance of liberal values in US policy is Arman Grigoryan, "Selective Wilsonianism: Material Interests and the West's Support for Democracy," *International Security* 44, no. 4 (spring 2020): 158–200; finding more support is Michael C. Desch, "America's Liberal Illiberalism: The Ideological Origins of Overreaction in U.S. Foreign Policy," *International Security* 32, no. 3 (winter 2007–8): 7–43.

79. Posen, *Restraint*; John J. Mearsheimer, *The Great Delusion: Liberal Dreams and International Realities* (Yale University Press, 2018); Stephen M. Walt, *The Hell of Good Intention: America's Foreign Policy Elite and the Decline of American Primacy* (Farrar, Straus, and Giroux, 2014). Disagreeing on a variety of points is Michael J. Mazarr, "Rethinking Restraint: Why It Fails in Practice," *Washington Quarterly* 42, no. 2 (summer 2020): 7–32.

80. On the poor prospects for foreign-imposed regime change to produce democracy, see Alexander B. Downes and Jonathan Monten, "Forced to Be Free: Why Foreign-Imposed Regime Change Rarely Leads to Democratization," *International Security* 37, no. 4 (spring 2013): 90–131.

81. If current US de-risking policies move toward full/hard decoupling, then US grand strategy could shade toward a form of Liberal Primacy.

terms of geography—East and West, Pacific and Atlantic—but in terms of values. We're living through a global struggle between autocracies and democracies."[82] This overall framing goes beyond explaining the competition as stemming from opposing regime types and their different foreign policy goals. It also reflects liberal values by judging that democracy is superior to autocracy along multiple dimensions. This framing does not preclude cooperation with China, but it likely does make it more difficult. Arguably, it becomes unnecessarily difficult, as the United States focuses on the adversary's regime type and not its policies; US prospects for influencing the latter are far greater than the former (at least in a reasonable time frame). This framing paints the relationship in irrevocably adversarial terms, thereby supporting policies that are overly competitive and overlooking possibilities for cooperation and moderation.[83] Although the framing does not call for efforts to spread democracy to China, there are, as discussed in chapter 1, influential American experts who have essentially called for regime change (albeit not via the use of force), and Chinese leaders see US efforts to promote democracy as a threat to China, a call for regime change.

Second, and more important, democracy and human rights are among the United States' key interests in Taiwan.[84] The United States maintains an ambiguous commitment to protect Taiwan, and much of US military planning in East Asia is dedicated to its protection. The risks of the US commitment are large—most observers believe Taiwan is by far the most likely locus of a major war between the United States and China and that a Chinese attack against Taiwan is not unlikely over the next couple of decades. While there are a number of reasons for the United States to come to Taiwan's defense, protecting Taiwan's vibrant democracy is frequently included among them.

Analysts disagree on whether this risk is warranted. Those who place greater weight on liberal values relative to security values will tend to favor the commitment more strongly. And there are reasons that the United States will be especially determined to protect Taiwan's democracy. In contrast to the post–Cold War cases in which the United States used force to advance

---

82. Remarks by President Biden at the US Naval Academy's Class of 2022 Graduation and Commissioning Ceremony, https://www.whitehouse.gov/briefing-room/statements-releases/2022/05/27/remarks-by-president-biden-at-the-united-states-naval-academys-class-of-2022-graduation-and-commissioning-ceremony/.

83. On the gap between ideology and interests, see James Goldgeier and Bruce W. Jentleson, "A Democracy Summit Is Not What the Doctor Ordered: America, Heal Thyself," *Foreign Affairs* (December 14, 2020), https://www.foreignaffairs.com/articles/2020-12-14/democracy-summit-not-what-doctor-ordered.

84. Taiwan is the subject of chapter 4. Other US interests include the credibility value of maintaining the US commitment, the possible military value of denying China control of Taiwan, and the economic value of maintaining access to Taiwan's production of advanced semiconductors. It is also important to note that the United States established its commitment before Taiwan became a democracy.

democracy, in Taiwan, the United States would be defending an established and vibrant democracy instead of building one from the ground up. It would also be protecting the norm of state sovereignty. These differences—between preserving and changing the ideological status quo—likely add to US determination to protect Taiwan.

My own assessment is that democracy and human rights are the largest values at stake in Taiwan, exceeding the reputational, strategic, and economic costs. States, however, should almost always give priority to protecting their core security, not their ideological values. Taiwan is not an exception: The security costs and risks of protecting Taiwan exceed all other benefits. Chapter 4 provides a full assessment. Let it suffice here to say that liberal values—while a defining feature of the United States—are leading the United States astray once again. And unlike the post–Cold War cases in which the costs and risks were large but limited, the risks in the case of Taiwan are extremely large.

Third, the US commitment to liberal values—including democracy and international institutions, such as NATO, its East Asian alliances, and the WTO—is reflected in US support for the liberal international order (LIO), now more commonly referred to as the rules-based international order. While the United States should strive to maintain many features of the LIO, framing the preservation of the LIO itself as a goal distorts US policy. By assuming that all features of the LIO need to be preserved and that the United States is uniquely capable of judging the legitimacy of global norms and rules, Liberal Hegemony's commitment to preserving all features of the rules-based order builds in a status quo bias. During periods of significant change in the distribution of power, a (relatively) declining state needs to critically assess which goals and commitments to preserve; Liberal Hegemony via its unwavering commitment to the LIO fails to do.[85] This, in turn, contributes to the US failure to adequately consider the need for partial retrenchment.

Bottom-line Assessments

COMPARING THE GRAND STRATEGIES

The debate over US grand strategy is decades-long and contains many intricacies; this chapter cannot fully adjudicate it. That said, my overall assessment is that two of the grand strategies—Neoisolation and Deep En-

---

85. Charles L. Glaser, "A Flawed Framework: Why the Liberal International Order Concept Is Misguided," *International Security* 43, no. 4 (spring 2019): 51–87. On the link between a state's power and its ability to maintain an international order, see Christopher Layne, "The US-China Power Shift and the End of the Pax Americana," *International Affairs* 94, no. 1 (2018): 89–111.

gagement—provide sound arguments; Offshore Balancing, in its strongest variant, is also sound. There is not a clear winner. The case for Primacy is weaker than the others because, among other reasons, military dominance is not in general required for the United States to adequately meet its alliance commitments. Looking more specifically in terms of the implications of China's rise, the case for Primacy is further weakened because the United States has poor prospects for achieving its military requirements and because Primacy fails to strike a reasonable balance between the requirements of deterrence and nonprovocation. Liberal Hegemony—understood as the combination of Deep Engagement with policies designed to achieve a variety of liberal values—has a poor record regarding the use of military force to achieve liberal values, but it could be reconstituted on more solid footing. However, China's rise weakens the case for giving America's liberal values—manifest most importantly in the US commitment to Taiwan—a prominent role in its grand strategy.

One variant of Offshore Balancing—which emphasizes preventing a regional hegemon because it might roam into the Western Hemisphere—is weak. However, that argument can be replaced by the Deep Engagement argument concerning the danger of being drawn back into a major-power war and, in turn, the importance of preserving the United States' alliances. With this change, Offshore Balancing is essentially a conditional subset of Deep Engagement's security arguments.[86] Choosing between Deep Engagement and Offshore Balancing then depends on a variety of specific judgments about the probability of a major-power war in Europe and in East Asia, the speed with which potential hegemons could win these wars, the challenges of rebuilding alliance institutions and force structure if the United States needed to reestablish large forward-deployed forces, and the importance of reducing US defense spending. If the probability of quick hegemonic victories is sufficiently high, then Offshore Balancing's prescriptions begin to converge with Deep Engagement's bottom line.

China's rise strengthens the cases presented by both Neoisolation and Deep Engagement. For Neoisolation, the greater probability of a war in East Asia increases the importance of ending US alliances and thereby avoiding involvement in a major-power war. In contrast, for Deep Engagement, the increased probability of war created by China's rise means that the probability of getting drawn back into an East Asian war is greater, which increases the importance of preserving the United States' alliances to prevent those wars. The same could be true for the revised version of Offshore Balancing that prescribes forward deployment in East Asia, but only if China could win a war against Japan or South Korea quickly—that is,

---

86. They could still diverge on the economic value of alliances, which Offshore Balancing has said relatively little about.

before the United States could redeploy its forces to the region to come to their defense. However, if quick victory is not possible, which seems likely, then China's rise would support the maintenance of US alliances and the preservation of large forces based in the United States but not forward-deployed forces. In short, in broad terms, China's rise strengthens both Neoisolation and Deep Engagement and does not clearly favor one over the other. Both sets of arguments remain strong, and the choice between them remains a close call. In comparison, China's rise and improving military capabilities may be insufficient to make Offshore Balancing with forces forward-deployed to East Asia (that is, onshore) as attractive an option.

A more nuanced comparison does, however, favor Neoisolation. The choice between ending and preserving US alliances depends heavily on whether the United States can better avoid a major-power war by remaining in the region to deter it or by terminating its alliance to avoid it. Both approaches have risks. Maintaining US alliances essentially guarantees that the United States will be involved in the war. In contrast, leaving likely increases the probability of war, which in and of itself does not pose a security threat to the United States (except possibly via nuclear proliferation) but leaves the United States with the temptation or necessity of joining the war.

Although more complicated to adjudicate than the preceding arguments, the United States' alliances and partnerships in East Asia do not sufficiently reduce the probability of war between the United States and China to make Deep Engagement or Offshore Balancing the United States' best bet. The key danger is a conflict over Taiwan. Given the importance that China places on unification and its increasing capability to prevail in a conflict with Taiwan, the United States may be unable to deter a war over the next couple of decades, even if China believes the United States will come to Taiwan's aid. Although difficult to assess probabilities, many experts are increasingly worried about the possibility of a war involving Taiwan. Given this specific danger, ending US alliances and its commitment to Taiwan, and withdrawing from East Asia is likely the United States' best option.

A MISSING OPTION: ARE US COMMITMENTS
AN ALL-OR-NOTHING CHOICE?

Because the grand-strategy debate focuses on regions of the globe, it does relatively little to consider possible variations within regional commitments. This leads to an important gap in the evaluation of the United States' grand strategy options in East Asia. The United States could end some of its commitments while keeping others.

Specifically, the United States could end its ambiguous commitment to Taiwan—make clear that it would not use force to defend Taiwan—while maintaining its alliance commitments with Japan, South Korea, and the

CHAPTER 3

Philippines and its other regional allies and partners. This would radically change the grand-strategy calculus: The probability of war involving the United States and its allies would drop quite dramatically. As a result, the case for preserving these alliances would be much stronger. Once again, the choice between Neoisolation and this narrowed version of Deep Engagement would be a close call.

Given this option, I would then choose to preserve the United States' East Asian alliances. There is wisdom in the argument that a shift to Neoisolation would "in essence entail a massive experiment."[87] There is a strong case for running that experiment when the United States, via its alliances and partnerships, is running a not insignificant and increasing risk of a major-power war and has poor prospects for reversing this trend. That is the situation the United States faces today. However, if the probability of a major-power war is much lower—as would be the case if the United States ended its commitment to Taiwan while maintaining its treaty alliances and other partner relationships in East Asia—then preserving US alliance commitments to counter China becomes United States' best bet. In Asia, the United States should shift its grand strategy to Deep Engagement Minus.

---

87. Brooks and Wohlforth, *America Abroad*, 195–99, quote at 195.

CHAPTER 4

Taiwan

Should the United States Maintain Its Commitment?

If the United States retains its current grand strategy of Deep Engagement, the most important question it will face in East Asia is whether to retain its commitment to Taiwan. This commitment is much more dangerous than the US commitments to its treaty allies in Northeast Asia—Japan, South Korea, and the Philippines. China believes Taiwan is an essential part of its homeland and is determined to gain full control of the island. In addition, China's decades of military modernization have greatly increased its ability to win a war over Taiwan, which increases the probability that China will use military force to achieve its goal of integrating Taiwan into China. China is less militarily capable of invading Japan and South Korea, and China is less interested in trying.[1] China's President Xi Jinping has highlighted the importance of the unification of Taiwan with the mainland, stating that the issue "cannot be passed from generation to generation."[2]

Tensions over Taiwan have grown significantly since the mid-2010s, following a period of relative calm across the Taiwan Strait. Taiwan's 2016 presidential election brought to power the political party that favors greater political distance from China; in 2024, a new president from the same party was elected. Largely in response, China has employed political, economic, and military approaches to increase pressure on Taiwan, including dispersing

---

1. Although most of the same US forces would be relevant to these invasions, Japan is farther from China than Taiwan is and has a larger landmass, population, economy, and military.
2. "China's Xi says political solution can't wait forever," Reuters, October 6, 2013. For a similar statement in 2019, see "Xi says 'China must be, will be reunified' as key anniversary is marked," http://www.xinhuanet.com/english/2019-01/02/c_137714898.htmee. See, however, Richard C. Bush, *Difficult Choices: Taiwan's Quest for Security and the Good Life* (Brookings Institution, 2021), 133–41, on Xi's speech, who argues that "some Chinese leaders may in fact believe that 2049 is the unification deadline" (140) but rejects the idea of a deadline and concludes, "Xi's remarks do not suggest a sense of danger looming or urgency to resolve the issue" (141).

disinformation, launching cyberattacks, and operating its military forces increasingly close to Taiwan.[3] The United States, starting during the first Trump administration and continuing since then, has added to tensions, provoking China by deepening US ties to Taiwan.[4] House Speaker Nancy Pelosi's 2022 visit to Taipei resulted in large-scale joint exercises, including ballistic missiles that flew over Taiwan, that indicated China's growing ability to blockade the island.[5]

The increased tension has generated substantial attention from the US national security community. Policy experts have offered careful and detailed analyses of US options.[6] Much debate has focused on whether the United States should change its currently ambiguous commitment to defend Taiwan to a certain commitment.[7] Other analyses have explored how Taiwan can increase its ability to defend itself and better contribute to US defense efforts.[8]

This chapter argues that a still more fundamental, and much more significant, revision of US policy is needed—the United States should end its commitment to come to Taiwan's defense. Taiwan is not a vital US interest, although it is an important one. The probability of war over Taiwan is worryingly high. As discussed later in this chapter, in the early 2020s, some military and civilian experts judged that a war over Taiwan was likely before the end of the decade; during the summer of 2022, some officials in the Biden administration were reported to have believed that China might attack Taiwan within a year and a half.[9] Although many question this end-of-the-decade timeline, few experts

---

3. Bush, *Difficult Choices*, chap. 12; Ben Lewis, "China Is Running Out of Lines to Cross in the Taiwan Strait," *New York Times*, February 26, 2024.

4. Ryan Haas and Jude Blanchette, "The Right Way to Deter China from Attacking Taiwan: American Hard Power Is Not Enough," *Foreign Affairs*, November 8, 2023, argue that US policies have "enflamed Beijing's grievance that the United States is hollowing out its 'one China' policy." At the outset of his second term, Trump has not clarified his policies toward Taiwan.

5. Paul Haenle and Nathaniel Sher, "How Pelosi's Taiwan Visit Has Set a New Status Quo for US-China Tensions," Carnegie Endowment for International Peace, August 12, 2022, https://carnegieendowment.org/2022/08/17/how-pelosi-s-taiwan-visit-has-set-new-status-quo-for-u.s-china-tensions-pub-87486.

6. See, for example, Patrick Porter and Michael Mazaar, *Countering China's Adventurism Over Taiwan: A Third Way* (Lowy Institute, May 20, 2021); Robert D. Blackwill and Philip Zelikow, *The United States, China, and Taiwan: A Strategy to Prevent War*, Council Special Report No. 90, Council on Foreign Relations, February 2021.

7. The current round of debate was launched by Richard Haass and David Sacks, "American Support for Taiwan Must Be Unambiguous: To Keep the Peace, Make Clear to China That Force Won't Stand," *Foreign Affairs*, September 2, 2020; for opposing views, see Bonnie Glaser, Michael J. Mazarr, Michael Glennon, Richard Haass, and David Sacks, "Dire Straits: Should American Support for Taiwan Be Ambiguous?," *Foreign Affairs*, September 24, 2020.

8. William S. Murray, "Revisiting Taiwan's Defense Strategy," *Naval War College Review* 61, no. 3 (summer 2008); James Timbie and Adm. James O. Ellis Jr., "A Large Number of Small Things: A Porcupine Strategy for Taiwan," *Texas National Security Review* 5, no. 1 (winter 2021/22): 83–93.

9. Edward Wong, David E. Sanger, and Amy Qin, "US Officials Grow More Concerned About Potential Action by China on Taiwan," *New York Times*, July 25, 2022.

believe China is very unlikely to use force against Taiwan over the next couple of decades. A war over Taiwan would, at a minimum, be a large conventional war. Nuclear war, although not likely, could result from escalation along several plausible paths.[10] Thus, the risk the United States incurs by its commitment to protect Taiwan, even though it is ambiguous, is enormous.

This apparent mismatch—running enormous risks to protect a not-vital interest—demands a full reevaluation of the US commitment to Taiwan. What would be the benefits of ending the commitment? What are the different rationales for ending it? What would be the costs and risks of terminating the commitment? Are there options for reducing these costs?

I conclude that the United States should end its commitment to Taiwan based on a combination of the logics of appeasement and retrenchment.[11] Ending the commitment might largely satisfy China's geopolitical goals— China would be appeased. However, China might not be satisfied. As described in chapter 2, its identity and status goals might combine to generate a desire for regional hegemony, even once the security problem posed by Taiwan is solved. And, as described in chapter 1, many China and foreign policy experts believe China desires regional hegemony. If this is the case, retrenchment would enable the United States to avoid the large risks of war over Taiwan. The remaining risks in East Asia would be much smaller because the United States is more militarily capable of deterring China's pursuit of regional hegemony than of deterring attacks against Taiwan. Moreover, China appears much less determined to achieve regional hegemony than to control Taiwan. These two factors—China's capability and interests—work together to greatly reduce the risks the United States would be accepting in maintaining its East Asian treaty alliances.

---

10. Recent wargames have identified a variety of escalation paths and logics; see Stacie Pettyjohn, Becca Wasser, and Chris Dougherty, *Dangerous Straits: Wargaming a Future Conflict over Taiwan*, Center for a New American Security, June 2022, https://s3.amazonaws.com /files.cnas.org/CNAS+Report-Dangerous+Straits-Defense-Jun+2022-FINAL-print.pdf; Mark Cancian, Matthew Cancian, and Eric Heginbotham, *Confronting Armageddon: Wargaming Nuclear Deterrence and Its Failures in a U.S.-China Conflict over Taiwan*, Center for Strategic and International Studies, December 2024, https://csis-website-prod.s3.amazonaws .com/s3fs-public/2024-12/241213_Cancian_Confronting_Armageddon.pdf?VersionId=Wyq ddCThZRiniczNwXHKcQHgOmUP8CH8.

11. Others have raised the possibility of accommodation on Taiwan. Lyle J. Goldstein, *Meeting China Halfway: How to Defuse the Emerging US-China Rivalry* (Georgetown University Press, 2015), proposes a series of reciprocal conciliatory steps designed to remove Taiwan as a barrier to improved US-China relations. See also Charles W. Freeman Jr., "Beijing, Washington, and the Shifting Balance of Prestige," remarks to the China Maritime Studies Institute, Newport, RI, May 10, 2011, who questions the wisdom of the United States' commitment to Taiwan: "Perhaps it's once again time to throw off the intellectual shackles imposed by long-standing policy and address the imperatives of long-term strategic interests"; see also Zbigniew Brzezinski, "Balancing the East, Upgrading the West: US Grand Strategy in an Age of Upheaval," *Foreign Affairs* 91, no. 1, January/February 2012, 103, and Bill Owens, "America Must Start Treating China as a Friend," *Financial Times*, November 17, 2009.

I previously argued that a grand bargain was the United States' best option.[12] The bargain required the United States to end its commitment to Taiwan, and China to peacefully resolve its disputes in the South China and East China Seas, and to officially accept the United States' long-term military security role in East Asia. But this option no longer appears feasible, as China's growing commitment to national rejuvenation and increased assertiveness have greatly reduced the likelihood that China would be willing to make these concessions. The United States is left with a less good option—ending the US commitment without Chinese concessions.

In broad terms, US accommodation of China deserves serious analysis for two reasons. First, both intuition and international relations (IR) theory suggest that a rising power, especially one that has experienced tremendous growth, can reasonably expect to increase its geopolitical influence and to more fully achieve its goals, especially when these goals involve its national identity. Bargaining theories maintain that the probability of war is greater when there is a larger disparity between the distribution of benefits in the existing territorial status quo and the balance of power.[13] As sketched in the introduction and developed further in this chapter, accommodation that reduces this disparity—via appeasement or partial retrenchment—can, under some conditions, reduce the probability of war and increase the declining state's security.

Second, as explained in chapter 1, international structure should allow China to rise peacefully, which, somewhat counterintuitively, increases the potential value of accommodation. If international structure were relentlessly driving the United States and China toward a major conflict, then only large concessions on vital interests might moderate the intense competition. But, because the structure of the international system is not creating such intense pressures, concessions that do not compromise vital US interests may greatly diminish the probability of a major war and therefore be worth pursuing.

More concretely, only one dispute—Taiwan—stands out as important enough to bring the United States and China into a large war. There are, of course, other possibilities, including disputes in the South China Sea, which are analyzed in chapter 5, and China's possible desire for regional hegemony, but the risks posed by Taiwan are far greater.

Accommodation would bring risks and costs of its own. Ending the US commitment to Taiwan would jeopardize US security if it convinced China that the United States lacked the resolve to protect its vital national inter-

---

12. Charles L. Glaser, "A US-China Grand Bargain? The Hard Choice Between Military Competition and Accommodation," *International Security* 39, no. 4 (spring 2015): 49–90.

13. Robert Powell, *In the Shadow of Power: States and Strategies in International Politics* (Princeton University Press, 1999), chap. 3. On related arguments, see Robert Gilpin, *War and Change in World Politics* (Cambridge University Press, 1983), and Randall L. Schweller and Xiaoyu Pu, "After Unipolarity: China's Visions of International Order in an Era of US Decline," *International Security* 36, no. 1 (summer 2011): 41–72.

ests, which could in turn lead China to adopt a more assertive foreign policy. This danger would be especially large if China turned out to place great value on achieving regional hegemony by forcing the United States out of East Asia. Accommodation might also raise serious concerns among US allies—most importantly, Japan—about the reliability of US security guarantees, thereby undermining alliances that are widely judged to be essential to the security of the United States. I argue, however, that the United States can adopt policies that should greatly reduce or even eliminate these credibility costs. Finally, ending the United States' commitment to Taiwan would likely sacrifice important US nonsecurity interests, including support for democracy and individual liberties.

This chapter proceeds as follows. The first section provides some basic information on Taiwan and its place in the US-China relationship. The following section analyzes the general logic of a policy of territorial accommodation, distinguishes between the more specific options of retrenchment and appeasement, and explores the factors that influence their benefits, costs, and risks. The third section explores the benefits of ending the US commitment to Taiwan, which include reducing the probability of a large conventional war with China and a nuclear war, and possibly improving US-China relations over the long term. The fourth section assesses the downsides of this change to US policy, including the increased probability that China would undermine Taiwan's democracy and repress its people, the possible reduction in US credibility for defending its allies, and the military implications of China controlling Taiwan. The fifth section considers alternatives to ending the US commitment, including bluffing, a grand bargain, and a concert of Asian powers. The closing section summarizes the case for ending the US commitment to Taiwan and considers whether the United States should then continue to arm Taiwan—a "Ukraine option" for Taiwan.

Taiwan Basics

Taiwan has a population of over twenty-three million and is now a multiparty democracy and a de facto independent state.[14] It lies roughly one hundred miles across the Taiwan Strait from the Chinese mainland. It is an advanced industrial economy, with a gross domestic product (GDP) of approximately $750 billion in 2023, which ranked roughly twentieth globally; its per capita GDP is roughly three times China's.[15] Taiwan dominates the

---

14. Paragraphs in the section draw on Charles L. Glaser, "The Sources and Consequences of Deepening US-China Competition," in *After Engagement: Dilemmas in US-China Security Relations*, ed. Jacques deLisle and Avery Goldstein (Brookings Institution, 2021).
15. International Monetary Fund, https://www.imf.org/external/datamapper/profile/TWN.

global fabrication of advanced semiconductors, which has complicated and strained US-China relations.[16]

China considers Taiwan to be an essential part of its homeland and a core or vital interest that it is determined to bring under full sovereign control.[17] In addition to its possible geostrategic value, as discussed in chapter 2, Taiwan is central to China's national identity and its international status concerns as an emerging superpower.[18] China believes that gaining control of Taiwan is essential to overcoming its century of humiliation and achieving national rejuvenation. Unification of Taiwan is China's paramount territorial goal.[19]

China continues to prefer that unification occur peacefully but for decades has made clear its willingness to go to war to prevent Taiwan from becoming independent.[20] Whether China will wait indefinitely to gain full control of Taiwan, even if Taiwan does not move toward independence, is increasingly unclear.[21] In 2005, China passed the Anti-Secession Law, which states that China would use "non-peaceful" means if "possibilities for a peaceful reunification should be completely exhausted," as well as to prevent Taiwan from seceding.[22] In a 2019 speech, President Xi Jinping stated that the Taiwan situation reflected China's weakness and, therefore, reunification must be part of China's rejuvenation, observing, "That the two sides of the strait are still not fully unified is a wound to the Chinese history."[23]

In contrast, the United States does not take a position on the substance of the resolution of the dispute over Taiwan and has, instead, emphasized the

---

16. Richard Cronin, *Semiconductors and Taiwan's "Silicon Shield": A Wild Card in US-China Technological and Geopolitical Competition*, Stimson Center, August 16, 2022, https://www.stimson.org/2022/semiconductors-and-taiwans-silicon-shield/.

17. M. Taylor Fravel, *Strong Borders, Secure Nation: Cooperation and Conflict in China's Territorial Disputes* (Princeton University Press, 2008), chap. 5.

18. Alan M. Wachman, *Why Taiwan? Geostrategic Rationales for China's Territorial Integrity* (Stanford University Press, 2007).

19. Zheng Wang, *Never Forget National Humiliation: Historical Memory in Chinese Politics and Foreign Relations* (Columbia University Press, 2012), esp. 129–33.

20. See, for example, Thomas J. Christensen, "Chinese Realpolitik: Reading Beijing's World-View," *Foreign Affairs* 75, no. 5, September/October 1996, 45–52; Michael D. Swaine, "Trouble in Taiwan," *Foreign Affairs* 83, no. 2, March/April 2014, 39–49; Yew Kun Tian and Ben Blanchard, "China Will Never Renounce Right to Use Force Over Taiwan, Xi says," Reuters, October 16, 2022, https://www.reuters.com/world/china/xi-china-will-never-renounce-right-use-force-over-taiwan-2022-10-16/.

21. For summary and analysis of political, economic, and military trends, see Scott L. Kastner, *War and Peace in the Taiwan Strait* (Columbia University Press, 2022).

22. "Full Text of Anti-Secession Law," https://www.europarl.europa.eu/meetdocs/2004_2009/documents/fd/d-cn2005042601/d-cn2005042601en.pdf.

23. Chris Buckley and Chris Horton, "Unification Plan from China Finds Few Takers in Taiwan," *New York Times*, January 3, 2019, 4; he also repeated that the problem cannot be passed between generations. On growing domestic pressure to make progress on Taiwan, see Jia Qingguo and Alan D. Romberg, "Taiwan and Tibet," in *Debating China: The US-China Relationship in Ten Conversations*, ed. Nina Hachigian (Oxford University Press, 2014).

process by which changes to the status quo are achieved, insisting they not be achieved via coercion or the actual use of force.[24] The official US position is that it will accept any resolution that is achieved peacefully. The United States has an ambiguous political (not legal) commitment to militarily defend Taiwan if attacked by China. During the Clinton and George W. Bush administrations, US policy was a form of "dual deterrence," in which "the United States implicitly warned Beijing that it would defend Taiwan in the event of an unprovoked attack and implicitly warned Taipei that US support would be in doubt if Taiwan provoked the conflict."[25] The United States sells Taiwan arms, consistent with the Taiwan Relations Act, which calls for the United States "to provide Taiwan with arms of a defensive character . . . as may be necessary to enable Taiwan to maintain a sufficient self-defense capability."[26]

Although the United States does not take a position on the eventual resolution of Taiwan's status, US policies are at odds with China's interests, and China has long viewed them this way.[27] While US policy allows for outcomes consistent with China's preferences, the United States is committed to supporting a status quo that China views as unacceptable.[28] The result is that the United States and China have a direct conflict of interests, albeit not as complete as if the United States rejected the possibility of unification. The nature of the disagreement is deepened because many US policies appear threatening to China. US opposition to the use of force to resolve the conflict runs counter to China's understanding of the Taiwan issue as an internal dispute and reduces China's options for dealing with it. China worries that US policies that enhance Taiwan's ability to defend itself increase the probability that Taiwan will move toward independence. Similarly, increases in the ability of the United States and its allies to come to Taiwan's aid reduce China's ability to coerce Taiwan.

---

24. On the subtlety and complexity of the US position, see Richard C. Bush, *A One-China Policy Primer*, East Asia Policy Paper 10, Brookings Institution, March 2017, https://www.brookings.edu/research/a-one-china-policy-primer/.

25. Richard C. Bush, *Uncharted Strait: The Future of China-Taiwan Relations* (Brookings Institution, 2013), 215.

26. "Public Law 96–8—APR 10, 1979," https://www.congress.gov/96/statute/STATUTE-93/STATUTE-93-Pg14.pdf. On China's view that the United States has failed to meet agreed limitations on arms sales, see Andrew J. Nathan and Andrew Scobell, *China's Search for Security* (Columbia University Press, 2012), 99–105.

27. Wachman, *Why Taiwan?*, 110–17.

28. There are hints that this may be changing, however. For example, in 2021, Ely Ratner, assistant secretary of defense for Indo-Pacific Security Affairs, testified that Taiwan's security is so important because Taiwan's location "is critical to the region's security and critical to the defense of vital US interests in the Indo-Pacific"; statement before the 117th Congress, Committee on Foreign Relations, United States Senate, December 8, 2021, https://www.foreign.senate.gov/imo/media/doc/120821_Ratner_Testimony.pdf.

The situation is not at its core driven by a pure security dilemma because the United States and China disagree about the status quo. In a pure security dilemma situation, the problem could be solved if both countries could be made confident that the other would not use its military forces to attack. But unlike in a pure security dilemma, in this case, the information would be incorrect: It would mean that China would not use force if Taiwan declared independence or use force to change the status quo if the odds of Taiwan accepting unification became too small. Similarly, the problem cannot be solved by the deployment of entirely defensive forces because this would require China to forgo the option of coercing Taiwan. At the same time, however, the competition over Taiwan does have some flavor of a security dilemma because China sees its goal as security that would be achieved by unifying its homeland, even though this requires changing the status quo.[29] Both the United States and China see themselves pursuing policies designed to preserve legitimate territorial integrity, but they disagree on what is being protected. Each country sees itself as acting with defensive motives, but because they disagree about the nature of the status quo, they see each other's policies as threatening.[30] The ensuing interaction therefore does have a security dilemma dynamic.

Logics of Territorial Accommodation: Retrenchment and Appeasement

To lay the foundation for evaluating whether the United States should end its commitment to defend Taiwan, this section distinguishes between two types of territorial concessions—retrenchment and appeasement—and considers their costs, benefits, and risks. Although territorial accommodation is frequently viewed as a deeply flawed strategy—often associated with British concessions to Germany at the 1938 Munich conference—under certain conditions, concessions can be a state's best option for protecting its vital interests.

By appeasement, I mean territorial concessions designed to satisfy an adversary that wants to expand. In contrast, by retrenchment, I mean territorial concessions designed simply to eliminate the specific dispute.[31] The adversary may or may not be satisfied; the retrenching state may anticipate having to confront its adversary over other territorial issues.

---

29. IR theories typically assume that states hold a shared view of the status quo. In cases in which the status quo itself is disputed, states will experience greater disagreement about each other's motives, making such situations both more complicated and more dangerous.

30. For a full discussion of this point in the context of the US-Japan alliance, see Thomas J. Christensen, "China, The US-Japan Alliance, and the Security Dilemma in East Asia," *International Security* 23, no. 4 (spring 1999): 49–80.

31. On definitions and understandings of retrenchment and appeasement, see notes 10 and 11 in the introduction.

POTENTIAL BENEFITS

There are several paths via which retrenchment and appeasement can increase the security of the conceding state. They share some logics but diverge on a key one. Appeasement works by satisfying an adversary that wants to change the status quo.[32] If the adversary has limited aims, appeasement has the potential to completely satisfy it. In this case, following accommodation, a greedy state that had limited aims in the prior status quo becomes a security seeker in the new status quo, the states' conflicting interests are eliminated, and war should not occur.

In contrast, retrenchment works because the state essentially gets out of its adversary's way—the possibility of war over the conceded territory is eliminated by the concession. In contrast to appeasement, the success of retrenchment does not depend heavily on whether the adversary has limited aims—the state makes the concession whether or not the adversary will be satisfied. If it does not have limited aims and, therefore, is not satisfied by the territorial concession, war over other issues remains a recognized possibility.[33]

Retrenchment could nevertheless be a state's best option. If the probability and/or costs of war over the remaining issues are sufficiently low, then avoiding war with certainty over the conceded territory could make sense. Importantly, this could be true even if the probability of war on these remaining issues was increased by making the concession. War could be unlikely both because the adversary values the remaining issues less than the conceded issue and because defending the remaining issues is much easier than defending the conceded issue. Retrenchment could also be a state's best option if war over the remaining issues is likely to be much less costly than a war over the conceded issue.

In addition, retrenchment could increase the conceding state's security by freeing up resources that were previously devoted to defending the con-

---

32. The state's decision is more complicated if it is a declining power. See Robert Powell, "Uncertainty, Shifting Power, and Appeasement," *American Political Science Review* 90, no. 4 (December 1996): 749–64.

33. This comparison overlooks similarities that are captured in a more complete description. A potential appeaser would estimate the probability that its adversary would be satisfied, and the extent of other aims if not satisfied, not simply assume the adversary would be satisfied. The appeaser would also consider how concessions would influence its ability to defend if the adversary has more than limited aims. The difference, then, is that a potential retrencher would be assuming that the adversary would not be satisfied. The retrencher is therefore making essentially the appeaser's worst-case assumption. If the retrencher and appeaser estimate the same probability of conflict over remaining issues, then retrenchment requires a higher cost of war if the concession is not made, a lower value on the concession, and/or a lower cost of war on the possible remaining issues. Alternatively, a more complete assessment of whether to retrench would include an estimate of whether the adversary would be satisfied; in this formulation, the costs and benefits of the two approaches are identical, even though the framings differ significantly.

ceded territory, which the defender can then reallocate to defend against the adversary in other disputes. This reallocation would also be possible under appeasement, but it typically gets less attention because the hope with appeasement is that concessions will eliminate the probability of war, which makes reallocation less important.

Other paths via which territorial accommodation could increase the accommodator's security are shared by appeasement and retrenchment. One such path involves increasing the adversary's security, which in turn increases the state's security. For example, territorial accommodation could directly increase the adversary's security if the state had deployed forces on the conceded territory or elsewhere that were dedicated to protecting that territory, if these forces threatened the adversary. Accommodation could also increase the adversary's security, as explained by defensive realism, by signaling that the conceding state is a security seeker or even that it has more limited hostile aims than the adversary previously believed.

Another, partially related path involves increasing both states' security by making unnecessary the military competition that the states would have engaged in while pursuing capabilities to defend or attack the territory in question. Under certain conditions, this military competition could have reduced both states' capabilities or could have communicated greedy motives, or both; this negative political spiral could make war more likely.

The magnitude of these benefits depends on the state's ability to deter its adversary in the current status quo. For example, if the state can deter its adversary with high confidence, then accommodation designed to reduce the probability of conflict provides smaller benefits than if the state's prospects for successful deterrence are poor. In addition, the benefits of accommodation should be evaluated across time. For example, if the status quo is characterized by competition that is increasing the probability of war, and if accommodation would moderate this competition, then the benefits of accommodation are larger than if the probability of war were constant.

POTENTIAL COSTS AND RISKS

International relations theorists and policy commentators have long warned of the costs and risks of territorial accommodation. Although framed differently, appeasement and retrenchment will generate essentially the same costs and risks.[34] First, there is the direct cost of the concession itself; that is, what the state loses by giving up the territory, measured in terms of its security, prosperity, ideological goals, prestige, and so on. If the losses are larger than the risks of competition and war, then the state should not employ a strategy of accommodation.

34. See note 33.

Second, instead of satisfying the adversary, territorial concessions could enable and/or encourage it to demand or forcibly pursue additional concessions. Whether these dangers exist depends on the adversary's motives and the extent of its aims. An accommodation that would fully satisfy an expansionist adversary with limited aims, thereby eliminating the probability of war, could instead increase the probability of war if the adversary has unlimited aims or even limited aims that significantly exceed the scope of the concessions. In addition, concessions could increase the adversary's expansionist goals. One possibility is that concessions could strengthen the domestic standing of hardliners who hold more ambitious aims. The state will almost always face some uncertainty about the nature and extent of the adversary's aims—current and future—so territorial concessions will rarely be risk-free.

Given this uncertainty, territorial accommodation can be dangerous if it improves the adversary's ability to conquer additional territory. Territorial concessions can enhance the adversary's potential offensive capabilities by increasing its wealth or access to critical resources, by providing it with territory that enhances its ability to fight on the offensive, and by freeing up military forces that were previously committed to challenging the conceded territory.

In addition, territorial accommodation can also be dangerous if it decreases the adversary's assessment of the state's credibility for defending its interests, thereby increasing the adversary's willingness to launch additional challenges. The IR theory literature is divided on how a state's actions influence an adversary's assessment of its credibility. A key strand holds that a state's credibility is connected across issues; making unmatched concessions on one issue will reduce a state's credibility for defending its other interests.[35] Although the broadest version of this argument—concessions on any issue anywhere damage a state's credibility on all other issues everywhere—seems implausible, a more conditional argument is logically

---

35. There is a large, divided literature on the connectedness of the credibility of commitments. My arguments are broadly consistent with those that find *conditional* connectedness, including Iain D. Henry, "What Allies Want: Reconsidering Loyalty, Reliability, and Alliance Interdependence," *International Security* 44, no. 4 (spring 2020): 45–83, https://doi.org/10.1162/isec_a_00375, Alex Weisiger and Keren Yarhi-Milo, "Revisiting Reputation: How Past Actions Matter in International Politics," *International Organization* 69, no. 2 (spring 2015): 473–95, https://doi.org/10.1017/S0020818314000393, and Robert Jervis, "Deterrence Theory Revisited," *World Politics* 31, no. 2 (January 1979): 319–22, https://doi.org/10.2307/2009945. Prominent skeptics include Jonathan Mercer, *Reputation and International Politics* (Cornell University Press, 1996), and Daryl G. Press, *Calculating Credibility: How Leaders Assess Military Threats* (Cornell University Press, 2005). For early arguments about the connectedness of credibility, see Glenn H. Snyder, *Deterrence and Defense: Toward a Theory of National Security* (Princeton University Press, 1961), 30–40.

sound.[36] Specifically, concessions on an issue that an adversary believes is similar along one or more dimensions to a second issue will reduce the state's credibility for defending the second issue. The relevant dimensions along which issues can be similar include geography, the magnitude of the interest, and, related but separable, the nature of the interest (security, economic, identity, etc.). For rational decision-makers, an opposing state's credibility is directly related to its understanding of that state's interest in the specific issue. The connectedness logic requires that the adversary be uncertain about the nature or extent of the state's interests. The state's action on the first issue provides the adversary with information about the extent of the state's interest in that issue. Because the two issues share significant similarities, the action then also provides information about the extent of the state's interest in the second issue.

For example, ending an alliance could lead an adversary to reduce its assessment of how likely the state would be to meet certain other alliance commitments. The magnitude of the change would depend on the size of the accommodation, the extent of uncertainties about the state's interests, and the similarity between the terminated and the continuing alliances. In addition, if the adversary believes that a structural change caused the state to adopt accommodation, it will see a similarity across otherwise disparate issues that are affected by the structural change and will, therefore, reduce its assessment of the state's credibility on all of these issues. More specifically, a shift in the balance of power could fuel this type of reevaluation.

The opposing strand of the credibility debate holds that a state's past actions do not influence its credibility. According to this line of argument, credibility depends only on an opposing state's power and interests, both of which are known.[37] This formulation, however, mischaracterizes the question of connectedness by assuming that the adversary essentially knows the extent of the state's interests. Uncertainty about the state's interests lies at the core of the adversary's uncertainty about the state's credibility. This in turn creates a mechanism by which past actions influence current assessments of credibility.

Finally, the state's territorial accommodation could reduce its allies' assessments of its credibility for meeting its commitments to them.[38] As a result, accommodation could damage a state's alliances, thereby reducing the state's security, possibly more than offsetting the direct benefits that accommodation provided vis-à-vis the state's adversary. The rationalist argument

36. A related but different question is whether leaders believe the broad version of the argument; Press contends that they do; Press, *Calculating Credibility*, 21.

37. Press, *Calculating Credibility*, 21.

38. Not all analysts agree that some reduction in US credibility for meeting its alliance commitments would have a negative impact on its security, arguing that the United States' high credibility leads its allies to shirk and/or adopt provocative policies. See Stephen M. Walt, *Taming American Power: The Global Response to US Primacy* (W. W. Norton, 2006), and Barry R. Posen, *Restraint: A New Foundation for US Grand Strategy* (Cornell University Press, 2014).

parallels the connectedness argument with respect to adversaries, which I summarized above. According to this argument, an ally that is uncertain about the extent of the state's interest in protecting it will observe how the state acts toward other allies to acquire information about the state's interest in it. The information these actions provide depends on the ally's similarity to the other ally, which could be understood along a variety of dimensions, including possibly the size of the allies' economies, their geographic location, their strategic value to the state, and their regime types.[39]

In sum, a strategy that involves territorial accommodation—whether appeasement or retrenchment—can generate a mix of benefits and costs. The nature and extent of the adversary's motives, whether concessions would significantly increase the adversary's military potential and/or raise doubts about the state's credibility for defending its interests, and how allies would interpret the state's concessions can all influence the desirability of accommodation.

Benefits of Ending the US Commitment to Taiwan

This section evaluates a range of benefits of ending the US commitment to Taiwan, including reducing the probability of conventional war and nuclear war, improving US-China relations, and reducing the value that China places on achieving regional hegemony.

AVOIDING CONVENTIONAL WAR

The most direct and important benefit of ending the United States' ambiguous commitment to use force to protect Taiwan would be the virtual elimination of the probability of war between the United States and China over Taiwan. This is a large benefit because the probability of conventional war over the next few decades is worryingly high, the war would at a minimum be a large conventional war, and it could escalate to nuclear war along several plausible paths. The expected benefits to the United States of accommodation—of ending its commitment to Taiwan—are larger when its prospects for deterring Chinese attack are poorer and the costs of war are higher.

Although gauging the probability of war is difficult, many China experts believe that the probability of China attacking Taiwan over the next two or three decades is high.[40] Maybe not high in absolute terms, but high in terms of

---

39. An alternative perspective, built on social psychological arguments, holds that an ally will damage its reputation for resolve and, in turn, its credibility by backing down, but it will not enhance its reputation by standing firm; see Mercer, *Reputation and International Politics*.

40. For analysis in the context of the bargaining model of war, see Kastner, *War and Peace in the Taiwan Strait*, chaps. 5 and 6.

a major-power war between countries with nuclear weapons. A 2022 survey of 64 experts—including 28 former high-level US government officials, 23 former US government policy and intelligence analysts, and 13 top experts from academia and think tanks—found that 84 percent believed that "Beijing is willing to wait for unification but will not accept the status quo permanently"; over 50 percent thought that China has a firm deadline for unification by 2049; and 41 percent believed that during his third term (2022–27), President Xi will give priority to peaceful unification but is willing to use large-scale military force.[41]

Many considerations support the conclusion that war is becoming significantly more likely. First, as reviewed above, China places tremendous importance on unification with Taiwan, and its determination to achieve this goal appears to be growing. Possession of Taiwan is central to China's national identity, and its determination is reinforced by concern for its international status as a rising, increasingly established superpower. China's desire is not new. However, while China was for decades willing to focus on ensuring that Taiwan did not declare independence and to wait for peaceful unification, its patience is now less certain. As noted above, President Xi has made unification with Taiwan central to his priority goal of national rejuvenation and stated that China should not wait indefinitely to achieve it. We can reasonably expect that China's willingness to wait will decrease as its economic and military capabilities continue to grow and as it becomes more firmly established as a superpower. It will be less willing to accept that its improved status and power have not enabled it to revise the status quo.[42] While this impatience would largely result from the leadership's perspective, China's leaders could also face pressure from its population to act on Taiwan. Writing in 2014, a prominent Chinese scholar argued that "political pressures on the Chinese government when it comes to Taiwan are tremendous and growing. In the past, the Chinese people knew that China was weak and could not stop the United States from selling weapons to Taiwan. Now, many believe that China should no longer tolerate such insulting behavior. Confronted with this mounting domestic pressure, the CCP [Chinese Communist Party] is finding it increasingly difficult to justify its weak responses."[43]

Second, China has greatly improved its military capabilities, which likely increases its willingness both to start and to escalate a Taiwan crisis. In the mid-

41. Bonny Lin et al., *Surveying the Experts: China's Approach to Taiwan*, Center for Strategic and International Studies, September 19, 2022, https://chinapower.csis.org/survey-experts-china-approach-to-taiwan/. There were some divides between types of experts, with former US government officials tending to think China was more willing to wait indefinitely and more open to believing that Xi would not need to make significant progress toward unification during his third term.

42. Instead of continuing to improve, some analysts believe that China's military capabilities, as well as its economy, will peak over the next decade, thereby creating incentives for China to act before its decline begins; see Hal Brands and Michael Beckley, *Danger Zone: The Coming Conflict with China* (W. W. Norton, 2022).

43. Qingguo and Romberg, "Taiwan and Tibet," in *Debating China*, 179.

1990s when the United States sailed aircraft carriers through the Taiwan Strait in response to China's missile exercises, China had little capability to invade or blockade Taiwan. Since at least the mid-2010s, China could begin to imagine success in both of these missions and its capabilities have improved significantly since then.[44] A thorough 2015 assessment found that although the United States continues to have greater aggregate military capabilities, "Chinese military modernization, in combination with the advantages conferred by geography, have endowed China with a strong military position vis-à-vis the United States in areas close to its own territory."[45] Much of the concern about China's so-called antiaccess/area-denial (A2/AD) capabilities—including missiles, submarines, and reconnaissance assets—focuses on China's ability to reduce the US ability to come to Taiwan's aid.[46]

China has two primary options for gaining control of Taiwan—blockade and invasion.[47] Blockade is generally believed to be easier militarily and might be attractive to China because a blockade could be less escalatory than an invasion.[48] Blockade, however, comes with major political uncertainties about whether even a militarily successful blockade would compel Taiwan to concede its independence. Historically, coercion via punishment of populations—whether by airpower or blockade—has a poor record of success.[49]

A Chinese campaign to blockade Taiwan would likely start with missile attacks against Taiwan's warning and surveillance assets and its long-range precision strike systems. The next phase would be designed to achieve air dominance, targeting air defenses, airfields, and combat aircraft. The following phase would pursue sea dominance, attacking submarines and surface

---

44. Jim Thomas, John Stillion, and Iskander Rehman, "Hard ROC 2.0: Taiwan and Deterrence through Protraction," Center for Strategic and Budgetary Assessments, 2014. See also David A. Shlapak et al., *A Question of Balance: Political Context and Military Aspects of the China-Taiwan Dispute* (RAND, 2009). On how improved Chinese capabilities could fuel Chinese misperceptions, see Steve Tsang, "The US Military and American Commitment to Taiwan's Security," *Asian Survey* 52, no. 4 (July/August 2012): 777–97. For earlier assessments, see David A. Shlapak, David T. Orletsky, and Barry Wilson, *Dire Strait? Military Aspects of the China-Taiwan Confrontation and Options for US Policy* (RAND, 2000), and Michael O'Hanlon, "Can China Conquer Taiwan?," *International Security* 25, no. 2 (fall 2000): 51–86.

45. Eric Heginbotham et al., *The US-China Military Scorecard: Forces, Geography, and the Evolving Balance of Power, 1996–2017* (RAND, 2015), 342.

46. Roger Cliff et al., *Entering the Dragon's Lair: Chinese Antiaccess Strategies and Their Implications for the United States* (RAND, 2007).

47. Other Chinese options include the seizure of some of Taiwan's small islands—which would not achieve its central objective of controlling Taiwan—and punishment attacks inflicted by Chinese missiles. On these scenarios, see Rachel Esplin Odell et al., *Active Denial: A Roadmap to a More Effective, Stabilizing, and Sustainable US Defense Strategy in Asia*, Quincy Paper No. 8, Quincy Institute for Responsible Statecraft, June 2022, 81–85.

48. Michael E. O'Hanlon, *Can China Take Taiwan?: Why No One Really Knows* (Brookings Institution, 2022).

49. Robert A. Pape, *Bombing to Win: Air Power and Coercion in War* (Cornell University Press, 1966).

combatants; China could deploy mines to increase the danger of approaching Taiwan's ports.[50] If successful, China would then be well-positioned to interrupt access to Taiwan. In contrast to the United States, China would benefit from fighting near its mainland. Maybe most important, improvements in antiship missiles and surveillance and reconnaissance technology are making ships at sea highly vulnerable. Mobile land-based missiles will be much more survivable than targets at sea, providing China with an advantage near its maritime periphery.[51]

China would likely be able to effectively blockade Taiwan if the United States does not intervene, but there is disagreement in the expert community about China's prospects if the United States does come to Taiwan's defense.[52] Some analysts believe that China currently has an effective capability, while others question whether China could sustain a successful blockade.[53] A basic model suggests that in a scenario in which China attacks first and is able to preserve its surveillance and reconnaissance capabilities, China would have good prospects for succeeding in an extended blockade. However, whether China's intelligence, surveillance, and reconnaissance capabilities would remain effective is one of many uncertainties. The model's broad finding is that both China and the United States would face large uncertainties about their prospects for success.[54]

In comparison, invasion would be militarily more difficult for a variety of reasons. For starters, amphibious invasions are logistically demanding because, among other reasons, the invader must transport vast quantities of people and materiel across water. China would likely have to send several

---

50. Michael Casey, "Firepower Strike, Blockade, Landing: PLA Campaigns for a Cross-Strait Conflict," in *Crossing the Strait: China's Military Prepares for War with Taiwan*, ed. Joel Wuthnow et al. (National Defense University Press, 2022).

51. Stephen Biddle and Ivan Oelrich, "Future Warfare in the Western Pacific: Chinese Antiaccess/Area Denial, US AirSea Battle, and the Command of the Commons in East Asia," *International Security* 41, no. 1 (summer 2016): 7–48. Their assessment explores capabilities in 2040; they argue that in 2016, China did not have the ability to blockade Taiwan.

52. Philip C. Saunders and Joel Wuthnow, "Crossing the Strait: PLA Modernization and Taiwan," 12, in *Crossing the Strait: China's Military Prepares for War with Taiwan*, ed. Joel Wuthnow et al. (National Defense University Press, 2022).

53. For a range of analyses of the former, see Biddle and Oelrich, "Future Warfare in the Western Pacific"; Owen R. Coté Jr., "One if By Invasion, Two if By Coercion: US Military Capacity to Protect Taiwan from China," *Bulletin of the Atomic Scientists* 78, no. 2 (2022): 65–72, who explains some of the difficulties in defeating a blockade but does not preclude the possibility, and Oriana Skylar Mastro, "The Taiwan Temptation: Why Beijing Might Resort to Force," *Foreign Affairs* 100, no. 4, July/August 2021, 58–67; on the latter, Rachel Esplin Odell and Eric Heginbotham, "Don't Fall for the Invasion Panic," *Foreign Affairs* 100, no. 5, September/October 2021, 217–18. On the difficulty of predicting the outcome of a Chinese attempt to blockade Taiwan, see O'Hanlon, *Can China Take Taiwan?*

54. O'Hanlon, *Can China Take Taiwan?* For an earlier model, see Michael A. Glosny, "Strangulation from the Sea? A PRC Submarine Blockade of Taiwan," *International Security* 28, no. 4 (spring 2004): 125–60.

hundred thousand troops across the Taiwan Strait, with some estimates reaching well over a million. These troops would have to land at a small number of beaches that, due to their terrain, are relatively easy to defend.[55] Second, the technologies that increasingly render ships at sea vulnerable—and which would enhance China's ability to impose a blockade—would make invasion more difficult by enabling the United States and Taiwan to impose high rates of attrition on China's ships. China would likely attempt to blunt these capabilities by launching missile attacks before sending its invasion forces across the strait. However, relying on mobility and dispersal should enable the defenders to make their forces sufficient survivability to pose a major threat to China's ships. Finally, once on the island, China would have to defeat Taiwanese forces and gain control of its population centers.

As with blockade, there is disagreement within the expert community about China's ability to successfully invade Taiwan. In widely quoted 2021 testimony, Admiral Phillip Davidson, then commander of US Indo-Pacific Command, stated, "They [China] have long said that they want to [supplant the United States] by 2050, I am worried about them moving that target closer. Taiwan is clearly one of their ambitions before then, and I think the threat is manifest this decade, in fact, in the next six years."[56] In 2022, when asked about Davidson's testimony in a congressional hearing, Director of National Intelligence Avril Haines said, "I think it is fair to say that it [the threat to Taiwan] is critical or acute between now and 2030."[57] Also in 2022, former Undersecretary of Defense Michèle Flournoy wrote that "it is possible that sometime in the next five years Xi will consider taking Taiwan by force" because, among other reasons, US deterrent capabilities were inadequate.[58] In contrast, in 2021, other experts held that China's prospects for a successful invasion would be poor for at least the next decade.[59] Yet

---

55. Ian Easton, "Why a Taiwan Invasion Would Look Nothing Like D-Day," *Diplomat* (May 26, 2021).

56. Committee on Armed Services, United States Senate, Hearing to Receive Testimony on the United States Indo-Pacific Command in Review of the Defense Authorization Request for Fiscal Year 2022 and the Future Years Defense Program, Stenographic Transcript, March 9, 2021, 48, https://www.armed-services.senate.gov/imo/media/doc/21-10_03-09-2021.pdf. This was not a coordinated US government position; see Saunders and Wuthnow, "Crossing the Strait," 13.

57. Committee on Armed Services, United States Senate, Hearing to Receive Testimony on Worldwide Threats, Stenographic Transcript, March 10, 2022, 82.

58. Michèle Flournoy and Michael Brown, "Time Is Running Out to Defend Taiwan: Why the Pentagon Must Focus on Near-Term Deterrence," *Foreign Affairs*, September 14, 2022, https://www.foreignaffairs.com/china/time-running-out-defend-taiwan.

59. Odell and Heginbotham, "Don't Fall for the Invasion Panic," 216. In an earlier analysis, Heginbotham et al., *The US-China Military Scorecard*, 342, anticipated the possibility of a tipping point, possibly as early as 2020, in which China could succeed in the early phases of an invasion; although the United States would likely prevail, it would incur high combat losses.

others have argued that the coming decade is likely the most dangerous because China currently has good prospects to conquer Taiwan, and its capabilities may decrease as its economic growth slows and the United States' capabilities increase beginning in the 2030s.[60]

Among the fullest assessments available of a Chinese invasion of Taiwan is a series of twenty-four analytic war games run in 2022. The results are reasonably promising for Taiwan and the United States.[61] In the base case model, which assumed the most likely values for key parameters, the coalition either defeated China or achieved a stalemate that China was likely to eventually lose. A set of pessimistic scenarios explored how changing key parameter values to favor China—including assuming that US long-range air-launch cruise missiles lacked antiship capabilities, the United States delayed its decision to join the conflict, Taiwan's ground forces were less effective than expected, and Japan prohibited the use of Japanese forces outside of its water and airspace—would influence the outcome.[62] None of the pessimistic assumptions resulted in China winning the war, but some resulted in stalemate or stalemate favoring China. China successfully invaded Taiwan only in the game that assumed the United States stayed out of the conflict. Even in the scenarios in which the defense of Taiwan is successful, the costs are high: The United States and its allies "lose dozens of ships, hundreds of aircraft, and thousands of personnel." Losses are significantly higher in some of the pessimistic scenarios. Overall, the results are not promising for China. Nevertheless, if China's leaders make optimistic, yet not unreasonable, assumptions about the invasion scenario, they could foresee paths to success, possibly including a stalemate followed by bargaining determined by China's greater interest in the outcome.

Given the difficulty of invasion, China might well prefer to blockade Taiwan instead of invading it. However, invasion would have two advantages. First, unlike blockade, successful invasion would eliminate the political uncertainties that plague blockade—China would impose its will, not rely on Taiwan giving in to its compellent demands. Second, China might launch an invasion with the hope of achieving its objectives quickly, thereby putting the United States in the situation of having to retake the island and avoiding the need to implement a prolonged blockade.[63] The prospects of a

60. Brands and Beckley, *Danger Zone*.
61. Mark F. Cancian, Matthew Cancian, and Eric Heginbotham, *The First Battle of the Next War: Wargaming a Chinese Invasion of Taiwan*, Center for Strategic and International Studies, January 2023, https://www.csis.org/analysis/first-battle-next-war-wargaming-chinese-invasion-taiwan; quote from 83.
62. On Japan's thinking about and options for a Taiwan conflict, see Mike Mochizuki, "Tokyo's Taiwan Conundrum: What Can Japan Do to Prevent War?" *Washington Quarterly* 45, no. 3 (fall 2022): 81–107.
63. Casey, "Firepower Strike, Blockade, Landing."

quick victory would be improved by a surprise attack against US and Taiwanese forces, which might enable China to win before the United States sends most of its forces into the region.[64] China would have to weigh this benefit against the possibility that the United States would not come to Taiwan's defense if US forces were not attacked.

In addition to its improved conventional capabilities, China's nuclear modernization could change its Taiwan calculus. China is deploying a larger and more survivable force, thereby increasing its ability to retaliate massively following a large US counter-nuclear attack.[65] The United States' previous possession of a significant damage-limitation capability—its ability to destroy most or all of China's nuclear force—arguably would have enhanced its bargaining position in a severe crisis or conventional war over Taiwan. Consequently, China's nuclear modernization may make China more willing to start a crisis, less willing to compromise once conflict occurs, and more willing to escalate to limited nuclear war.[66]

Overall, then, while much is uncertain about how China might attack Taiwan and what the outcome would be, there is no doubt that China's military capabilities have improved dramatically since the mid-1990s. China can now reasonably contemplate military success in a blockade and even possibly in an invasion of Taiwan, especially if its leaders believed the United States would not quickly come to Taiwan's aid and/or that Japan might not fully support the United States. China might also expect that the United States would not escalate to nuclear war, or might at least largely discount the possibility, because the United States has lost its significant nuclear advantage and Taiwan is not a vital US interest.[67] At the same time, any reasonable Chinese assessment should understand that the outcome was uncertain and the conflict would be costly, likely extremely costly for blockade scenarios that involve attacks against the Chinese mainland and US ships and bases, and for all invasion scenarios. This is why many experts believe that China will be deterred from attacking Taiwan. Hopefully, they are correct.

The third factor making war more likely is that China is increasingly likely to conclude that peaceful unification with Taiwan is impossible or too

---

64. Given the size of the forces required for invasion, strategic surprise seems highly unlikely; China might achieve tactical surprise, which would be far less valuable.

65. See chapter 6 for detailed analysis.

66. Evan Braden Montgomery and Toshi Yoshihara, "The Real Challenge of China's Nuclear Modernization," *Washington Quarterly* 45, no. 4 (winter 2023): 45–60, argue that the greater danger is that China may believe that its advantage in theater nuclear forces will deter the United States from coming to the defense of its regional allies and partners.

67. However, Henrik Stalhane Hiim, M. Taylor Fravel, and Magnus Langset Troan, "The Dynamics of an Entangled Security Dilemma: China's Changing Nuclear Posture," *International Security* 47, no. 4 (spring 2023): 157–60, observe that China believes that changes in US nuclear doctrine and force posture are increasing the likelihood that the United States would rely on limited nuclear attacks to compensate for its conventional inferiority.

CHAPTER 4

unlikely to be held out as a plausible path forward. Survey data shows that an increasing percentage of Taiwan's population identify as Taiwanese, a very small percentage identify as Chinese, and a large majority favor preserving the status quo, with less than 2 percent favoring a quick move toward unification. In addition, China's violation of its promise to allow a high degree of political autonomy in Hong Kong has undermined the credibility of a "one country, two systems" outcome for Chinese unification of Taiwan.[68] The lack of peaceful unification options would leave China with only the threat and use of force to achieve its goal.

Fourth, there is the possibility that China will attack Taiwan because it believes that Taiwan has moved too close to independence. Taiwan's former president Tsai Ing-wen refused to accept the 1992 Consensus, which China's president Xi Jinping understands as acknowledging that China and Taiwan are a single country.[69] Taiwan's new president, Lai Ching-te, who was elected in 2024, holds a similar if not stronger position.[70] In fact, the 1992 Consensus included disagreement from the beginning about what was meant by "one China," but the governments agreed to use this ambiguity to allow cooperation on other issues.[71] It remains to be seen how much further Taiwan can push its position without Beijing concluding that Taiwan has essentially declared independence. And there is the possibility that China could use even the appearance of additional movement toward independence as an excuse for attacking.

Fifth, the United States may be adding to China's incentives by diluting the United States' one-China policy, which is an important element of China's understanding and acceptance of the status quo. During the first Trump administration, and continuing during the Biden administration, the United States deepened its connections with Taiwan. For example, the United States has relaxed restrictions on interactions between American and Taiwanese officials; US House Speaker Nancy Pelosi's visit to Taipei in August 2022 led China to launch large-scale military exercises around Taiwan, raising tensions to a level not reached in decades.[72] In addition, the

68. Philip C. Saunders, "Three Logics of Chinese Policy Toward Taiwan: An Analytic Framework," in Saunders and Wuthnow, "Crossing the Strait."
69. Derek Grossman, "Is the '1992 Consensus' Fading Away in the Taiwan Strait?" *Diplomat*, June 2, 2020.
70. Dean P. Chen and Kiely Paris-Rodriguez, *The Role of the 1992 Consensus in Taiwan's 2024 Presidential Elections*, East-Western Center Occasional Paper 6, January 2024, https://www.eastwestcenter.org/publications/role-1992-consensus-and-taiwans-2024-presidential-elections.
71. Alyssa Resar, "The 1992 Consensus: Why It Worked and Why It Fell Apart," *Diplomat*, July 18, 2022.
72. Julian E. Barnes and Amy Qin, "State Dept. Moves to Ease Restrictions on Meeting with Taiwan Officials," *New York Times*, January 18, 2021; Paul Haenle and Nathaniel Sher, "How Pelosi's Taiwan Visit Has Set a New Status Quo for US-China Tensions," Carnegie Endowment for International Peace, August 17, 2022, https://carnegieendowment.org/2022/08/17/how-pelosi-s-taiwan-visit-has-set-new-status-quo-for-u.s-china-tensions-pub-87696.

United States has changed its policy for supporting Taiwan's self-defense capabilities. The December 2022 Taiwan Enhanced Resilience Act, for the first time, authorizes the use of Foreign Military Financing—direct loans and loan guarantees—of up to $2 billion per year, and makes Presidential Drawdown Authority available to Taiwan.[73] China could interpret these moves as watering down the United States' one-China policy to a point that it was meaningless, which China could find unacceptable. China could also reasonably interpret these policies as reflecting a shift in the US commitment to defend Taiwan—from ambiguous toward certain and independent of whether the Chinese attack was provoked—that would make Taiwan's move toward declaring independence more likely.[74]

Finally, China's transition to an increasingly personalist authoritarian regime, as discussed in chapter 2, likely increases the probability of war over Taiwan. If President Xi is leaning toward running the risks of invasion, his advisors will be less likely to try to dissuade him and less able to succeed if they try. This could be especially dangerous because, as summarized above, there will be substantial uncertainties about the outcome of a Chinese invasion of Taiwan. If Xi chooses to focus on the rosier possibilities and his military leaders are reluctant to highlight the probability of military failure, he will decide based on exaggerated prospects for success, and deterrence will be more likely to fail.[75]

In sum, while the great importance of Taiwan to China is long-standing, improvements in China's military capabilities could well change China's calculus. The probability of war is further increased by the declining prospects for peaceful unification as well as the possibility that China will judge, correctly or incorrectly, that Taiwan is moving toward independence. China experts give varying weight to these arguments and reach divergent conclusions about their combined effects. Some conclude that the probability that China will use force has risen significantly, while others find that China will continue to pursue peaceful unification far into the future.[76] Virtually all are concerned about China's growing military capabilities and want the United States and Taiwan to pursue policies to offset China's advances. Taken as a whole, these arguments and expert assessments paint a worri-

---

73. Caitlin Campbell, *Taiwan: Defense and Military Issues*, Congressional Research Service, September 19, 2023, https://crsreports.congress.gov/product/pdf/IF/IF12481.

74. This conclusion is supported by former President Joe Biden's repeated statements that the United States would come to Taiwan's defense, even though aides consistently walked back these statements.

75. For a broad discussion of false optimism leading to war, see Stephen Van Evera, *Causes of War: Power and the Roots of Conflict* (Cornell University Press, 1999), chap. 2.

76. See, for example, Oriana Skylar, "The Taiwan Temptation" and responses by Rachel Esplin Odell et al., "Strait of Emergency: Debating Beijing's Threat to Taiwan," *Foreign Affairs* 100, no. 5, September/October 2021, 216–29. See also Andrew J. Nathan, "Beijing Is Still Playing the Long Game on Taiwan: Why China Isn't Poised to Invade," *Foreign Affairs*, June 23, 2022.

CHAPTER 4

some picture. A Chinese attack may be unlikely in the next few years—the 2025–28 time frame—although some take a more pessimistic view, but there is a not insignificant probability of conventional war over the next two or three few decades. A 10 or 20 percent chance of a war may not sound very dangerous, but this fails to appreciate that we are talking about a major conventional war between nuclear powers.

These arguments address only the Chinese side of the decision for war over Taiwan. The United States could avoid a war over Taiwan simply by deciding not to come to Taiwan's defense. Its ambiguous commitment explicitly creates leeway to do this. Moreover, the United States could wait to see if Taiwan could succeed without US help, then join only if the negative outcome became clear.[77]

However, for a variety of reasons, maintaining its commitment, ambiguous though it is, significantly increases the probability that the United States would, in fact, come to Taiwan's defense. Maybe most important, the commitment creates the domestic expectation—within the government, including the military, with foreign policy elites, and with the US public—that the United States would fight to defend Taiwan. In addition, the United States views China as a major threat to its security in large part due to the threat it poses to Taiwan, which in turn would make failing to come to Taiwan's defense still more politically difficult. Plus, China's expectation that the United States would join the war creates substantial incentives for China to attack US forces based in Northeast Asia, which would ensure the United States' entry into the conflict. Ending the US commitment would not fully eliminate these pressures and incentives, but it would greatly reduce them, especially as time passed and the US recharacterization of the threat posed by China became more deeply internalized by the United States. I address a related issue, the option of bluffing—keeping the commitment but planning not to join the war—in a later section.

AVOIDING NUCLEAR WAR

A conventional war over Taiwan could escalate to nuclear war along several plausible paths. If China lost the conventional war, it could escalate to limited nuclear attacks to attempt to compel the United States and Taiwan to end the war on terms favorable to China. Given the stakes, both for

---

77. I do not address the latter point in the text, but two key points deserve mention. Taiwan is likely to be unable to defend itself, so the United States would eventually need to join the conflict. In addition, waiting to join the conflict would make prevailing more difficult and possibly impossible; therefore, US leaders will face pressures to respond quickly.

China and the CCP, Chinese leaders might be unwilling to lose. They might believe that China has a bargaining advantage because China cares much more about Taiwan than does the United States; this judgment would be correct. China might even turn to nuclear threats to try to convince the United States not to come to Taiwan's defense. Further, as noted above, China's acquisition of a large nuclear retaliatory capability (and likely an assured destruction capability before the end of the 2020s) fully levels the nuclear playing field, eliminating whatever nuclear bargaining advantage the United States possessed in earlier decades. Consequently, China might see smaller risks in a limited nuclear attack since the United States would lack incentives to escalate to an all-out nuclear war.[78]

Chinese escalation would violate China's no-first-use (NFU) doctrine, but there are reasons to anticipate this possibility. Experts report that China has created some ambiguity about its NFU policy. China might consider a conventional attack against its nuclear forces as crossing a threshold that warranted the first use of nuclear weapons, especially if its nuclear retaliatory capability were seriously threatened. More directly relevant to the Taiwan case, China might make an exception if it were losing a conventional war over truly vital interests and, therefore, be willing to threaten nuclear first use or even use nuclear weapons first.[79]

In addition, the large conventional war could itself create military incentives for nuclear escalation. The conventional war might destroy some Chinese nuclear weapons and command and control assets that are colocated with its conventional forces. China's deployment of an increasingly sophisticated assured destruction capability should eliminate, or at least dramatically reduce, China's concern about these losses. But there is, nevertheless, the possibility that while enduring an intense conventional war, China's leaders would lose confidence in the survivability of their nuclear forces or fear that the United States believes it can launch an effective damage-limitation campaign. In response, China might then launch a limited nuclear attack to destroy US conventional forces that were destroying its nuclear

---

78. Many of the possibilities surfaced in a high-level war game; see Stacie L. Pettyjohn and Becca Wasser, "A Fight Over Taiwan Could Go Nuclear: War Gaming Reveals How a U.S.-Chinese Conflict Might Escalate," *Foreign Affairs*, May 20, 2022.

79. Thomas J. Christensen, "The Meaning of the Nuclear Evolution: China's Strategic Modernization and US-China Security Relations," *Journal of Strategic Studies* 35, no. 4 (August 2012): 474–81; among possible evidence for exceptions to China's NFU policy, Christensen notes a military author who held that "China could use nuclear weapons, whenever 'China's core national security and development interests are fundamentally undermined'" (479). For nuanced disagreements on this question, see Fiona S. Cunningham and M. Taylor Fravel, "Dangerous Confidence? Chinese Views on Nuclear Escalation," *International Security* 44, no. 2 (fall 2019): 84–88, and Tong Zhao, "China and the International Debate on No First Use of Nuclear Weapons," *Asian Security* 18, no. 3 (2022): 206–9.

forces or to signal its resolve, thereby pressuring the United States to end its conventional campaign.[80] Pressures for escalation could also be generated by conventional attacks against dual-capable communication and reconnaissance assets, including satellites and ground-based radars, that both the United States and China would see as valuable targets in a conventional war.[81]

Finally, there is the possibility that the United States would escalate to limited nuclear attacks if it was losing the conventional war over Taiwan. Although the risks generated by this escalation might appear to dwarf US interests, US leaders could act believing that the war had increased the stakes by killing a large number of US military personnel, destroying a large fraction of US aircraft and naval forces, putting US credibility for protecting its allies on the line, and transforming US domestic politics in ways that made conceding appear unacceptable. Recent analysis has called for the United States to plan for using nonstrategic nuclear weapons against China's invasion forces to deter a Chinese invasion.[82]

Given the costs of a large conventional war and the variety of paths via which it could escalate to nuclear war, the risks generated by the US commitment to Taiwan are truly enormous, and, therefore, the benefits of ending the US commitment would be as well.

IMPROVING US-CHINA RELATIONS

Beyond the direct benefit of avoiding war, ending the US commitment to Taiwan could contribute to improving US-China relations, thereby reducing the probability of war over other issues. Given the current downward spiral in the relationship, improvement may be hard to imagine. But the US-China competition is likely to play out over many decades. Some factors will remain constant, maybe most important their different systems of governance, which may place limits on improvements in the relationship. But US and Chinese policies will also significantly influence the trajectory of their relationship. Because (as explained in chapter

---

80. Caitlin Talmadge, "Would China Go Nuclear?: Assessing the Risk of Chinese Nuclear Escalation in a Conventional War with the United States," *International Security* 41, no. 1 (spring 2017): 50–92.

81. James A. Acton, "Escalation Through Entanglement: How the Vulnerability of Command-and-Control Systems Raises the Risks of Inadvertent Nuclear War," *International Security* 43, no. 1 (summer 2018): 56–99. See also Avery Goldstein, "First Things First: The Pressing Danger of Crisis Instability in US-China Relations," *International Security* 37, no. 4 (spring 2013): 49–89, on a variety of plausible escalation paths.

82. Matthew Kroenig, *Deterring Chinese Strategic Attack: Grappling with the Implications of China's Strategic Forces Buildup*, Atlantic Council, November 2021, 17, https://www.atlantic council.org/in-depth-research-reports/report/deterring-chinese-strategic-attack-grappling -with-the-implications-of-chinas-strategic-forces-buildup/.

1) international structure does not create large pressures for US-China security competition, regional issues are key to the US-China security relationship.

US support for Taiwan is probably the most important policy-driven source of China's suspicions about US motives and intentions. Beginning with the first Trump administration, trade has increasingly strained the US-China relationship. However, the two countries share significant common interests in trade, as past US-China experience demonstrates, and policies are available that can greatly dampen trade tensions. In contrast, long-standing American and Chinese positions on Taiwan are largely irreconcilable. Although the United States does not take a position on what the final outcome should be, China considers US support of Taiwan a key source of "strategic distrust." In 2012, two leading authorities on US-China relations—Kenneth Lieberthal and Wang Jisi—concluded that Beijing views US arms sales to Taiwan "as confirming American arrogance and determination to interfere in China's domestic affairs and to prevent peaceful unification from occurring, thereby harming a clearly-articulated Chinese core interest." In a similar vein, their report argues that "continuing to provide Taiwan with advanced weapons . . . is viewed as pernicious in Chinese eyes and has added to suspicion that Washington will disregard Chinese interests and sentiments as long as China's power position is secondary to America's."[83] Andrew Nathan and Andrew Scobell conclude that "most Chinese see strategic motives at the root of American behavior. They believe that keeping the Taiwan problem going helps the US tie China down."[84] Xu Hui, a professor at China's National Defense University, holds that "US policies toward Taiwan have been and are the fundamental cause of some anti-American sentiment among the Chinese public. . . . I assure you that a posture change of the US policy on Taiwan will remove the major obstacle for our military-to-military relations and also strengthen Sino-American cooperation by winning the hearts and minds of 1.3 billion Chinese people."[85] In short, ending the US commitment to Taiwan

---

83. Kenneth Lieberthal and Wang Jisi, *Addressing US-China Strategic Distrust* (Brookings Institution, 2012), 45–46, 13. The authors wrote the first quoted statement together; Wang wrote the second one. *Strategic distrust* is their term.

84. Nathan and Scobell, *China's Search for Security*, 105. See also Bush, *Uncharted Strait*, 210.

85. Christopher P. Twomey and Xu Hui, "Military Developments," in *Debating China: The US-China Relationship in Ten Conversations*, ed. Nina Hachigian (Oxford University Press, 2014), 162. Similarly, Jia Qingguo writes, "In China, the Taiwan problem is considered the most important and most sensitive issue between China and the United States. . . . Such sales reinforce Chinese suspicions that the United States has an evil intention of splitting Taiwan from China forever. This strategic distrust hampers China-US cooperation on many other issues." See Qingguo and Romberg, "Taiwan and Tibet," in *Debating China*, ed. Hachigian, 177, 183. See also Andrew Bingham Kennedy, "China's Perceptions of the US Intentions Toward Taiwan: How Hostile a Hegemon?" *Asian Survey* 47, no. 2 (March/April 2007): 217.

has the potential to improve US-China relations, which in turn could reduce the probability of competition and conflict over other issues.

In addition, ending the US commitment to defend Taiwan could greatly moderate the intensifying military competition between the United States and China, which continues to strain their relationship. Most directly, the United States' conventional military strategy for East Asia is designed to counter China's A2/AD capabilities, which are intended primarily to undermine the US ability to come to Taiwan's aid.[86] The impact of the US commitment to Taiwan on China's military requirements and capabilities, however, arguably reaches still further. China worries that in a conflict over Taiwan the United States will interrupt its sea lines of communication (SLOCs).[87] This vulnerability would leave China open to US coercion during severe crises and conventional wars.[88] China relies heavily on seaborne trade, especially in oil and advanced technologies. Because the imported oil comes primarily from the Persian Gulf, the relevant SLOCs reach across the Indian Ocean, which the United States dominates. The requirement for both China and the United States to control these SLOCs during a crisis or war creates a second-order security dilemma, which adds to strains in the US-China relationship. There is no military-technical solution to this security dilemma, however, because two countries cannot control the same space. A decision by the United States to end its commitment to Taiwan could moderate this security dilemma: By eliminating the scenario that is most likely to bring the United States and China into a large war, accommodation should significantly reduce the importance that China places on controlling its SLOCs.

The positive political impact of the United States ending its commitment to defend Taiwan would depend on the extent of China's regional goals. If primarily driven by Taiwan and security, the impact could be quite large. In contrast, if China is heavily driven by its national identity and desire for international status to pursue regional hegemony, and its accompanying sphere of influence in East Asia, then the impact would likely be smaller. The impact of ending its Taiwan commitment would also depend on other dimensions of US policy toward Taiwan. As discussed in a later section, if the United States continues to arm and train

---

86. Andrew F. Krepinevich, "Why AirSea Battle?," Center for Budgetary and Strategic Assessment, 2010, Jan Van Tol et al., "AirSea Battle: A Point-of-Departure Operational Concept," Center for Budgetary and Strategic Assessment, 2010), and chapter 7 of this book.

87. Michael McDevitt, *China as a Twenty-First-Century Naval Power: Theory, Practice, and Implications* (Naval Institute Press, 2020).

88. Sean Mirski, "Stranglehold: The Context, Conduct and Consequences of an American Naval Blockade of China," *Journal of Strategic Studies* 36, no. 3 (June 2013): 385–421, and Fiona S. Cunningham, "The Maritime Rung on the Escalation Ladder: Naval Blockades in a US-China Conflict," *Security Studies* 29, no. 4 (2020): 730–68.

Taiwanese forces after ending its commitment to use force to protect Taiwan, the positive impact will be smaller.

REDUCING THE VALUE THAT CHINA PLACES
ON REGIONAL HEGEMONY

Ending the US commitment to Taiwan could reduce China's desire to have the United States end its East Asian alliances and leave the region. As discussed in chapter 1, although most China experts believe China would prefer to be the sole great power in its region—that is, to be the regional hegemon—they disagree about how much China values this goal. The US commitment to Taiwan creates a strong security rationale for China to achieve regional hegemony because US alliances—especially with Japan—significantly increase the US ability to defend Taiwan. To the extent that China's preference for regional hegemony is driven largely by security rationales, ending the US commitment to Taiwan should therefore significantly reduce its value. Even if China's desire for regional hegemony is driven by national identity and status rationales, as well as security concerns, which seems likely, ending the US commitment to Taiwan should still have a large impact because states tend to place the greatest weight on security.

Ending the US commitment, however, would not eliminate this security rationale because China could not be confident that the United States would not reverse itself once a severe crisis or war had begun. US forces deployed to the region and those committed to defending its allies could be used to protect Taiwan.

Costs and Risks of US Accommodation on Taiwan

Retrenchment or appeasement regarding Taiwan would bring a variety of costs and risks for the United States, including compromising certain US values, reducing US credibility with China and US allies, and reducing the US military capability to defend its allies.

US IDEOLOGICAL AND HUMANITARIAN VALUES

The United States has a significant interest in promoting and protecting freedom and democracy around the globe. Cutting the US commitment to Taiwan would put these values in greater jeopardy. While the feasibility of "one country, two systems" has always been at best uncertain, China's crackdown on Hong Kong rendered it an empty promise. If China were to gain control over Taiwan, its authoritarian government would almost certainly be unwilling to accept the political institutions and personal freedoms that Taiwan's people currently enjoy. Many proponents of preserving the US commitment to Taiwan point to the importance of protecting these values.[89] In 2022, the *Economist* argued, "Were Taiwan still a military dictatorship full of political prisoners, it would be a niche cause in Washington. As it is, bipartisan support for Taiwan is at its strongest in years."[90] A 2023 Council on Foreign Relations task force report on Taiwan included democracy among its "array of important, even vital, US interests."[91]

These are important values that Washington should be reluctant to jeopardize. I believe these costs would be the most significant that would result from ending the US commitment, larger than the credibility and military costs addressed later in this section. States, however, usually should, and usually do, give priority to their key national security interests. The United States should not be an exception: It should pursue these political and ideological interests only if the risks to its national security are relatively small in comparison, which, in this case, they are not.

CHINA'S ASSESSMENT OF US CREDIBILITY

Ending the US commitment to protect Taiwan might reduce China's assessment of the United States' credibility for protecting its interests in Northeast Asia. As discussed above, territorial accommodation can lead an adversary to doubt the state's resolve to protect other interests, which is dangerous if the state's concessions do not leave the adversary fully satisfied.[92] Two mechanisms could be at work here. One mechanism depends on

---

89. Among many possible examples, see Nancy Bernkopf Tucker and Bonnie Glaser, "Should the United States Abandon Taiwan?" *Washington Quarterly* 34, no. 4 (fall 2011): 34, and Haass and Sacks, "American Support for Taiwan Must be Unambiguous. On the importance that US elites place on protecting democracy in Taiwan, see Kennedy, "China's Perceptions of the US Intentions Toward Taiwan," 279–82.

90. "Few Painless Options Left: China's Chilling Plans for Governing Taiwan," *Economist* October 10, 2022.

91. Susan M. Gordon and Michael G. Mullen, chairs, *US-Taiwan Relations in a New Era: Responding to a More Assertive China*, Independent Task Force Report No. 81, Council on Foreign Relations, 2023, 9–10, https://www.cfr.org/task-force-report/us-taiwan-Relations-in-a-new-era.

92. Another danger is that concessions could increase the domestic political influence of Chinese proponents of more assertive policies—including nationalists and the military—thereby resulting in China becoming greedier and more expansionist. These are standard second-image reversed arguments. See Peter Gourevitch, "The Second Image Reversed: The International Sources of Domestic Politics," *International Organization* 32, no. 4 (fall 1978): 881–912, and Charles L. Glaser, "Political Consequences of Military Strategy: Expanding and Refining the Spiral and Deterrence Models," *World Politics* 44, no. 4 (July 1992): 519–25. For discussions that allude to this type of interaction in the Chinese context, see Kenneth Lieberthal in Kenneth Lieberthal and Wang Jisi, "An Overview of the US-China Relationship," in *Debating China: The US-China Relationship in Ten Conversations*, ed. Nina Hachigian (Oxford University Press, 2014), 4, and Thomas J. Christensen, "Fostering Stability or Creating a Monster?: The Rise of China and U.S. Policy Toward East Asia," *International Security* 31, no. 1 (summer 2006): 111.

China seeing a similarity across one or more features of the potentially connected interests, including their geography, the nature and extent of the US interests, and the US history of involvement with these interests. The second mechanism comes into play if China believes that US accommodation on Taiwan reflects a change in a variable that also affects US decisions on these other issues. The broad change that is currently most relevant is the shifting balance of deployed military power in East Asia. If China's leaders believe that the United States chose accommodation in response to China's growing regional military capabilities, then they would also reasonably conclude that the United States is more likely to make concessions on other regional issues.

These mechanisms are reflected in prominent and long-standing arguments against the United States accommodating Beijing on Taiwan. For example, Nancy Tucker and Bonnie Glaser argued that "China would respond to appeasement as have virtually all governments: It would conclude that a weaker United States lacking vision and ambition could be pressured and manipulated."[93] Richard Bush asserted, "Should the United States concede to Beijing on Taiwan, the lessons that China would learn about the intentions of the region's dominant power would likely discourage moderation and accommodation on other issues, like Korea or maritime East Asia."[94] Rush Doshi claims that ending the US commitment will "startle" US allies and "may even induce bandwagoning behavior if they fear balancing is futile, undermining the US position in the region."[95]

These are important arguments that the United States needs to take seriously, especially given the possibility that China is determined to achieve regional hegemony. There is a clear geographic similarity across the disputes—they are all located in East Asia. Thus, China could be expected to reason that US accommodation on one of these disputes indicates a greater willingness to make concessions on the others. Arguably, ending the US commitment to Taiwan might even lead China to believe that its growing power will enable it to convince the United States to fully exit East Asia. In addition, China's view of the shifting balance of power could reinforce these conclusions: Many Chinese officials believe that the shifting balance of power partly reflects the failings of the US domestic political system and the superiority of China's system of governance and development; the result is a new international system in which China's growing power should generate greater influence and the major powers should acknowledge its rising status.[96] Because this transformation influences all issues in East

---

93. Tucker and Glaser, "Should the United States Abandon Taiwan?," 33.

94. Bush, *Uncharted Strait*, 232.

95. Rush Doshi, *The Long Game: China's Grand Strategy to Displace American Order* (Oxford University Press, 2021), 305.

96. Wang Jisi in Lieberthal and Wang, *Addressing US-China Strategic Distrust*, 8–11.

Asia, US accommodation on Taiwan could validate these expectations and put other US interests at greater risk.

Fortunately, the United States has options that should preserve most, possibly all, of its credibility with China. The United States could pursue policies (and it already is) that make clear that East Asia is its top defense priority. These policies include increasing its defense spending, tailoring weapons acquisition to the challenges of deterring and fighting China, deepening and expanding its alliances in the region, and working to increase and improve ties with partners throughout the Indo-Pacific. Important examples include AUKUS, the QUAD, and the US-Japan-South Korea partnership established in 2023.[97] If the United States anticipated not coming to its allies' defense or eventually leaving the region, it would be far less likely to pursue these policies. These policies, therefore, constitute costly signals—the United States is investing political and military resources that it would be less likely to do if it were not intending to defend its allies. Thus, US policies should make clear to China that Taiwan is the exception and that the United States' treaty commitments in the region remain unchanged or are even deepening.

Of course, if the United States weakens these alliances for other reasons, as some worry President Donald Trump did during his first term and is doing once again during his second term, then US credibility will be put in jeopardy. But this loss of credibility would reflect an overall shift in US priorities and policy that is largely if not entirely independent of its policy toward Taiwan.

Even though deepening US alliance commitments should theoretically preserve US credibility, many regional experts worry that in practice they will fail. States frequently misinterpret actions and signals.[98] In addition, China tends to exaggerate its own successes and therefore might emphasize US concessions and discount US signals of commitment. For example, China was too quick to conclude that the 2008 global financial crisis—in which it fared better than the United States—was a telling indicator of reduced US prosperity, capabilities, and influence.[99] Thus, US efforts to preserve its credibility might not fully succeed; even if the United States pursues policies that should preserve its credibility, it will be running some risk.

The magnitude of this risk depends on the importance that China places on achieving regional hegemony in East Asia. As discussed in chapters 1

---

97. White House, "The Spirt of Camp David: Joint Statement of Japan, the Republic of Korea, and the United States," August 18, 2023, https://www.whitehouse.gov/briefing-room/statements-releases/2023/08/18/the-spirit-of-camp-david-joint-statement-of-japan-the-republic-of-korea-and-the-united-states/.

98. Robert Jervis, Richard Ned Lebow, and Janice Gross Stein, *Psychology and Deterrence* (Johns Hopkins University, 1986).

99. Xiaoyu Pu and Chengli Wang, "Rethinking China's Rise: Chinese Scholars Debate Strategic Overstretch," *International Affairs* 94, no. 5 (September 2018): 1019–35, https://doi.org/10.1093/ia/iiy140.

and 2, China likely does prefer to be the regional hegemon for both national identity and status reasons. However, the possibility, even the likelihood, that China does not place great inherent value on achieving regional hegemony in the short to medium term reduces the risks. If in the future China comes to place great value on achieving regional hegemony—that is, becomes willing to fight a major war to achieve it—the United States will have had plenty of time and opportunity to restore any lost credibility.

ALLIES' ASSESSMENTS OF US CREDIBILITY

Ending the US commitment to Taiwan might also reduce its allies' assessments of US credibility for coming to their aid if attacked by China. More specifically, critics believe that ending the US commitment to Taiwan could lead to such severe Japanese doubts about America's commitment that the alliance would be destroyed, which would in turn reduce US security. Tucker and Glaser argue, "A US decision to abandon Taiwan—leading to the unification of an unwilling Taiwan with China—would be particularly alarming to Japan. . . . If Japan begins to doubt US reliability, that could deal a fatal blow to the US-Japan alliance."[100] Elbridge Colby argues that ending the US commitment to Taiwan would "significantly reduce the United States differentiated credibility as the external cornerstone balancer of an anti-hegemonic coalition."[101]

Although ending the US commitment to Taiwan would certainly send political shock waves racing across the region, these concerns are overstated. There are similarities between the US commitments to Taiwan and Japan but also clear differences. Likely most important, the United States has a clear rationale for ending its commitment to Taiwan that does not apply to Japan and its other regional allies: China believes Taiwan is part of China; it does not believe this about Japan. Consequently, the value that China places on Taiwan is much greater, as is the probability of war over Taiwan. Related, the US commitment to Taiwan strains the US-China relationship in ways and to an extent that the US commitment to Japan does not. Also important, US security interests in Japan are greater; as a result, the alliance involves stronger political commitments and the deep integration of US and Japanese military capabilities. Japan should appreciate these differences and therefore recognize that ending the US commitment to Taiwan would not indicate a coming diminution of the US commitment to Japan. US leaders should emphasize to their Japanese counterparts the extent of these differences.

100. Tucker and Glaser, "Should the United States Abandon Taiwan?," 33. Also voicing concern about US alliances are Shelley Rigger, "Why Giving Up Taiwan Will Not Help Us with China," American Enterprise Institute for Public Policy Research, November 2011, 3, and Nathan and Scobell, *China's Search for Security*, 239.

101. Elbridge A. Colby, *The Strategy of Denial: American Defense in an Age of Great Power Conflict* (Yale University Press, 2021), 236; see also 63–64.

CHAPTER 4

In addition, the United States could continue to take actions that starkly distinguish its policies toward Japan from its policies toward Taiwan, which should reduce credibility fears that accommodation on Taiwan might create. As noted above, the United States is already adopting many of these policies as part of its response to China's growing capabilities and the United States' increasingly negative assessments of China's goals. Most specifically regarding Japan, the United States could continue to increase the size and improve the quality of the forces it commits to Japan's protection and to the region more broadly. Other policies include further deepening US-Japan joint military planning and continuing high-level discussions of the requirements for extending nuclear deterrence to Japan. Growth in Chinese conventional and nuclear forces spurred these policies by the late 2000s.[102] They would be still more valuable if the United States ends its commitment to Taiwan and should go a long way toward preserving US credibility.

Finally, as China's power continues to grow, Japan's need for US security guarantees will also grow. Doubts about US reliability are therefore likely to convince Japan to work harder to strengthen the US-Japan alliance, not to abandon it or to bandwagon with China.[103]

All this said, two qualifications are required. First, US allies in Northeast Asia have complicated domestic politics that could undermine US efforts to maintain its credibility, especially as China's economic influence grows in the region. There is thus some possibility that ending the US commitment to Taiwan would reduce US credibility with its East Asian allies.[104] My assessment is that well-designed US policies can keep this probability quite small. But, as with China's assessment of US credibility, there would be some risk with US allies.

Second, and currently more important, a qualification already offered above requires repeating: The wild card in this assessment is President

---

102. James L. Schoff, *Realigning Priorities: The US-Japan Alliance and the Future of Extended Deterrence* (Institute for Foreign Policy Analysis, March 2009), and Richard J. Samuels and James L. Schoff, "Japan's Nuclear Hedge: Beyond 'Allergy' and Breakout," in *Strategic Asia 2013–2014: Asia in the Second Nuclear Age*, ed. Ashley J. Tellis, Abraham M. Denmark, and Travis Tanner (National Bureau of Asian Research, 2013), 233–64.

103. On the basic alliance logic for security-seeking states, see Stephen M. Walt, *The Origins of Alliances* (Cornell University Press, 1987); on preservation of alliances by a declining power, see Jasen J. Castillo and Alexander B. Downes, "Loyalty, Hedging, or Exit: How Weaker Alliance Partners Respond to the Rise of New Threats," *Journal of Strategic Studies* 46, no. 2 (2023): 227–268. Another possibility is that Japan would decide to acquire nuclear weapons. See Samuels and Schoff, "Japan's Nuclear Hedge," and Mike M. Mochizuki, "Japan Tests the Nuclear Taboo," *Non-Proliferation Review* 14, no. 2 (July 2007): 303–28. Analysts disagree about how dangerous this would be; see chapter 3.

104. On general concerns about US credibility, see Hiroyuki Akita, "Time for Asia to Rethink Its Deep Dependence on US for Security," *Nikkei Asia*, March 3, 2019, https://asia.nikkei.com/Spotlight/Comment/Time-for-Asia-to-rethink-its-deep-dependence-on-US-for-security.

Trump and the at least temporary shift in Republican support for US allies. With good reason, US allies in Europe and Asia are coming to believe that the United States is no longer a reliable ally. Consequently, convincing allies that ending the US commitment to Taiwan did not foreshadow the ending of other alliances has become significantly more difficult. The issue here, however, is not Taiwan but broader and deeper changes to US foreign policy.

US MILITARY CAPABILITIES

A very different type of potential cost is that ending the US commitment to Taiwan could reduce the US military capabilities necessary for protecting its allies. The most obvious impact of controlling Taiwan would be that China could move its forces—most importantly, missiles—farther east by about two hundred miles.[105] This difference, however, seems unlikely to add a critical increment to the range of China's capabilities.[106]

The more important possibility is that control of Taiwan would give China more direct access to the open Pacific, which might significantly increase its ability to destroy US forces.[107] Chinese analysts have long identified the importance of Taiwan for enabling China to get through the barrier created by Japan, including the Ryukyu Islands, Taiwan, and the Philippines.[108] Described more fully, "Control of Taiwan . . . would allow the PLA to erect its own Great Wall at sea, giving Beijing some say over the exercise of foreign naval and military power in nearby seas and skies. . . . Analysts view Taiwan as the one geographic asset that can grant Chinese forces direct access to the Pacific. If the island is a guard tower in an offshore Great Wall, then its offensive value is unmatched."[109]

Dissecting the strategic value of greater access to the Pacific requires assessing how Chinese control of Taiwan would influence China's ability to perform specific military missions. A key possibility is that control of Tai-

---

105. For discussion of a range of geostrategic considerations, see Wachman, *Why Taiwan?*

106. On this point, see Robert S. Ross, "Navigating the Taiwan Strait: Deterrence, Escalation Dominance, and US-China Relations," *International Security* 27, no. 2 (fall 2002): 55–56; James Steinberg and Michael E. O'Hanlon, *Strategic Reassurance and Resolve: U.S.-China Relations in the Twenty-First Century* (Princeton University Press, 2014), 242–43, and Porter and Mazaar, *Countering China's Adventurism Over Taiwan*.

107. Another possible danger is that control of Taiwan would enable China to redirect its military efforts to other military missions in East Asia and beyond. However, China would have to invest much more than it already is because invading or blockading Taiwan is easier that other ambitious missions. Consequently, control of Taiwan is unlikely to be decisive in enabling China to make the necessary investments.

108. Wachman, *Why Taiwan?*, 138.

109. Toshi Yoshihara and James R. Holmes, *Red Star Over the Pacific: China's Rise and the Challenge of U.S. Maritime Strategy* (Naval Institute Press, 2010), 20–21. See also the second edition of *Red Star Over the Pacific* (2018), 83–87, and Vincent Wei-cheng Wang, "The Chinese Military and the 'Taiwan Issue': How China Assesses Its Security Environment," *Southeast Review of Asian Studies* 29 (2007): 130.

wan would enhance China's A2/AD capabilities by increasing its ability to send submarines into the Philippine Sea, which would increase the threat to US carrier battle groups. Owen Coté explains that Taiwan plays an important role in enabling the United States "to form effective acoustic barriers through which Chinese SS/SSGs [diesel attack submarines/guided missile diesel submarines] must pass in transiting" from the shallow waters along China's coast into the deep water of the Philippine Sea.[110] In the most extensive analysis to date, Brendan Green and Caitlin Talmadge argue that the United States likely deploys multiple antisubmarine warfare (ASW) barriers that would enable it to track Chinese submarines as they transit to or from the Philippine Sea during peacetime and to impose high levels of attrition during a war. According to their analysis, Chinese control of Taiwan would severely reduce US ASW capabilities by eliminating key acoustic barriers that connect to Taiwan.[111] The increased ability of Chinese submarines to pass into and operate in the Philippine Sea would increase the risk of operating US surface ships there, which would reduce the United States' ability to attack Chinese naval and land-based forces. In addition, Green and Talmadge argue that control of Taiwan could significantly improve China's ocean surveillance capability by enabling China to deploy deep sound channel sonar arrays on the eastern shore of Taiwan. This capability would fill a critical gap in China's wartime surveillance capability, thereby increasing the vulnerability of US naval forces.

Questions remain, however, about how large the military effects of Chinese control of Taiwan would be. First, as Green and Talmadge point out, there will be a "battle for the barriers": China may be able to defeat current US ASW barriers by cutting sensor cables or sending large numbers of submarines (and possibly drones) across the barrier at the same time. On the flipside, the United States might be able to establish new barriers that do not depend on connecting to Taiwan.[112] If feasible, either of these possibili-

---

110. Owen R. Coté Jr., "Assessing the Undersea Balance Between the US and China," working paper (Massachusetts Institute of Technology Security Studies Program, February 2011), 12. Guided missile submarines carry antiship cruise missiles that pose a threat to US ships. Coté found that diesel submarines likely pose a larger threat than the nuclear attack submarines that China will be able to build in the short to medium term. See Coté, "Assessing the Undersea Balance," 11–12. See also Owen R. Coté Jr., "Invisible Nuclear-Armed Submarines, or Transparent Oceans? Are Ballistic Missile Submarines Still the Best Deterrent for the United States?," *Bulletin of the Atomic Scientists* 75, no. 1 (2019): 30–35.

111. Brendan Rittenhouse Green and Caitlin Talmadge, "Then What? Assessing the Military Implications of Chinese Control of Taiwan," *International Security* 47, no. 1 (summer 2020): 7–45, esp. 17–23. For a critique of these many of these arguments and further analysis, see Jonathan D. Caverley, "So What: Re-assessing the Military Implications of Chinese Control of Taiwan," Texas National Security Review (forthcoming 2025). In addition, ownership of Taiwan would enable China to deploy fighters that could greatly reduce the ability of ASW aircraft (which prosecute contacts) to operate within approximately five hundred kilometers of Taiwan. I thank Eric Heginbotham for this point.

112. Green and Talmadge, "Then What?," 22.

ties would reduce or even eliminate the ASW value of Taiwan. Second, China is developing and deploying a variety of ways, other than submarines, to attack US naval forces at increasingly long distances, including antiship cruise missiles that can be launched from a diverse array of platforms, antiship ballistic missiles that are becoming capable of hitting moving targets, and hypersonic glide vehicles that would make Chinese ballistic missile attacks harder to intercept.[113] The United States can pursue a variety of approaches to interrupt the Chinese "kill chain" that enables these missiles to be effective, including masking the location of navy ships, jamming China's maritime surveillance, using decoys to confuse missiles as they approach targets, and missile defenses for destroying the antiship missiles.[114] As with the battle of the barriers, there will be a battle over the missile kill chains, with uncertainty about the outcome. The greater the extent to which Chinese missiles prevail, the less important any reduction in ASW capabilities that would result from China's control of Taiwan.

Third, China will likely have other options—besides the deep sonar arrays—for filling the current gap in its ocean surveillance capabilities. As Green and Talmadge point out, "If China deploys many, new large imagining satellites" or a large number of small imagining satellites, then the deep sonar array would be less valuable.[115] Finally, the United States has options for attacking China that could greatly reduce the importance of attacking from the sea. Likely most important, the United States could launch attacks from outside the Pacific Theater, relying on long-range bombers carrying cruise missiles to target Chinese naval and land forces.[116] In sum, although further analysis is required, the negative impact of Chinese control of Taiwan on the United States' ability to destroy Chinese forces is unlikely to be large and could be quite small.

Ending the US Commitment to Defend Taiwan

The case for ending the US commitment to Taiwan is, in a sense, straightforward. The risks of the commitment are simply too large: The probability of a conventional war over the next two or three decades is significant, the conventional war itself would be very costly, and there is some real chance

---

113. Ronald O'Rourke, *China Naval Modernization: Implications for US Naval Capabilities—Background and Issues for Congress* (Congressional Research Service; updated November 10, 2022): 11–15; see also appendix B, which addresses countermeasures the United States can pursue, and Evan Braden Montgomery, "Contested Primacy in the Western Pacific: China's Rise and the Future of U.S. Power Projection," *International Security* 38, no. 4 (spring 2014): 130–39.
114. O'Rourke, *China Naval Modernization*, appendix B.
115. Green and Talmadge, "Then What?," 36.
116. See chapter 7 for a short discussion of this possibility.

that a conventional war would escalate to a nuclear war. The nuclear war could start as a limited nuclear attack and escalate, or it could start as a large nuclear attack. Taiwan is an important but not vital US interest. Given the risk of conventional and nuclear war, the interests at stake do not warrant the US commitment. Ending the US commitment would essentially eliminate these risks.

Of course, this simplified conclusion does not capture the nuance and complexity of the preceding assessment. However, my conclusion based on a more complete assessment remains the same. Against the benefits of avoiding a large major-power war, the costs, although not small, are dwarfed. The key cost is to US political, ideological, and humanitarian values—ending the US commitment would increase the probability of China crushing Taiwan's democracy and restricting a range of political freedoms. Of course, if war over Taiwan were quite unlikely, then the expected costs of war (probability times cost) might be smaller than the expected costs to these American values. However, the probability of war is not nearly this small.

The other costs of ending the US commitment are simply too small, if correctly handled, to outweigh the benefits. Although concerns about US credibility with both China and US allies are frequently voiced, these risks should be manageable if the United States demonstrates strong support for its allies more generally. The United States can demonstrate its continuing commitment to its allies by explaining why they are so different from Taiwan and by pursuing a variety of military and diplomatic policies that require large investments that are tailored to the region. Of course, there is no guarantee that US efforts will succeed—allies' domestic politics could produce unreasonable outcomes—but the prospects for success are high because, among other reasons, the United States would remain the allies' best available provider of security. The military implications of Chinese control of Taiwan are potentially more problematic, although a variety of arguments suggest that the United States' ability to protect Japan and other allies would not be greatly reduced, especially if the United States continues to design its military forces to defeat China's A2/AD capabilities. Likely, the more telling point, however, is that even a decrease in US military capabilities would be worth accepting because China does not appear determined to conquer Japan. Consequently, a reduction in US military capabilities is quite unlikely to meaningful increase the probability of war with Japan; any increase would be dwarfed by the reduced risk of war over Taiwan.

Deciding to end the commitment raises the question of how a state can end an already ambiguous commitment in a convincing manner. Unlike in certain formal alliances—for example, the US alliances with Japan and South Korea—the United States does not forward-deploy forces on Taiwan, does not engage in joint training exercises, and so on. Nevertheless, there are meaningful steps that would indicate the change in US policy. For example, the United States would stop planning and exercising its military for a Taiwan scenario. Likely more important, stating clearly that the United States will not use force to come to Taiwan's defense would change expectations in the United States, reframing the issue for US decision-makers and reducing, albeit not eliminating, domestic pressures to respond to a Chinese attack on Taiwan. Arguably, the impact would be greater for US decisions than for China's perception of the US commitment, as China's leaders might well remain skeptical that the United States would not intervene. But, perhaps counterintuitively, this would have advantages: If China doubts the United States has changed its policies, then there would be little if any reduction in the US ability to deter a Chinese invasion or blockade; at the same time, if deterrence fails, the United States would be more likely to stay out of the war. The United States would get the benefits of bluffing that it would respond to a Chinese attack, without the risks, which are discussed later in this chapter.

SHOULD THE UNITED STATES THEN HELP ARM TAIWAN?

Ending its commitment to Taiwan—that is, making clear that the United States would not come to Taiwan's defense if attacked by China—would leave the United States with an important question: Should the United States continue to sell arms to Taiwan and train its military forces?[117] Arming Taiwan could enable the United States to pursue its interests—primarily ideological and humanitarian—while avoiding the direct risk of war with China.

Taiwan is unlikely to be able to defend itself if fighting alone, but there are policies it could pursue to make China's success more costly and thereby enhance deterrence. Among the most important, Taiwan can shift more fully to a strategy that makes use of the defensive advantages of water and current technology—a so-called porcupine strategy.[118]

US arming and training might contribute significantly to Taiwan's prospects. In 2023, Taiwan spent $19 billion on defense, which is 2.4 percent of its GDP. US support on the order of billions of dollars per year would therefore constitute a significant increase. The United States, which has sold

---

117. For a more extensive analysis of this question, see Charles L. Glaser, "Considering a US-Supported Self-Defense Option for Taiwan," *Washington Quarterly* 48, no. 1 (spring 2025): 187–204.

118. See footnote 8 as well as Jim Thomas, John Stillion, and Iskander Rehman, *HARD ROC 2.0: Taiwan and Deterrence Through Protraction*, Center for Strategic and Budgetary Assessments, 2014, https://csbaonline.org/research/publications/hard-roc-2-0-taiwan-and-deterrence-through-protraction.

weapons to Taiwan for decades, changed its policy in 2022 to increase its support of Taiwan.[119] As already noted, the December 2022 Taiwan Enhanced Resilience Act authorizes the use of Foreign Military Financing of up to $2 billion per year and makes Presidential Drawdown Authority available, "authorizing the drawdown from Department of Defense stocks of up to $1 billion annually."[120] The United States could afford to make still-larger contributions to Taiwan's defense.

The arming option could take two broad forms—arming during peacetime and arming during both peacetime and war. The first would be far less risky because China would be less likely to interrupt or destroy US weapons shipments during peacetime. The second creates an escalatory path to a US-China war in which China attacks US weapons shipments and the United States concludes that it needs to respond. Although China might limit its attacks to Taiwan's ports, transit hubs, and weapons storage depots, US ships and planes approaching Taiwan would be lucrative targets. Once US forces were attacked, the United States would likely retaliate against Chinese forces, thereby taking its first steps into a war with China.

A cost of arming Taiwan is that it would greatly reduce, if not eliminate, the political benefits that ending the US commitment might otherwise produce—improved US-China relations. China would, correctly, see the United States continuing to actively oppose its achievement of a fundamental goal. China might also worry that the United States was supporting Taiwan's independence because the United States would be losing some of its ability to constrain Taiwan.

Whether to continue to provide Taiwan with arms is a difficult call. The easy, and possibly correct, answer is to provide arms, at least during peacetime, in the hope of enabling Taiwan to deter China, thereby protecting US interests. Doing so would also signal to America's allies a continuing commitment, which might reduce still further the possibility that ending its Taiwan commitment would damage US credibility. And, at an emotional level, arming Taiwan could feel better than completely ending US support for Taiwan. The downside, however, is potentially large, if one judges that ending the US commitment might otherwise lead to significant improvements in US-China relations. There is also the possibility that providing military support would increase the probability of the United States deciding to come to Taiwan's defense—getting drawn back in—by somehow blurring the end of the US commitment.

---

119. For an assessment of previous US arms sales, see Pin-Fen Kok and David J. Firestein, *Threading the Needle: Proposals for US and Chinese Arms Sales to Taiwan* (EastWest Institute, 2013).

120. Caitlin Campbell, *Taiwan: Defense and Military Issues*, Congressional Research Service, September 19, 2023, https://crsreports.congress.gov/product/pdf/IF/IF12481.

Given the current poor state of US-China relations and the multiple barriers to near-term improvements, I lean toward providing Taiwan with quite substantial arms during peacetime. As the US-China relationship evolves, the United States should reevaluate whether to end this military support for Taiwan.

Alternative Policies

Three broad alternatives to ending the US commitment to Taiwan and continuing with current US policy deserve consideration: bluffing, a grand bargain, and a concert of Asian powers.

BLUFF

An alternative to ending the US commitment would be to bluff—maintain the current ambiguous US commitment (or even make it certain), but plan not to come to Taiwan's defense. Cast in its starkest terms, this option would provide the deterrent benefits of the commitment while eliminating the risks of actually fighting a war with China.

Attractive as it may sound, bluffing would bring a variety of risks and costs. Most importantly, bluffing would be harder to successfully carry out than it sounds. The United States might fool itself, that is, end up coming to Taiwan's defense because it had said it would. Given its commitment, the United States would need to continue to plan and exercise its forces as though it were giving priority to a Taiwan contingency. The United States would continue to define the threat posed by China largely in terms of the danger it posed to Taiwan, which increases the probability it would intervene. Only a few people at the very top of the US leadership could know it was a bluff, and this understanding would have to be passed from one administration to the next. The US military would likely not be included in this bluffing cabal and would therefore be strongly inclined to support US involvement. The overall result would be a widely shared expectation within the US government, the US military, and the US public that the United States would come to Taiwan's aid.

Even if the United States ends its commitment to Taiwan, a Chinese invasion would create pressures for the United States to join the war. Consider US experiences joining other wars that it was not committed to fighting, including the First and Second World Wars and, maybe more directly parallel, the Korean War. Bluffing, even with an ambiguous commitment, would significantly increase these pressures. The US president would face tremendous pressure to defend Taiwan and might well do so. If the United States should not come to Taiwan's defense, as I have argued above, then the

CHAPTER 4

United States needs to create barriers to joining the war if China attacks Taiwan. Thus, the United States should not bluff regarding Taiwan.[121]

Other costs are more speculative. If ending the US commitment to Taiwan would improve US-China relations over the long term, bluffing would forgo these benefits. Related but separable, ending the US commitment would greatly reduce the military challenges the United States faces in East Asia, even as it continues to prepare to defend its allies. This would make the United States feel more secure, clarifying that China was a smaller threat to US vital interests than the growing conventional wisdom suggests. Bluffing would forgo this benefit, resulting in an odd type of threat inflation.

GRAND BARGAIN

In an earlier analysis of US policy toward Taiwan, I recommended a grand bargain: The United States would end its commitment to Taiwan; China would resolve its disputes in the South China Sea and East China Sea on "fair" terms and officially accept the United States' long-term security role in East Asia, including its alliances and forward-deployed forces.[122]

This grand bargain would have a variety of advantages. Most obviously, China's acceptance of the grand bargain would indicate that its aims were limited (at least for the time being). Closely related, it would demonstrate a degree of reasonableness in Chinese foreign policy priorities and decision-making, given that the value of Taiwan dwarfs the value of the territorial disputes in the South China Sea (see chapter 5 for discussion).

Insisting on Chinese concessions would also have demonstrated US resolve to protect American and allied interests. In addition, a resolution of the maritime disputes would have directly increased US security by eliminating disputes that, via its alliance commitments and determination to preserve the rules-based order, could draw the United States into dangerous crises with China.

Although a grand bargain would clearly be preferable to unilateral accommodation/retrenchment, the grand bargain now appears infeasible. China's tougher positions on sovereignty issues and the South China Sea indicate that it is unlikely to make major concessions on these maritime disputes. As explored in chapters 1 and 2, China likely places some value on achieving regional hegemony, which somewhat reduces the probability it would officially accept the US military presence in its region. More con-

---

121. In chapter 5, I argue that the United States could bluff with regard to its commitments in the South China Sea. In contrast to Taiwan, these disputes do not drive US military planning; in addition, they are less likely to generate strong US domestic pressures for the United States to intervene.

122. The United States is not directly involved in these disputes, but it could encourage or pressure its allies to make compromises.

cretely, although there have been periods when China viewed the US-Japan alliance relatively favorably, which made the grand bargain seem possibly feasible, a variety of factors, including the decline of Soviet power, the redefinition of the US-Japan alliance starting in the mid-1990s, and China's growing power came together to reduce, if not eliminate, China's positive assessment.[123] By the mid-2010s, Chinese elites began expressing harshly negative views.[124]

Whereas China's acceptance of a grand bargain would have provided information that reduced the risks of ending the US commitment to Taiwan, the changes in China's policies since the mid-2010s have provided information that indicates the opposite. I argued above that these risks are worth accepting, but there is no getting around the fact that they now appear larger.

CONCERT OF ASIAN POWERS

A third very different alternative would be a concert of Asia's major powers.[125] In the broadest terms, the concert would require the United States and China to share power in East Asia. In the early 2010s, Hugh White proposed an Asian concert in which "the major powers [agree] not to seek primacy in a strategic system" and "members agree not to try to deprive one another of the status of a great power." Among other requirements, the success of this concert would depend on members accepting the legitimacy of the others' political systems and committing to oppose any state that tries to dominate another member. In addition, members would have the right to use force to protect their interests and to build the forces this requires, but "forces strong enough to threaten the independence of other great powers are not acceptable." White argued that agreeing to the requirements of the concert would be difficult and costly for both the United States and China. The United States would find it challenging to accept the legitimacy of China's political system and to treat China as a military and political

---

123. Jianwei Wang and Xinbo Wu, "Against Us or with Us? The Chinese Perspective of America's Alliances with Japan and Korea," Asia/Pacific Research Center, Stanford University, May 1998; Xinbo Wu, "The End of the Silver Lining: A Chinese View of the US-Japan Alliance," *Washington Quarterly* 29, no. 1 (winter 2005/6): 119–30.

124. Helene Cooper and Jane Perlez, "US Sway in Asia Is Imperiled as China Challenges Alliances," *New York Times*, May 31, 2014; Timothy R. Heath, "China and the US Alliance System," *Diplomat*, June 11, 2014, http://thediplomat.com/2014/06/china-and-the-u-s-alliance-system.

125. Hugh White, *The China Choice: Why America Should Share Power* (Black, 2012). For analyses of White's argument, see Yuen Foong Khong, "Primacy or World Order? The United States and China's Rise—A Review Essay," *International Security* 38, no. 3 (winter 2013/14): 153–75, and Denny Roy, "The Problem of Premature Appeasement," *Survival* 55, no. 3 (June/July 2013): 182–202.

peer, which would include accepting "China's growing capability to limit US military options in the Western Pacific." For its part, China would have to "forgo its dream of leading Asia" and "accept that even as the world's richest power, it will not exercise primacy in Asia as America has done."[126]

Although White's Asian concert would include valuable political understandings between the United States and China, it would fall short primarily because it fails to address the key dangers facing the United States and China. It would contribute little to resolving the region's sovereignty and maritime disputes and would therefore leave largely unchanged the probability of severe crises and escalating military competition. Further, giving priority to getting the United States and China to forgo military postures designed to dominate the region would do little to alleviate the key regional danger because a large war between the United States and China is most likely to escalate from disputes that were not initially intended to overturn the system, most importantly, a conflict over Taiwan. In any event, as with a grand bargain, China's policies since the mid-2010s have made a concert virtually infeasible, leaving the United States without this option. In addition, the increasing importance the United States is placing on China's authoritarian regime—both its illegitimacy and the threat it poses to US interests—has further reduced the prospects for an East Asian concert.

The dangers posed by the US commitment to Taiwan leave the United States with only bad options. Current US policy, which is defined by an ambiguous commitment to defend Taiwan from China, entails very large risks: A conventional war over the next couple of decades is not unlikely, nor is its escalation to nuclear war. And the trend line is worrisome. China's military capabilities against Taiwan are increasing, and US prospects for reversing this trend are poor. Taiwan's population is increasingly opposed to unification with China, which leaves Beijing with only the option of using force to achieve its goal. And China's President Xi has made the unification of Taiwan a priority, one that he likely hopes to achieve under his watch. US prospects for defeating a Chinese invasion remain quite good and are hopefully sufficient to deter China. However, there are plausible scenarios in which a risk-accepting Chinese leader could reasonably convince himself, or be convinced, that China's chances were sufficiently good to roll the dice. Scenarios in which the United States does not respond to a Chinese attack or responds slowly, and in which Japan does not allow the United States to use its bases all fall into this category. There are also scenarios that begin with

---

126. White, *The China Choice*, chap. 8, quotes at 133, 134, 135, 148, 141–42. Although Japan and India do not play a central role in White's analysis, he includes them as the other major-power members of the concert. Among the challenges White sees is the need for Japan to assume its major-power responsibilities, which, he implies, would require it to acquire nuclear weapons. See White, *The China Choice*, 149.

smaller risks but then escalate—for example, a blockade that fails and then leaves China with only riskier options. And there is the possibility that China comes to believe that Taiwan has moved too close to independence, leaving China without options except for the use of force.

As reviewed above, the costs of ending the US commitment would be primarily in US ideological and humanitarian values, not US security. These costs would be significant but are too small to warrant the risk of fighting to protect Taiwan. Lacking other preferable options, the United States should explicitly end its commitment to defend Taiwan. Retrenchment is the United States' best option.

Having made this break, the United States would still need to decide whether to continue arming Taiwan and training its forces. I conclude in favor of arming, but this conclusion is not clear-cut and should be reevaluated if US-China relations improve along multiple other dimensions.

A key argument against this far-reaching change in US policy is that China will remain deeply dissatisfied. According to this perspective, once it gains control of Taiwan, China will pursue regional hegemony; appeasement will not only fail but will also encourage and enable China. However, China does not need to be satisfied for US policy to succeed. Ending the US commitment based on the logic of retrenchment—which does not assume that the adversary has limited aims and therefore will be satisfied by the concession—is a sound policy. The United States, working with its treaty allies, should have excellent prospects for deterring attacks against them. Virtually all experts agree that China is far less motivated to achieve regional hegemony than to reunify with Taiwan and that the military challenges of achieving regional hegemony are much greater. In short, retrenching enables the United States to avoid the possibility of war over Taiwan while preserving excellent prospects for protecting its other interests in East Asia.

Following the ending of its ambiguous commitment to Taiwan, the United States should take a variety of actions to reinforce the credibility of its remaining commitments. Most obviously, the United States should continue to respond to China's improving military capabilities and further deepen its alliance relationships. The United States is already doing much of what is required—planning its force structure and deployments for a major war in East Asia, exercising more extensively with Japan and other allies, and increasing consultation with its allies on conventional and nuclear planning.[127]

---

127. Of course, once again the caveat concerning Trump's undermining of US credibility with its allies requires mentioning. On increased consultation with South Korea on nuclear issues, established by the Washington Declaration, see Scott Snyder, "The Washington Declaration: Expanding the Nuclear Dimension of the US-South Korean Alliance Response," Council on Foreign Relations, April 27, 2023, https://www.cfr.org/blog/washington-declaration-expanding-nuclear-dimension-us-south-korean-alliance-response.

In addition, the United States is expanding and deepening its alliance commitments and partnerships, as evidenced by the 2021 AUKUS security pact, the evolution of the QUAD, and the Pacific Deterrence Initiative.[128] In short, the United States should balance and compete intensively.

Although increased US military forces, and deepening and expanding alliances, will likely appear somewhat threatening to China, the risks will be worth running. By ending its commitment to Taiwan, the United States will already have largely dealt with China's overriding security concern. Consequently, China should view the US ability to disrupt its SLOCs as much less threatening and understand that US military capabilities are intended to defend US allies, not Taiwan. This should reduce China's perceptions of the threat posed by the United States. Moreover, given uncertainty about China's goals, generating some insecurity is warranted by the deterrence benefits. When uncertain about an adversary's motives or when facing a state with mixed motives—a combination of security seeking and greed—a state should pursue a mix of policies designed to balance deterrence and provocation.[129] If China turns out to be very determined to push the United States out of East Asia, which is unlikely but not impossible, the deterrent capability of US forces will be quite valuable.

---

128. On the Pacific Deterrence Initiative, see *The Pacific Deterrence Initiative: A Budgetary Overview*, Congressional Research Service, January 9, 2023, https://sgp.fas.org/crs/natsec/IF12303.pdf.

129. Robert Jervis, *Perception and Misperception in International Politics* (Princeton University Press, 1976), chap. 3, and Charles L. Glaser, *Rational Theory of International Politics: The Logic of Competition and Cooperation* (Princeton University Press, 2010), 81–85, 94–102.

CHAPTER 5

South China Sea

How Much Risk Should the United States Run?

China's assertiveness in the South China Sea poses an especially vexing set of policy choices for the United States.[1] For decades, the South China Sea disputes appeared to be limited to small islets, rocks, and reefs claimed by several countries. These small bits of land were a source of international concern because they fueled numerous limited conflicts, but they were themselves of little material value or strategic importance.

Now, however, China appears to want to control a vast body of water in a critical region of the world. Around 2008, China started adopting more assertive policies in the South China Sea. Since then, it has seized control of Scarborough Shoal, built artificial islands in the Spratly Islands (and constructed large military bases on three of them), rejected an international tribunal ruling that invalidated Chinese claims to historic rights within the "nine-dash line," and harassed and intimidated Vietnamese and Malaysian vessels within their Exclusive Economic Zones (EEZs). Taken together, China's actions suggest that it is intent on dominating the South China Sea.

China's behavior in the South China Sea played a central role in transforming US assessments of China's ambitions. In contrast with the 2000s, when the United States believed its relationship with China could be primarily cooperative,[2] by 2022, the US Indo-Pacific Strategy stated that China "pursues a sphere of influence in the Indo-Pacific and seeks to become the world's most influential power. The PRC's [People's Republic of China] coercion and aggression spans the globe, but it is most acute in the Indo-

---

1. This chapter draws heavily on an article I coauthored with Taylor Fravel: M. Taylor Fravel and Charles L. Glaser, "How Much Risk Should the United States Run in the South China Sea?," *International Security* 47, no. 2 (fall 2022): 88–134.

2. Barack Obama, *National Security Strategy*, White House, May 2010, 43, https://obamawhitehouse.archives.gov/sites/default/files/rss_viewer/national_security_strategy.pdf.

Pacific."[3] The shift in official US assessments largely mirrors a significant negative shift across the US foreign policy community.

Many experts place great importance on the South China Sea. For example, in 2017, Ely Ratner, who became a senior official at the US Department of Defense in the Biden administration focused on the Indo-Pacific, held that China "is now poised to seize control of the sea. Should it succeed, it would deal a devastating blow to the United States' influence in the region, tilting the balance of power across Asia in China's favor."[4]

The South China Sea is considered a likely locus of conflict between the United States and China. Although a large conventional war is most likely to occur over Taiwan, analysts have explored incentives for escalation that could push a crisis in the South China Sea into a large conventional war or even a nuclear war.[5]

This chapter analyzes how strenuously, and at what risk, the United States should resist China's efforts to dominate the South China Sea. As emphasized throughout this book, China's rise requires the United States to reevaluate all its commitments and decide whether to adopt more competitive or less competitive strategies for defending them. Where US interests are relatively small and China's rise significantly increases the risks of protecting them, the United States may need to trim its commitments. In contrast, where its interests are large, the United States may need to deepen its commitments and compete intensively to protect them, even if the dangers posed by China's rise are greater.

Building on the analysis of the grand strategy debate discussed in chapter 3, this chapter assumes that the United States retains the core of its current grand strategy, including its security commitments to its East Asian treaty allies. The analysis also assumes that the United States retains its ambiguous commitment to Taiwan. Although contrary to the conclusion of chapter 4, the United States is likely to retain a commitment to come to

3. Joe Biden, *Indo-Pacific Strategy of the United States*, White House, February 2022, 5, https://www.whitehouse.gov/wp-content/uploads/2022/02/US-Indo-Pacific-Strategy.pdf. For the Donald Trump administration's characterization, see Donald J. Trump, *National Security Strategy of the United States of America*, December 2017, 25.

4. Ely Ratner, "Course Correction: How to Stop China's Maritime Advance," *Foreign Affairs* 96, no. 4, July/August 2017, 64, https://www.jstor.org/stable/44823892. See also Patrick M. Cronin and Ryan Neuhard, *Total Competition: China's Challenge in the South China Sea* (Center for a New American Security, January 2020), 1, and Hal Brands and Zack Cooper, "Getting Serious About Strategy in the South China Sea," *Naval War College Review* 71, no. 1 (winter 2018): 16, https://digital-commons.usnwc.edu/nwc-review/vol71/iss1/3.

5. Avery Goldstein, "First Things First: The Pressing Danger of Crisis Instability in US-China Relations," *International Security* 37, no. 4 (spring 2013): 49–89, https://doi.org/10.1162/ISEC_a_00114; Caitlin Talmadge, "Would China Go Nuclear? Assessing the Risk of Chinese Nuclear Escalation in a Conventional War with the United States," *International Security* 41, no. 4 (spring 2017): 50–92.

Taiwan's defense for the foreseeable future (although President Trump does make this less certain); therefore, this is a productive position from which to analyze US options in the South China Sea.

I analyze three options along a continuum: from increased resistance to China's assertive policies on one end to partial South China Sea retrenchment on the other, with current US policy in the middle. More intense military resistance could include explicitly committing to use force to prevent China from gaining control of additional South China Sea features, interfering with trade and resource extraction, or infringing on the United States' ability to conduct military surveillance and exercises, as well as using force if China pursues any of these actions. In contrast, under a policy of partial South China Sea retrenchment, the United States would not use force to protect regional states' contested claims in the South China Sea, including their territorial claims and maritime rights, even though it has the capability to do so. The United States, however, would remain committed to protecting the mainland territory of its allies and maintain its capability to deny China the ability to operate in the South China Sea during a war. The United States could also continue to send naval ships through the South China Sea during peacetime, including to conduct freedom of navigation operations (FONOPs), and it would use economic and diplomatic means, including sanctions and shaming, to demonstrate that it continues to find China's actions to be illegitimate.[6] Partial retrenchment would grant China a limited sphere of influence over the South China Sea. Critically, partial retrenchment would not allow China to achieve regional hegemony—the United States would retain its treaty alliances and maintain the ability to fight a major war in East Asia to defend them.

Current US policy falls between these two positions. The United States has not taken sides on sovereignty disputes over South China Sea islands and reefs, nor has it specified how it would respond to China's seizure of additional features. It has not employed force to protect countries' resource rights, although it did signal its willingness to use force if China attempted to reclaim land at Scarborough Shoal. The United States continues to call on China to abide by the 2016 tribunal ruling that rejected the legality of China's claims to historic rights and to conduct FONOPs to uphold its interpretation of navigational rights under the United Nations Convention on the

---

6. This chapter assumes that the United States is not already in a full-scale trade war with China and, therefore, has the option to significantly increasing economic sanctions. In spring 2025, however, unrelated to the South China Sea, the Trump administration imposed high tariffs against China; the goals were unclear, but appeared to focus on economic issues, not geopolitical issues. Extensive decoupling of the US economy from China's during peacetime deprives the United States of potentially large deterrent leverage. See Stephen G. Brooks and Ben A. Vagle, "The Real China Trump Card: The Hawk's Case Against Decoupling," *Foreign Affairs* 104, no. 2 (March/April 2025): 76–89.

Law of the Sea (UNCLOS). Moreover, the United States has increased its air and naval presence in these waters and sanctioned firms involved in enhancing China's South China Sea presence to indicate its opposition to some of China's intimidation of littoral states.

I conclude that current US policy is preferable to both increased military resistance and partial South China Sea retrenchment. Because US security interests are quite limited, a significantly firmer policy, which would generate an increased risk of a high-intensity war with China, is unwarranted. Especially with the growing consensus for competing more intensively against China, the United States will require a clear understanding that its interests are very limited to avoid shifting toward this option. In comparison, given the caution that China has demonstrated, the risks of current US policy appear to be relatively small and consistent with US interests, the most important of which is preserving its credibility in the region. Consequently, at least for the time being, the United States should maintain its current level of resistance.

If, however, China's future actions indicate that it is willing to run a much higher risk to control these waters—for example, using force to take control of features claimed by US allies—the United States should then shift to a policy of partial South China Sea retrenchment. Today's policy—including the possibility of not responding to China's aggression—provides the United States with deterrent and credibility benefits at acceptable risk. If facing a more determined China, the US risk calculus shifts—given its quite limited security interests, the higher risks of a war would be unwarranted. The United States would have to redouble other efforts to preserve its credibility with both China and its allies. A partial Chinese sphere of influence in the South China Sea may be a natural outcome of China's rise.[7]

The first and second sections of this chapter review China's claims and behavior in the South China Sea. The third section explores the factors that motivate China's policies in the South China Sea because they can influence the proper degree of US military resistance to these policies. The fourth section reviews US interests in the South China Sea, given the current US grand strategy. The fifth section addresses threats that China's South China Sea policies pose to US interests. Contrary to many expert claims, I find that China's actions in the South China Sea pose little direct threat to US security and peacetime economic interests. The concluding section assesses cur-

---

7. On spheres of influence, see Lindsey O'Rourke and Joshua Shifrinson, "Squaring the Circle on Spheres of Influence: The Overlooked Benefits," *Washington Quarterly* 45, no. 2 (2022): 105–24, Van Jackson, "Understanding Spheres of Influence in International Politics," *European Journal of International Security* 5, no. 3 (October 2020): 255–73, and Graham Allison, "The New Spheres of Influence: Sharing the Globe with Other Great Powers," *Foreign Affairs* 99, no. 2, March/April 2020, 30–40.

rent and future US policy options to determine the proper degree of US military resistance in the South China Sea.

Conflicting Claims in the South China Sea

The South China Sea disputes involve competing claims to territorial sovereignty and maritime jurisdiction.[8] China claims sovereignty over three different groups of islands in these waters. The first is the Paracel (Xisha) Islands, which Vietnam and Taiwan also claim. Since a clash in 1974, China has controlled all the Paracels, which previously were divided between China and Vietnam.[9] The second is Macclesfield Bank (Zhongsha), most of which is submerged and thus not subject to claims of territorial sovereignty. However, Scarborough Shoal, a large reef with several rocks that are permanently above high tide, is contested by China and the Philippines. The third and largest group of islands in the South China Sea is the Spratly (Nansha) Islands, which consists of roughly 230 features, including small islands, islets, and coral reefs, only some of which are permanently above the waterline. China, Taiwan, and Vietnam claim sovereignty over all the Spratly Islands, while the Philippines and Malaysia each claim some features (fifty-three and twelve, respectively).[10] Vietnam currently occupies twenty-nine features, the Philippines occupies nine features, China seven, Malaysia five, and Taiwan one.[11] Although China has not fought another country since 1988 to acquire control of contested features in the South China Sea, it did seize Mischief Reef in 1994 and gain effective control of Scarborough Shoal in 2012. China is believed to have been deterred from beginning land reclamation there in 2016 after President Barack Obama signaled to China that this would violate a redline that could lead to military escalation.[12]

Another component of the South China Sea disputes is conflicting claims to maritime jurisdiction. UNCLOS, which was signed in 1982 and came into force in 1994, delineates different kinds of maritime rights or entitlements that states may claim in zones that are adjacent to their coastlines or

---

8. Ronald O'Rourke, *US-China Strategic Competition in South and East China Seas: Background and Issues for Congress*, Congressional Research Service, August 26, 2024, https://crsreports.congress.gov/product/pdf/R/R42784/153.

9. M. Taylor Fravel, *Strong Borders, Secure Nation: Cooperation and Conflict in China's Territorial Disputes* (Princeton University Press, 2008), 272–87.

10. Greg Austin, *China's Ocean Frontier: International Law, Military Force, and National Development* (Allen & Unwin, 1998), 153–54.

11. Fravel, *Strong Borders, Secure Nation*, 267–99.

12. Demetri Sevastopulo, Geoff Dyer, and Tom Mitchell, "Obama Forced Xi to Back Down Over South China Sea Dispute," *Financial Times*, July 12, 2016.

other land features, such as islands. The first of these is the territorial sea, which extends twelve nautical miles seaward from a state's baselines. Within the territorial sea, states enjoy full sovereignty over the water, seabed, and airspace. Nevertheless, coastal states must allow the "innocent passage" of foreign ships transiting through these waters, including both military and commercial vessels.

A second maritime right is the EEZ, which extends seaward two hundred nautical miles from a state's coast. Within the EEZ, coastal states enjoy the exclusive right to the resources in the water column and the seabed, as well as jurisdiction over other activities, such as marine scientific surveys. Other states enjoy "high-seas freedoms" in the EEZ, defined as freedoms of navigation and overflight. None of the claimants to the Spratly Islands have issued baselines—usually the low waterline—around any of the claimed land features and thus have not delineated the scope of any territorial sea or EEZ claims.

In 2016, China clarified that its maritime claims in the South China Sea included a territorial sea, EEZ, and continental shelf from all island groups. China also asserted "historic rights in the South China Sea" but did not define the scope or content of those rights.[13] Most analysts view this as a claim to rights within the nine-dash line that appears on Chinese maps.[14] An authoritative Chinese scholar describes historic rights as rights to fishing, resource development, and navigation.[15] The 2016 tribunal, however, rejected broad claims to historic rights and found that none of the land features that China (or any other claimant) controls in the Spratly Islands are an "island," which means that they are not entitled to EEZs.

As shown in figure 1, China's claims to maritime jurisdiction overlap with those of the littoral states in the South China Sea, especially where China's nine-dash line overlaps with their coastal EEZs. China's claims to maritime jurisdiction also create conflicts with nonclaimant states, especially the United States, which exercise various high-seas freedoms in the South China Sea. First, China requires foreign military ships to receive prior permission to transit through its territorial sea—that is, for innocent passage—a position that the United States rejects. Since 2015, many US FONOPs have challenged this Chinese position. Second, China has op-

13. Ministry of Foreign Affairs of the People's Republic of China, "Statement of the Government of the People's Republic of China on China's Territorial Sovereignty and Maritime Rights and Interests in the South China Sea," July 12, 2016, https://www.fmprc.gov.cn/mfa_eng/wjdt_665385/2649_665393/201607/t20160712_679472.html.

14. On the origins of the nine-dash line, see Chris P. C. Chung, "Drawing the U-Shaped Line: China's Claim in the South China Sea, 1946–1974," *Modern China* 42, no. 1 (2016): 38–72.

15. Hong Nong, "Interpreting the U-Shape Line in the South China Sea," *China-US Focus*, May 15, 2012, https://www.chinausfocus.com/peace-security/interpreting-the-u-shape-line-in-the-south-china-sea.

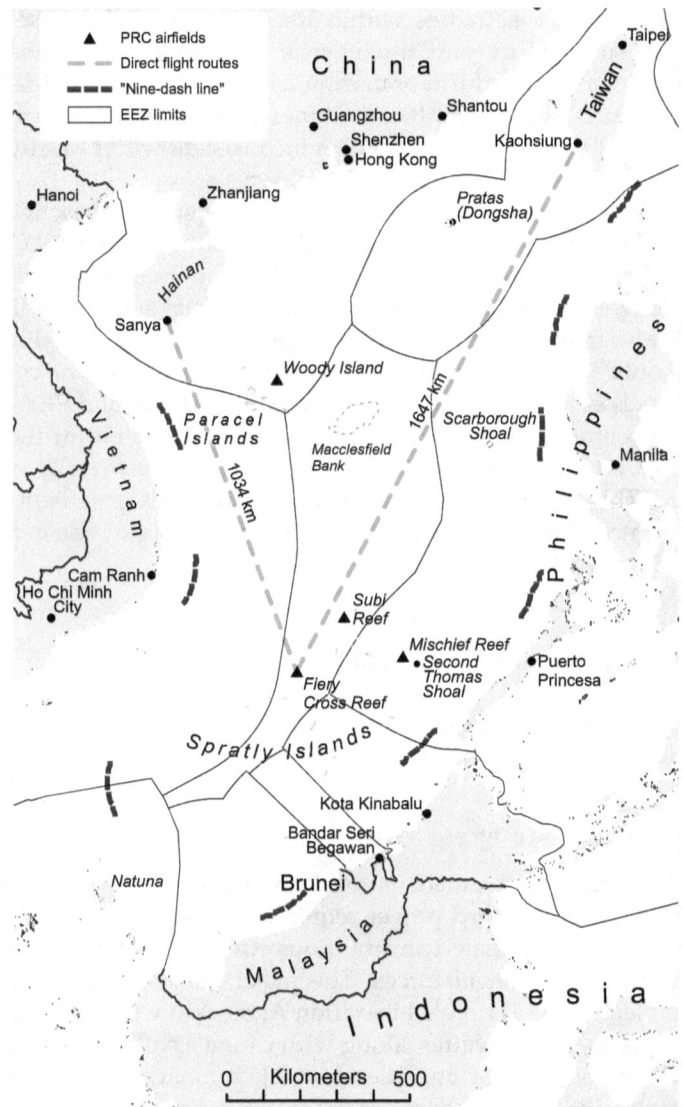

Figure 1. Exclusive Economic Zones (EEZs) in the South China Sea and China's nine-dash line. Map by Andrew Rhodes. EEZs were drawn using data from Flanders Marine Institute, Maritime Boundaries Geodatabase, version 11 (2019), https://doi.org/10.14284/382. The map does not show EEZ claims from disputed territory such as the Paracel Islands. When the breadth between two states is less than 400 nautical miles, the map shows either the maritime boundary determined by a treaty or agreement between the two states or a notional median line. China's claimed EEZ would include the entirety of Taiwan's EEZ as shown on the map

CHAPTER 5

posed some military activities within its EEZ, especially those that are linked with surveillance and intelligence gathering near China's coast, which China claims are a form of marine scientific research that falls under coastal state jurisdiction. Unofficial Chinese legal commentaries also underscore how US military surveillance is inconsistent with peaceful use and the idea of "due regard" for coastal state interests.

Third, the United States opposes China's use of straight baselines, which create internal waters on their landward side. In the Paracels, China has used straight baselines to create a large body of internal waters over which it could deny entry of foreign vessels. Quasiofficial sources indicate that China will also treat the Spratly Islands as an "integral whole," which would create not only a large area of internal waters over which China could deny foreign vessels entry but also much larger territorial seas and EEZs.[16]

Finally, uncertainty remains over the scope and content of the historic rights that China claims within the nine-dash line, especially regarding navigation. This is potentially the most significant disagreement between the two countries because US naval vessels transit and exercise in the South China Sea for a variety of purposes.

China's Behavior in the South China Sea

In addition to reviewing China's behavior in the South China Sea, this section considers actions that China has not taken.[17]

GROWING MARITIME PRESENCE

China has greatly expanded its maritime presence in the South China Sea, which gives it the hard power required to assert its claims. Since the late 1990s, China has pursued an ambitious effort to modernize its military, especially its air and naval forces. The major surface combatants in the South Sea Fleet of the People's Liberation Army Navy (PLAN) include destroyers, frigates, and corvettes, along with China's ballistic missile submarines (SSBNs) and nuclear and diesel attack submarines.[18] All destroyers would be classified as "modern" in terms of their capabilities, and most

---

16. Chinese Society of International Law, "The South China Sea Arbitration Awards: A Critical Study," *Chinese Journal of International Law* 17, 2 (June 2018): 207–748.

17. On changes in China's behavior, see Andrew Chubb, "PRC Assertiveness in the South China Sea: Measuring Continuity and Change, 1970–2015," *International Security* 45, no. 3 (winter 2020/21): 79–121, https://doi.org/10.1162/isec_a_00400, and Ketian Zhang, "Cautious Bully: Reputation, Resolve, and Beijing's Use of Coercion in the South China Sea," *International Security* 44, no. 1 (summer 2019): 117–59.

18. International Institute for Strategic Studies, *The Military Balance 2020* (Routledge, 2020), 266.

have been commissioned since 2010.[19] Some of these naval forces are part of China's growing antiaccess/area denial (A2/AD) capability in the region, which are discussed later in this chapter.[20]

The China Coast Guard (CCG) has over two hundred vessels, making it the largest coast guard in Asia and probably the world. The CCG has played a prominent role in asserting China's rights and claims, from escorting seismic survey vessels in contested waters and enforcing fishing bans to blockading land features held by other claimants and escorting Chinese fishing fleets in disputed waters.[21]

The People's Armed Forces Maritime Militia complements PLAN and CCG forces. These units are composed mostly of fishers, some of whom receive training from the PLAN and are then activated on demand. Militia forces have been involved in many efforts by China to assert its maritime claims, including the 2009 harassment of the US Navy's USS *Impeccable* and China's presence since 2018 around Philippine-held Thitu Island.[22]

A final component of China's maritime presence is the seven military installations atop the reefs that it controls in the Spratly Islands. As part of a large-scale land reclamation in the Spratly Islands, China transformed Fiery Cross, Mischief, and Subi Reefs into forward-operating bases with runways, hardened hangars for fighter aircraft, hardened shelters for antiair and antiship missiles, radars, communications equipment, and large harbors. The wartime utility of these bases is discussed later in this chapter. The peacetime utility, however, is significant—these bases can be used to sustain a forward presence of CCG, maritime militia, and fishing vessels in the southern half of the South China Sea.

ASSERTION OF RIGHTS TO RESOURCES

A key way that China has pursued dominance in the South China Sea has been by asserting its rights to resources. China often describes itself as reacting to the actions of other states that challenge or do not defer to China's

---

19. Michael A. McDevitt, *China as a Twenty-First-Century Naval Power: Theory, Practice, and Implications* (Naval Institute Press, 2020).

20. On China's antiaccess/area denial (A2/AD) capabilities, see US Department of Defense, *Military and Security Developments Involving the People's Republic of China 2020*, Annual Report to Congress (Office of the Secretary of Defense, 2020), esp. 72–76, and Stephen Biddle and Ivan Oelrich, "Future Warfare in the Western Pacific: Chinese Antiacess/Area Denial, US AirSea Battle, and Command of the Commons in East Asia," *International Security* 41, no. 1 (summer 2016): 7–48.

21. Ryan D. Martinson, *Echelon Defense: The Role of Sea Power in Chinese Maritime Dispute Strategy* (China Maritime Studies Institute, US Naval War College, 2018).

22. Conor M. Kennedy and Andrew S. Erickson, *China's Third Sea Force, The People's Armed Forces Maritime Militia: Tethered to the PLA*, China Maritime Report No. 1 (US Naval War College, 2017).

sovereignty claims. Even if reactive, however, China's responses are often disproportionate in scope and scale and have contributed to escalating tensions in the past decade.[23] First, China has asserted its right to develop resources within other countries' EEZs when they overlap with the nine-dash line. Since the first decade of the 2000s, China has threatened that foreign oil companies exploring in Vietnam's waters would lose access to China's market. It also opened blocks for exploration that appeared to be within Vietnam's EEZ.[24] In 2014, China deployed a drilling rig between two Vietnamese blocks. Vietnam's attempt to prevent the rig from drilling sparked battles between coast guard vessels from both sides.[25]

Second, China has harassed or interfered with the hydrocarbon exploration and development activities of other states within their respective EEZs. Since 2010, for example, Chinese government vessels have interfered with Vietnamese exploration activities within Hanoi's EEZ, "expelled" a Philippine seismic survey vessel that was within the Philippines' EEZ, challenged Malaysia's exploration activities within its EEZ and continental shelf, and challenged Indonesia drilling within its EEZ.[26] In one instance, Chinese pressure, including military threats, led Vietnam to suspend exploration and drilling activities by a Spanish company in its EEZ.[27]

Third, China has asserted its rights to fishing within the coastal EEZs of other states. Since 1999, China has instituted a unilateral fishing ban in the South China Sea above twelve degrees north, which includes traditional fishing grounds of littoral states. Since 2016, China and Indonesia have repeatedly clashed over the presence of Chinese fishing vessels inside Indonesia's EEZ near the Natuna Islands, where it overlaps with the nine-dash line.[28]

---

23. You Ji, *Deciphering Beijing's Maritime Security Policy and Strategy in Managing Sovereignty Disputes in the China Seas* (S. Rajaratnam School of International Studies, 2013).

24. M. Taylor Fravel, "China's Strategy in the South China Sea," *Contemporary Southeast Asia* 33, no. 3 (December 2011): 301, https://www.jstor.org/stable/41446232; M. Taylor Fravel, "The South China Sea Oil Card," *Diplomat*, June 27, 2012.

25. Michael Green et al., *Countering Coercion in Maritime Asia: The Theory and Practice of Gray Zone Deterrence* (Center for Strategic and International Studies [CSIS], 2017), 202–23.

26. Michael D. Swaine and M. Taylor Fravel, "China's Assertive Behavior—Part Two: The Maritime Periphery," *China Leadership Monitor* 35 (summer 2011), https://www.hoover.org/research/chinas-assertive-behavior-part-two-maritime-periphery; "China and Malaysia in Another Staredown over Offshore Drilling," Asia Maritime Transparency Initiative, CSIS, November 25, 2020, https://amti.csis.org/china-and-malaysia-in-another-staredown-over-offshore-drilling/; "Nervous Energy: China Targets New Indonesian, Malaysian Drilling," Asia Maritime Transparency Initiative, CSIS, November 12, 2021, https://amti.csis.org/nervous-energy-china-targets-new-indonesian-malaysian-drilling/.

27. Bill Hayton, "South China Sea: Vietnam 'Scraps New Oil Project,'" BBC News, March 23, 2018.

28. Leo Suryadinata, "Recent Chinese Moves in the Natunas Riles Indonesia," *Perspective*, ISEAS Yusof Ishak Institute, February 19, 2020.

BRUTE FORCE, COERCION, AND INTIMIDATION

China has also used its growing maritime power to coerce claimants and other states. Perhaps the most noteworthy incident occurred over Scarborough Shoal. After the Philippines attempted to arrest Chinese fishers within the reef in 2012, a multimonth standoff evolved into a contest for control of the entrance to the reef and its surrounding waters. After reneging on an agreement to enact a mutual withdrawal, China gained effective control of the shoal.[29]

Elsewhere, China has used its CCG and maritime militia to harass and intimidate other claimants, often by maintaining an overwatch position. Starting in 2013, for example, China has maintained a near-continuous presence near two shoals: the Philippine-held Second Thomas Shoal (sometimes preventing the Philippines from resupplying the few marines stationed atop the shoal),[30] and the South Luconia Shoals, within Malaysia's EEZ (including harassing Malaysian oil and gas operations in that location).[31] The frequency of Chinese interference has increased at the Second Thomas Shoal. Over the course of a few years, beginning in 2021, China used force ten times to contest Philippine resupply missions, including a 2024 incident that resulted in damage to Philippine ships and injuries to its personnel.[32] Since 2018, Chinese vessels have swarmed Thitu Island, the largest Spratly Islands feature held by the Philippines, to monitor infrastructure upgrades.[33] These Chinese actions seek to bolster Chinese claims and deter other claimants from strengthening their own claims or positions.

China has also sought to intimidate US naval and air forces. Disagreement over military surveillance operations in China's EEZ "appears to be at the heart" of the incidents between US and Chinese ships and aircraft.[34] In 2009, China interfered with the navigation of the USS *Impeccable*, which was conducting a survey off the coast of Hainan Island, inside China's EEZ. The purpose was to object to what China viewed as an increase in US "close-in" military surveillance along its coast.[35] The United States has also reported "unsafe" maneuvers by Chinese aircraft when they have intercepted US

---

29. Green et al., *Countering Coercion in Maritime Asia*, 95–123.
30. Green et al., *Countering Coercion in Maritime Asia*, 169–201.
31. "Malaysia Picks a Three-Way Fight in the South China Sea," Asia Maritime Transparency Initiative, CSIS, February 21, 2020, https://amti.csis.org/malaysia-picks-a-three-way-fight-in-the-south-china-sea/.
32. Asia Maritime Transparency Initiative, "Shifting Tactics at Second Thomas Shoal," August 22, 2024, https://amti.csis.org/shifting-tactics-at-second-thomas-shoal/.
33. "The Long Patrol: Staredown at Thitu Island Enters Its Sixteenth Month," Asia Maritime Transparency Initiative, CSIS, March 5, 2020, https://amti.csis.org/the-long-patrol-staredown-at-thitu-island-enters-its-sixteenth-month/.
34. O'Rourke, *US-China Strategic Competition*, 46.
35. Green et al., *Countering Coercion in Maritime Asia*, 52–65.

surveillance aircraft; in 2023, the United States reported an "alarming increase in the number of risky aerial intercepts and confrontations at sea" of US and other countries' forces.[36] Although China shadows US vessels conducting FONOPs, it generally does not interfere with them. The one exception occurred in 2018, when a PLAN destroyer sailed on a vector to collide with a US destroyer, forcing it to change course to avoid a collision.[37]

DIPLOMACY

Although China continues to call for negotiations on the South China Sea, its diplomacy reflects its desire to stall in order to increase control in these waters. This is reflected in China's efforts to influence the Association of Southeast Asian Nations (ASEAN) and its statements regarding the South China Sea. In 2012, for example, it leaned on Cambodia to block ASEAN foreign ministers from issuing a joint communiqué to prevent any mention of Scarborough Shoal, which China had seized earlier in the year. China was trying to legitimate its efforts to increase control over the shoal and to preempt public criticism of its seizure. In 2016, Cambodia, likely acting on China's behalf, blocked an ASEAN joint statement from mentioning the arbitral tribunal's ruling.

In addition, China has engaged in a protracted negotiation with ASEAN over a code of conduct for the South China Sea, building on a 2002 declaration. When a draft negotiating text was prepared in 2018, China proposed language that reflected a desire to exclude external states from the region. Specifically, China proposed that the signatories must provide consent for "joint military exercises with countries from outside the region"; this language would have allowed China to veto US military exercises with ASEAN states in the South China Sea.[38] Other Chinese proposed language stipulated that oil and gas development "shall not be conducted in cooperation with companies from countries outside the region."[39] Although ASEAN

---

36. From 2016 to 2018, the US Pacific Fleet reported eighteen "unsafe and/or unprofessional interactions with China." See Ryan Browne, "US Navy Has Had 18 Unsafe or Unprofessional Encounters with China Since 2016," *CNN*, November 3, 2018. Jim Garamone, "Defense Leaders See Increase in Risky Chinese Intercepts," *DOD News*, June 8, 2023, https://www.defense.gov/News/News-Stories/Article/Article/3421766/defense-leaders-see-increase-in-risky-chinese-intercepts/.

37. "US Says Chinese Destroyer Came Dangerously Close to US Ship," Associated Press, October 2, 2018, https://apnews.com/d3d9c8cc8f2e4d16ad54ea240725dbaa/US-says-Chinese-destroyer-came-dangerously-close-to-US-ship.

38. Single Draft Code of Conduct (CoC) in the South China Sea Negotiating Text, October 25, 2018. Regarding a 2023 effort to accelerate progress on the code of conduct, see Prashanth Parameswaran, "What's Behind the New China-ASEAN South China Sea Code of Conduct Talk Guidelines?," Indo-Pacific Program, Wilson Center, July 25, 2023, https://www.wilsoncenter.org/blog-post/whats-behind-new-china-asean-south-china-sea-code-conduct-talk-guidelines.

39. Single Draft Code of Conduct (CoC) in the South China Sea Negotiating Text.

and China are still negotiating the text of the code, neither proposal is likely to be part of the final agreement, given opposition from Vietnam and other claimants. Nevertheless, these phrases reveal China's preference to limit the involvement of non–South China Sea states.

ACTIONS THAT CHINA HAS NOT (YET) TAKEN

Although China's assertiveness in the South China Sea remains persistent, the actions that China has not yet taken since the beginning of its rise in the 1990s suggest that its pursuit of South China Sea dominance has been calibrated to avoid major escalation. China has not sought to seize those Spratly Islands' features currently held by other claimants, though its acquisition of Scarborough Shoal is a partial exception.[40] China has not sought to prevent the US military from navigating in or above the South China Sea, especially beyond the twelve-nautical-mile territorial sea, nor has it declared an air defense identification zone in the South China Sea. China has primarily limited its efforts to contesting close-in surveillance along the Chinese coast in the far northern reaches of the South China Sea. China has not sought to interfere in or prevent military exercises involving the United States and other countries in the South China Sea. China has not garrisoned the forward-operating bases at Fiery Cross, Mischief, and Subi Reefs with power projection forces such as fighter squadrons. China has not drawn straight baselines around the Spratly Islands, although it has indicated that it will.[41] China has not used its economic and other sources of leverage to try to terminate the US-Philippine alliance or to deny US forces access to other South China Sea states. Finally, China has not tried to interrupt or block seaborne commerce.

To pursue its claims in ways that avoid armed conflict, China has employed "gray zone" actors, such as the CCG and maritime militia. When US resistance to China's actions in the South China Sea has increased—including after the 2010 ASEAN Regional Forum and after China completed land reclamation at the end of 2015—China has paused. China's caution matters for my analysis because it indicates that China has been unwilling

---

40. China has used force in the more distant past; in 1974, it fought Vietnam to gain full control of the Paracel Islands.

41. China did, however, in 2024 announce baselines for Scarborough Shoal, which is within the Philippines' EEZ. China reacted to the Philippines' passage of legislation that clarified the right of passage of foreign vessels and aircraft in its waters. The legislation aligns Philippine law with UNCLOS. See Sebastian Strangio, "China Declares Baselines Around Disputed South China Sea Shoal," *Diplomat*, November 12, 2024, https://thediplomat.com/2024/11/china-declares-baselines-around-disputed-south-china-sea-shoal/, and Sebastian Strangio, "Philippines' Marcos Signs Law Aimed at Strengthening Maritime Claims," *Diplomat*, November 11, 2024, https://thediplomat.com/2024/11/philippines-marcos-signs-laws-aimed-at-strengthening-maritime-claims/.

CHAPTER 5

to generate a large risk of conflict while it asserts its claims and pursues increased control.

Factors That Motivate China's Behavior

Understanding China's motives for trying to increase its dominance in the South China Sea provides insight into the feasibility and risks of various US–South China Sea policy options. Building on the analysis in chapter 2, this section assesses the security, resource, national identity, and international status motives for China's behavior.

SECURITY

China's security goals include protecting its mainland, increasing its military capabilities against Taiwan, preserving access to trade, and securely basing its SSBNs. The core of China's efforts to achieve these security goals is its ongoing military modernization, not its actions in the South China Sea that are described in the previous section. In addition, China has security interests related to its territorial claims and maritime rights in the South China Sea.

First, China would like to create a maritime buffer for its wealthy coastal provinces that abut the South China Sea.[42] To protect these regions, China would endeavor to create a layered defense at sea to prevent an adversary from easily striking its mainland. China's emphasis in its naval strategy on "island chains," which include the South China Sea as a critical part of the first island chain, reflects this desire to create a maritime buffer.[43]

The second security motive concerns Taiwan. The People's Liberation Army's (PLA) current approach for an amphibious assault of the island envisions two landing zones: one on the central part of the island's west coast, and the other near the island's southern tip.[44] Defending an assault on Taiwan's southern tip would require sea control in adjacent areas, including the northern reaches of the South China Sea, especially if US forces were based in the Philippines.

A third security motive is to secure the sea lines of communication (SLOCs) that pass through the South China Sea and terminate at various

---

42. Andrew Chubb, "Chinese Popular Nationalism and the PRC Policy in the South China Sea," PhD diss., University of Western Australia, 2016, 48–49.

43. Andrew S. Erickson and Joel Wuthnow, "Barriers, Springboards, and Benchmarks: China Conceptualizes the Pacific 'Island Chains,'" *China Quarterly* 225 (March 2016): 1–22, https://doi.org/10.1017/S0305741016000011.

44. Keoni Everington, "Leaked Map Shows China Plans to Invade S. Taiwan After Taking Kinmen, Penghu," *Taiwan News*, January 20, 2020, https://www.taiwannews.com.tw/en/news/3861097.

Chinese ports. Although many countries, including Japan and South Korea, rely on trade that transits through the South China Sea, the majority terminates in China.[45] China wants to be able to defend these SLOCs because it fears that the United States could interrupt trade through them to gain leverage during a conflict over Taiwan.

China's fourth security motivation concerns the sea leg of its evolving nuclear deterrent. China currently bases its SSBNs on Hainan Island. China has deployed a submarine-launched ballistic missile on its second-generation SSBN that may be capable of reaching the United States from the South China Sea; its next-generation missile will definitely be able to. Given these capabilities, China may use the South China Sea itself as a bastion because its current SSBNs are relatively noisy, which likely renders them vulnerable to US antisubmarine warfare (ASW) capabilities in the open ocean.[46] In addition, control of the South China Sea would facilitate "flushing" China's SSBNs into the western Pacific through deep water in the northern half of the South China Sea.

Finally, China has security interests in the South China Sea itself, generated by its claims to all of the land features, as well as to maritime rights related to these features and the nine-dash line. Although arguably much less important than its other security concerns, China has occasionally described the Spratly Islands as involving its core interests, suggesting that China understands its South China Sea claims as part of its national territory and maritime jurisdiction.

RESOURCES

Resources, specifically hydrocarbons, are frequently mentioned as a key Chinese interest in the South China Sea. Even though China's efforts to assert its claims have stressed resource-related issues, the need for access to resources themselves does not appear to be an important driver.[47] Hydrocarbon estimates for this vast body of water vary widely.[48] One standard for evaluating natural resources as a driver is the extent to which they can reduce China's import dependence.

Chinese control of the South China Sea would not significantly reduce China's dependence on oil imports. Although the South China Sea is estimated to

---

45. "How Much Trade Transits the South China Sea?" China Power Project, CSIS, August 2, 2017, updated January 25, 2021, https://chinapower.csis.org/much-trade-transits-south-china-sea/.

46. For more on China's sea-based nuclear leg and citations, see chapter 6.

47. Because fish stocks have already been rapidly depleted, I do not discuss them in this chapter. U. Rashid Sumaila and William W. L. Cheung, *Boom or Bust: The Future of Fish in the South China Sea* (Ocean Recovery Alliance, 2015).

48. *South China Sea Analysis Brief*, US Energy Information Administration, US Department of Energy, February 2013, https://www.eia.gov/international/analysis/regions-of-interest/South_China_Sea.

have 11.5 billion barrels of proven/probable reserves, the US government estimates that the waters around the Spratly Islands have "virtually no proved or probable reserves."⁴⁹ Instead, most oil deposits lie on the continental shelves of Malaysia, Brunei, and Vietnam, a good portion of which lies outside even the nine-dash line. Given that China consumed around 5.3 billion barrels in 2019, two-thirds of which was imported, control of all the proven and probable South China Sea reserves would do little to reduce China's dependence on imports, especially because its oil consumption continues to grow.⁵⁰ Similarly, of the estimated 190 trillion cubic feet of natural gas reserves, only one hundred billion cubic feet are located in the waters around the Spratly Islands.⁵¹ Much of the remainder lies in the northern half of the South China Sea, within China's EEZ. As China now consumes more than eleven trillion cubic feet per year, which may double by 2040, these reserves around the Spratly Islands would have only a modest impact on China's natural gas imports.⁵²

Looking ahead, new exploration of the waters in the South China Sea might identify new potential reserves. For now, however, China's pursuit of these resources largely reflects concerns about its international status and national identity.

NATIONAL IDENTITY

As described in chapter 2, a country's motives for wanting to control territory need not be determined by material considerations. Both a country's national identity and its desire for status can also matter. National identity can influence the territory that a state believes belongs to it and that it should control. Once this identity is established, the state has a security interest in acquiring or protecting this territory.

China's modern national identity is frequently characterized in terms of two defining strands—historical glory and a century of humiliation—that support its drive for national rejuvenation. Gaining control of a territory it claims in the South China Sea is part of this identity narrative.

China's claims to the islands in the South China Sea have been an established component of the PRC's national identity since 1949. In 1951, during

---

49. *South China Sea Analysis Brief*.

50. "China's Crude Oil Imports Surpassed 10 Million Barrels Per Day in 2019," US Energy Information Administration, US Department of Energy, March 23, 2020, https://www.eia.gov/todayinenergy/detail.php?id=43216. Assuming that only one-quarter of proven or probable oil reserves lie inside the nine-dash line, a twenty-five-year development time frame, and no growth in China's oil consumption, these reserves would constitute about 2 percent of China's oil consumption per year over twenty-five years.

51. *South China Sea Analysis Brief*.

52. Using assumptions similar to those in our oil estimate, these reserves would make up about 18 percent of China's current gas consumption per year.

the Treaty of San Francisco peace negotiations, Premier Zhou Enlai declared that the islands had "always been Chinese territory."[53] Chinese statements since the mid-1950s have used the strong language of "indisputable sovereignty" (*wuke zhengyi zhuquan*) over the Spratly and Paracel Islands to characterize the country's claims. By contrast, China has never used such absolutist language to describe the more numerous territorial disputes on its land borders. A thorough study of China's South China Sea policies concludes that "the political-symbolic significance of the South China Sea dispute is probably sufficient to explain China's consistent refusal to compromise on any of its claims to sovereignty over disputed *territories*, as well as its dogged insistence on the nine-dash line map."[54]

At the end of the Hu Jintao era, China began to change the language that it used to describe its claims. In 2010, China reportedly informed the United States that the South China Sea touched on China's core interests, implying a greater willingness to fight over it and a reduced willingness to compromise. Subsequent research indicated that China had not yet made such a clear-cut declaration, especially in contrast to declarations over areas such as Taiwan, Tibet, and Xinjiang that are now routinely described specifically as core interests.[55]

After becoming the Chinese Communist Party's general secretary, Xi Jinping began to use much more strident language to describe China's general position on sovereignty. In 2013, at the end of a Politburo study session on becoming a maritime power, Xi remarked that while "it is necessary to resolve disputes peacefully and through negotiations . . . in the South and East China Seas, [but] . . . we must not give up our legitimate rights and interests, let alone sacrifice our national core interests."[56] In 2018, Xi underscored that "we cannot lose an inch of the territory left behind by our forefathers."[57]

These leadership statements may, however, mask a more nuanced debate among China's policy elites. Studies show that Chinese elites have not

---

53. Fravel, *Strong Borders, Secure Nation*.
54. Chubb, "Chinese Popular Nationalism and the PRC Policy in the South China Sea," 52–55, quote at 53–54.
55. Michael D. Swaine, "China's Assertive Behavior—Part One: On 'Core Interests,'" *China Leadership Monitor* 34 (2010): 10.
56. Xi Jinping, "Xi Jinping guanyu jianshe haiyang qiangduo de lunshu" ["Xi Jinping's Remarks on Construction Maritime Great Power"], *Taipingyang xuebao* [*Pacific Journal*], July 30, 2013, http://www.pacificjournal.com.cn/CN/news/news263.shtml. See also Xi Jinping, "Xi Jinping: Genghao tongchou guonei guoji liangge daju, hangshi zuo heping fazhan daolu de jichu" ["Xi Jinping: Better Manage the Two Overall Situations at Home and Abroad, Consolidate the Foundation of the Road to Peaceful Development"], *Renmin Ribao* [*People's Daily*], January 30, 2013, http://cpc.people.com.cn/n/2013/0130/c64094-20368861.html.
57. "Xi Jinping huijian Meiguo guofang buzhang Madisi" ["Xi Jinping Meets with US Defense Secretary Mattis"], Xinhua News Agency, June 30, 2018, http://www.xinhuanet.com/politics/leaders/2018-06/27/c_1123046180.htm.

achieved a consensus on the South China Sea. Some consider it a core interest, others do not; some are prepared to generate significant international opposition to China's rise to achieve gains in the South China Sea, while others prioritize maintaining support for its rise.[58] Thus, although China has moved toward increasing the standing of the South China Sea in its national identity, its long-term position on the South China Sea appears not to be fully resolved.

Unlike national identity, popular nationalism does not appear to greatly influence China's South China Sea policy. The public's awareness of these disputes and the general importance of sovereignty does raise the costs for China's leaders of pursuing genuine compromises. But the hardening of China's position does not appear to be a response to public opinion. For example, Chinese police prevented domestic protests during the 2012 Scarborough Shoal standoff as well as in the 2014 oil rig confrontation with Vietnam.[59]

In sum, although the South China Sea has become increasingly important to China, its territorial claims are long-standing and have not expanded in scope. This is not to say that China's claims are reasonable, which they are not, or that they are not the source of serious international conflict, which they are. The point is simply that China's claims are not expanding, which is significant especially in light of its growing power. China is not in the process of creating a new national identity that includes claims that reach beyond those that it established when the PRC was founded. Of course, countries can change their national identities over time. But, overall, the news is good—nothing in this dimension of China's statements and narrative suggests that dominance of the South China Sea is the first step toward further territorial expansion. At the same time, though, the South China Sea's increasing importance in China's national identity does suggest that policies that depend on China compromising on its South China Sea claims are less likely to succeed.

STATUS

A final driver of China's behavior in the South China Sea could be China's desire for both regional and global status. Status desires can influence

---

58. Nie Wenjuan, "China's Domestic Strategic Debate and Confusion over the South China Sea Issue," *Pacific Review* 31, no. 2 (2018): 188–204, https://doi.org/10.1080/09512748.2017.1370608; Feng Zhang, "Chinese Thinking on the South China Sea and the Future of Regional Security," *Political Science Quarterly* 132, no. 3 (2017): 435–66, https://doi.org/10.1002/polq.12658.

59. Jessica Chen Weiss, "Here's What China's People Really Think About the South China Sea," *Washington Post*, July 14, 2016. See also Andrew Chubb, "Assessing Public Opinion's Influence on Foreign Policy: The Case of China's Assertive Maritime Behavior," *Asian Security* 15, no. 2 (2019): 159–79, https://doi.org/10.1080/14799855.2018.1437723.

a state's expectations about the rights and deference that it should receive from others. Rising powers have tended to believe that they have not achieved changes in the political, economic, geographic, and/or institutional status quo that are commensurate with their power. As a result, the rising power may want a sphere of influence and the military capabilities and weapons systems that are associated with greater status. Although a great power could desire these changes simply for material or identity reasons, it could also desire them because they would provide the status associated with being recognized as a major power, the regionally dominant power, or a superpower.[60]

In addition to the broad finding about China's status desires, which were summarized in chapter 2, the argument that major powers will value and demand status recognition from smaller states is especially important in the context of the South China Sea, because China's disputes are with smaller states.[61] Chinese statements hint at the role of status in driving its South China Sea ambitions. For example, at the 2010 meeting of the ASEAN Regional Forum, the United States rallied many countries, including some claimants, to express concerns about recent Chinese behavior in the South China Sea. Staring at his Singaporean counterpart, PRC Foreign Minister Yang Jiechi said that "China is a big country and other countries are small countries, and that's just a fact."[62] Similarly, in 2014, Foreign Minister Wang Yi stressed, in the context of territorial disputes, that "we will never accept smaller countries who make trouble [*qunao*]," implying that China expects deference from other claimants.[63]

Given the limited material value of the South China Sea islands and reefs themselves and the large international costs that China has incurred for its assertive policies, status appears to help explain China's policies. By the time China decided to establish a physical presence in the Spratly Islands in the mid-1980s, the most desirable land features were already held by other claimants. In less than a year, from 2014 to 2015, China's land reclamation reversed this situation. China's physical presence now matches the standing that it expects as the most powerful state in the region and in the South China Sea disputes in particular. As a Chinese scholar remarked after the land reclamation, "We are the big brother now" in the South China Sea.[64]

---

60. For a more extensive summary and citations, see chapter 2.
61. Alex Yu-Ting Lin, "Contestation from Below: Status and Revisionism in Hierarchy," *International Studies Quarterly* 68, no. 3 (2024).
62. John Pomfret, "US Takes a Tougher Tone with China," *Washington Post*, July 30, 2010.
63. Ministry of Foreign Affairs of the People's Republic of China, "Waijiaobu buzhang Wang Yi jiu Zhongguo waijiao zhengce he duiwai guanxi huida Zhongwai jizhe tiwen" [Foreign Minister Wang Yi Responds to Questions from Chinese and Foreign Journalists on China's Foreign Policy and External Relations"], March 8, 2014, https://www.fmprc.gov.cn/chn//pds/wjb/wjbz/xghd/t1135388.shtml.
64. Taylor Fravel conversation with Chinese scholar, Beijing, July 2015.

CHAPTER 5

Concerns about status may also help to explain China's focus on asserting rights to oil and gas resources, given the limited value of the resources. Such assertions are a way for China to demonstrate its desire for dominance and insist upon deference. China likely cares less about the resources and more about whether the other claimants will concede to China's demands for joint development in those parts of their EEZs that overlap with the nine-dash line and thus recognize China's historic rights in the South China Sea.

US Interests in the South China Sea

We should not simply assume that the United States has large interests in the South China Sea. Whether it does depends on causal links between the South China Sea and the fundamental US interests of security and prosperity. As a starting point, I bound the analysis by assuming that the United States retains its current grand strategy—Deep Engagement, as explored in chapter 3, which identifies the following derivative interests in East Asia: US security via the security of its allies in the region, and US prosperity via the region's open trade, investment, and prosperity.[65]

The question then becomes how the South China Sea influences these derivative interests. This section identifies the most prominent links between the South China Sea and (1) the security of US treaty allies and partners, (2) the regional rules-based order, and (3) the military bases that China has built on South China Sea islands.

SECURITY OF ALLIES AND PARTNERS IN EAST ASIA

The United States' commitments to East Asia reflect first and foremost its judgment that the security of US allies is important, even vital, for US security and prosperity. Most importantly, this judgment is manifest in US treaty commitments to Japan and South Korea and, to a lesser extent, the Philippines. In addition, although the United States has not made an unambiguous commitment to defend Taiwan, the broad expectation is that it would do so in the case of an unprovoked attack.[66] As examined in chapter 4, there is disagreement about whether Taiwan is a US security interest. I argued that Taiwan is primarily a political-ideological interest; others be-

---

65. On derivative interests, see Charles L. Glaser, "Rational Analysis of Grand Strategy," in *The Oxford Handbook of Grand Strategy*, ed. Thierry Balzacq and Ronald R. Krebs (Oxford University Press, 2021), 107–22.

66. Richard C. Bush, *The United States Security Partnership with Taiwan*, Brookings Institution, July 13, 2016, https://www.brookings.edu/research/the-united-states-security-partnership-with-taiwan/.

lieve that protecting Taiwan is necessary to preserve US credibility in the region or that Chinese control of Taiwan would undermine necessary US military capabilities.

The importance of the South China Sea to US wartime capabilities varies by country. The United States does not need to pass through or fight from the South China Sea to protect Japan and South Korea; US forces could approach from other directions. In contrast, the US ability to protect Taiwan and the Philippines does depend on its access to the South China Sea, although this dependence could be reduced by using the growing US arsenal of long-range standoff missiles, which can attack targets from a substantial distance.

In addition to its military capabilities, the US ability to protect its allies will depend on preserving its credibility, which in turn depends on not only preserving its military capabilities but also establishing policies that communicate its willingness to fight to protect them. Consequently, the following section explores whether China's increasing ability to control these waters and US responses would put US credibility at risk.

RULES-BASED ORDER IN EAST ASIA

The United States is frequently said to have an interest in preserving the regional order or the rules-based order in East Asia, including most importantly UNCLOS.[67] Some analysts also include the principle of not using force to settle international disputes, which has been a "key element of the US-led international order that has operated since World War II."[68]

Part of UNCLOS addresses activities that the United States engages in to increase its ability to protect its allies and to support maritime norms globally, including rights to the freedom of navigation and overflight in the high seas and EEZs. In peacetime, the United States relies on access to the South China Sea to exercise its naval and air capabilities, train with allies and partners, gather intelligence, transit to other theaters, and demonstrate its commitment to the region. Open access to these waters and the commitment to keeping them open also underpin the region's prosperity, which relies heavily on seaborne transport, including both trade among Southeast Asian states and trade between Southeast Asia and US allies in Northeast Asia.

The value of these rules, and thus the extent of US interest in the rules-based order, depends on their concrete implications. First, their value depends on whether the United States would actually fight from the South

---

67. On orders as means, not ends, see Charles L. Glaser, "A Flawed Framework: Why the Liberal International Order Concept Is Misguided," *International Security* 43, no. 4 (spring 2019): 57–58, https://doi.org/10.1162/isec_a_00343.

68. O'Rourke, *US-China Strategic Competition*, 3–6.

China Sea. As China's A2/AD improves, the ability of the United States to operate surface ships and aircraft in the South China Sea in a large war with China will become unacceptably risky (especially in its northern portion), which would reduce the military value of conducting exercises there.[69] Second, the value of military exercises and other activities depends on the availability of alternative activities that provide similar value. For example, among other purposes, US military presence is intended to signal its commitment to the region. Especially if the United States would fight primarily from east of the South China Sea, in the Philippine Sea, exercising from there should demonstrate its commitment. Of course, whether it actually would demonstrate such a commitment depends on the vagaries of states' assessments of credibility. Third, although UNCLOS rules do not directly affect US prosperity, certain Chinese violations of these rules damage the prosperity of US allies and partners; US failure to prevent China's violations might therefore damage US credibility.

In addition to protecting rights, states' acceptance of rules can reduce the probability of unintended confrontations by coordinating expectations. UNCLOS serves these functions by granting specific rights regarding activities in maritime spaces and access to resources. During peacetime, shared understandings of these rights can reduce military accidents, avoid generating political tensions when the United States operates naval vessels in the South China Sea, and reduce crises between China and other claimants, all of which reduce the probability of the United States getting drawn into conflict. When these understandings are not shared, however, the rules can cause friction or conflict, as they now do in the South China Sea.

SOUTH CHINA SEA AND MILITARY BASES

Although the features of the Spratly Islands are themselves of little value to the United States, having access to the resources of the South China Sea (e.g., fish and petroleum) is valuable to US allies and partners, especially those with growing energy demands and large domestic fishing industries, such as Vietnam and the Philippines.

Whether the United States has an interest in China not having military bases on the South China Sea islands depends on whether China's Spratly bases reduce the United States' ability to protect its allies and partners. The assessment of their military value, in the following section, finds that these bases pose little threat to US military capabilities.

---

69. Biddle and Oelrich, "Future Warfare in the Western Pacific"; Eugene Gholz, Benjamin Friedman, and Enea Gjoza, "Defensive Defense: A Better Way to Protect US Allies in Asia," *Washington Quarterly* 42, no. 4 (2019): 171–89, https://doi.org/10.1080/0163660X.2019.1693103.

Chinese Military Threats to US Interests

Given US interests, how large a threat do China's efforts to dominate the South China Sea pose to the United States? The key military challenges that the United States faces reflect China's overall military expansion and modernization, including regional power projection capabilities. Although not typically the focus of US South China Sea debates, China's improving A2/AD capabilities are significantly reducing the US ability to fight a large war close to China's coast, including in the northern half of the South China Sea, thus limiting US access to Northeast Asia via the South China Sea during wartime. The extent of the threat these new capabilities pose to US interests is the subject of substantial debate. Expert analysis finds that because of limits on the reach of China's improving A2/AD capabilities, they will not undermine the US ability to defend its treaty allies in Northeast Asia (i.e., South Korea and Japan),[70] but they will increase the challenge.[71] In contrast, as described in chapter 4, China's military modernization has already greatly reduced US capabilities in a conflict over Taiwan. Moreover, China's naval expansion has begun to increase China's ability to project power and has significantly increased its ability to maintain a permanent presence in the South China Sea.

China's new bases in the South China Sea deserve special attention because they have played a defining role in apprehensions about China's South China Sea policies and its goals more broadly. These new bases should be assessed in the context of China's improving A2/AD and power projection capabilities, not in isolation.

The following analysis considers four possible scenarios that would engage US interests: interruption of trade, a war over Taiwan, a war between China and the United States over a Spratly feature, and a conflict between China and a regional state that the United States does not join. We also consider their impact on China's ability to protect a bastion for its SSBNs in the South China Sea. Our analysis shows that, unlike China's A2/AD capabilities, China's militarization of the Spratly Islands has contributed little or

---

70. Biddle and Oelrich, "Future Warfare in the Western Pacific." For dissenting views, see Andrew S. Erickson et al., "Correspondence: How Good Are China's Antiaccess/Area-Denial Capabilities?" *International Security* 41, no. 4 (spring 2017): 202–13, https://doi.org/10.1162/ISEC_c_00278. Analysts have explored changes in US and allied military doctrine that can improve these countries' ability to offset China's A2/AD capabilities; see, for example, Eric Heginbotham and Richard J. Samuels, "Active Denial: Redesigning Japan's Response to China's Military Challenge," *International Security* 42, no. 4 (spring 2018): 128–69, https://doi.org/10.1162/isec_a_00313.

71. The increased challenge will be especially large for defending South Korea; see Eric Heginbotham and Richard J. Samuels, "Vulnerable US Alliances in Northeast Asia: The Nuclear Implications," *Washington Quarterly* 44, no. 1 (2021): 157–75, https://doi.org/10.1080/0163660X.2021.1894709.

nothing to the increased challenges that the United States faces in defending its Northeast Asian allies.

INTERRUPTION OF TRADE

Many commentators have argued that China's growing military capabilities threaten the extensive trade that flows through the South China Sea.[72] US prosperity and the prosperity of countries across the globe depend on these major trade routes. The danger posed by China's military capabilities is, however, greatly exaggerated.

To start with, because a blockade during peacetime would likely be viewed as an act of war, China would almost certainly refrain from such a provocation unless it was already involved in a war with the United States or its allies, or expected to be imminently. Thus, despite China's growing military capabilities, there is no significant threat to the region's trade and prosperity during peacetime.[73]

In addition, most shipping could take alternative routes around the South China Sea. During a war, shipping from the Strait of Malacca to South Korea, Japan, and Taiwan could go through the archipelagic waters of Indonesia and the Philippines, which would take only between one and two days longer than if it traveled through the South China Sea.[74] Although not insignificant, these shipping delays pale in importance when compared with an action as provocative as blocking international trade in the South China Sea, let alone fighting a major war. In contrast, China, which itself depends on seaborne trade through these waters more than any other state, does not have any alternative wartime routes. This largely explains why China has long worried about the vulnerability of its Southeast Asian SLOCs.[75]

Finally, whatever capabilities the Spratly bases provide are largely redundant for the interruption of trade. China's overall military modernization already provides this capability for at least the northern reaches of the South China Sea.[76] It is true that these bases increase the ease and speed

---

72. See, for example, Brands and Cooper, "Getting Serious About Strategy in the South China Sea," 16.

73. This lack of a peacetime threat may be somewhat overstated because it does not address the possibility of China blockading Southeast Asian states that are not US allies.

74. Benjamin Herscovitch, *A Balanced Threat Assessment of China's South China Sea Policy*, Policy Analysis No. 820, CATO Institute, August 28, 2017, 7–12.

75. On China's focus on the vulnerability of sea lines of communication (SLOCs), see McDevitt, *China as a Twenty-First-Century Naval Power*, and Zha Daojiong, "China's Energy Security: Domestic and International Issues," *Survival* 48, no. 1 (2006): 179–90, https://doi.org/10.1080/00396330600594322.

76. On China's antisurface capabilities, see Eric Heginbotham et al., *The US-China Military Scorecard: Forces, Geography, and the Evolving Balance of Power, 1996–2017* (RAND, 2015): 153–200. See also Biddle and Oelrich, "Future Warfare in the Western Pacific."

with which China could interrupt trade in the southern South China Sea and contribute to China's ability to intimidate South China Sea states. But if China cares enough, it does not need these bases to interrupt that trade.

TAIWAN WAR INVOLVING THE UNITED STATES

At the other end of the conflict spectrum, we need to consider how the militarization of the Spratly Islands could contribute to China's capability in a large regional war involving the United States. A conflict over Taiwan is the most likely and important scenario in this category. It is widely accepted that China's military modernization has greatly reduced the US ability to defend Taiwan, with a blockade possibly posing the most likely threat.

However, whether China's Spratly bases add much to China's military capabilities in a war over Taiwan is a different question altogether. Some experts have concluded that these bases (as well as China's Woody Island in the Paracels) will contribute significantly to China's overall capabilities.[77] For a variety of reasons, however, China's bases in the Spratly Islands are likely to be of little consequence. First, and most important, the United States would not need to move naval forces through the South China Sea to support its operations in the Taiwan theater. US forces would likely be coming from Japan, Guam, Hawaii, and the continental United States. If the United States needed to bring forces from the Middle East, these forces could bypass the South China Sea by going east of the Philippines after passing through the Strait of Malacca.[78]

Second, the Spratly Islands are roughly 1,400 to 1,600 kilometers from Taiwan, which would put China's growing arsenal of ballistic missiles and unrefueled bombers deployed on these islands largely, if not entirely, out of reach of the center of a battle over Taiwan. Third, most forces that China would employ in a Taiwan scenario are much closer to Taiwan, which further reduces the marginal value of Chinese forces deployed in the Spratly Islands. For example, in 2017, China had thirty-nine air bases within eight hundred kilometers of Taiwan.[79]

Finally, even if these bases were militarily valuable, a modest, albeit not insignificant, diversion of US forces would be sufficient to destroy them. For example, rough estimates suggest that initial attacks against Spratly air

---

77. Gregory Poling, "The Conventional Wisdom on China's Island Bases Is Dangerously Wrong," *War on the Rocks*, January 10, 2020, https://warontherocks.com/2020/01/the-conventional-wisdom-on-chinas-island-bases-is-dangerously-wrong/.

78. Rachel Esplin Odell, "Assessing the Effect of China's Expanded Presence in the South China Sea on the US-China Military Balance," working draft, December 2016, 27–28. Even if the South China Sea features were not militarized, the United States would likely avoid the South China Sea because of submarine and surface ship threats.

79. Heginbotham et al., *The US-China Military Scorecard*, 139.

CHAPTER 5

bases (plus Woody Island in the Paracels) designed to destroy air defenses, disable runways, and damage aircraft would require about 5 percent of the rapidly growing US force of air-launched standoff missiles. The United States has procured over four thousand Joint Air-to-Surface Standoff Missiles (JASSM)—long-range, stealthy cruise missiles—and plans to acquire up to ten thousand, including increasingly capable variants. If necessary, early in a conflict, the United States has a variety of platforms that would be available to attack these bases.[80]

US-CHINA SPRATLY SCENARIO

In this scenario, the United States and China fight over control of one or more of the Spratly Islands. The 2015 RAND *US-China Military Scorecard* posits an illustrative scenario: A dispute over oil and gas resources leads China to occupy an island, and the United States decides to push Chinese forces off the island.[81] The most politically salient contingency in which the United States and China would fight over a Spratly Islands feature would involve islands held by the United States' ally, the Philippines.

We can envision two versions of this scenario: one in which China relies only on forces deployed in the Spratly Islands, and another in which China employs forces based on the mainland as well. As noted above, the United States could destroy the forces deployed on China's bases in the Spratly Islands with a medium-sized attack and prevail in this conflict. The US attack would kill some number of Chinese military personnel deployed on these islands and possibly on Chinese surface ships. To reduce the risks of escalation, the United States could target only those Chinese forces used in the attack while withholding strikes against the Spratly bases.

There are several ways that a conflict of wider scope, involving Chinese mainland-based forces, could develop. China could employ these forces as the United States was defeating its Spratly-based forces or could include mainland forces in its initial operations. Alternatively, the United States could escalate to attacks against mainland bases in anticipation of China's escalation.

---

80. On the bases' vulnerability, see Odell, "Assessing the Effect of China's Expanded Presence," 31–35. On the availability of US forces, see Olli Pekka Suorsa, "The Conventional Wisdom Still Stands: America Can Deal with China's Artificial Island Bases," *War on the Rocks*, February 6, 2020, https://warontherocks.com/2020/02/the-conventional-wisdom-still-stands-america-can-deal-with-chinas-artificial-island-bases/. On their limited military value, see Shahryar Pasandideh, "Do China's New Islands Allow It to Militarily Dominate the South China Sea?" *Asian Security* 17, no. 1 (2021): 1–24, https://doi.org/10.1080/14799855.2020.1749598. On joint air-to-surface standoff missiles (JASSMs), see Sara Sirota, "Air Force, Lockheed Martin Finalize $818 Million JASSM-ER Contract," *Inside Defense*, April 1, 2020, https://insidedefense.com/insider/air-force-lockheed-martin-finalize-818-million-jassm-er-contract.

81. Heginbotham et al., *The US-China Military Scorecard*, 14.

As with the narrower conflict, the United States should also prevail in this one, at least given the currently deployed forces. According to the RAND *Scorecard* (which did not factor in the Spratly bases because their construction had just begun at the time of the study), the United States maintains an overall advantage in this scenario even though China has significantly improved its capabilities. A key difference between the Taiwan scenario—in which China could possibly defeat US forces—and the Spratly scenario is geography. Compared with Taiwan, the Spratly Islands are much farther from Chinese mainland bases and proportionally farther from the relevant US bases in Northeast Asia. Consequently, putting aside China's South China Sea bases, US prospects in a Spratly scenario would be both much better than in a Taiwan scenario and reasonably promising. Although the PLAN surface fleet has been substantially modernized and expanded, the US Navy is planning to purchase more than sixteen hundred antiship missiles by 2025 (e.g., the Long-Range Anti-Ship Missile, the Naval Strike Missile, and the SM-6 Missile) and is upgrading all of its Tomahawks with an antiship capability.[82]

Nevertheless, if China continues to invest in its mainland-based forces, by around 2030, "PLA forces could gain local or temporary air and naval superiority during initial battles." While the United States would still prevail in such a scenario, "US success might entail sustained combat and significant losses."[83]

In short, until 2030 or so, the United States should be able to prevail in a conflict over a Spratly feature. But China's overall military modernization will continue to increase the military cost of this fight, including the risks to US soldiers and the risks of escalation to a broader conflict. The United States would face a deteriorating military environment even if China had not militarized its Spratly features. This militarization contributes to China's capabilities, but it is unlikely to be decisive in determining the outcome of this Spratly scenario.

CHINA VERSUS A REGIONAL STATE

The final set of scenarios involves cases in which China challenges a US ally or partner, and the United States does not join the conflict. There are

---

82. On antiship missiles, see David B. Larter, "As China Expands Navy, US Begins Stockpiling Ship-Killing Missiles," *DefenseNews*, February 11, 2020, https://www.defensenews.com/naval/2020/02/11/as-china-continues-rapid-naval-expansion-the-us-navy-begins-stockpiling-ship-killing-missiles/. On Tomahawk upgrades, see David B. Larter, "US Navy Set to Receive Latest Version of the Tomahawk Missile," *DefenseNews*, March 17, 2021, https://www.defensenews.com/naval/2021/03/17/us-navy-set-to-take-delivery-of-the-latest-version-of-its-tomahawk-missile/.

83. Heginbotham et al., *The US-China Military Scorecard*, 342. See also 338–42.

three types of scenarios: China uses force to gain control of a Spratly feature or resources; China attacks a US ally or partner to compel concessions; and China uses its Spratly bases to harass and interfere with a state's resource extraction. These three scenarios would not directly threaten the US interests, but they could threaten a US ally, the Philippines, as well as principles embodied in the rules-based order that the United States seeks to uphold, and could be linked to regional assessments of US credibility.

China's Spratly bases enhance its capability in each of the scenarios but would not be decisive in any. China increasingly can succeed in these scenarios from its mainland bases and infrastructure. Just as China's mainland-based capability to fight the United States in the Spratly Islands has increased significantly and is expected to continue to improve, China's ability to launch attacks against regional states—including the Philippines and Vietnam—is increasing. At the same time, because aircraft based on the mainland would be close to their range limits in some of these scenarios, especially in the southern portion of the South China Sea, the option to deploy aircraft to its Spratly bases would increase China's capabilities in some instances.

Some experts conclude that China's new bases are designed primarily to coerce Southeast Asia states, forcing them to forgo their resource and maritime claims and providing China dominance of the South China Sea.[84] China, however, can accomplish these activities without relying on its Spratly bases. China's expanded and modernized coast guard can operate effectively across the entire South China Sea, with some ships able to reach beyond it. Nevertheless, China's Spratly bases do enable it to increase the tempo of these operations and to sustain a permanent presence in the southern half of the South China Sea. This likely does intimidate the much smaller claimants and, with sufficient numbers of ships, could increase China's ability to control the waters that these claimants might contest.[85]

BASTION FOR BALLISTIC MISSILE SUBMARINES

China may deploy its SSBNs in a bastion in the South China Sea, which China would defend with its conventional forces. To enhance its ability to find US nuclear attack submarines that are hunting for its SSBNs, China is deploying ASW aircraft. Flying these aircraft from its Spratly bases could increase their operational tempo in the central and southern portions of the

---

84. Poling, "The Conventional Wisdom on China's Island Bases Is Dangerously Wrong."
85. Joshua Hickey, Andrew S. Erickson, and Henry Holst, "China Maritime Law Enforcement Surface Platforms: Order of Battle, Capabilities, and Trends," in *China's Maritime Gray Zone Operations*, ed. Andrew S. Erickson and Ryan D. Martinson (China Maritime Studies Institute, Naval Institute, 2019), 129.

South China Sea.[86] Once a conflict starts, China's regional power projection capabilities would help protect its bastion by preventing US surface ships and ASW aircraft from operating freely in the region. Whether China's ASW capabilities will be significantly increased by flying from Spratly bases is unknown, but the United States would be able to destroy these bases early in a war.

How large a threat China's ability to protect its SSBNs poses to US security depends on the feasibility and value of undermining China's pursuit of an assured destruction capability. If the value is low, and possibly even negative (which chapter 6 argues it is), then even if the Spratly bases enhance the survivability of China's SSBNs, they do not threaten US security. At the same time, China views the current US nuclear strategy as seeking to deny China a secure second-strike capability, which increases the value of SSBNs and a bastion strategy for using them.[87] Thus, an effective bastion would increase China's security without reducing US security.

Chinese Threats to UNCLOS and US Credibility

This section assesses additional threats to US interests—China's challenges to the rules and institutions designed to guide behavior in East Asia (i.e., UNCLOS), to US credibility with China, and to US credibility with its East Asia allies. The most significant danger is that reduced US military resistance to China's effort to dominate the South China Sea could reduce US credibility with both China and US allies. Although the United States retains options that, in principle, should enable it to maintain its credibility—including deepening its alliance commitments—such actions may not be completely successful.

CHINA'S INTERPRETATIONS OF UNCLOS

China's interpretation of UNCLOS requires that foreign military vessels request permission from China before transiting through its territorial waters. This interpretation challenges the principle of freedom of navigation that the United States seeks to uphold not just in the South

---

86. Lyle J. Goldstein, "China Girds for Undersea Battle in the South China Sea," *National Interest*, December 11, 2018, https://nationalinterest.org/feature/china-girds-undersea-battle-south-china-sea-38452.

87. Fiona S. Cunningham and M. Taylor Fravel, "Assuring Assured Retaliation: China's Nuclear Posture and US-China Strategic Stability," *International Security* 40, no. 2 (fall 2015): 7–50, https://doi.org/10.1162/ISEC_a_00215.

China Sea but also globally.[88] China also rejects the legitimacy of US surveillance and intelligence gathering within its EEZ as a form of marine scientific research, which coastal states enjoy the exclusive right to conduct. The United States and China also disagree over the ruling of the 2016 tribunal.

China has not aggressively imposed its interpretation of UNCLOS on the United States. China's opposition to US surveillance is as much political as it is legal—China views these acts as hostile regardless of their legality. Nevertheless, China has not sought to prevent the United States from navigating in the South China Sea, with notable exceptions in 2009 and 2018. Chinese vessels shadow but rarely interfere with or prevent the US naval activities that China opposes, especially FONOPs. Thus, the main danger is the risk of an accident during a shadowing operation or an aerial intercept, which would be small scale and unlikely to escalate.

In the future, China could change either its interpretation of UNCLOS or its determination to impose its current interpretation. It could also pressure the United States to halt its surveillance or FONOPs, and it could expand the scope of the area covered by its current interpretation, most importantly by drawing straight baselines around the Spratly Islands. Moreover, China could expand the list of activities that it would use force to prevent within its EEZ, most notably military exercises.[89] It is also possible, however, that China will change its position on freedom of navigation to reflect the PLAN's increasing ability to conduct surveillance operations near distant countries. This would bring China's position into closer alignment with the US position and reduce friction over this issue.

In short, although a source of military and political friction, China's divergent interpretation of and associated actions related to UNCLOS pose a relatively small security threat to the United States. Perhaps more important is China's insistence on its interpretation and especially its rejection of the tribunal's ruling in 2016. China demonstrated its willingness to ignore international law and incur the ensuing substantial reputational costs. This stance suggests that China may be more willing than previously believed to pursue dominance of the South China Sea, even when facing extensive international objections, and possibly that it is more likely to pursue regional hegemony.

---

88. If enough other countries adopt China's interpretations, then the perceived legitimacy of US operations and activities could be weakened around the globe.

89. China has been largely consistent in its positions on innocent transit, surveillance in its EEZ, and military exercises in EEZs, which suggests significant change is less likely. On China's positions, see Rachel Esplin Odell, "*Mare Interpretatum*: Continuity and Evolution in States' Interpretations of the Law of the Sea," PhD diss., Massachusetts Institute of Technology, 2020, 237–88.

US CREDIBILITY WITH CHINA

China's assertive policies in the South China Sea pose a potential challenge to US security interests by creating conditions that require the United States to respond to preserve its credibility. If the United States does not push back, especially if it stops militarily resisting China's efforts to control the South China Sea, China might conclude that the United States is less resolved to protect its other interests in East Asia. China might conclude that the United States is less determined to protect its allies and partners in the South China Sea region, is less willing to fight to protect Taiwan, and, most worrisome, is more likely to terminate its East Asian alliances and withdraw from the region. China might then adopt a variety of more assertive foreign policies and an intensified military buildup designed to achieve regional hegemony.

These possible Chinese reactions follow directly from the connectedness of credibility logic, which was discussed in chapter 4: When a state makes concession on one set of issues, an adversary may infer that the state will be less likely to uphold its other commitments, if there are relevant similarities across the issues.[90] As in the case of Taiwan, there are similarities between the South China Sea issues and China's possible further expansion in East Asia.

Although the United States should be concerned about its credibility, reducing its resistance to China's efforts to dominate the South China Sea need not significantly reduce US credibility. The United States should be able to sever this credibility link between South China Sea claims and its allies because the extent of US interests in East Asia varies greatly. As a first step, therefore, if it decides to decrease its military resistance to China's pursuit of South China Sea control, the United States should make clear to China that it cares orders of magnitude more about protecting its allies' mainland territory and preventing China's regional hegemony than about protecting states' territorial claims to small features in the South China Sea or even preventing China's dominance of the South China Sea.

Words are cheap, however. Therefore, if the United States reduces its resistance to China's pursuit of South China Sea dominance, it should take costly actions to make clear to China that the United States remains deeply committed to protecting its allies. As with the case of ending the US commitment to Taiwan, these could include maintaining and increasing US military capabilities dedicated to protecting its allies and deepening regional alliances and partnerships. Thus, a well-implemented policy of partial South China Sea retrenchment should be able to preserve US credibility with China for protecting its allies and would therefore be acceptably risky.

---

90. See note 35 in chapter 4 for basic citations.

CHAPTER 5

US CREDIBILITY WITH ALLIES

If the United States does not help to protect its allies' territorial claims and maritime rights in the South China Sea, they may lose them. The United States, however, would not suffer any direct losses. The potential cost to the United States is that its allies and partners might question US credibility for protecting their truly vital interests—their homelands and economies—if it fails to protect their sovereignty and economic interests in the South China Sea disputes. This could weaken or even destroy the alliances, which would in turn damage US security. The Philippines, Vietnam, and Malaysia all face extensive challenges from China. US decisions not to help resist these challenges could create doubts among other countries that have South China Sea claims or interests, as well as among US allies outside Southeast Asia, especially Japan.

The connectedness of credibility logic, which was employed above to analyze US credibility vis-à-vis China, provides the link between US South China Sea policies and its credibility with allies and partners. And the same basic arguments apply here as well: The United States can pursue a variety of military, economic, and diplomatic policies that should sufficiently demonstrate its commitments to its allies. In addition, the United States is by far the best security option available to these countries, which should significantly increase US prospects for preserving its alliances.[91] There are, however, no guarantees—as discussed in chapter 4, Chinese leaders and US allies in Northeast Asia face complex domestic and international environments, which could result in them not following this logic. Thus, although well-designed US policies should be able to maintain US credibility, partial South China Sea retrenchment would generate some risks.

The United States would face still greater credibility challenges in Southeast Asia. Southeast Asia is a diverse region in which countries' inclinations to lean toward or against the United States vary quite substantially.[92] Preserving credibility with the Philippines may be the most difficult because it has urged the United States to clarify that the Philippines' South China Sea claims are covered by the mutual defense treaty.[93] In addition, for decades, the United States' inconsistent attention to the region has generated doubts

---

91. On a declining power's ability to preserve its alliances, see Jasen J. Castillo and Alexander B. Downes, "Loyalty, Hedging, or Exit: How Weaker Alliance Partners Respond to the Rise of New Threats," *Journal of Strategic Studies* 46, no. 2 (2023): 227–268.

92. David Shambaugh, "US-China Rivalry in Southeast Asia: Power Shift or Competitive Coexistence?" *International Security* 42, no. 4 (spring 2018): 85–127, https://doi.org/10.1162/isec_a_00314.

93. Gregory Poling and Eric Sayers, "Time to Make Good on the US-Philippine Alliance," *War on the Rocks*, January 21, 2019, https://warontherocks.com/2019/01/time-to-make-good-on-the-u-s-philippine-alliance/.

about the extent of its interests and commitments, which has increased the opportunities available to China.[94] China has gained regional influence by developing deep economic ties with many Southeast Asian countries—ASEAN is now China's largest trading partner, surpassing the United States and the European Union—which it has used both to demand acquiescence to its interests and to dampen the political costs of its bullying.[95] In part, the United States' inconsistent prioritization of the region reflects its belief that Southeast Asia plays, or at least has played, a limited role in US security.

How Hard Should the United States Resist China?

Although US policy toward the South China Sea comprises a variety of elements, in broad terms, the choice facing the United States is how hard to resist China's efforts to control the South China Sea. This requires the United States to weigh the risks and benefits of different levels of resistance to China's efforts. The key risk of resistance is the possibility of escalation to armed conflict. In addition, increased US resistance could further worsen US-China relations. The key benefit of resistance concerns US credibility with China and with US allies, which can be increased by intensified US resistance.

I conclude that, at least for the time being, the United States should maintain roughly its current level of resistance to China's assertive policies in the South China Sea. Although the risks generated by a policy of reduced resistance are acceptable, current US policy provides benefits that reduced resistance does not. Within this range of current policies, the United States should lean toward less competitive actions. For example, it should consider planning not to respond militarily in the most dangerous scenario—China's military seizure of additional South China Sea features. As explained later in this section, bluffing may sometimes be the United States' best option.

A key reason for retaining the current level of resistance is that China can likely be deterred, which means the risks of the US policy are relatively small. Before its increased assertiveness in the past decade, China pursued a slow and steady approach to increasing its control in the South China Sea.

---

94. Joseph Chinyong Liow, *Ambivalent Engagement: The United States and Regional Security in Southeast Asia After the Cold War* (Brookings Institution, 2017). See also Lynn Kuok, "America Is Losing Southeast Asia: Why US Allies in the Region Are Turning Toward China, *Foreign Affairs*, September 3, 2024, https://www.foreignaffairs.com/united-states/america-losing-southeast-asia.

95. Feng Zhang, "Is Southeast Asia Really Balancing Against China?" *Washington Quarterly* 41, no. 3 (2018): 191–204, https://doi.org/10.1080/0163660X.2018.1520573.

CHAPTER 5

Even by 2025, however, China had not moved to take the roughly forty-five islets and rocks currently controlled by other countries. China has also not moved to limit or restrict foreign military vessels from transiting, patrolling, or exercising in these waters, nor has it attempted to coerce littoral states to stop hosting US forces that operate in the South China Sea. Furthermore, China has sought to increase its control of the South China Sea by relying primarily on its coast guard and maritime militia forces, while depending on the PLAN to back them up only if necessary, which suggests that China is reluctant to provoke a major armed conflict. China's caution suggests that it can likely be deterred.

Nevertheless, because the United States has quite limited interests in the South China Sea, the risks of increased military resistance would be unwarranted. Increased commitments and tighter redlines could appear to directly challenge China's territorial sovereignty claims and its status goals, provoking more forceful Chinese behavior. They could also further strain US-China relations, creating additional incentives for China to strive to push the United States out of East Asia. Additionally, firmer commitments would reduce US leeway for not responding to certain actions and create expectations within the US government and public that the United States should respond to more Chinese provocations.

The United States should continue to update its assessments of China's determination to dominate the South China Sea, which would be reflected in a shift toward even more assertive policies. These could include seeking to reclaim land at Scarborough Shoal and build an additional base in these waters, attacking and seizing features held by other claimants or coercing them to relinquish them, or coercing littoral states to stop hosting US forces (especially the Philippines, which signed the Enhanced Defense Cooperation Agreement in 2014).[96]

If China's future actions indicate that it is much more determined than it is today and, therefore, that US deterrent policies are more likely to fail, then the United States should shift to a policy of partial South China Sea retrenchment. Shifting to a less competitive policy in the face of more assertive Chinese behavior may appear counterintuitive, but this is the logical conclusion. Given the increased risk posed by China, pursuing the benefits of current policy would no longer be warranted. Shifting to partial retrenchment would enable the United States to avoid increasingly dangerous confrontations with China. The risks of reduced resistance, as argued above, should be small if the United States pursues well-designed policies to maintain its credibility with China and US allies.

96. Carl Thayer, "Analyzing the US-Philippines Enhanced Defense Cooperation Agreement," *Diplomat*, May 2, 2014, https://thediplomat.com/2014/05/analyzing-the-us-philippines-enhanced-defense-cooperation-agreement/.

Under a policy of partial US retrenchment, China would be able to militarily dominate the countries of Southeast Asia along their South China Sea periphery. The United States would not use force to protect those countries' territorial or maritime claims in the South China Sea. There would be an exception for treaty allies—specifically the Philippines—for which the United States would protect access to trade in addition to the security of Philippine homeland territory. Critically, the United States would maintain its ability to deny China the ability to operate in the South China Sea during war. It would also continue to send naval ships through the South China Sea during peacetime, including to conduct FONOPs. But, for example, the United States would not engage in operations to break a Chinese blockade of a Southeast Asian country that is not a US ally. This policy of partial retrenchment would, in effect, accept a Chinese limited sphere of influence over the South China Sea, while maintaining the US ability to fight a major war in East Asia. The United States would continue to use nonmilitary means—including sanctions and shaming—to indicate its opposition to China's assertiveness.

The following subsections consider the components of a US policy that continues to resist China's assertiveness in the South China Sea, including the seizure of features, intimidation, further militarization of features, and denial of navigational rights to US naval vessels. US decisions about these components would determine the specifics of its overall policy and the extent of the risks it generates.

The analysis focuses on policy options that bear directly on increasing or decreasing the risk of crises and war because they most significantly influence the risks of resisting China in the South China Sea. Although I do not address them in this chapter, the United States should continue to pursue other policies that do not significantly alter the risk of armed conflict between the United States and China in the South China Sea. These include increasing the capability of littoral states to monitor, patrol, and defend their waters—through maritime domain awareness and naval and law enforcement capacity building—and continuing to call for China to abide by the ruling of the 2016 tribunal regarding maritime claims and the legitimacy of coastal states' rights in their own EEZs.

DETERRING AND RESPONDING TO CHINA'S SEIZURE OF FEATURES

So long as the United States continues to militarily resist Chinese South China Sea dominance, its most consequential policy choice will be whether and how to prevent China from expanding its control over South China Sea land features held by other claimants. These scenarios are the most dangerous because they could involve direct and possibly large-scale conflict between US and Chinese forces.

CHAPTER 5

The United States has a range of options for trying to deter China from seizing a large number of the islands and reefs held by others. The United States could intensify its resistance by explicitly committing itself to use force to defend an ally's or partner's South China Sea interests. The United States could also establish redlines for territorial claims and abandon its current policy of neutrality regarding the underlying claims to sovereignty over the islets and rocks in the South China Sea. The United States has shifted in this direction by partially clarifying the reach of its treaty commitments to the Philippines. In 2019, it included attacks against "Philippine forces, aircraft, or public vessels in the South China Sea" as falling under the US-Philippines Mutual Defense Treaty.[97] The US statement only partially clarified this US commitment because it did not specifically reference the Spratly features controlled or claimed by the Philippines. Thus, the United States could go further and include these features in the treaty with the Philippines and extend similar protections to Vietnam, Malaysia, and Taiwan. To prevent allies and partners from taking advantage of the US guarantee to pursue more assertive policies, the United States could adopt a policy of dual deterrence—promising protection only when China's actions were not provoked by the ally's overtly assertive action. Given limited US interest, these policies are too risky.

Alternatively, instead of clarifying its commitment to respond to China's forceful expansion, the United States could maintain its more ambiguous position. To achieve this, the United States would not further clarify its commitment under the US-Philippines Mutual Defense Treaty, nor would it extend explicit protection to other countries' forces or South China Sea claims. This ambiguity is advantageous because it gives US leaders greater leeway to make decisions that factor in the nuances of specific situations or crises, and it avoids provoking China. The downside, however, is that the ambiguity option could contribute less to deterrence. This set of policies achieves a reasonable balance between the United States' interests and the risks it would be running.

Under either of these policies, the United States could knowingly bluff—threaten to respond to Chinese aggression but plan not to. Bluffing could enhance the US ability to deter Chinese expansion yet avoid fighting if deterrence fails, and it avoids jeopardizing US credibility with its allies. A policy of bluffing might be harder to implement if the United States makes

---

97. Michael R. Pompeo, "Remarks with Philippines Foreign Secretary Teodoro Locsin, Jr. at a Press Availability," US Department of State, March 1, 2019, https://2017–2021.state.gov/remarks-with-philippine-foreign-secretary-teodoro-locsin-jr/index.html. President Biden reiterated the US position in 2024; Bernd Debusmann Jr., "Biden Vows to Defend Philippines in the South China Sea," *BBC*, April 11, 2024, https://www.bbc.com/news/world-us-canada-68794803.

explicit deterrence commitments because US leaders might feel greater pressure from both the public and within the government to meet such commitments, and they might be less likely to critically question the risks and benefits of fighting.[98] Best of all would be if China is deterred, conflict is avoided, and US credibility is preserved. But if China decides to expand, conflict is still avoided, although US credibility would likely be damaged by bluffing. In contrast to the case of Taiwan, where bluffing has many downsides, for the South China Sea, bluffing looks attractive. The South China Sea plays a much smaller role in defining the China threat, is far less important in shaping US military requirements and planning, and is less prominent in the US debate over China. Consequently, US leaders have significantly better prospects for bluffing effectively on this issue.

If deterrence fails and China seizes features held by other claimants, the US response should be influenced by the extent of China's expansion. If China seizes many features simultaneously, the United States could launch military operations to retake those features from China and then to defend them against counterattacks. Such a response would likely result in a much wider conflict with China, which could extend beyond the South China Sea. The risks would be too large; the United States should not fight to retake these features. Moreover, China would have demonstrated significantly increased resolve to dominate the South China Sea, which would support a US shift toward partial South China Sea retrenchment.

Reducing US military resistance in response to extensive Chinese expansion would not entail tacit approval of China's actions. In this scenario, the United States should further intensify military cooperation with its allies and partners, enact substantial economic sanctions, and pursue shaming measures to make clear that China's assertive policies violate widely accepted international norms and agreements.[99] Especially in combination, these policies might deter China from seizing more features in the South China Sea. Even if they do not, these measures would highlight US disapproval of China's actions, which should contribute to preserving US alliances against China.

The US calculus should be different if China seizes only a single feature, such as the Philippine-held Second Thomas Shoal. In this case, China's action would not signal significantly greater determination to control the

---

98. There is, however, extensive debate on audience costs. See, for example, Jayme R. Schlesinger and Jack S. Levy, "Politics, Audience Costs, and Signaling: Britain and the 1863–4 Schleswig-Holstein Crisis," *European Journal of International Security* 6, no. 3 (August 2021): 338–57, https://doi.org/10.1017/eis.2021.7.

99. Michael O'Hanlon develops the case for relying on sanctions in these low-value, high-risk situations. Michael E. O'Hanlon, *The Senkaku Paradox: Risking Great Power War Over Small Stakes* (Brookings Institution, 2019). As noted at the beginning of this chapter, the United States is assumed here not to be in a major trade war with China and, therefore, to have the option of imposing costly economic sanctions.

CHAPTER 5

South China Sea, and the risks of continuing US resistance might not have increased. Consequently, the US decision would be more complicated. To preserve its ability to deter further Chinese expansion, the United States might need to take actions to demonstrate its continuing commitment. Attempting to retake the feature would be too risky, but other actions could be appropriate. These could include imposing economic sanctions, further clarifying the scope of the US treaty with the Philippines, and temporarily or permanently deploying surface and air forces near other features that China might threaten.[100] Although such responses to limited expansion would bolster US credibility with allies and China, deepening the US commitment (except for sanctions) could increase the probability of direct conflict because deterrence of subsequent expansion might nevertheless fail.

DETERRING AND RESPONDING TO CHINA'S INTIMIDATION

China has frequently violated the resource rights of Southeast Asian states and used force to intimidate them. The United States has not used force to prevent China from violating states' rights within their EEZs. One reason why the US Navy has increased its general presence in the South China Sea is to counter Chinese intimidation of Malaysian and Vietnamese oil exploration within their respective EEZs.[101] These presence operations implicitly suggest that the United States would respond to Chinese efforts to disrupt a country's activities, thereby hoping to reduce the fear that China intends to generate.

The United States could extend this type of counterintimidation to all Southeast Asian countries; it could also extend its scope to include harassment and interruption of fishing. The United States could state clear guidelines for when it will engage in counterintimidation operations or leave its policy rather ad hoc. An explicit policy would deepen the US commitment to the Philippines and to nonallied claimant states, contribute more to US credibility for protecting allies' and partners' interests, and increase the salience of China's transgressions. Of course, the United States should only do so if desired by these states, which must manage their own relations with China.

This type of counterintimidation policy would generally be less risky than policies that commit the United States to deter and defeat China's forcible acquisition of islands and reefs. In counterintimidation operations, the

---

100. See O'Hanlon, *The Senkaku Paradox*.
101. Niharika Mandhana, "US Warships Support Malaysia Against China Pressure in South China Sea," *Wall Street Journal*, May 13, 2020; Drake Long, "China's Coast Guard Shows Up at Vanguard Bank Again," Radio Free Asia, July 7, 2020, https://www.rfa.org/english/news/china/vietnam-southchinasea-07072020183440.html.

United States is unlikely to engage in fighting. If actual fighting were to occur, either intentionally or accidentally, the prospects for keeping the conflict from escalating should be reasonably good given the conflict's limited size and stakes. For example, if a US naval ship engages in a skirmish with a Chinese naval ship while trying to counter Chinese intimidation of a South China Sea state that is exploring oil reserves, the incident would take place far from other military forces, the countries would not already be mobilizing their militaries for war, and their leaders would have available many explanations for containing the incident. The credibility benefits of counterintimidation operations could accumulate rather quickly because China's encroachments have occurred relatively frequently. Yet the frequency of China's encroachments means that there would be more events that could escalate to the use of force if China chose to use its naval ships to escort its commercial vessels.

An alternative variant that avoids the increased probability of military conflict would be to respond to Chinese intimidation by imposing economic sanctions instead of employing military threats. For example, the United States could sanction Chinese individuals or firms that seek to extract resources from within the EEZs of Vietnam, Malaysia, and the Philippines. Another alternative would be for the United States to provide public guarantees to protect US firms that are involved in projects or operating in the EEZs of these states. These alternatives are likely preferable to the expanded counterintimidation option because US interests do not warrant even that level of greater risk.

RESPONDING TO CHINA'S MILITARIZATION OF FEATURES

Whatever level of resistance to China's assertiveness the United States chooses, it must ensure that China understands that its South China Sea bases do not significantly reduce the US ability to defend its allies in a large war. The United States should therefore deploy any additional forces (e.g., air-launched standoff missiles) that might be required to confidently defeat China's buildup in the Spratly Islands and make clear that it will continue to offset improvements to these Chinese bases.[102] This policy should put to rest concerns that China's South China Sea bases are weakening US capabilities by requiring the country to divert forces that would otherwise be committed to essential missions in other parts of the East Asia theater. Because the additional forces are small relative to the overall US force, this acquisition will not unduly burden the US defense budget.

---

102. In fact, the United States is already doing this; see note 80 on acquisition of standoff missiles.

CHAPTER 5

The United States should not, however, place great political significance, as opposed to military significance, on China's Spratly bases, given that China already occupies them.[103] Instead, it should view this military buildup as another component of China's ongoing military modernization and enlargement, and plan to offset it.

PROTECTING THE NAVIGATIONAL RIGHTS OF US NAVAL VESSELS

The United States will need to preserve its military capabilities for fighting a large war in East Asia even if it decides to reduce its opposition to China's efforts to dominate the South China Sea. Whether this requires continuing to exercise its naval forces and to gather intelligence in the South China Sea will depend on the evolution of China's regional military capabilities. As long as the United States plans to fight from the South China Sea, it should continue to exercise the full range of high-seas freedoms, including transiting through these waters and airspace, operating in these waters (including surveys and surveillance), and conducting exercises in these waters with other states. Given China's current positions on UNCLOS, surveillance is the only source of explicit friction in China's EEZ. If, however, China clarifies its position on the nine-dash line to include denying high-sea freedoms, expanding its restriction on military operations in its EEZ, or issuing baselines around the Spratly Islands (and thus formally claiming a much greater area of jurisdiction under UNCLOS), then the US-China mismatch will grow much larger.

The United States should also continue to occasionally conduct FONOPs. These operations are part of exercising high-seas freedoms but are arguably less important than the simple practice of navigation and presence in these waters. Unlike the military exercises discussed above, which are designed to enhance US military capabilities, FONOPs demonstrate that the United States is unwilling to accept China's interpretation of UNCLOS and any effort to limit navigation in the South China Sea. There is little material value in transiting through territorial waters, but failing to exercise this right might mislead China into believing that the United States will accept more problematic Chinese claims about its historic rights in the South China Sea and straight baselines in the Spratly Islands. Given this purpose, the United States should reduce if not eliminate the publicity of individual FONOPs because it incites Chinese nationalist reactions without doing much to advance the FONOP's relatively narrow purpose of asserting the US interpretation of UNCLOS.

In addition, the United States should consider possibilities for reducing clashes and friction while preserving its military capabilities and credibil-

---

103. For an opposing view, see Ratner, "Course Correction," 69–70.

ity. For example, the United States might be able to reduce somewhat the scope and tempo of surveillance activities, especially if other means can be used to gather the same intelligence, even though China's continued modernization may increase the demand for such operations. Similarly, the United States should keep the frequency of FONOPs relatively low. The United States also should remember that China's key positions on UNCLOS—including on innocent passage and surveillance within EEZs—are longstanding, dating back to the early discussions of the convention and restated when China accepted the overall package encompassed by the treaty. Therefore, China's opposition to FONOPs does not reflect a fundamental change in its position.[104]

This chapter has analyzed the challenges that China's more assertive policies in the South China Sea pose to US interests. It summarized China's policies, examined US interests, and identified three broad US options—increased resistance, current US policy, and partial retrenchment.

I concluded that the United States' best option is to maintain its current level of resistance to China's efforts to dominate the South China Sea. This policy brings dangers—the possibility that US deterrent policies would fail and that a conflict would escalate to a larger war—but these escalatory risks currently appear to be limited and in line with US interests. Intensified US resistance would tend to generate still greater risks, which would exceed US interests.

If China becomes much more assertive in the South China Sea and more willing to fight to achieve its objectives, the risks of the current policy would no longer be warranted. The cost of reducing US resistance and shifting to partial retrenchment would be small if the United States could retain its credibility with its allies and China. Although this should be possible, it might not be easy.

Given the uncertainty about the future, the United States should take steps now to deepen its credibility, which could include enhancing its regional force structure, selling military and maritime awareness equipment to allies and partners, increasing joint exercises with South China Sea claimants, sharing information, furthering integration across alliance partners, and consistently prioritizing East Asia. Although US policies will likely appear somewhat threatening to China, this risk is warranted given the possibility of future increases in China's South China Sea ambitions.

If China's policy becomes more assertive, US allies and partners are likely to seek intensified security cooperation with the United States. Chinese behavior that increases states' insecurity will encourage intensified balancing

---

104. Odell, "*Mare Interpretatum*," 261. See also Ronald O'Rourke, *Maritime Territorial and Exclusive Economic Zone (EEZ) Disputes Involving China: Issues for Congress*, Congressional Research Service, March 24, 2018, 8–9.

with the United States—allies are likely to become more open to basing US forces on their respective territories and sharing defense responsibilities with the United States. The result would be a decrease in the risk of partial South China Sea retrenchment.

In closing, it is important to emphasize again that while maintaining its current level of military resistance to Chinese control of the South China Sea, the United States must keep the stakes in mind. Although China's assertive policies in the South China Sea violate international norms and create reasonable fears that China will become still more assertive, there is very little of material value at stake for the United States. Exaggerating the value of the South China Sea could undermine US policy by fueling overly competitive policies in the South China Sea and more broadly against China. To avoid this pitfall, the United States must be vigilant in critically assessing its interests in the South China Sea.

PART III. US MILITARY STRATEGY

CHAPTER 6

Nuclear Strategy

Should the United States Pursue a Damage-limitation Capability?

China is increasing the size, diversity, and sophistication of its nuclear arsenal.[1] At the beginning of the century, China lacked a large nuclear retaliatory capability against the United States and possibly any retaliatory capability at all. Now China has or soon will have a truly massive retaliatory capability against US economic, logistical, and population targets—an "assured destruction capability" in the lingo of nuclear strategy.

The implications for US security are potentially quite significant. In the past, the United States' ability to destroy most or even all of China's nuclear force likely contributed to its ability to deter Chinese conventional attacks against US allies and partners.[2] Today, China's leaders could reasonably judge that US nuclear escalation is less likely because China possesses a massive retaliatory capability. Also worrying, US allies took some comfort in the US nuclear advantage; the loss of the US damage-limitation capability is thus generating doubts about the adequacy of US nuclear extended deterrence commitments. And, of course, the US nuclear advantage provided a more direct benefit—the United States would have suffered far less damage in an all-out nuclear war than it would today.

The reduction in US deterrent capabilities is all the more salient because China has greatly improved its conventional military capabilities—most importantly, its ability to blockade and even invade Taiwan, as discussed in

---

1. This chapter draws heavily on an article that I coauthored with Steve Fetter: Charles L. Glaser and Steve Fetter, "Should the United States Reject MAD?: Damage Limitation and US Nuclear Strategy Toward China," *International Security* 41, no. 1 (summer 2016): 49–98.

2. Jacob Stokes, *Atomic Strait: How China's Nuclear Buildup Shapes Security Dynamics with Taiwan and the United States,* Center for a New American Security, February 2023, 1, https://www.cnas.org/press/press-release/atomic-strait-how-chinas-nuclear-buildup-shapes-security-dynamics-with-taiwan-and-the-united-states.

chapter 4. In addition, under President Xi Jinping, China appears more determined to unite with Taiwan, through the use of force if necessary, and possibly to become the hegemonic power in East Asia. The combination of China's increased capability and increased determination means the US requirements for deterrence have increased. Unfortunately, this is occurring at the same time as the ability of US nuclear forces to contribute to deterrence has decreased.

The United States therefore must decide whether to attempt to regain a significant damage-limitation capability—that is, the ability to meaningfully reduce the costs that China can inflict in a retaliatory attack. Given the benefits, that answer might seem obvious. Moreover, the pursuit of a damage-limitation capability is required by current US nuclear strategy. Although it emphasizes deterrence, US strategy implies a role for damage limitation and emphasizes the targeting of adversary nuclear forces, which is required for damage limitation.[3] Not pursuing damage limitation would require a fundamental change in long-standing US nuclear strategy.

There are, however, a variety of reasons for questioning US pursuit of damage limitation. First is feasibility: Regaining a significant damage limitation capability against China promises to be exceedingly challenging, likely impossible. As China increases the size of its force, and especially as it deploys its forces in more survivable basing modes, the technological difficulty of significantly limiting damage grows dramatically. Second, the strategic, political, and economic costs of pursuing a damage-limitation capability could be large. The forces the United States would have to deploy would create pressures during a crisis or war for deliberate escalation by both countries, for an accidental launch by China, and for miscalculations by China that could fuel unwarranted escalation. In addition, the competitive military policies required to maintain a damage-limitation capability would likely strain the US-China relationship, thereby making serious crises and conflict more, rather than less, likely. And a damage-limitation strategy would require the United States to make larger investments in its strategic nuclear forces. Third, the benefits are easily exaggerated: Anything short of a highly effective, high-confidence capability would not add much to deterrence. In part, this is because even when China has an assured destruction capability, US nuclear weapons can contribute significantly to deterrence.

Whether to pursue a damage-limitation capability is far and away the most important nuclear policy decision facing the United States. It will define the essence of US nuclear strategy and the overall US-China nuclear relationship, determining how competitive US strategy is and how threatening

---

3. US Department of Defense, *2022 Nuclear Posture Review*, October 27, 2022, 8, https://apps.dtic.mil/sti/trecms/pdf/AD1183514.pdf.

its nuclear forces appear to China. A damage-limitation strategy is inherently competitive, requiring the United States to defeat China's efforts to make its nuclear forces survivable. As a result, a damage-limitation strategy will require much greater innovation and investment in US nuclear capabilities. In contrast, if the United States accepts China's acquisition and maintenance of an assured destruction capability, current US forces would be adequate to support US strategy.[4] US and Chinese force requirements would be largely compatible; both states would simultaneously be able to satisfy their deterrence requirements, and arms competition between them should taper off. In other words, if the United States understands its nuclear requirements in terms of its ability to inflict damage, then nuclear weapons largely eliminate the nuclear security dilemma between the United States and China.

The United States certainly faces other important nuclear decisions. Improvements in China's overall military capabilities are raising questions about whether the United States needs to revise how it extends nuclear deterrence to Japan and South Korea. China's deployment of theater nuclear forces has generated calls for the United States to pursue nuclear sharing arrangements with these allies.[5] And the problem of "two nuclear peers," created by China's maturing nuclear force and Russia's nuclear arsenal, has generated a good deal of concern and debate.[6] Decisions on these issues, however, will have much smaller implications than the US decision about whether to pursue a damage-limitation decision or will simply reflect it.

This chapter begins with a brief overview of China's expansion and modernization of its strategic nuclear force. The second section explores the concept of damage limitation, including the question of where the threshold for a damage-limitation capability should be drawn, which influences the requirements for achieving one. The third section analyzes the United States' prospects for achieving a significant damage-limitation capability, assuming that China responds to preserve its own assured destruction capability. The following sections assess the potential benefits and cost of US pursuit of damage-limitation capability.

---

4. US nuclear forces would still require replacement, but primarily because they are aging, not because their capabilities need to be enhanced. On current plans, see Amy F. Wolff, "US Strategic Nuclear Forces: Background, Developments, and Issues," Congressional Research Service, December 14, 2021.

5. Evan Braden Montgomery and Toshi Yoshihara, "The Real Challenge of China's Nuclear Modernization," *Washington Quarterly* 45, no. 4 (winter 2023): 45–60.

6. For opposing positions of this debate, see *Study Group Report, China's Emergence as a Second Nuclear Peer: Implications for US Nuclear Deterrence Strategy*, Lawrence Livermore, 2023, https://cgsr.llnl.gov/content/assets/docs/CGSR_Two_Peer_230314.pdfLivermore study, and Charles L. Glaser, James M. Acton, and Steve Fetter, "The US Nuclear Arsenal Can Deter Both China and Russia: Why America Doesn't Need More Missiles," *Foreign Affairs*, October 5, 2023, https://www.foreignaffairs.com/united-states/us-nuclear-arsenal-can-deter-both-china-and-russia.

These assessments engage an ongoing debate about nuclear strategy. Skeptics of damage limitation build their arguments largely on the theory of the nuclear revolution, which expects that the tremendous destructive potential of nuclear weapons tends to strongly favor retaliation over damage limitation in competition between major powers and, therefore, that competition will result in both countries possessing assured destruction capabilities. The result is a world of mutual assured destruction (MAD) capabilities. The theory of the nuclear revolution sees little or no value in targeting an adversary's nuclear forces when the adversary possesses an assured destruction capability and emphasizes the strategic and political implications of massive societal vulnerability for states' security. In contrast, proponents of damage limitation argue that the history of the Cold War nuclear competition raises serious doubts about whether states can maintain their massive retaliatory capabilities and holds that a modest damage-limitation capability, or even the possibility of having acquired such a capability, is valuable for deterrence.[7]

I conclude that the United States should forgo efforts to regain its damage-limitation capability. In part, this assessment reflects a technical judgment. China is continuing to deploy a larger and more mobile force, and improving its nuclear command and control (C2) capabilities. If the United States deploys the systems required to find and target China's mobile intercontinental ballistic missiles (ICBMs)—most importantly, space-based radars (SBRs)—China should be able to employ countermeasures that defeat them. As important, however, is that the value of a damage-limitation capability to the United States is small. If such a capability were necessary for protecting vital US interests, then a case could be made for investing great sums in intense military competition to acquire one, even if the probability of limited success were low. The United States faces a much less daunting security environment, however. It will be able to continue to meet its extended deterrence commitments to its East Asian treaty allies without a damage-limitation capability. Most importantly, the combined conventional capabilities of the United States and these allies, especially Japan, should be sufficient to prevent China from winning a major conventional war and thereby to deter large Chinese conventional attacks. In addition, even without a US damage-limitation capability, the possibility that a large conventional war could escalate to a nuclear war should contribute signifi-

---

7. Robert Jervis, *The Meaning of the Nuclear Revolution: Statecraft and the Prospect of Armageddon* (Cornell University Press, 1990); Charles L. Glaser, *Analyzing Strategic Nuclear Policy* (Princeton University Press, 1990); Austin Long and Brendan Rittenhouse Green, "Stalking the Secure Second Strike: Intelligence, Counterforce, and Nuclear Strategy," *Journal of Strategic Studies* 38, nos. 1–2 (2015): 38–73; Brendan Rittenhouse Green, *The Revolution That Failed: Nuclear Competition, Arms Control, and the Cold War* (Cambridge University Press, 2020); Keir A. Lieber and Daryl G. Press, *The Myth of the Nuclear Revolution: Power Politics in the Atomic Age* (Cornell University Press, 2020).

cantly to deterring a large Chinese conventional attack. If the United States and its allies conclude that the credibility of US extended deterrence commitments needs to be enhanced, they will have a variety of options, including enhancing alliance conventional capabilities and deploying theater nuclear forces in the region. Consequently, the marginal deterrent value of a significant damage-limitation capability is small, and the value of a modest damage-limitation capability is even smaller.

Compared to these limited benefits, the potential costs and risks of the United States striving to regain its damage-limitation capability are large. Doing so could increase a variety of escalatory dangers, including accidental and unauthorized Chinese attacks resulting from a Chinese shift to a launch-on-warning (LOW) posture and possibly to predelegation of launch authority, inadvertent nuclear escalation driven by US attacks against China's dual-capable forces and C2, early Chinese intentional limited nuclear escalation driven by China's fears of US preemptive attacks, and incentives for the United States to launch large counterforce attacks in a crisis or early in a conventional war. In addition, US pursuit of a damage-limitation capability would fuel strategic nuclear competition and further strain already troubled US-China relations.

The requirements for protecting Taiwan are the possible exception. As addressed in chapter 4, Taiwan is much harder to defend and China is much more determined to prevail. Fortunately, Taiwan is not a vital US interest. If, however, the United States retains its commitment—whether ambiguous or certain—to come to Taiwan's defense, then there is a case for pursuing a damage-limitation capability. There are scenarios in which China might be willing to challenge the United States' and Taiwan's conventional capabilities, and China would enjoy an advantage in resolve in bargaining over Taiwan. Competing for a damage-limitation capability, even if the United States were unsuccessful, might communicate US resolve and increase China's assessment that the United States would escalate to nuclear war, based on the belief that the United States believed that it possessed at least some damage-limitation capability. Although this is the strongest case for the United States to pursue a damage-limitation capability against China, I find that it, too, falls short.

My overall conclusion fits well with this book's effort to identify policies that manage the security dilemma by striking a healthy balance between providing necessary deterrent capabilities and avoiding creating Chinese insecurity. From this perspective, US acceptance of China's acquisition of an assured destruction capability is an easy call. A US strategy that accepts China's assured destruction capability and emphasizes deterrence via threats to China's economic, industrial, and population centers, instead of via targeting its nuclear forces, provides the vast majority of deterrence that is feasible. Pursuing a damage-limitation capability promises little additional deterrence but a great deal of Chinese insecurity, numerous pressures and incentives for escalation in a severe crisis or war, and intense US-Chinese military competition.

CHAPTER 6

Overview of China's Nuclear Forces and Motivations

China has significantly modernized and expanded its strategic nuclear arsenal over the past couple of decades. It is working toward an increasingly capable triad of forces, composed of land-based and sea-based intercontinental ballistic missiles and long-range bombers.

The land-based missile leg is currently the most important. At the beginning of this century, China had only about twenty ballistic missiles (DF-5s) capable of reaching the United States, which were deployed in silos that were highly vulnerable to US attack. By 2025, China had deployed roughly 170 ICBMs capable of reaching the continental United States. Almost 120 of these were road mobile—DF-31s and DF-41s. At least some of the DF-41s are equipped with multiple independently targetable reentry vehicles (MIRVs) and can carry three warheads; some of China's newest mobile ICBMs are reported to have off-road capabilities.[8] China is constructing over three hundred new ICBM silos and likely has begun to deploy missiles in some of them.[9] Whether China will deploy missiles in all of the silos is uncertain; it might instead leave some empty, using a "shell game" that could require an attacker to target all of these silos even though only some contained missiles. In addition, China is building some new silos for DF-5s and is constructing new bases for mobile ICBMs, which indicates it plans to continue to increase their number.

China has deployed six ballistic missile submarines (SSBNs), each of which can carry twelve submarine-launched ballistic missiles (SLBMs). These submarines have carried the JL-2 SLBM, which could reach Alaska and Hawaii from China's littoral waters, but could not reach the continental United States. China has begun deploying a longer-range SLBM—the JL-3—and may have replaced all of the JL-2s. The JL-3 appears to be capable of targeting the northwestern parts of the continental United States from China's northern coastal waters; if adapted to carry a single warhead, it should be able to reach the East Coast of the United States from the South China Sea. China is expected to begin construction of its next-generation SSBN by the middle of

---

8. Hans M. Kristensen, Matt Korda, Eliana Johns, and Mackenzie Knight, "Chinese Nuclear Weapons, 2025," *Bulletin of the Atomic Scientists* 81, no. 2 (March 12, 2025), 135–60, https://www.tandfonline.com/doi/epdf/10.1080/00963402.2025.2467011?needAccess=true. This includes thirty ICBMs estimated to be deployed in new silos.

9. Shannon Bugos and Michael Klare, "Pentagon: Chinese Arsenal Exceeds 400 Warheads," *Bulletin of the Atomic Scientists* (January/February 2023), https://www.armscontrol.org/act/2023-01/news/pentagon-chinese-nuclear-arsenal-exceeds-400-warheads; US Department of Defense, *Military and Security Developments Involving the People's Republic of China, 2023*, Annual Report to Congress, https://media.defense.gov/2023/Oct/19/2003323409/-1/-1/1/2023-MILITARY-AND-SECURITY-DEVELOPMENTS-INVOLVING-THE-PEOPLES-REPUBLIC-OF-CHINA.PDF.

the 2020s. The current generation of Chinese SSBNs are relatively noisy and would therefore be vulnerable to US antisubmarine warfare (ASW) in the open ocean. China is likely, therefore, to adopt a bastion strategy—deploying its SSBNs in its coastal waters and protecting them with conventional forces. China's next generation SSBNs should be quieter, possibly much quieter—Russia has been reported to have provided China with assistance in reducing the noise produced by the submarines' propulsion system.[10]

The least developed leg of China's nuclear force is its strategic bombers force, but here, too, China is modernizing. In 2020, it fielded a bomber that can carry a nuclear air-launched ballistic missile (ALBM). If refueled and paired with a new long-range ALBM, this bomber would be able to attack the United States without having to penetrate US airspace. Otherwise, this bomber will be limited to theater missions. China is expected to increase the size of its bomber force and to develop a stealth bomber.[11]

The key motive for China's nuclear modernization is likely China's long-standing concern about the adequacy of its retaliatory capabilities.[12] In addition to ensuring against a surprise attack, a large retaliatory capability increases China's ability to deter US escalation of a conventional war that the United States is losing. China could fear that the United States, if losing a conventional war, would escalate to nuclear weapons to weaken China's conventional capabilities and/or to compel China to accept defeat. Further, China could believe that the United States is more likely to escalate if it can limit the damage it would suffer in an all-out nuclear war. By essentially eliminating the possibility of significant damage limitation, China's modernization would, therefore, reduce the probability of US nuclear escalation, which would in turn reduce the US ability to deter Chinese conventional

---

10. Anthony Capaccio, "China Has Put Longer-Range ICBMs on Its Nuclear Subs, US Says," Bloomberg, November 18, 2022, 13, https://www.bloomberg.com/news/articles/2022-11-18/us-says-china-s-subs-armed-with-longer-range-ballistic-missiles?leadSource=uverify%20wall; Kristensen et al., "Chinese Nuclear Weapons, 2025."

11. Stacy Pettyjohn and Jennie Matuschak, *Long Shadows: Deterrence in a Multipolar Age*, Center for a New American Security, May 2022, https://www.cnas.org/press/press-release/new-cnas-report-long-shadows-deterrence-in-a-multipolar-nuclear-age. On the ALBM, see Thomas Newdick, "China's H-6k Bomber Seen Firing Air-Launched Ballistic Missile for First Time," *WarZone*, May 1, 2024, https://www.twz.com/air/chinas-h-6k-bomber-seen-firing-air-launched-ballistic-missile-for-first-time.

12. Henrik Stalhane Hiim, M. Taylor Fravel, and Magnus Langset Troan, "The Dynamics of an Entangled Security Dilemma: China's Changing Nuclear Posture," *International Security* 47, no. 4 (spring 2023): 147–87; David C. Logan and Phillip C. Saunders, *Discerning the Drivers of China's Nuclear Force Development: Models, Indicators, and Data*, Center for the Study of Chinese Military Affairs, National Defense University, July 2023; Fiona S. Cunningham, "Cooperation Under Asymmetry? The Future of US-China Arms Control," *Washington Quarterly* 44, no. 2 (2021): 163. My brief description in this paragraph covers what Logan and Saunders term the "secure second strike" model and the "nuclear shield" model.

aggression, especially over Taiwan.[13] In addition, as noted in chapter 2, China sees its nuclear arsenal contributing to its great-power status. Consequently, it may build a force that is larger and more technologically advanced than if it wanted only a flexible assured destruction capability.[14]

The Concept of Damage Limitation

Before evaluating whether the United States should pursue a damage-limitation capability, it is essential to consider what is meant by and required for damage limitation. A damage-limitation attack is designed to reduce the adversary's ability to inflict damage in a retaliatory attack. To achieve damage limitation, the United States would attack China's nuclear forces, as well as the C2 capabilities that China relies on to launch these forces. It would also employ ballistic missile defenses (BMD) to intercept the warheads that China could launch with missiles that survived the US counterforce attack.

A state could benefit from a damage-limitation capability in two different, albeit related, ways. First, an effective damage-limitation capability, by definition, would reduce the costs the adversary could inflict in a retaliatory attack. In an all-out war, if the state launched a damage-limitation attack before its adversary had launched an all-out countervalue attack, the state would suffer less than if its adversary had launched an unimpeded all-out countervalue attack. Second, a damage-limitation capability could enhance a state's deterrent capability, which is the most frequently discussed mission for US nuclear forces. A deterrent strategy is designed to influence an adversary's behavior: The United States attempts to convince China not to attack by threatening sufficiently credible and costly retaliation. A damage-limitation capability, by reducing the cost the adversary can inflict in retaliation, can enhance a country's ability to deter and to compel by increasing the credibility of its nuclear threats.

WHAT COUNTS AS SIGNIFICANT DAMAGE LIMITATION?

By definition, a damage-limitation capability would enable the United States to achieve a meaningfully better outcome in an all-out nuclear war than if it lacked such a capability. The feasibility of a US damage-limitation capability vis-à-vis China depends on the level to which the United States

---

13. Brian Radzinsky, "The Strategic Implications of the Evolving US-China Nuclear Balance," *Washington Quarterly* 44, no. 4 (2022): 163–82, argues also that modernization increases China's retaliatory and signaling options; Abraham Denmark and Caitlin Talmadge, "Why China Wants More and Better Nukes," *Foreign Affairs*, November 19, 2021, https://www.foreignaffairs.com/articles/china/2021-11-19/why-china-wants-more-and-better-nukes.

14. Logan and Saunders, *Discerning the Drivers of China's Nuclear Force Development*, 14–15.

would need to reduce the damage from a Chinese retaliatory attack to produce such an outcome. The lower this level of death and destruction is set, the more difficult damage limitation is to achieve.

During the Cold War, the United States set the threshold for damage limitation at a high level. To limit damage, the United States needed to deny the Soviet Union an assured destruction capability. In the early 1960s, US Secretary of Defense Robert McNamara defined "assured destruction" as the ability of the United States to destroy, in retaliation, 20 to 25 percent of the Soviet population and 50 percent of the Soviet industrial base. US calculations estimated that the delivery of two hundred one-megaton warheads could inflict this level of destruction.[15] This analysis assumed that if the Soviet Union could not reduce the effects of a US retaliatory attack below this level, Soviet leaders would conclude that they could not limit damage to a meaningful extent and therefore would have virtually no incentive to launch a massive counterforce attack. These judgments about the level of damage required for assured destruction largely reflected the fact of strongly diminishing marginal returns in the damage that additional US warheads could inflict. Importantly, they did not reflect assessments of how Soviet leaders viewed the implications of various levels of damage or how much damage they were willing to tolerate.

A Soviet assured destruction capability was envisioned as inflicting roughly the same level of retaliatory damage on the United States. Consequently, a US damage-limitation capability was understood to require reducing Soviet retaliation to below roughly the same level—that is, two hundred equivalent megatons (EMT).[16]

As the United States evaluates its nuclear strategy toward China, the threshold for what constitutes meaningful damage limitation requires careful scrutiny. McNamara established the damage-limitation threshold and the amount of equivalent megatonnage that would produce this level of damage to demonstrate that damage limitation was infeasible. This analysis was not weakened by adopting an unnecessarily high threshold because the analysis showed that the United States could not reduce Soviet retaliatory damage to even that high level. In contrast, determining whether meaningful damage limitation is feasible requires first identifying a threshold (or a range) above which additional damage does not result in significantly worse outcomes for the United States and below which less damage

---

15. Alain C. Enthoven and K. Wayne Smith, *How Much Is Enough? Shaping the Defense Program, 1961–1969* (RAND, 1971), 207.

16. The equivalent megatonnage of a nuclear weapon is a measure of the area that the weapon can destroy compared to the area that a one-megaton weapon can destroy. The area destroyed by blast overpressure of a weapon is proportional to the two-thirds power of the yield of the weapon, measured in megatons. For a summary of the Cold War debate on US damage-limitation requirements, see Glaser, *Analyzing Strategic Nuclear Policy*, 30–35.

begins to result in a significantly better outcome. Once this threshold is established, we can assess the size of the nuclear attack required to inflict it and the US counterforce attack required to deny this level of damage.

Both steps are analytically challenging. There is more than one way to conceptualize the damage-limitation threshold. One variant sets the threshold at a given level of economic and population damage that reflects a subjective judgment about the overall societal costs that a specific nuclear attack would inflict on the United States: Outcomes in which damage exceeds the threshold are considered not significantly or meaningfully worse than those at the threshold; although not literally totally destroyed, the costs at this level are judged to be essentially indistinguishable from still large attacks. Above the damage-limitation threshold, whatever nuclear weapons a US damage-limitation attack destroyed would not have significantly increased the costs inflicted by the adversary's retaliatory attack. McNamara's damage threshold is commonly understood in this way, even though it did not originate from this type of judgment.[17]

A second variant sets the threshold by considering a country's ability to recover from a nuclear attack. At some level, the extent of economic and infrastructure damage and population loss, and the resulting social and political collapse, might prevent a country from recovering from a nuclear war in anything resembling its current form. While this understanding raises many questions of its own—recover how quickly? recover along what dimensions? recover in absolute terms or relative to the adversary?—it offers a different perspective. The issue becomes not only the immediate damage inflicted but also the long-term implications of that damage, including environmental effects.[18]

A third variant conceives of the damage-limitation threshold as the level above which the United States should be unwilling to risk even a small increase in the probability of nuclear war to reduce the damage of an all-out nuclear war. This trade-off is of concern if the forces and war plans required for damage limitation would increase the probability of war via the creation of preemptive or other escalatory incentives. This conception is still more complicated than the first two because it incorporates judgments about the impact of pursuing damage-limitation capabilities on the likeli-

---

17. His flat-of-the-curve logic captured the relationship between additional megatons and additional damage, not the relationship between additional damage and additional costs to the country that was attacked.

18. The environmental impacts could be enormous; reductions in crop yields would put at risk of starvation a billion people worldwide. See Mutlu Özdoğan, Alan Robock, and Christopher J. Kucharik, "Impacts of a Nuclear War in South Asia on Soybean and Maize Production in the Midwest United States," *Climatic Change* 116, no. 2 (January 2013): 373–87, and Xia Lili et al., "Decadal Reduction of Chinese Agriculture After a Regional Nuclear War," *Earth's Future* 3, no. 2 (February 2015): 37–48.

hood of nuclear war. Although some analysts understand the infeasibility of damage limitation in this way, it is very difficult to determine the threshold because the relationship between the damage-limitation efforts and the probability of war is complex and controversial.

A fourth variant shifts the focus from the outcomes the United States would suffer to the adversary's beliefs about how US leaders understand these outcomes. When damage limitation is included as part of a state's deterrent strategy, it is the adversary's beliefs that become most important. How effective would a projected US damage-limitation attack need to be for Chinese leaders to believe that US leaders were more likely to escalate to nuclear war than if the United States lacked a damage-limitation capability?

Once a threshold is identified, analyzing whether a nuclear attack would inflict that level of damage becomes a largely technical question. However, adequate analysis requires much more comprehensive and realistic models than employed by McNamara. The damage estimates produced during the McNamara era were based largely on the blast effects of nuclear weapons—the destruction of buildings by the explosion's shock wave—based on the US bombings of Hiroshima and Nagasaki. But thermonuclear weapons, which have much higher yields than did the Hiroshima and Nagasaki bombs, also produce a pulse of thermal radiation that ignites fires over a wider area.[19] Later estimates that included fire effects indicated that the detonation of as few as seventy 1-megaton weapons would kill 20 percent of the Soviet population.[20] Similar calculations for the United States indicated that forty 1-megaton weapons could kill 20 percent of the US population.[21]

Beyond correcting damage calculations for fire effects, an adequate assessment needs to address a fuller range of effects—including the systemic impact of destroying critical infrastructure, including, among other things, energy systems, communication and information systems, and major ports and other transportation nodes.[22] In other words, the analysis would address the vulnerability to nuclear attack of a highly integrated

---

19. On why US estimates did not include fire effects, see Lynn Eden, *Whole World on Fire: Organizations, Knowledge, and Nuclear Weapons Devastation* (Cornell University Press, 2006).

20. Barbara G. Levi, Frank N. von Hippel, and William H. Daugherty, "Civilian Casualties from 'Limited' Nuclear Attacks on the USSR," *International Security* 12, no. 3 (winter 1987/88): 168–89.

21. Levi, von Hippel, and Daugherty, "Civilian Casualties from 'Limited' Nuclear Attacks on the USSR," fig. 4. See also William Daugherty, Barbara Levi, and Frank von Hippel, "The Consequences of 'Limited' Nuclear Attacks on the United States," *International Security* 10, no. 4 (spring 1986): 3–43.

22. Cold War studies of the impact of large attacks include Arthur M. Katz, *Life After Nuclear War: The Economic and Social Impact of Nuclear Attacks on the United States* (Ballinger, 1982), and Office of Technology Assessment, *The Effects of Nuclear War* (Government Printing Office, 1979). On the impact of a small attack, see M. Anjali Sastry, Joseph J. Romm, and Kosta Tsipis, *Nuclear Crash: The US Economy After Small Nuclear Attacks*, Report #17, Program in Science and Technology for International Security, MIT, June 1987, at https://apps.dtic.mil/sti/pdfs/ADA359603.pdf.

and potentially fragile modern economy. Results based on a less complete analysis should be recognized as underestimating the damage and arguments built on them should be treated with caution.

While this chapter cannot further explore this set of issues, a key takeaway is that a US decision to pursue damage limitation needs to fully engage these complex issues. Otherwise, the United States risks pursuing capabilities that it believes will provide significant protection in an all-out war, but they will not.

That said, to give some sense of what might be required for damage limitation, the following analysis draws on the first two conceptions of damage limitation and, instead of a specific threshold, identifies a range: at the lower end, ten medium-yield warheads dropped on ten cities, reflecting the possibility that such an attack would generate partial or widespread systemic collapse, and at the higher end, forty EMT on cities, which is the corrected Cold War/McNamara threshold for killing approximately 20 percent of the US population, although the full effects would undoubtedly be much worse.[23] Analysts who disagree with these thresholds/ranges can adjust the findings by setting their own thresholds.

DAMAGE LIMITATION VERSUS DETERRENCE

Having revisited the question of what counts as damage limitation, we need to keep in mind the distinction between damage limitation and deterrence. The level of retaliation required to deter a nuclear attack is almost certainly much lower than the level required to achieve damage limitation.[24] Deterring an adversary from pursuing an action requires the adversary to anticipate that the expected costs of retaliation would exceed the benefits it expects to receive. There are very few, if any, actions that US leaders would pursue if they believed that such an action would result in the certain destruction of even one US city. This basic position was articulated in an often-quoted statement by McGeorge Bundy, who served as the national security advisor to Presidents John F. Kennedy and Lyndon Johnson: "Think-tank analysts can set levels of 'acceptable' damage well up in the tens of millions of lives. They can assume that the loss of dozens of great cities is somehow a real choice for sane men. They are in an unreal world. In the real world of real political leaders—whether here or in the Soviet Union—a decision that would bring even one hydrogen bomb on one city

---

23. The costs inflicted by an attack, however, are unlikely to be proportional to the damage. For example, ten 200-kiloton warheads targeted on the centers of the ten largest US cities would effectively directly eliminate economic activity in metropolitan areas that are responsible for more than one-third of total US gross domestic product.

24. To simplify the discussion, this claim glosses over the fact that the state would need to threaten greater damage when its deterrent threat is not fully credible than when it is fully credible; nevertheless, the basic point stands.

of one's own country would be recognized in advance as a catastrophic blunder; ten bombs on ten cities would be a disaster beyond history; and a hundred bombs on a hundred cities are unthinkable."[25]

Bundy's position, however, is largely consistent with the judgment that a nuclear attack that reduced the damage inflicted on the US homeland but nevertheless allowed the destruction of ten or more US cities could qualify as meaningful damage limitation. Whether the threat of nuclear damage would deter a leader from pursuing a specific action and whether that leader would judge the outcome of two nuclear attacks on her country to have inflicted meaningfully different costs are entirely distinct questions. The deterrence question arises when the leader is comparing pursuing the action and risking retaliation to not pursuing the action. In sharp contrast, the damage-limitation question arises when a country is already in a severe crisis or war and the leader believes that the adversary may launch a massive nuclear attack against her country. The choice at this point is between possibly suffering a first strike and suffering a second strike.[26]

Although deterrence and damage limitation are fundamentally different concepts, possession of a damage-limitation capability can enhance a country's ability to deter. An adversary might doubt that a state would retaliate to either a conventional attack or a limited nuclear attack because the adversary could then escalate further, inflicting massive damage on the state. By reducing or even eliminating this counterdeterrent threat, a damage-limitation capability could enhance the state's ability to deter.

The contribution of a damage-limitation capability to a state's deterrent is likely to be greater for attacks against a state's allies than against the state's homeland. Retaliatory threats by a vulnerable state tend to be more credible when designed to protect interests that a state values more. Because states value their own territory more than their allies' territory, credibility is harder to achieve when protecting allies, which makes the potential contribution of a damage-limitation capability greater.

The effectiveness of a damage-limitation capability is another factor that influences its contribution to a state's deterrent. If the retaliatory damage the United States expects to suffer would remain so high that it dwarfs the interests at stake, then its damage-limitation capability would do less to enhance the credibility of US threats to escalate.[27]

---

25. McGeorge Bundy, "To Cap the Volcano," *Foreign Affairs* 48, no. 1, October 1969, 1–20, quotation at 10.

26. Although this is the standard formulation, a state might have a third option that would lead to a different outcome—surrender to avoid war altogether. See Robert Powell, *Nuclear Deterrence Theory: The Search for Credibility* (Cambridge University Press, 2008), chap. 5.

27. More precisely, because the credibility of the US is judged by its adversary, it is the adversary's beliefs about the damage the United States expects to suffer and the extent of the US interests at stake that would determine the credibility of the US threat.

CHAPTER 6

Feasibility of a US Damage-Limitation Capability Against China

Until around 2010, the United States was capable of destroying the vast majority of China's relatively small strategic nuclear force.[28] China's deployment of mobile ICBMs began to increase the survivability of its strategic force, but as late as 2015, the United States likely had some damage-limitation capability. However, the continued expansion and modernization of China's strategic nuclear force—including the deployment of additional mobile ICBMs, but also its deployment of a longer-range SLBM (which can probably reach the United States from China's maritime periphery) and improved nuclear command and control (NC2)—has essentially eliminated the US damage-limitation capability.[29]

To reduce China's ability to inflict retaliatory damage, the United States could rely on a mix of systems to destroy China's nuclear forces. It could employ nuclear missiles against China's ICBMs and ASW forces against China's SSBNs, as well as engage in nuclear or conventional attacks against China's C2 assets. In addition, the United States could employ BMD to intercept any warheads China was able to launch.[30]

TARGETING ICBMS

US nuclear forces pose a potent threat to China's silo-based ICBMs. US ICBMs and SLBMs are now very accurate, making them highly capable of destroying hard silos. The United States has further improved the effectiveness of its missile force by adding fusing devices that reduce the implications of inaccuracy and maintaining the ability to rapidly retarget its missiles to account for missile failures.[31] If the United States attacked each of China's twenty DF-5 silos with two warheads, there would be a 90 percent or greater chance that no more than one missile would survive and virtual certainty that no more than two missiles would survive. Such an attack could be carried out with ten Trident-II or forty Minuteman-III missiles, representing only a small percentage of the currently deployed US strategic

---

28. China did, however, have mobile nuclear systems capable of hitting Japan, Taiwan, and Guam that would have been much harder for the United States to destroy and that therefore provided China with a significant retaliatory capability.

29. For a comparison to estimates from 2016, see Glaser and Fetter, "Should the United States Reject MAD?" This finding pertains to politically meaningful scenarios in which China could reasonably mobilize its nuclear forces, not to a surprise attack.

30. In addition, a country can, at least in principle, try to limit damage by civil defense, protecting its population from nuclear weapons that explode on its territory.

31. Lieber and Press, *The Myth of the Nuclear Revolution*, 70–76. On reprogramming counterforce strikes, see, for example, Lynn E. Davis and Warner R. Schilling, "All You Ever Wanted to Know about MIRV and ICBM Calculations But Were Not Cleared to Ask," *Journal of Conflict Resolution* 17, no. 2 (June 1973): 218.

force. If it is possible to detect missile failures and to rapidly reprogram and launch replacement Trident or Minuteman missiles, the probability of no DF-5A missiles surviving would be 90 percent or greater, and the probability of no more than one missile would be more than 99 percent.

The United States' ability to destroy the new silos that China is building will be comparable. The results will depend upon the hardness of the new silos. If all of these silos are filled with missiles and the United States dedicated two warheads to each silo, there would be a roughly 90 percent chance that one or fewer silos would survive if the silos are hard, and that ten would survive if the silos are very hard.[32] The more important impact of the new silos/missiles may be that attacking them with six hundred warheads could reduce the US ability to target other Chinese forces, most importantly, its mobile ICBMs.

Mobile missiles present the United States with a very different challenge because the United States will have to locate them. How difficult this will be depends partly on how effectively China operates its mobile ICBMs. It will also depend upon US capabilities for finding and tracking China's missiles and China's ability to undermine these capabilities.[33]

Mobile missiles deployed in their peacetime garrisons will be extremely vulnerable. For China to maintain a highly survivable mobile ICBM force will require, in a crisis or war, that it have a significant number of its mobile ICBMs armed with nuclear weapons and deployed in the field over a large area, away from bases and other fixed sites known to be associated with the missiles.

Historically, in peacetime, Chinese missiles and their transporter-erector-launchers (TELs) were stored together in garrison; nuclear warheads were stored separately.[34] However, the 2022 Pentagon report on China's military developments finds that China now practices maintaining its nuclear force at higher alert, including "assigning a missile battalion to be ready to launch, and rotating to standby position, on about a monthly basis for unspecified periods."[35] In a crisis, warheads not mated with ICBMs would be transported by road or rail from central to base-level storage facilities. Warhead

---

32. These estimates are for 2,000 psi and 10,000 psi, using the single kill probabilities for a 100kt warhead on a Trident II, in Hans M. Kristensen, Matthew McKinsie, and Theodore A. Postol, "How US Nuclear Force Modernization Is Undermining Strategic Stability, *Bulletin of the Atomic Scientists* (March 1, 2017), https://thebulletin.org/2017/03/how-us-nuclear-force-modernization-is-undermining-strategic-stability-the-burst-height-compensating-super-fuze/#post-heading.

33. For an assessment that reaches different conclusions about the survivability of China's mobile missiles, based on different political and operational assumptions, see Wu Riqiang, "Living with Uncertainty: Modeling China's Nuclear Survivability," *International Security* 44, no. 4 (spring 2020): 84–118.

34. Mark A. Stokes, "China's Nuclear Warhead Storage and Handling System" (Project 2049 Institute, March 12, 2010).

35. US Department of Defense, *Military and Security Developments Involving the People's Republic of China, 2022,* 95.

shipments reportedly use specialized rail cars and vehicles on designated rail lines and roads. These operations likely have distinctive signatures that US intelligence could identify. This raises the possibility that the United States would have warning that China was placing its nuclear forces on alert, moving to a more survivable posture. Such warning would provide opportunities for US counterforce attacks that could destroy warhead storage facilities or missile garrisons, or the roads and rail lines linking them. There may be choke points in China, such as rail or road tunnels, bridges, or narrow passages that, if destroyed, would prevent Chinese warheads from being delivered to missiles or prevent missiles from leaving their garrisons. Such attacks could be carried out with low-yield nuclear weapons and possibly with precision conventional weapons, if available.[36]

A key question, therefore, is how early in a crisis China would move to put its mobile missiles on high alert. Moving quickly to place missiles on alert could escalate a crisis by signaling that China believed the United States was preparing to launch a nuclear attack; waiting until a crisis or war is so severe that a nuclear attack is no longer unlikely increases the probability of a US damage-limitation attack. Given these dangers, China may increase the number of mobile ICBMs mated with warheads during peacetime and increase further the number of mobile ICBMs that are regularly on higher alert.

China's mobile ICBMs would be more survivable once they were deployed in the field together with their nuclear warheads, but the degree of survivability would depend on other operational details that are not publicly known. The TELs for China's mobile ICBMs are the largest vehicles found on Chinese roads and would be accompanied by command-and-control and other vehicles, which would give this combination of vehicles a distinctive signature. To escape detection, China could move its missiles at night or when no US photoreconnaissance satellites were known to be overhead, and TELs might hide, for example, by moving into tunnels when satellites were overhead.

Until around the mid-2010s, Chinese crews trained to launch their mobile missiles from prepared sites, presumably to reduce launch time and minimize exposure to attack.[37] If, as seems likely, US intelligence has identified many of these prepared launch sites, the United States could destroy the sites by using nuclear or even long-range precision conventional weap-

---

36. On US prompt conventional strike programs, see James M. Acton, *Silver Bullet? Asking the Right Questions About Conventional Prompt Global Strike* (Carnegie Endowment for International Peace, 2013), Bruce M. Sugden, "Speed Kills: Analyzing the Deployment of Conventional Ballistic Missiles," *International Security* 34, no. 1 (summer 2009): 113–46, and Austin Long, Dinshaw Mistry, and Bruce M. Sugden, "Correspondence: Going Nowhere Fast: Assessing Concerns About Long-Range Conventional Ballistic Missiles," *International Security* 34, no. 4 (spring 2010): 166–84.

37. Launch preparation times of less than thirty minutes have been reported. See Li Bin, "Tracking Chinese Strategic Mobile Missiles," *Science and Global Security* 15 (2007): 10–11.

ons (if they are available). Therefore, for its mobile ICBMs to survive, China must be able to launch them from unprepared sites. China is reported to have achieved this capability in at least one of its mobile ICBMs, the DF-31G, and likely has this capability in the DF-41.[38]

If the United States can locate a Chinese TEL and it is then stationary for more than thirty minutes, the United States could easily destroy it. If a TEL is located while it is moving, the United States could destroy it with a barrage attack of nuclear weapons. A TEL spotted while moving down a highway could be destroyed with high probability by a few to a dozen US nuclear warheads.[39] Some of China's mobile missiles are reported to have the ability to operate off road (the DF-31AG), which would increase the area to which they could travel and, therefore, increase the number of US warheads required for an effective barrage. Thus, if the United States can reliably detect China's mobile missiles, it could destroy China's current force of 120 mobile missiles with as few as 120 nuclear or long-range precision conventional weapons if the TELs are stationary, or with roughly 360 to 1,400 nuclear weapons if they are moving along a road. The upper end of this range is approaching the number of warheads the United States has deployed and that are allowed under the New START treaty (which is expected to remain in force until 2026).[40] The required number of US warheads would be still larger if some Chinese ICBMs can operate off road.

Since the 1991 Gulf War, in which the United States had great difficulty destroying Iraqi Scud missiles, US nuclear policy has identified the importance of improved capabilities for finding mobile missiles.[41] The key technology for locating China's mobile ICBMs will be space-based radars. The

---

38. Fiona Cunningham, "Nuclear Command, Control, and Communication Systems of the People's Republic of China," NAPSNet Special Reports, July 18, 2019, https://nautilus.org/napsnet/napsnet-special-reports/nuclear-command-control-and-communications-systems-of-the-peoples-republic-of-china/

39. This estimate assumes a weapon can be delivered on target an hour after the target is identified; a TEL of hardness between 5 and 15 pounds per square inch, moving in one direction at an average speed between 10 and 50 kilometers per hour, and a 100-kiloton or 475-kiloton warhead. The required number could be somewhat increased by forks in the roads. Much larger numbers of weapons would be required for barrage attacks if the TEL could drive in any direction after being spotted, but this would require a dense network of suitable roads, which seems unlikely, or off-road capability.

40. Shannon Bugos, "US Strategic Forces Under New Start," Arms Control Association, April 2022, https://www.armscontrol.org/factsheets/USStratNukeForceNewSTART#:~:text=Under%20New%20START%2C%20the%20United,capable%20bombers%2C%20and%20240%20SLBMs.&text=As%20of%20September%202020%2C%20the,which%20have%20a%20single%20warhead.

41. See, for example, US Department of Defense, "Nuclear Posture Review" [excerpts], January 8, 2002, http://imi-online.de/download/Nuclear_Posture_Review.pdf, which was leaked to the press, US Department of Defense, "Quadrennial Defense Review Report," February 6, 2006, 57, and Li, "Tracking Chinese Strategic Mobile Missiles."

CHAPTER 6

"2022 Missile Defense Review" found that "Because of their global nature, persistence, and greater access to denied regions, resilient space-based infrared, radar" will play a critical role in US efforts to combine offensive and defensive capabilities to defend the US homeland.[42]

The advantage of SBR is that it provides an ability to track targets—particularly moving targets on the ground—during day and night and under almost any weather condition. Unlike airborne radar platforms, such as the Joint Surveillance Target Attack Radar System or Global Hawk, SBR can track targets deep in the interior of large countries that have deployed good air defenses. The challenge with SBR is that the long distance from space to ground results in correspondingly high radar power requirements. Until recently, these requirements combined with the high cost of building and placing equipment in space made SBR very expensive, which led the United States in 2005 to decide against pursuing these systems.[43]

Recent advances in microelectronics and signal processing have facilitated the miniaturization of small, highly capable satellites, while improvements in space launch have dramatically decreased the cost of putting satellites into orbit. Consequently, a high-density constellation of small satellites that provides continuous or near-continuous coverage of China is now technologically and financially feasible.[44] The United States has not yet deployed such a constellation of SBR but appears headed in that direction, although specifics are scarce. The Department of Defense (DoD) 2024 budget request includes funding to integrate air and space sensors that track moving targets. This reflects efforts over the past few years by the US Space Force to design and develop a space-based ground moving target indicator capability.[45]

Assuming the United States deploys a highly capable SBR constellation, China could pursue a variety of countermeasures that would degrade and

---

42. US Department of Defense, "2022 Missile Defense Review," which is included in "2022 National Defense Strategy of the United States, Including the 2022 Nuclear Posture Review and the 2022 Missile Defense Review," October 27, 2022, 8, https://apps.dtic.mil/sti/pdfs/AD1183539.pdf.

43. See Joseph A. Post and Michael J. Bennett, "Alternatives for Military Space Radar," Congressional Budget Office, January 2007; House Committee on Appropriations, *Report of the Committee on Appropriations*, Department of Defense Appropriations Bill, 2005, House Report 108–553: 312–14.

44. Steve Fetter and Jaganath Sankaran, "Emerging Technologies and Challenges to Nuclear Stability," *Journal of Strategic Studies* 48, no. 2 (2025): 255–65.

45. Brian Everstine, "Space Force Developing Concept of Operations for GMTI from Orbit," *Aviation Week*, April 19, 2023, https://aviationweek.com/defense-space/space-force-developing-concept-operations-gmti-orbit; Courtney Albon, "US Space Force Wants Funding for a New Mission—Tracking Ground Targets," C4ISRNET.com, January 19, 2022, https://www.c4isrnet.com/2022/01/19/us-space-force-wants-funding-for-a-new-mission-tracking-ground-targets/, and Courtney Albon, "Defense Budget Includes Plans for Space-Based Tracking, Kendall Says," C4ISRNET, March 7, 2023, https://www.c4isrnet.com/battlefield-tech/space/2023/03/07/defense-budget-includes-plans-for-space-based-tracking-kendall-says/.

likely undermine the SBR's capability. Among the possibilities are deploying mobile decoys; deploying mobile missiles in mountainous terrain that blocks radar signals; employing stealth technology to reduce the TELs' radar cross section, thereby generating a requirement for a still larger US SBR constellation; and using electronic warfare and antisatellite weapons to jam or destroy SBR and other US intelligence, surveillance, and reconnaissance (ISR) capabilities.[46]

Of course, the United States could pursue countermeasures to these countermeasures. For example, it could target Chinese jammers. In anticipation of this response, China could proliferate jammers, which are cheap. Although there is always the possibility that China would fail to effectively pursue countermeasures in the ensuing countermeasures action-reaction cycles, the competition between survivable missiles and SBR detection appears to significantly favor survivability.[47]

In addition to investing in SBR, the United States could also deploy small, inexpensive imaging satellites. Until recently, imaging satellites that provided continuous coverage were plagued by the same cost problems as SBR. Here, too, however, the cost and coverage problem is being solved by the possibility of small, highly capable imaging satellites that collect visible, ultraviolet, and infrared light that can now be built and launched into orbit at a fraction of the previous cost. Imaging satellites would work only during the daytime and clear weather but would augment the capabilities of SBR by providing the United States with the ability to enhance target characterization and discrimination, thereby degrading the effectiveness of Chinese decoys and camouflage. However, as with SBR, China could pursue a variety of approaches that would likely be effective in defeating these imaging satellites.

Another possibility for locating mobile missiles is signals intelligence (SIGINT). During the Cold War, the United States made large investments in SIGINT dedicated to tracking Soviet mobile ICBMs and had some success using these capabilities to locate Soviet missiles. US SIGINT assets have improved since then.[48] Fully evaluating the potential effectiveness of US SIGINT against Chinese mobile missiles is difficult because there is relatively little information about US programs available in the open literature, and even less is known about how China operates its nuclear force. Nevertheless, China likely has available approaches for significantly reducing this potential vulnerability, including communicating to satellites via burst

---

46. Li, "Tracking Chinese Strategic Mobile Missiles," 15–25.

47. For extensive analysis, see Thomas MacDonald, "Tracking Mobile Missiles," *Journal of Strategic Studies* 48, no. 2 (2025): 297–333. For earlier debate, see Brendan Rittenhouse Green, Austin Long, Matthew Kroenig, Charles Glaser, and Steve Fetter, "Correspondence: The Limits of Damage Limitation," *International Security* 42, no. 1 (summer 2017): 193–207.

48. Long and Green, "Stalking the Secure Second Strike," 51–56, 60–64.

transmissions, relying less during crises on satellite links for communication, and relying more heavily on landlines.

In short, China's mobile missiles are likely to be highly survivable if they are deployed in the field with nuclear weapons relatively early in a crisis; if China could launch its mobile missiles from unprepared or unidentified sites; and if Chinese missile forces adopt best practices to avoid detection while in the field. In the future, the United States might deploy large constellations of SBR and imaging satellites that would be able to detect and track China's mobile missiles. China, however, should be able to adopt countermeasures that would significantly degrade the capability of these satellites.

In addition, even if China is unable to defeat US satellite surveillance, the United States' nuclear force could be too small to target all Chinese silos and barrage its mobile missiles. Depending on the number of warheads required to barrage an on-road mobile missile—three to twelve—the US force is already too small. If the United States needs seven warheads to barrage each mobile missile, then its entire ICBM and SLBM force would be required to adequately target China's silos and mobile missiles, leaving the United States without warheads available for other military targets and a reserve force that could be employed against Chinese infrastructure and economic targets.[49] As China continues to deploy more mobile missiles, the US force would need to grow to keep pace.[50]

The qualitative race is likely to be more consequential than the quantitative race. Instead of trying to outbuild the United States, China is more likely to succeed, at lower cost, by winning the countermeasures race. The combination of qualitative and quantitative competitions gives China still better prospects for maintaining a large number of survivable ICBMs.

TARGETING SSBNS

The challenge that the United States would face in finding and destroying China's SSBNs depends on how China deploys them. One option is

---

49. For a rough estimate, assume the United States targets two warheads on each Chinese silo (640) and that one hundred mobile missiles are out of garrison, requiring seven hundred warheads. The US missile force includes four hundred ICBM warheads. If ten of its fourteen SSBNs were at sea, carrying an average of ninety warheads per submarine, then the United States would have nine hundred SLBM warheads available. On the US force, see Hans M. Kristensen and Matt Korda, "Nuclear Notebook: United States Nuclear Weapons, 2023," *Bulletin of the Atomic Scientists* (January 16, 2023), https://thebulletin.org/premium/2023-01/nuclear-notebook-united-states-nuclear-weapons-2023/. The shortfall will be even greater if the United States decides it needs a force capable of deterring Russia as well as China. Some analysts argue that the current US force is too small, even without adding in the large requirement generated by barrage attacks; see for example, *Study Group Report, China's Emergence as a Second Nuclear Peer*.

50. Some of this shortfall could be covered by uploading weapons that the United States removed from its force to meet New START limits, once the treaty is no longer in force.

for China to deploy them in the open ocean, which would require its submarines to transit from their base on Hainan Island in the South China Sea into the Philippine Sea, via gaps in the first island chain. The United States can use underwater sensor arrays that are likely deployed in these straits—most importantly, between Taiwan and the Philippines and between Taiwan and the Ryukyu Islands—to detect Chinese SSBNs as they exit the South China Sea. Once detected, the United States could trail the submarine and/or use different sensors to try to track it in the Western Pacific.

The problem for China is that its current SSBNs are relatively noisy, noisier than the Soviet SSBNs that the United States was able to track during the Cold War.[51] Consequently, even if not detected as they pass through straits, the United States would likely be able to detect and track them in the open ocean. China will find it challenging to produce submarines within the next decade that are quiet enough to reliably evade open-ocean detection by the United States.[52]

The less technically demanding alternative is for China to adopt a bastion strategy. China would deploy its SSBNs in its coastal waters, inside the first island chain, and defend them against US ASW forces—most importantly with attack submarines but also with mines, ships, and aircraft that carry dedicated ASW sensors. Many experts believe that a bastion strategy is better matched to China's geography and current capabilities. The most promising location is likely the South China Sea. The possible northern locations have the advantage of being closer to the continental United States but are probably not suitable for sustained SSBN operations.[53]

---

51. Tong Zhao, *Tides of Change: China's Nuclear Ballistic Submarines and Strategic Stability*, Carnegie Endowment for International Peace, 2018, 26–28, https://carnegieendowment.org/files/Zhao_SSBN_final.pdf; Wu Riqiang, "Survivability of China's Sea-Based Nuclear Forces," *Science and Global Security* 19, no. 2 (2011): 91–120.

52. This judgment is based on the Soviet experience during the Cold War. See Coté, *The Third Battle*. However, the newer variant of China's current SSBN, the Type 094A, is significantly quieter than the earlier variant. David C. Logan, *China's Sea-Baser Nuclear Deterrent: Organizational, Operational, and Strategic Implications*, China Maritime Report No. 33, China Maritime Studies Institute, US Naval War College, December 2023, 3–4, https://digital-commons.usnwc.edu/cmsi-maritime-reports/33/. In addition, as noted in a previous section, there is some possibility that technology transfer from Russia will enable China's next generation SSBNs to be dramatically quieter.

53. Zhao, *Tides of Change*, identifies the East and Yellow Seas, but notes they are too shallow for ideal submarine operations. The Department of Defense 2022 report on Chinese power identifies the Bohai Gulf as a possible location; see US Department of Defense, *Military and Security Developments Involving the People's Republic of China, Annual Report to Congress 2022*, 96, https://media.defense.gov/2022/Nov/29/2003122279/-1/-1/1/2022-MILITARY-AND-SECURITY-DEVELOPMENTS-INVOLVING-THE-PEOPLES-REPUBLIC-OF-CHINA.PDF. However, the Bohai Gulf is quite shallow, likely too shallow, for sustained SSBN operations.

CHAPTER 6

This strategy requires SLBMs that are capable of reaching the United States from the bastion. The JL-3 is reported to have a range of approximately ten thousand kilometers, which would enable it to reach much of the western part of the continental United States from northern bastions, but not from the South China Sea.[54] One possibility is for China to remove warheads from the JL-3—a MIRVed missile—which would increase its range. If its estimated range of ten thousand kilometers assumes the missile is carrying three warheads, then the JL-3's range with one warhead would be sufficient to reach the East Coast of the United States.[55] China's next-generation SSBN will be larger than the current one and would be able to carry a larger, longer-range SLBM.

How effective the United States would be in finding and destroying Chinese SSBNs deployed and protected in a bastion is something of an open question largely because the interactions between US and Chinese forces would be complex.[56] China has improved its own ASW capabilities over the past decade but still faces a variety of shortcomings, some of which it is likely to reduce in coming decades. It does have very quiet diesel submarines, an advanced version of which can remain submerged for weeks at a time. China would use its attack submarines and mines, and possibly its surface- and air-based ASW assets, to try to keep US SSNs out of its bastion. This will be difficult, however, because China currently lacks sufficient numbers of attack submarines to effectively patrol the perimeter of its South China Sea bastion. If US SSNs get into the bastion, China would need to get its SSBNs out of port without being detected and trailed. To reduce US prospects, China could use surface ships equipped with sonar arrays to clear lanes from the port and a variety of evasive tactics. Once into the Chinese bastion, US SSNs searching for Chinese SSBNs would have an acoustic advantage over Chinese nuclear submarines, but maybe not over its diesel submarines. With enough time, the United States would likely find China's SSBNs but would also probably suffer some losses. The amount of search

---

54. However, US Department of Defense, *Military and Security Developments Involving the People's Republic of China, Annual Report to Congress 2022*, 96, suggests that the JL-3 would enable China to target the continental United States from the South China Sea. There is some uncertainty about the range of the JL-3, with some reports saying that the range exceeds 10,000 kilometers.

55. Based upon calculations by Steve Fetter.

56. On bastion basics and US prospects against Soviet SSBNs in bastion, see Tom Stefanick, *Strategic Antisubmarine Warfare and Naval Strategy* (Lexington Books, 1987), esp. 53–62. Specifically on possible US efforts against a Chinese bastion, see Elizabeth Freund, "Blind Man's Bluff: Strategic Anti-Submarine Warfare and US-China Nuclear Stability," unpublished paper, May 21, 2020, and Tom Stefanick, "Undersea Nuclear Forces: Survivability of Chinese, Russian, and US SSBNs," *Journal of Strategic Studies* 48, no. 2 (2025): 334–406, which argues that advances in signal processing, uncrewed underwater vehicles, and sensors will tend to increase the survivability of SSBNs deployed in bastions.

NUCLEAR STRATEGY

time available to the United States would depend on the scenario, including whether the possibility of US nuclear escalation for damage limitation was preceded by a long conventional war during which the United States began waging its ASW campaign.

In sum, improvements in China's sea-based nuclear leg mean that the United States can no longer completely discount its contribution to China's nuclear deterrent, as was the case as recently as 2015. At least based on publicly available information, the United States would need to worry that some Chinese SSBNs would survive against US ASW. The challenge facing the United States will grow in coming years as China deploys more SSBNs, a new-generation SSBN that will be larger and quieter than the current generation, and a still-longer-range SLBM.

TARGETING NUCLEAR COMMAND AND CONTROL

A nuclear retaliatory capability requires not only that a state's nuclear weapons and delivery systems can survive attack but also that the state has the ability to launch the surviving weapons. If the United States could fully destroy China's NC2 systems before China launched its nuclear forces, the United States would have a highly effective damage-limitation capability. Even partially destroying China's NC2 could complement other US counterforce capabilities by reducing the fraction of surviving weapons that China could launch.

A state has three broad approaches for addressing NC2 vulnerability: (1) ensuring that the political leadership and the communication links between leaders and launch commanders are survivable, (2) predelegating launch authority down the political and military chains of command, and (3) preparing to launch on warning (LOW) of a US attack. None of these approaches provides an easy route to adequate NC2. During the Cold War, the United States developed an elaborate system of sensors, mobile platforms, and organizational procedures to overcome the vulnerability of its NC2. These extensive efforts were unable to avoid difficult trade-offs between ensuring the United States' ability to launch a retaliatory attack and increasing the probability of an accidental or unauthorized launch of its nuclear weapons.[57]

Any fixed Chinese leadership and communication assets that the United States has located would be vulnerable to US nuclear attack. Even deep underground facilities can be compromised by attacks on surface features, such as entrances and ventilation, communication, and power facilities. A

---

57. See Ashton B. Carter, John D. Steinbruner, and Charles A. Zraket, eds., *Managing Nuclear Operations* (Brookings Institution, 1987), and Bruce G. Blair, *Strategic Command and Control: Redefining the Nuclear Threat* (Brookings Institution, 1985).

partial solution to this vulnerability during a crisis or conventional war would be to disperse political and military leaders to hidden locations and/or put them on mobile air-based or ground-based platforms. After surviving a US attack, these mobile platforms would need to be able to communicate with China's mobile ICBMs and its SSBNs, which is itself a challenging but feasible task. Among other possibilities, China could rely on airborne command posts, which would be highly survivable when flying well within its territory, to communicate over long distances to mobile transmitters and mobile ICBMs that survived a US attack.[58]

China would not want its ability to retaliate to depend on its top leader giving a launch command following a US nuclear attack. Relying on a single leader leaves the entire Chinese nuclear arsenal vulnerable to "decapitation"—a small attack that killed the leader or destroyed his ability to communicate with China's nuclear forces would effectively disable the country's entire force.[59] To address this vulnerability, China could predelegate launch authority down the political or military chain of command, or both, thereby greatly increasing the number and diversity of targets that the United States would need to destroy to fully disrupt China's ability to launch. Predelegation of launch authority directly to field commanders early in a crisis would reduce the need to make the Chinese leadership and communications survivable. Predelegation has a major downside, however: Early and deep predelegation increases the probability of an unauthorized launch of Chinese nuclear weapons. From what is publicly known, China has made this trade-off in favor of control—it has not predelegated launch authority.[60]

The third approach—LOW—avoids China's need to deploy survivable NC2 by instead enabling its nuclear forces to launch before a US attack can destroy critical targets. LOW is technically and organizationally demanding: China would have thirty minutes or less to reliably detect by satellite the launch of US missiles, provide the attack information to decision-makers, order the launch of its nuclear weapons, and launch them.[61] Even the most carefully planned systems and procedures cannot eliminate the risk of launching when not under attack and not launching when under attack.

58. James M. Acton, "The Survivability of Nuclear Command-and-Control Capabilities," *Journal of Strategic Studies* 48, no. 2 (2025): 430–32.

59. For an early discussion of this danger in the US-Soviet context, see John D. Steinbruner, "Nuclear Decapitation," *Foreign Policy* (winter 1981/82): 16–28.

60. Cunningham, "Nuclear Command, Control, and Communication Systems of the People's Republic of China," 7.

61. The warning time could be closer to fifteen minutes for a US attack launched from an SLBM. On LOW, see Richard L. Garwin, "Launch Under Attack to Redress Minuteman Vulnerability?" *International Security* 4, no. 3 (winter 1979/80): 117–39, and Office of Technology Assessment, *MX Missile Basing* (Government Printing Office, 1981), chap. 4.

NUCLEAR STRATEGY

According to DoD reports, China is implementing a LOW posture. China has long been interested in LOW and is now well along in acquiring the components of this capability. As of 2022, China likely had at least three early warning satellites in addition to several large ground-based phased array radars; in combination, these would provide comprehensive early-warning coverage.[62] It will likely rely on its new silo-based ICBM for the LOW mission.[63]

In sum, although China appears not to have pursued the full panoply of approaches for ensuring its ability to prevent decapitation, it has deployed the basic capabilities required for LOW. In a recent thorough analysis, James Acton found that although firm conclusions are not possible due to the opacity of the Chinese C2 system, "given the technology available to China and Russia, they would have had to badly mismanage the development of their nuclear C3I systems if the United States could undermine their retaliatory capabilities by attacking those systems."[64] If China does meet its technological potential in these systems, this would further dim US prospects for acquiring a significant damage-limitation capability and should greatly reduce any US confidence in its ability to do so.

BALLISTIC MISSILE DEFENSE

Ballistic missile defenses can be used in combination with counterforce attacks to attempt to limit damage. Current and planned US BMD systems are designed and intended to counter limited missile attacks by regional powers, such as North Korea and Iran, against the United States and its allies.[65] China, however, remains unconvinced by US statements and instead perceives US BMD as a strategic threat that could eventually undermine its ability to retaliate after a US nuclear attack. And Chinese officials point to the "2019 Missile Defense Review," which states that "in the event of con-

---

62. For this assessment, see James Acton, https://twitter.com/james_acton32/status/1640704913847058432?s=20 Twitter, who notes that information about the performance of Chinese early warning capabilities is not available. In addition, there are gaps in China's ability to acquire dual phenomenology.

63. US Department of Defense, *Military and Security Developments Involving the People's Republic of China, 2022*, 99. On earlier Chinese interest, see Gregory Kulacki, "The Chinese Military Updates China's Nuclear Strategy," Union of Concerned Scientists, 2015, http://www.ucsusa.org/sites/default/files/attach/2015/03/chinese-nuclear-strategy-full-report.pdf, and Fiona S. Cunningham and M. Taylor Fravel, "Assuring Assured Retaliation: China's Nuclear Posture and US-China Strategic Stability," *International Security* 40, no. 2 (fall 2015): 30–31, 39.

64. Acton, "The Survivability of Nuclear Command-and-Control Capabilities," 451.

65. Department of Defense, "2022 Missile Defense Review," https://media.defense.gov/2022/Oct/27/2003103845/-1/-1/1/2022-NATIONAL-DEFENSE-STRATEGY-NPR-MDR.PDF.

flict, [the Ground-based Midcourse Defense system] would be used to defend, to the extent feasible, against a ballistic missile attack upon the US homeland from any source" in support of their concern.[66] Chinese experts worry that the United States could combine improving US long-range conventional strike weapons with BMD to undermine China's nuclear retaliatory capability without employing nuclear weapons.[67]

China has long been critical of US theater missile defense (TMD) plans in East Asia. Chinese concerns grew with the 2016 deployment by the United States of the Terminal High Altitude Area Defense (THAAD) missile defense system in South Korea, in reaction to North Korea's missile and nuclear weapons tests.[68] However, the interceptors deployed or planned for deployment in East Asia—SM-3s, which are deployed on US Navy ships—have no capability against Chinese ICBMs.[69] In addition, deploying ICBMs further inland—as China has done with its new silo bases—greatly increases the interceptor velocities required for TMD to be effective and, therefore, should provide China with confidence that US TMD systems are not at threat to these missiles.

A potentially larger military challenge than TMD is posed by the United States' Ground-based Midcourse Defense (GMD) system, which consists of forty-four ground-based interceptors (GBIs), plus space-based sensors and radars (including radars deployed in Japan, as part of a TMD system, which provide tracking information for the GBI). The United States plans to deploy an additional twenty next-generation GBIs beginning in 2028.[70] The GMD system is intended to defend against a small number of single-warhead ICBMs, not equipped with countermeasures, that might be launched by North Korea or Iran. These GBIs would be capable, at least in theory, of engaging ICBM warheads launched from China against the United States.

There are good reasons, however, to doubt that the United States will be able to deploy a highly effective missile defense against China. For starters, after over twenty years of development and testing, the GMD program has

---

66. Hiim, Fravel, and Troan, "The Dynamics of an Entangled Security Dilemma," 161–68. Quote from Department of Defense, "2019 Missile Defense Review," Office of the Secretary of Defense, 2019, 41.

67. China's concerns are long-standing: Christopher P. Twomey and Michael S. Chase, "Chinese Attitudes Toward Missile Defense," in *Regional Missile Defense from a Global Perspective*, ed. Catherine McArdle Kelleher and Peter Dombrowski (Stanford University Press, 2015), 197–216; Cunningham and Fravel, "Assuring Assured Retaliation, 16–19.

68. Hiim, Fravel, and Troan, "The Dynamics of an Entangled Security Dilemma," 162.

69. Personal communication from Jaganath Sankaran and Jaganath Sankaran, *The United States' European Phased Adaptive Approach Missile Defense System: Defending Against Iranian Missile Threats Without Diluting the Russian Deterrent* (RAND, 2015).

70. Arms Control Association, "Current U.S. Missile Defense Programs at a Glance," January 2025, https://www.armscontrol.org/facantisheets/current-us-missile-defense-programs-glance.

struggled to meet its basic operational requirements.[71] Still more important, there is a yet unsolvable technical challenge facing national missile defense: midcourse discrimination. The midcourse phase of the warhead's trajectory takes place in the vacuum of outer space; because it is a vacuum, all objects follow a similar trajectory. Therefore, the defender must be able to identify the ICBM warhead within a cloud of debris (the spent final stage, unburned propellant, and separation debris). In addition, the attacker can greatly complicate the defender's challenge by deploying MIRVs, decoys, and penetration aids. These countermeasures are relatively inexpensive and within the technical abilities of states that can build sophisticated ICBMs.[72] A 2012 National Academy of Sciences committee judged that combining high-resolution data from X-band radars with the infrared data collected by optical sensors on the missile-defense interceptor offered the best chance of discrimination against emerging missile states such as North Korea and Iran.[73] China, however, is capable of deploying sophisticated countermeasures, such as antisimulation decoys—which disguise the warhead to appear like a decoy—and warheads with very low infrared signatures and radar cross sections, for which discrimination remains extremely difficult, if not impossible. And China has pursued a variety of countermeasures, including not only decoys but also programs designed to undermine key subsystems of the missile defense, including space-based sensors.[74] Because the technological relationship in the competition between missile defense and countermeasures strongly favors countermeasures, China's ability to defeat US BMD is likely to far outpace the United States' ability to improve it. Moreover, emerging technologies—including space-based directed energy systems, advanced sensors, and machine learning—hold little prospect of significantly shifting this competition in favor of BMD.[75]

A BMD countermeasure that has received less attention is direct or indirect attacks on BMD ground-based sensor systems. GMD uses data from

---

71. Jaganath Sankaran and Steve Fetter, "Defending the United States: Revisiting National Missile Defense Against North Korea," *International Security* 46, no. 3 (winter 2021/22): 51–86.

72. Andrew M. Sessler et al., *Countermeasures: A Technical Evaluation of the Operational Effectiveness of the Planned US National Missile Defense System* (Union of Concerned Scientists, April 2000).

73. Committee on an Assessment of Concepts and Systems for US Boost-Phase Missile Defense in Comparison to Other Alternatives, *Making Sense of Ballistic Missile Defense: An Assessment of Concepts and Systems for US Boost-Phase Missile Defense in Comparison to Other Alternatives* (National Academies, 2012).

74. Tong Zhao, *Narrowing the US-China Gap on Missile Defense: How to Help Forestall a Nuclear Arms Race* (Carnegie Endowment for International Peace, 2020), 45–50, https://carnegieendowment.org/files/Zhao_USChina_MissileDefense.pdf.

75. Laura Grego, "Do Technology Advances Allow Missile Defense to Make Up Ground?," *Journal of Strategic Studies* 48, no. 2 (2025): 465–509.

several radar systems, including ultrahigh-frequency (UHF) early warning radars and X-band radars, to establish the missile track used to launch interceptors to a predicted intercept point. The X-band radars necessary for discrimination are forward-based; China would have good prospects for destroying these radars with conventional attacks.

If these attacks failed, China would have the option of escalation to nuclear attacks in outer space to interfere with US radars and infrared sensors. A single nuclear explosion at an altitude of 100 to 1,000 kilometers (where the midcourse intercepts would take place) would cause ionization over a very large volume of space.[76] A nuclear explosion would make accurate radar tracking of objects behind the ionized region impossible for UHF early warning radars. Although X-band radars would have much smaller location errors, warhead radar cross sections (and therefore detection ranges) can be much smaller at these higher frequencies, and the fluctuations in the radar signatures of the warhead and other target objects would make discrimination even more difficult. Nuclear detonations would also generate large infrared signals, making it impossible for the sensors on the interceptor kill vehicle to detect incoming warheads against this background over a similarly large area.[77] These effects would greatly—probably impossibly—complicate midcourse discrimination.

In summary, it is extremely unlikely that the United States would be able to deploy a midcourse defense that would be effective against a sophisticated and responsive adversary. China has the ability to deploy a wide variety of countermeasures that would defeat US BMD systems and is reported to be pursuing many of them.

Infeasibility of Damage Limitation

The overall finding of the preceding assessment is that China's modernization and expansion of its nuclear force has virtually eliminated the US damage-limitation capability, or will soon. Around the turn of the century, the United States had a highly effective counterforce capability against China, and BMD held out the possibility of enhancing this capability.[78] As recently

---

76. For example, a 1-megaton burst at an altitude of 400 kilometers would create an ionized region 440 kilometers in diameter and extending from 270 kilometers to more than 1,000 kilometers in altitude. Radar tracking of any targets behind the ionized region would experience interference. See Philip J. Dolan, ed., *Capabilities of Nuclear Weapons, Part One: Phenomenology* (Defense Nuclear Agency, 1972), figs. 8–6.

77. A. T. Stair and Randall E. Murphy, *Background Assessment and Sensor Study* (A. T. Stair Associates, 1993).

78. Charles L. Glaser and Steve Fetter, "National Missile Defense and the Future US Nuclear Weapons Policy," *International Security* 26, no. 1 (summer 2001): 58, 81–84.

as 2015, the United States still retained some of this damage-limitation capability, but China's nuclear modernization had greatly decreased it. At that time, judged in terms of the damage-limitation range specified at the outset of this chapter, the United States had some prospect of limiting damage at the higher level (40 EMT) by destroying China's silo-based ICBMs, but it likely lacked the ability to protect itself at the lower level (ten warheads on cities).[79] The situation is now quite different.

China's roughly 120 mobile ICBMs are likely to be reasonably survivable. This conclusion covers only politically plausible scenarios—the United States attacks once a crisis has become severe or during a conventional war, not by surprise during peacetime or a minor crisis.[80] It also assumes that China alerts its forces early in a crisis, can launch its mobile ICBMs from unprepared positions, adopts best practices for operating its missiles, and can launch its mobile missiles following a US attack against its NC2. Uncertainty about the future effectiveness of China's mobile missile force stems from the possibility that the United States will deploy a highly capable SBR constellation, but China has excellent prospects for winning the action-reaction competition against US surveillance. The percentage of mobile missiles that would survive is difficult to estimate with any precision. The United States might be able to locate and barrage some of them, but most should be unlocatable due to the effectiveness of available diverse countermeasures. If mobile operations extend over weeks during a crisis and conventional war, some mobile launchers may break down and others may expose themselves via communication errors. A reasonable guestimate, quite possibly on the optimistic side from the US perspective, is that the United States locates a quarter of China's mobile missiles because they fail to defeat US SBR and locates another quarter that fail for a variety of operational and logistical reasons; the other half of China's mobile missiles would survive a massive US counterforce attack and be able to maintain communications with China's leaders.[81]

---

79. This assessment was consistent with RAND estimates; see Eric Heginbotham et al., *The US-China Military Scorecard: Forces, Geography, and the Evolving Balance of Power, 1996–2017* (RAND, 2015), table 12.7.

80. During the Cold War, the United States gauged the adequacy of its forces against a bolt-from-the-blue surprise attack; this might be an appropriate conservative force-planning criterion, but judging the United States' damage-limitation capability in a surprise attack is not useful because the scenario is politically implausible.

81. The United States might do less well than these possibilities suggest because (1) even if the United States identifies some mobile missiles, it would not attack immediately but instead continue to track these missiles until it decided to launch a massive attack; during this time, China would have options to hide its missiles and pursue measures to defeat US tracking, and (2) for similar timing reasons, China would have time to repair missile systems that breakdown.

CHAPTER 6

Some of the mobile ICBMs that survive a US nuclear attack are likely to suffer launch failures. A reasonable estimate of missile reliability is 80 percent. Given these assumptions, following a US counterforce attack, China would be able to launch close to fifty mobile ICBMs at the United States. If China employs midcourse decoys—which is highly likely—and attacks US tracking radars, the vast majority of the warheads it launches can be expected to reach the United States. Assuming that the mobile missiles carry warheads with a yield of 425 kilotons, China's retaliatory capability would be close to 40 EMT, which is the upper end of the range specified for assured destruction.[82] Because China is continuing to deploy mobile missiles, its retaliatory capability will increase. In addition, the United States would likely lack confidence in its ability to destroy half of the Chinese mobile missile force and, therefore, would have to anticipate the possibility of still larger Chinese retaliation.

In addition, China's retaliatory capability will no longer be provided only by mobile missiles. China will have deploy some number of silo-based ICBMs—still to be determined by how many they deploy in the three hundred new silos—that it should be able to LOW, if not now, then in the not-distant future. If China fills half of these silos and splits this deployment between DF-31s and DF-41s, which can carry up to three warheads, and if 80 percent of these launch, these silo-based missiles would be able to deliver over 130 EMT, which is far above the upper threshold of the damage-limitation range. If China fills more or all of the silos, its LOW capability will be still larger.[83]

In addition, China's deployment of a longer-range SLBM is giving it the capability to deploy its SSBNs in bastions and target at least some of the continental United States, and quite possibly all of it. Although how effective China will be in defeating US ASW forces remains an open question, its prospects appear to be good enough that the United States can no longer discount this leg of China's nuclear forces. These forces are likely contributing to putting significant damage limitation further out of US reach.

Finally, there is every indication that China is determined to deploy a strategic nuclear force that will provide a truly massive retaliatory capability against the United States. In addition, the technological nature of the competition favors the retaliator, which reflects, among other things, the ability of countermeasures to protect mobile missiles from SBRs and launched warheads from defeat by national missile defenses, the difficulty of defeating a LOW system, and the possible advantages of protecting SSBNs in bastions. Combining China's determination with the advantage of retaliation over

---

82. Using information from Kristensen et al., "Chinese Nuclear Weapons, 2025," on China's mobile missiles: 24 DF-31As, 72 DF-31AGs with single warheads, and 28 DF-41s with three warheads, and warhead yields that are reported to be 425 kilotons.

83. This estimate does not include the DF-5s, which China is reported to be increasing from 18 to 48.

damage limitation (defense/deterrence over offense) suggests that the United States will be unable to regain a damage-limitation capability by outcompeting China.

Benefits of a US Damage-Limitation Capability

The likely infeasibility of achieving a significant damage-limitation capability might seem sufficient to make unnecessary analysis of whether the United States should pursue it. And it largely is: At first order, there is no reason to pursue military capabilities that the United States cannot acquire.

There are, however, reasons for evaluating the benefits, risks, and costs of US possession and pursuit of a damage-limitation capability. As noted at the beginning of this chapter, the United States remains committed to damage limitation, even though it emphasizes the deterrent role of its nuclear weapons. Therefore, even if out of reach, the United States is likely to pursue these capabilities. Understanding the implications is therefore vitally important.

In addition, there are arguments that resurrect the case for damage limitation, even when military-technical analysis finds achieving it to be infeasible. There is always some possibility that China will not defeat US damage-limitation programs—it could fail to adopt best operational practices, to develop necessary technologies, and/or to deploy advanced countermeasures. This is a lesson that recent scholarship finds in the Cold War experience: The Soviet Union failed to quickly develop and operate some of its forces in the ways that were required to ensure their survivability.[84] If the benefits would be sufficiently large, or the risks and costs sufficiently small, the United States should try to regain its damage-limitation capability, even though the probability of success is quite low and depends upon China's failure to pursue policies that appear to be feasible and essential to its national security. Finally, even if infeasible, the United States might be able to convince China that it believes damage limitation is feasible and that it might escalate to all-out nuclear war to achieve it. If successful, this would enhance the US ability to deter China.[85] In an attempt to make the best case for damage limitation, the following analysis addresses these arguments.

If the United States were able to achieve a damage-limitation capability, it might provide four types of benefits: (1) reduced costs to the United States in an all-out nuclear war; (2) an improved ability to deter a nuclear attack against the US homeland; (3) an enhanced ability to deter attacks against US

---

84. See Long and Green, "Stalking the Secure Second Strike."
85. Green, *The Revolution That Failed*, makes this type of argument for damage limitation.

allies and an improved bargaining position if crises occur; and (4) enhanced reassurance of US allies, especially Japan, regarding the effectiveness of the United States' extended deterrent, thereby helping preserve the alliances and supporting allies' decisions to forgo nuclear weapons.[86] Exploring the magnitude of these benefits in the US-China context—specifically the marginal benefits, given the US ability to deter China without a damage-limitation capability—provides a necessary starting point for assessing whether to pursue damage-limitation when the prospects of success appear exceedingly poor.

REDUCING COSTS OF A NUCLEAR WAR

The most obvious and direct benefit of a damage-limitation capability is a reduction of the costs the United States would suffer in an all-out nuclear war with China. As discussed above, reasonable people disagree about what constitutes meaningful damage limitation. However, given that the United States cannot achieve a damage-limitation capability at even the upper of level of the range specified in this chapter, pursuit of a damage-limitation capability holds virtually no chance of providing this type of benefit.

Some proponents of damage limitation argue that this understates the potential benefits. They claim that any reduction in the size of a nuclear attack is worth pursuing because it would save some lives.[87] Yet the survivors would be in a country essentially destroyed. What if those surviving millions were fated to lives of misery, famine, and disease, struggling for mere survival in a "smoking radiating ruin?"[88] Saving those lives would have value, but far less than saving lives in today's United States. If saving these lives involved no economic costs, the United States could pursue a damage-limitation capability as insurance against an even worse outcome. But if the cost of being minimally successful were hundreds of billions of dollars per decade, the insurance might not be worth the price. Moreover, because the probability of all-out nuclear war with China is low, the expected value—that is, the probability multiplied by the value of the damage limitation—is orders of magnitude smaller. Other uses of US resources to save and improve the quality of American lives would have to be compared to the expected value of damage

---

86. These sections draw on and extend analysis of the benefits and costs of a damage-limitation capability against emerging nuclear powers in Charles L. Glaser and Steve Fetter, "Counterforce Revisited: Assessing the Nuclear Posture Review's New Missions," *International Security* 30, no. 2 (fall 2005): 84–126.

87. See, for example, Matthew Kroenig, "Correspondence: The Limits of Damage Limitation," *International Security* 42, no. 1 (summer 2017): 200.

88. This terminology is from David Alan Rosenberg, "'A Smoking Radiating Ruin at the End of Two Hours': Documents on American Plans for Nuclear War with the Soviet Union, 1954–1955," *International Security* 6, no. 3 (winter 1981/82): 3–38, which quotes the term from a 1954 US Air Force briefing of Strategic Air Command plans for attacking the Soviet Union.

limitation. Any such calculation would be complicated, but above some level of nuclear destruction, the investment in a marginal damage-limitation capability would fare poorly against the alternative uses of US resources.

An even more telling counterargument is that a damage-limitation capability would not only be economically costly; it could also increase the probability of nuclear war. As discussed later in this chapter, pursuit of the highly competitive policies required to preserve a US damage-limitation capability would strain the US-China relationship, which could increase the probability of both conventional and nuclear war. And it would create strategic incentives for both the United States and China to increase the alert rates of their nuclear forces and/or escalate to the use of nuclear weapons, and could increase the probability of the accidental and unauthorized use of nuclear weapons. Given the exceeding small benefits of damage limitation at such high levels of damage, the increased risk of nuclear war would dwarf the benefits, resulting in expected lives lost, not lives saved.

A very different line of argument holds that even if based on military-technical considerations China "should" be able to maintain an assured destruction capability, political or organizational factors might prevent it from succeeding. The Soviet Union failed to make its SSBNs survivable when technical analysis indicated it should have been able to, and the Soviets operated their mobile missiles poorly. Again, if there were no costs or risks in pursuing a damage-limitation capability, the United States should pursue one based on the slim hope that China would make similarly poor technical and operational choices, thereby enabling the United States to significantly reduce the costs of an all-out war. The costs and risks, however, are quite large. In addition, as argued earlier in this chapter, China's prospects for acquiring an assured destruction capability are quite good: Its continuing force modernization and expansion demonstrate the country's determination to deploy a massive retaliatory capability; and China's economic and technological potential, combined with the technological advantages of retaliation over damage limitation, favor success. Thus, at least according to publicly available information, US pursuit of a damage-limitation capability based upon this possibility is a bad bet.

ENHANCING DETERRENCE OF A NUCLEAR ATTACK AGAINST THE US HOMELAND

A damage-limitation capability might enhance the US ability to deter nuclear attacks against the US homeland. Whether a damage-limitation capability contributes a lot or a little to homeland deterrence depends on how effective the US homeland deterrent would be without one. If already highly effective, there is little room for a damage-limitation capability to contribute. This is the case for the United States.

CHAPTER 6

Credibly threatening to retaliate following an all-out nuclear attack against a nuclear state's homeland is generally considered to be easy. An opponent is unlikely to doubt a state's willingness to retaliate following such an attack because at that point, the state would have little left to lose. States that have survivable nuclear forces, and are therefore capable of nuclear retaliation, will be able to make highly credible retaliatory threats.

The amount of retaliatory damage the United States must be able to threaten depends on how much the adversary values attacking the US homeland. We therefore need to ask why China might want to attack the United States in the first place. Fortunately, there are no obvious reasons. Although popular discussions during the Cold War often envisioned a nuclear war starting with a surprise attack launched under peacetime conditions, a bolt-from-the-blue attack is especially unlikely.[89] The benefits during peacetime of destroying US military capabilities and economic capabilities would be small (or negative), and they would certainly be dwarfed by the enormous costs of a US retaliatory attack that destroyed even a few major Chinese cities and industrial centers.

Given the US ability to inflict massive society-destroying damage, the only potential weakness in the US homeland deterrent stems from the credibility of US retaliation following a limited Chinese nuclear attack. However, there are no politically plausible scenarios in which China launches a limited nuclear attack against the United States, except those that grow out of a war involving US allies. Avoidance of these attacks brings us to the challenges of extended deterrence.

ENHANCING EXTENDED DETERRENCE

Establishing sufficiently credible extended deterrence threats—that is, threats intended to deter attacks on US allies—is widely believed to be much more difficult than establishing sufficiently credible homeland deterrent threats.[90] Because US interests in protecting its allies are smaller than its interests in protecting itself, China is more likely to doubt that the United States would follow through on risky US threats designed to protect its al-

---

89. Preventive attacks intended to destroy a state's nuclear force in the early stages of development or deployment are the possible exception. On states' consideration of preventive attacks, see Rachel Elizabeth Whitlark, *All Options on the Table: Leaders, Preventive War, and Nuclear Proliferation* (Cornell University Press, 2021), Mark Trachtenberg, "A 'Wasting Asset': American Strategy and the Shifting Nuclear Balance, 1949–1954," *International Security* 13, no. 3 (winter 1988/89): 5–49, Marc Trachtenberg, "Preventive War and US Foreign Policy," *Security Studies* 16, no. 1 (January/March 2007): 1–31, and William Burr and Jeffrey T. Richelson, "Whether to 'Strangle the Baby in the Cradle': The United States and the Chinese Nuclear Program, 1960–64," *International Security* 25, no. 3 (winter 2000/1): 54–99.

90. For an early articulation of this position, see Glenn H. Snyder, *Deterrence and Defense: Toward a Theory of National Security* (Princeton University Press, 1961).

lies. Extended deterrence could involve deterring nuclear use by China. For example, if it were losing a conventional war, China might launch a small number of nuclear warheads against the US homeland or a US ally with the hope of compelling the United States to stop fighting.[91] Such an attack could communicate China's willingness to risk huge costs to prevail in the conflict and thereby convince the United States to back down. Extended deterrence could also involve deterring a conventional war by threatening to escalate to a limited nuclear war if the United States and its allies were losing a conventional war.

At least in theory, a significant damage-limitation capability could increase the credibility of these US threats to employ limited nuclear options (LNOs) by reducing the costs of an all-out war. Because the United States would face reduced risks, China should increase its estimate that the United States would carry out its threats to escalate to limited nuclear attacks. The US damage-limitation capability could also contribute to deterring China by increasing its estimate that the United States would launch a massive counterforce attack instead of an LNO. Fearing that the war was going to become unlimited, the United States would likely consider launching a damage-limitation attack to reduce the costs. The costs would still greatly exceed the stakes over which the war was being fought, but they would be smaller than if the United States suffered a full Chinese nuclear attack. If China appreciates these incentives, it would be more likely to be deterred from launching its limited nuclear attack in the first place. Recognition of these rationales for possible US retaliation might also contribute to deterring China from starting a crisis or conventional war that it imagined could lead to nuclear war.

The credibility of US LNOs, however, does not depend entirely, or even primarily, on a damage-limitation capability. The threat of a limited US nuclear attack on China should, at least in theory, be more credible than all-out retaliation because a limited attack preserves China's incentives for restraint. China, understanding that the United States expects a limited Chinese response, should find US threats of limited attack more credible. The Cold War produced an extensive literature and debate on LNOs, largely reflecting the challenges of extending deterrence in MAD.[92] The key point here is that LNOs could contribute to extended deterrence when the United

---

91. This escalation would seem to violate China's no-first-use doctrine, but China appears to have a somewhat malleable and ambiguous understanding of what constitutes first use. On relevant sources, see note 79 in chapter 4.

92. See, for example, Morton H. Halperin, *Limited War in the Nuclear Age* (John Wiley and Sons, 1963), and Andrew L. Ross, "The Origins of Limited Nuclear War Theory," in *On Limited Nuclear War in the 21st Century*, ed. Jeffrey A. Larsen and Kerry M. Kartchner (Stanford University Press, 2014), 21–48.

States lacks a damage-limitation capability. How much a damage-limitation capability would enhance the US ability to deter China should therefore be judged relative to the deterrent value of the United States' massive retaliatory capabilities and its LNOs.

Pursuing a damage-limitation capability could also enhance extended deterrence by communicating to China the high value the United States places on protecting its allies. Pursuing and maintaining a damage-limitation capability would require the United States to make large investments in forces designed to counter China's growing nuclear force. The United States' willingness to make these investments, especially when its prospects for success were poor, could signal to China that the United States places great value on protecting its allies.

Whether a state should use competitive military policies, of which damage limitation is one among many, to communicate resolve is part of a long-standing debate over the merits of competitive and cooperative international policies, which were addressed in chapter 1.[93] The risk is that competition may do more harm than good, communicating geopolitical ambition instead of resolve to protect security interests, which would then strain political relations, generate insecurity, and fuel intensified competition. The key determinant of the competition versus cooperation choice is the extent to which an adversary is driven by insecurity rather than by revisionist/greedy motives or a combination of the two. Thus, the wisdom of the United States pursuing a damage-limitation capability to communicate resolve depends partly on judgments about China's motives and goals. As discussed in the theory chapters (chapters one and two), China is a mixed type—an insecure greedy state, likely one with limited greedy aims. When facing this type of adversary, defensive strategies—those that deter without threatening—are highly desirable. This counts against competing to acquire an illusory, bluffing damage-limitation capability.

The value of a damage-limitation capability for enhancing conventional deterrence depends not only on overall US nuclear capabilities, but also on the adequacy of US and allied conventional capabilities, US credibility for using its conventional forces to protect its allies, and the value that China places on conquering the ally. The more likely that conventional capabilities are adequate to deter the adversary's attack, the smaller the marginal value of increasing the credibility of nuclear escalatory threats. The problem during the Cold War was that the North Atlantic Treaty Organization (NATO) believed that the Soviet Union might have a serious interest in conquering Western Europe and that NATO's conventional forces were inferior

---

93. On this rationale for US counterforce policies during the Cold War, see Glaser, *Analyzing Strategic Nuclear Policy*, 61–102, 240–42.

to those of the Warsaw Pact.⁹⁴ The situation the United States faces today in Northeast Asia is more promising. Although China's conventional capabilities have increased substantially (as described more fully in chapter 7), the United States' treaty allies, in combination with the United States, have good prospects for defeating and deterring large-scale invasion and blockade. Factors favoring the US-Japan alliance include Japan's distance across water from China, the defense advantage created by advances in intelligence, surveillance, and reconnaissance capabilities, as well as precision strike, and the ability of the United States to flow massive forces into the region. South Korea's situation is less favorable due to its geography—which leaves it more vulnerable to a blockade—but with US support, it has reasonably good prospects for defending itself.⁹⁵

Further supporting the adequacy of extended deterrence, the credibility of the United States for using its conventional forces to defend these allies is high. For example, in a large war with Japan, not only would vital US interests be at stake (according to the Deep Engagement grand strategy, as described in chapter 3); China would also almost certainly attack US conventional forces deployed in Japan, which it should expect would draw the United States into the war. China's antiaccess/area-denial strategy, which is designed to undermine the US military's ability to operate effectively in East Asia, envisions early attacks against US forces based in the Western Pacific, which include large deployments in Japan.⁹⁶ Consequently, in addition to providing the United States and its allies with a deterrence-by-denial capability, US conventional forces have a trip-wire function that parallels the role they played in Cold War Europe. The combination of effective deterrence-by-denial capabilities and the high credibility of the US commitment meets the requirements for conventional deterrence success. There is no plausible scenario in which Chinese leaders could reasonably foresee a quick and decisive victory.⁹⁷

Confidence provided by this deterrence logic is reinforced by political assessments. Although tensions between China and US allies have grown, fueling doubts about the adequacy of the US extended deterrent and increases in allies' defense spending, there is little indication that China

---

94. In fact, NATO conventional forces were likely much more capable than they were commonly given credit for. See John J. Mearsheimer, "Why the Soviets Can't Win Quickly in Central Europe," *International Security* 7, no. 1 (summer 1982): 3–39, and Barry R. Posen, "Measuring the European Conventional Balance: Coping with Complexity in Threat Assessment," *International Security* 9, no. 3 (winter 1984/85): 47–88.

95. Eric Heginbotham and Richard J. Samuels, "Vulnerable US Alliance in Northeast Asia: The Nuclear Implications," *Washington Quarterly* 41, no. 1 (spring 2021): 159.

96. On Chinese antiaccess/area-denial capabilities and operations, see Roger Cliff et al., *Entering the Dragon's Lair: Chinese Antiaccess Strategies and Their Implications for the United States* (RAND, 2007).

97. On this criterion for effective conventional deterrence, see John J. Mearsheimer, *Conventional Deterrence* (Cornell University Press, 1983).

places great value on conquering and controlling these countries. As described in chapter 2, although China would likely prefer to have the United States end its military commitments to East Asia, there is little to suggest that China would be willing to fight a major war to achieve this.

The recurring qualification concerns President Trump's undermining of the credibility of the United States for defending its allies, which reflects the low value he places on the United States' key allies. Because the source of this problem is deeply political, the solutions are not military, including pursuit and acquisition of a damage-limitation capability.

In sum, the benefits of a damage limitation for deterring Chinese attacks on US allies would be small because US prospects for successfully extending deterrence to these countries are very good even when China has an assured destruction capability. The combination of capable conventional forces and high US credibility for using them and US LNOs for escalation should convince China's leaders not to try to conquer these US allies. Further counting against pursuing damage limitation are the negative political effects that could outweigh the credibility benefits. Given its poor prospects for acquiring a significant damage-limitation capability, the case for pursuing damage limitation in the cause of extended deterrence is still weaker. If the United States believes its extended deterrent threat requires enhancement, adding to its already substantial conventional capabilities would be the better investment.[98]

The exception to this generally rosy picture is Taiwan. As summarized in chapter 4, since the beginning of this century, the growth and modernization of China's conventional forces has decreased the US ability to defeat, and thereby deter, an invasion of Taiwan. China has also increased its capabilities for coercing Taiwan via conventional missile attacks and blockade. In addition, and very importantly, China has long emphasized the tremendous importance of unification with Taiwan. Under President Xi, China has implied a timeline for achieving unification and has engaged in a steady stream of military harassment across the Taiwan Strait. In a crisis or war over Taiwan, the balance of interests would strongly favor China. Consequently, the United States' need to supplement its ability to deter invasion and coercion of Taiwan has grown, which increases the value of a damage-limitation capability for increasing the credibility of US nuclear threats.[99]

---

98. Abraham Denmark and Caitlin Talmadge, "Why China Wants More and Better Nukes: How Beijing's Nuclear Buildup Threatens Stability," *Foreign Affairs*, November 19, 2021, https://www.foreignaffairs.com/china/why-china-wants-more-and-better-nukes.

99. Although little is known publicly about US nuclear planning vis-à-vis China, a nuclear role for protecting Taiwan would not be new; see US Department of Defense, "Nuclear Posture Review," 16. For discussion of limited nuclear war that includes a possible scenario involving Taiwan, see Thomas G. Mahnken, "Future Scenarios of Limited Nuclear Conflict," in *On Limited Nuclear War in the 21st Century*, ed. Larsen and Kartchner, 138–40.

Whether the United States should pursue a damage-limitation capability to increase its ability to deter a Chinese conventional attack on Taiwan depends partially on the value the United States places on protecting Taiwan. Chapter 4 argues for ending the US commitment to Taiwan because US interests are not vital and the risks are large. However, US policy and the mainstream view among policy experts is to preserve the commitment, in one form or another. Given this policy, Taiwan appears to be the possible exception—pursuing a damage-limitation capability, even though it is almost certainly beyond the United States' reach, might be warranted. There is always some possibility that the United States might succeed or that China would believe it has, or that China would believe the United States believes it has, which would enhance deterrence. In the end, I oppose pursuing a damage-limitation capability to enhance US deterrence of attacks against Taiwan. Even if the United States maintains its commitment, the risks of pursuing a damage-limitation capability, which are explored in more detail in the following section, exceed the benefits. Nevertheless, if looking for the best case for pursuing damage limitation, protecting Taiwan is it.

ENHANCING ALLIES' CONFIDENCE IN US EXTENDED DETERRENCE

Even though the United States can meet its extended deterrence requirements without a damage-limitation capability, US allies might not be confident that the US extended deterrent is adequate. Allies are generally harder to reassure than adversaries are to deter. Preceding China's military buildup, Japan and South Korea were largely satisfied with US extended deterrence capabilities because China posed such a small conventional threat. As China's conventional capabilities have continued to improve, both countries have become more concerned about their own capabilities and those offered by the United States. In addition, South Korea is influenced by North Korea's growing nuclear capabilities.[100] Similarly, enlargement and improvements in China's nuclear force are raising questions about the adequacy of the US extended deterrent. Japan began to worry about the implications of China's improving nuclear capability when it was still at an early stage.[101] There is a precedent for Japan's anxiety: During the Cold War, some Japanese strategists argued that Soviet acquisition

---

100. Richard J. Samuels and James L. Schoff, "Japan's Nuclear Hedge: Beyond 'Allergy' and Breakout," in *Strategic Asia 2013–14: Asia in the Second Nuclear Age*, ed. Ashley J. Tellis, Abraham M. Denmark, and Travis Tanner (National Bureau of Asian Research, 2013), 245–46. More broadly on extending deterrence to Northeast Asia, see Brad Roberts *The Case for U.S. Nuclear Weapons on the 21st Century* (Stanford University Press, 2016), chap. 7.

101. Samuels and Schoff, "Japan's Nuclear Hedge," 250.

of nuclear parity had undermined the effectiveness of the US extended deterrent commitment.[102]

The United States and its allies have a variety of options for trying to maintain allied confidence in the adequacy of the US extended deterrent without the United States pursuing a damage-limitation capability. During the Cold War, the United States relied on a variety of approaches to maintain the credibility of its commitment to Western Europe and, in turn, its allies' confidence. These included enhancing its forward-deployed conventional forces, tightening the integration of its military capabilities with those of its NATO partners, deploying theater nuclear weapons on the soil of its NATO allies, and building LNOs into its strategic nuclear war plans. Because the threats facing the United States' East Asian alliances are less severe than that posed by the Soviet Union to NATO, there are strong grounds for concluding that these approaches should be sufficient to build confidence in the United States' extended deterrent.

The United States and its allies have already taken some steps to enhance extended deterrence. For example, the 2023 Washington Declaration with South Korea creates a consultative forum to discuss nuclear planning, calls for greater integration of South Korean conventional operations with US nuclear operations and increased joint planning of conventional operations, and commits the United States to "further enhance the regular visibility of strategic assets to the Korean Peninsula," as evidenced by SSBN visits.[103] The consultative arrangement parallels the Extended Deterrence Dialogue that the United States established with Japan during the Obama administration.[104] In response to growing Chinese capabilities, Japan has decided to significantly increase its defense budget.[105] Alliance consultations have ad-

---

102. Mike M. Mochizuki, "Japan Tests the Nuclear Taboo," *Nonproliferation Review* 14, no. 2 (July 2007): 312.

103. Ankit Panda, "The Washington Declaration Is a Software Upgrade for the US-South Korea Alliance," Carnegie Endowment, May 1, 2023, https://carnegieendowment.org/2023/05/01/washington-declaration-is-software-upgrade-for-US-south-korea-alliance-pub-89648; The White House, "Washington Declaration," April 26, 2023, https://www.whitehouse.gov/briefing-room/statements-releases/2023/04/26/washington-declaration-2/. The declaration also includes a South Korean reaffirmation to the Treaty on the Non-Proliferation of Nuclear Weapons.

104. On the Extended Deterrence Dialogue, see Roberts, "Extended Deterrence and Strategic Stability in Northeast Asia," 14; Government of the United States and Government of Japan, "The Guidelines for US-Japan Defense Cooperation," April 27, 2015, http://archive.defense.gov/pubs/20150427_-_GUIDELINES_FOR_US- https://mail.yahoo.com/?.intl=us&.lang=en-US&.partner=none&.src=finance&activity=uh-mail&pspid=1183300002 JAPAN_DEFENSE_COOPERATION.pdf.

105. Adam P. Liff, "No, Japan Is Not Planning to 'Double Its Defense Budget,'" Brookings Commentary, May 22, 2023, https://www.brookings.edu/articles/no-japan-is-not-planning-to-double-its-defense-budget/.

dressed enhancing coordination of ISR and targeting, expanding shared use of US and Japanese facilities in Japan, increasing US forward deployment of more versatile and mobile capabilities, and enhancing coordination of space capabilities.[106] If these steps fail to provide sufficient confidence, Japan and South Korea could call for the deployment of US nuclear weapons on their territories; control of the weapons could reside entirely with the United States or could be shared with the host country.[107]

Costs of a US Damage-Limitation Capability

As already touched on above, a US damage-limitation capability could create pressures for escalation during a severe crisis or war. This section explores those potential pressures more fully. It also addresses a second type of cost—US pursuit of damage limitation could reduce China's security and strain US-China relations—which could increase the likelihood of a crisis or war.[108]

ESCALATORY PRESSURES AND RISKS

A US damage-limitation capability could increase the probability of Chinese escalation to nuclear war along a variety of paths, including intentional escalation, accidental and unauthorized use, and inadvertent escalation. It could also create incentives for the United States to escalate to nuclear use early in a crisis or conventional war.

Unfortunately, many of these dangers would arise even if the United States does not succeed in acquiring a meaningful damage-limitation capability; pursuit of a damage-limitation capability could be sufficient to generate many of these pressures and incentives. One set of dangers could result from policies China adopted to undermine US damage-limitation forces and from US reactions to these policies. Other of these dangers could result from uncertainties and flawed Chinese evaluations of the US capabilities: if China believes the United States has a damage-limitation capability, even if it does not have one; and from Chinese misperceptions of US beliefs about its damage-limitation capabilities, for example, if China believes the United

---

106. US Department of Defense, "Joint Statement of the 2023 US-Japan Security Consultative Committee ('2+2'), January 11, 2023, https://www.defense.gov/News/Releases/Release/Article/3265559/joint-statement-of-the-2023-usjapan-security-consultative-committee-22/.
107. On possible ways for Japan to share US nuclear weapons deployed on its soil, see Samuels and Schoff, "Japan's Nuclear Hedge," 258–60.
108. A third cost, which is not analyzed here, is the economic cost of building the forces required to pursue a damage-limitation capability.

CHAPTER 6

States believes it has a damage-limitation capability, even if the United States does not believe this.[109]

The vulnerability of China's nuclear forces could create incentives for China to use them early in a crisis or conventional war. If China plans to rely on limited nuclear attacks to coerce the United States to back down in a conflict over Taiwan or some other regional dispute, it could feel pressure to escalate early, fearing the United States would attempt to deny this option to China by launching a damage-limitation attack early in the conflict.[110] China would hope that the war could be terminated before the United States judged that an all-out nuclear war was sufficiently likely to warrant a full-scale US counterforce attack. However, the time pressure created by the United States' damage-limitation capability (or believed capability) would reduce the prospects for terminating a war before it escalates to the nuclear level. Even if the United States lacked a significant damage-limitation capability, continued US pursuit of damage limitation could lead Chinese leaders to anticipate an American attack and therefore to make the decision to escalate.

A different type of escalatory danger could result if China adopts a LOW posture to reduce the effectiveness of a US damage-limitation attack, which it appears to have done. As noted in the discussion of NC2, China has adopted a LOW posture and, by 2023, had acquired most of the capability this requires. The danger created by a LOW posture is that China could decide to launch its nuclear weapons based on flawed information that led it to believe incorrectly that the United States had launched an attack against China's nuclear forces. Given the severe timelines required to launch on warning, a state is more likely to act on flawed information because it lacks time to adequately assess warning information.

The dangers of escalation would be even greater if China believed that the United States could cripple its NC2 facilities. As discussed above, even if a US attack against Chinese missiles would not by itself significantly limit damage, China could fear that the United States might succeed by also attacking its NC2, thereby decreasing or even eliminating China's ability to launch whatever missiles survive. To reduce this vulnerability, the Chinese leadership could predelegate launch authority and capability to the military officers who operate the weapons, enabling them to launch an attack if the Chinese command authority is destroyed. The danger is that field command-

---

109. On these types of dangers during the Cold War, see Glaser, *Analyzing Strategic Nuclear Policy*, 245–49.

110. This pressure is quite different and likely much weaker than the standard interlocking preemptive incentives that were the focus of much Cold War concern and analysis. That type of pressure does not currently exist because China lacks the ability to destroy enough of the US nuclear force.

ers might then launch an attack that the national leadership had not authorized, possibly because they believed their weapons were going to be destroyed or because they misunderstood an order from the leadership. In addition, the danger of an unauthorized launch might increase simply because, under tense and demanding conditions, there would be more individuals who were capable of launching a nuclear attack. Fortunately, Chinese leaders have given priority to maintaining centralized control over their nuclear systems and therefore are believed to be unwilling to predelegate launch authority.[111] If this priority holds, these dangers will be minimized.

During a conventional war, a very different escalatory path could result from US attacks against China's conventional forces and C2, which also "inadvertently" destroy some of China's nuclear forces, including its SSBNs, NC2, and space intelligence assets. The danger is that China could believe these attacks increased the effectiveness of a full-scale US damage-limitation attack and that the United States was preparing to launch one.[112] If this occurs, China would face time pressures to escalate, either to destroy some of the US damage-limitation capability or to try to coerce the United States before suffering a damage-limitation attack. If the United States lacks a damage-limitation capability—which, I have argued, it does or will soon—and China understands this, the unintended destruction of some Chinese nuclear capability would be much less dangerous. Nevertheless, once an intense conventional war has commenced, leaders may be inclined toward pessimistic assessments in the face of uncertainties that favor escalation.

The ability to destroy China's forces could also create incentives for the United States to attack earlier in a conventional conflict. If China has the capability to make its nuclear forces more survivable as a crisis deepens—as it would by increasing the alert rate and dispersal of its mobile missiles and SSBNs and possibly by predelegating launch authority—the United States would face time pressure to launch a counternuclear attack before China was able to fully institute these survivability measures. The United States would face a "tactical window" of opportunity that created time pressures to attack China's nuclear capabilities, even though the United

---

111. Cunningham, "Nuclear Command, Control, and Communication Systems of the People's Republic of China."

112. Avery Goldstein, "First Things First: The Pressing Danger of Crisis Instability in US-China Relations," *International Security* 37, no. 4 (spring 2013): 49–89; Caitlin Talmadge, "Would China Go Nuclear? Assessing the Risk of Chinese Escalation in a Conventional War with the United States, *International Security* 40, no. 4 (spring 2017): 50–92; James Acton, "Escalation Through Entanglement: How the Vulnerability of Command-and-Control Systems Raises the Risks of Inadvertent Nuclear Escalation," *International Security* 43, no. 1 (summer 2018): 56–99. Arguing that the risks of inadvertent escalation are small is Wu Riqiang, "Assessing China-US Inadvertent Nuclear Escalation," *International Security* 46, no. 3 (winter 2021/22): 128–62.

States would prefer that the conflict remain at the conventional level.[113] Adding to pressures to escalate, the United States might interpret China's alerting as indicating that China was planning to launch a nuclear attack, even though China was acting simply to increase the survivability of it forces. Given this interpretation, the United States would face increasing time pressure to launch a damage-limitation attack. It is, however, extremely unlikely that the United States would take advantage of this opportunity to attack in response to Chinese mobilization early in a crisis, unless it believed that nuclear war was quite likely.

Although I conclude that these damage-limitation-fueled escalatory pressures would reduce US security, there is a counterargument: They might enhance the US ability to deter a Chinese conventional attack and thereby increase US security. According to this line of argument (which I touched on while assessing how damage-limitation capabilities might enhance deterrence of Chinese attacks against Taiwan), without these escalatory pressures, China might believe that a conventional war was so unlikely to escalate to a nuclear war that it would essentially disregard, or at least heavily discount, the danger posed by US nuclear weapons. In other words, without creating these escalatory pressures, the contribution of US nuclear forces to conventional deterrence is undermined by the "stability-instability paradox." During the Cold War, there was an extensive debate over the magnitude of this paradox and how best to address it.[114]

Two points deserve emphasis. First, even without these counterforce-driven escalatory pressures, the possibility of a US-China nuclear war should contribute substantially to deterrence of major Chinese provocations. The United States would be able to threaten limited nuclear strikes that should be far more credible than an unlimited nuclear attack. Likely still more important, Chinese leaders should be concerned that a large conventional war, complicated by the "fog of war" and unforeseen twists and exigencies, could escalate.[115] Second, China's provocations could result in a large conventional war that China's leaders did not foresee when they launched their provocations. In this type of scenario, pressures to escalate to nuclear war would do nothing to deter the original provocation but would increase the probability of escalation to nuclear war and thereby increase its overall probability.

---

113. On window pressures, see Stephen Van Evera, *Causes of War: Power and the Roots of Conflict* (Cornell University Press, 1999), chap. 4.

114. See, for example, Glenn A. Kent and David E. Thaler, *First Strike Stability: A Methodology for Evaluating Strategic Forces* (RAND, August 1989); Glaser, *Analyzing Strategic Nuclear Policy*, 224–26; and Jervis, *The Meaning of the Nuclear Revolution*, 19–22.

115. Nevertheless, past evidence has suggested that Chinese leaders were confident it would not escalate. See Cunningham and Fravel, "Assuring Assured Retaliation," 34–47. This may be changing, however; see Hiim, Fravel, and Troan, "The Dynamics of an Entangled Security Dilemma."

In short, through a variety of potential paths, current US counterforce systems and future US efforts to regain a damage-limitation capability are likely to create pressures that increase the probability that a conventional war would escalate to nuclear war. Thus, even if US damage-limitation policies did enhance extended deterrence, the United States would face a complex trade-off. Given that US extended deterrent capabilities are adequate even when the United States lacks a damage-limitation capability (with the possible exception of a war over Taiwan), and the shortcomings of the stability-instability arguments, the United States should make this trade-off against the pursuit of a damage-limitation capability.

NEGATIVE POLITICAL IMPACT ON US-CHINA RELATIONS

As explained in chapter 1, a state's competitive military policies can reduce an adversary's security both by undermining military capabilities that it believes are necessary to protect its vital security interests and by communicating that the state has malign motives. Through the logic of the security dilemma, the adversary's increased insecurity can reduce the state's own security because a more insecure adversary is more likely to place greater value on expansion, to adopt riskier policies to prevail in disputes over territory, to pursue assertive foreign policies designed to divide the state's allies, and to compete intensely to improve its military capabilities. These policies can in turn lead the state to become more insecure and to feel compelled to adopt more competitive policies of its own. More specifically, US damage-limitation efforts could further convince China that the United States wants to continue to dominate Northeast Asia, contribute to China's determination to undermine US power projection capabilities, and encourage Beijing to pursue uncompromising policies in regional disputes.

Efforts by the United States to regain its damage-limitation capability are likely to set these dynamics in motion because they would be designed to deny retaliatory capabilities that China believes are necessary to protect its vital interests. In fact, China already sees US nuclear policy in this light—it is "frequently cited by Chinese experts as evidence of a destabilizing pursuit of nuclear superiority."[116] US full pursuit of a damage-limitation capability would lead to even more negative and intense interpretations. China is especially likely to interpret competitive US nuclear policies as reflecting malign US motives because the United States has the option of choosing a less threatening strategy that promises to be highly effective—a wide spectrum of nuclear retaliatory options without a damage-limitation capability. In other words, the United States would be choosing an offensive strategy—one that attempts to take away China's retaliatory capability and provide

---

116. Fiona S. Cunningham, "Cooperation Under Asymmetry": 162.

CHAPTER 6

the United States with a clear nuclear advantage—instead of a defensive strategy that relies on retaliatory capabilities and accepts China's possession of the same, thereby signaling malign motives. The interaction could be most acute over Taiwan, with the United States believing that it needs a true nuclear advantage to deter China, and China concluding that the United States is determined to prevent it from achieving its top foreign policy priority.

Because the United States already deploys key components of a damage-limitation capability—nuclear forces capable of destroying all fixed land-based targets and highly capable ASW assets—the most significant addition to its damage-limitation programs would likely be SBRs designed to track Chinese mobile missiles. Although, as discussed above, China would likely be able to defeat these US surveillance capabilities, it would correctly interpret them as deployed to undermine its nuclear retaliatory capability. Increasing the size of the US nuclear force, which will be required to target the fully alerted Chinese force if planning to barrage China's mobile missiles, would be another indicator of US pursuit of damage limitation. US BMD designed specifically to counter Chinese ballistic missiles would pose yet another significant addition. China has long worried that US BMD programs pose a threat to its retaliatory capabilities; a US program dedicated to intercepting Chinese missiles would generate much greater concern.[117] Prompt conventional weapons, if deployed in sufficiently large numbers, could raise the specter of a US damage-limitation capability that did not rely on nuclear weapons. These forces would be effective only if used before China alerted its nuclear forces, but they could appear especially threatening if China believes that the United States would be more likely to use them than its nuclear weapons.[118]

By forgoing deployment of these new systems, the United States would avoid sending China negative signals about its motives; China might even interpret this restraint as a positive signal about the extent of American goals. This signaling would be especially valuable because other efforts by the United States to send positive signals by reducing its existing damage-limitation capability would be harder to design and implement.

China's ongoing nuclear modernization program has or will soon provide it with an assured destruction capability. Even if the United States deploys

---

117. Jing-Dong Yuan, "Chinese Response to US Missile Defense: Implications for Arms Control and Regional Security," *Nonproliferation Review* 10, no. 1 (spring 2003): 75–96; Kulacki, "Chinese Concerns About US Missile Defense"; Twomey and Chase, "Chinese Attitudes Toward Missile Defense"; Cunningham and Fravel, "Assuring Assured Retaliation."

118. On growing Chinese concern about US conventional capabilities, see Hiim, Fravel, and Troan, "The Dynamics of an Entangled Security Dilemma."

the systems required to destroy China's mobile missiles—including SBRs and a larger nuclear force—China should be able to defeat these systems. In addition, China will be able to launch its silo-based ICBM on warning of a US attack. Although not yet as capable as its ICBM leg, China is making significant progress toward a survivable sea-based nuclear force—its current-generation SLBM can likely be deployed in a mode capable of reaching most or all of the United States from a protected bastion and its next-generation SLBM should have still greater range.

The United States should not try to regain its damage-limitation capability—its prospects for success would be poor, and the benefits would be small compared to the risks. China is a wealthy and technically advanced adversary, which gives it excellent prospects for winning this competition. Fortunately, the United States does not need a damage-limitation capability to effectively extend deterrence to its East Asian allies. Working with these countries, the United States can continue to meet the requirements for conventional deterrence without relying on the threat of nuclear escalation. Moreover, even without a damage-limitation capability, the possibility that an intense conventional war could escalate to a nuclear war should contribute significantly to deterring China from launching a large conventional attack against a US ally. Taiwan is the exception here because it is much more vulnerable to Chinese conventional capabilities and China is far more determined to achieve unification. But given the asymmetry of interests and the United States' limited interests, the increased risks that would be generated by US pursuit of a damage-limitation strategy are unwarranted.

These risks are both political and military. The intensified military competition that would unavoidably result would deepen strains in US-China relations, thereby increasing the probability of conflict between the United States and China by leading each country to see the other as more ambitious and threatening and, therefore, less willing to make political compromises. On the military side, US deployment of the forces required to pursue a damage-limitation capability would increase pressure for China to alert its nuclear forces early in a crisis, predelegate launch authority, prepare to launch its missile forces on warning, or all of these. The result would be an increased probability that a severe crisis or conventional war would escalate to nuclear war. These US counterforce systems could also encourage the United States to launch a nuclear war in the hope of achieving marginal damage limitation, when the war would otherwise have remained a conventional war or a limited nuclear war.

Although China will be more capable than in the past, the good news is that, even without a significant damage-limitation capability, the United States will retain highly effective nuclear deterrent forces and will be able to do so without engaging in intense military competition. Adopting this policy will require a fundamental change in US nuclear strategy—from its

CHAPTER 6

current emphasis on targeting adversary forces to a punishment/countervalue strategy—that is long overdue. Among its advantages, this change would reduce the dangers created by counterforce targeting and enable the United States to more accurately gauge the danger posed by China's nuclear force. More broadly, the change in nuclear strategy would lay the foundation for a nuclear policy that easily balances the dual goals that the United States should be pursuing—high-quality deterrent forces that pose relatively little threat to China's security.

CHAPTER 7

Conventional Strategy

How Much Offense Does the United States Need?

As with its nuclear force, China has dramatically improved its conventional forces since the beginning of this century. The implications for the United States and its security commitments are even larger than those that flow from China's deployment of an assured destruction capability. In the 1990s, if the United States came to Taiwan's defense, China lacked the ability to invade or blockade Taiwan. In contrast, by the early 2020s, China could reasonably envision scenarios in which its invasion would be successful. As reviewed in chapter 4, the weight of expert opinion still holds that China's invasion prospects are poor. Nevertheless, a military contest over Taiwan would now pose major challenges for the United States.

Beyond Taiwan, China's modernization and expansion of its conventional forces has greatly improved its capabilities throughout East Asia. China can now project military power to the southern reaches of the South China Sea, enabling it to challenge the maritime and resource claims of other littoral states. And China's conventional buildup has increased Japan's, and especially South Korea's, vulnerability. In combination with growing doubts about the reliability of the US extended deterrence commitments, these countries have become increasingly interested in acquiring nuclear weapons.[1]

China's conventional forces are designed to make the operation of US forces near its coastline and maritime periphery much more difficult. China's conventional missiles can target US bases in Japan and Guam, as well as Japanese and Taiwanese bases. China's antiship cruise and ballistic missiles, combined with improved intelligence, surveillance, and reconnaissance (ISR) capabilities, will make US ships vulnerable out to at least many

---

1. Eric Heginbotham and Richard J. Samuels, "Vulnerable US Alliances in Northeast Asia: The Nuclear Implications," *Washington Quarterly* 44, no. 1 (spring 2021): 157–75.

CHAPTER 7

hundred kilometers from China's coast. In addition, China's submarines and combat aircraft will further increase the risks to US forces operating within the first island chain—which includes Japan, Taiwan, and the Philippines, and bounds the South China and East China Seas as well as the Taiwan Strait. This combination of military assets is captured by the term *anti-access/area-denial* (A2/AD). Due to its improved conventional capabilities and the severely strained US-China political relationship, China is now officially the "pacing challenge" for US military forces.[2]

Looking beyond specific forces, the central question the United States must address is what conventional military strategy can best defend its interests against these Chinese capabilities. Given its current grand strategy, the United States needs to have the capability to aid in the protection of its treaty allies—including Japan, South Korea, the Philippines, and Australia—as well as Taiwan. If the United States were to shift to my recommended grand strategy—Deep Engagement Minus—then it would no longer need to plan to be able to protect Taiwan. But this change is unlikely for the foreseeable future.

Given the United States' commitment to Taiwan, defending Taiwan should be the United States' key planning scenario. It is the most demanding and the most likely of the major-war scenarios. China could attempt to gain control of Taiwan via invasion, blockade, or conventional countervalue attacks, and experts disagree about whether invasion or blockade is more likely.[3] China could also invade some of the smaller islands that are part of Taiwan. As discussed in chapter 4, both blockade and invasion have advantages for China. Blockade is likely easier, but even if militarily successful, it might fail to compel Taiwan to accept China's demand for unification. Invasion is harder but can produce a more direct and decisive outcome. Beyond Taiwan, China could employ similar options to gain control of Japan, although success would be much harder to achieve. And, as discussed in chapter 5, China could use its improved naval and air capabilities to gain control of additional land features in the South China Sea.

This chapter focuses on US strategy for deterring a Chinese invasion of Taiwan and for defending Taiwan if deterrence fails. Focusing on invasion is especially useful for assessing US strategy because this mission would stress US forces and decision making, and for understanding how the risks

---

2. Secretary of Defense Lloyd Austin, 2022 *National Defense Strategy of the United States of America (Security Strategy)*, Department of Defense, October 2022, 3.

3. Michael Casey, "Firepower Strike, Blockade, Landing: PLA Campaigns for a Cross-Strait Conflict," in *Crossing the Strait: China's Military Prepares for War with Taiwan*, ed. Joel Wuthnow et al. (National Defense University Press, 2022).

of escalation vary with US conventional strategy.⁴ The strategy that is focused on Taiwan would also be well matched to protecting Japan, although in the latter case, the military challenges would be smaller and the political implications would be far less negative.

Beyond deterring China, the design of US conventional strategy should include two other objectives. First, it should avoid decreasing China's security. An insecure adversary can be more dangerous because it may place greater value on expansion that will increase its security and because its efforts to regain its security by building up its arms can fuel an arms competition that leads both states to believe the opposing state is more ambitious/greedier, which can fuel a continuing negative political spiral. The security dilemma can be the primary cause of insecurity, in which case, the United States faces a trade-off between enhancing its deterrence capabilities and decreasing China's insecurity. Chapter 1 explored these issues and provided the theoretical foundation for exploring how best to strike this balance. Second, the United States' strategy should avoid creating pressures and incentives for escalation—from crisis to conventional war, and from conventional war to nuclear war.⁵ In some cases, there can be trade-offs between enhancing deterrence and decreasing escalatory pressures.⁶

The first section of the chapter makes a basic point about the political implications of defending Taiwan: The United States cannot maintain its commitment to defend Taiwan without creating Chinese insecurity. Chinese insecurity is unavoidable because, as explored in chapter 4, the source of this dispute between China and the United States is a fundamental disagreement about the status quo, not a security dilemma. Although this may not seem like the natural place to begin this chapter, the point is sufficiently important that it deserves highlighting at the outset.

---

4. This said, a US force optimized to defeat an invasion might differ from one designed against a blockade. The divergence could be largest for US allies and partners, who would face increased risks if they design their forces to support the United States' strategy but then the United States did not join the war. See Rachel Esplin Odell et al., *Active Denial: A Roadmap to a More Effective, Stabilizing, and Sustainable U.S. Defense Strategy in Asia*, Quincy Paper No. 8, Quincy Institute for Responsible Statecraft, June 2022, 81–82, 84, https://quincyinst.org/research/active-denial-a-roadmap-to-a-more-effective-stabilizing-and-sustainable-u-s-defense-strategy-in-asia/.

5. This criterion is more controversial than it might initially sound; escalatory pressures can be valuable if the adversary's awareness of them engenders caution and thereby deters crises and war. Consequently, a state may want its strategy and forces to create some escalatory pressures.

6. Concern about escalation is largely distinct from concern about how to manage a peacetime security dilemma. For example, escalatory dangers can directly decrease the state's own security; in contrast, when focusing on a security dilemma, the immediate effect of the state's policy is a decrease in the adversary's military capabilities and an increase in the state's own capabilities.

CHAPTER 7

The second section briefly reviews China's conventional forces and the military challenges they create for the United States. The third section begins the evaluation of the United States' broad choice of conventional strategy. I draw on the existing debate, which is not extensive, to characterize US options and the conditions under which they are most likely to succeed. The United States could pursue deterrence by punishment—threatening costs to convince China not to attack, or deterrence by denial—promising defeat to convince China not to attack. Within deterrence-by-denial strategies, there are two basic approaches, which I term *Offensive Denial* and *Defensive Denial*. Although punishment—which could take the form of a blockade—has some attractive features, I argue it is too unlikely to succeed to provide the foundation for US conventional strategy. Offensive Denial focuses on destroying the adversary's forces and overall military capability quickly, while Defensive Denial focuses more narrowly on defeating the forces the adversary is employing to achieve its key military mission. In the Taiwan scenario, Offensive Denial, in the form of the Air-Sea Battle concept that the United States adopted in the late 2000s, emphasizes early attacks deep into China's territory that are designed to destroy its air defenses, mobile missiles, and command-and-control capabilities.

In contrast, Defensive Denial focuses on destroying China's amphibious forces as they cross the Taiwan Strait and takes advantage of the US ability to bring forces into the theater as the war progresses. I conclude that Defensive Denial is better matched with the technological and geographic conditions the United States faces in East Asia. The good news is that current US doctrine is moving in this direction. The Joint Concept for Access and Maneuver in the Global Commons (JAM-GC), which the United States adopted in 2016, is more focused on defeating invading forces than was Air-Sea Battle. However, JAM-GC contains significant ambiguities, and some of the forces the United States plans to buy are not well matched with the doctrine's requirements.

The chapter's fourth section explores a variety of escalatory pressures that US conventional attacks could create and compares the extent to which Offensive and Defensive Denial would create them. The most basic type of escalation is deliberate escalation in response to losing. China might be willing to escalate to nuclear bargaining, especially since it likely believes its greater interest in Taiwan confers a bargaining advantage. There is little the United States can do to reduce this danger. There is also the possibility that, if losing the war, the United States would escalate to limited nuclear attacks to compel China to forgo its attempted conquest. Other escalatory dangers could arise from US attacks against the Chinese mainland and from conventional crisis instability and inadvertent escalation—pressures created by US conventional attacks that weaken China's nuclear retaliatory capability. Defensive Denial would create smaller escalatory pressures along some of these paths, but not others.

The fifth section addresses choices that would shape the United States' implementation of Defensive Denial. Long-range antiship missiles play a central role in Defensive Denial. The United States needs to decide on the proper balance among deploying them on allied territory, tactical aircraft, carrier-based air, and bombers based outside of East Asia. Each has advantages and disadvantages. The United States will need to decide whether to attack targets on China's mainland—although Defensive Denial aspires to forgo these attacks, their military value suggests the need to find a careful balance with the escalatory risks. The United States will also need to decide whether to launch kinetic antisatellite attacks, which could greatly reduce the risk of operating its naval forces relatively close to Taiwan. The trade-offs here involve the likely loss of US satellites due to Chinese retaliation and the risks of escalation due to the entanglement of satellites in conventional and nuclear operations. A final question is whether the United States should plan to deploy American troops to Taiwan to contribute to the defeat of Chinese forces that reach the island. The section does not set out to resolve these complicated issues but explains the considerations and analyses required to reach conclusions.

Taiwan and Chinese Insecurity

Unfortunately, the United States cannot defend Taiwan without threatening China—that is, generating Chinese insecurity. China and the United States have a disagreement over the political status quo. China believes that Taiwan is part of its homeland. In contrast, although the United States' official policy is that it will accept unification if achieved peacefully, it also provides Taiwan with military forces that reduce China's ability to invade and coerce Taiwan and, more importantly, has a commitment, albeit an ambiguous one, to protect Taiwan from a Chinese attack.

The result of this complicated situation is that the US ability to defend Taiwan creates Chinese insecurity, and improvements in the US ability to defend Taiwan increase this insecurity. China relies on its ability to invade or coerce to deter Taiwan from declaring independence. In addition, China believes it might need these capabilities even if Taiwan does not declare independence if peaceful unification clearly becomes politically infeasible. It is also possible that China will decide it is unwilling to wait any longer, even if the possibility of peaceful unification has not been clearly foreclosed.

Unlike a situation that is driven fundamentally by a security dilemma, deploying forces that favor defense and provide little offensive capability will not solve this insecurity problem. Even improving a purely defensive US-Taiwan capability increases Chinese insecurity. As discussed later in this chapter, US conventional capabilities for protecting Taiwan are in fact heavily oriented toward defense, with little strategic offensive capability. Nevertheless, China sees the US ability to defend Taiwan and its commitment to do so as problematic.

The point here is not that the United States should necessarily end its commitment to defend Taiwan. Defense policy unavoidably involves trade-offs, and the United States can quite reasonably trade enhanced deterrent capabilities for Chinese insecurity. However, the United States should not overlook how its strategy and capabilities look to China. Improvements in US capabilities will generate Chinese reactions, not because China has become more determined to control Taiwan but instead simply because China is trying to preserve what it sees as necessary capabilities. If the United States fails to appreciate the nature of this interaction, it may take other steps to reinforce its Taiwan policy that are unnecessarily provocative.

In contrast, if the United States were committed to defending Japan but not Taiwan, its military capabilities would generate far less Chinese insecurity. The difference is not the US forces involved—the United States would rely on essentially the same types of forces to defend Japan as it would to defend Taiwan. Instead, the key difference lies in the political situation: China does not consider Japan to be part of China; therefore, the combined ability of Japan and the United States to defend Japan is far less problematic. China might still find US forces undesirable, but for reasons of greed—for example, if it wants to be a regional hegemon and therefore wants the United States to leave East Asia. All this said, at this point, the distinction is a bit theoretical because the United States is committed to defending both Japan and Taiwan.

Given the political situation, efforts to reduce the risks generated by the United States' conventional strategy will be largely limited to operational considerations that influence the probability of escalation. Before turning to these issues, I briefly summarize the challenge that China's conventional forces present to the United States.

China's Invasion Requirements and Challenges

To assess US conventional strategy, we need first to understand the forces and missions that the United States and Taiwan need to be able to defeat. To invade Taiwan, China would need to transport hundreds of thousands of troops and large amounts of heavy equipment (including tanks and artillery) across the Taiwan Strait, as well as supplies to sustain its military forces. China would then likely attempt to occupy Taipei (Taiwan's capital)—which would require a major ground battle—and to compel Taiwan's leaders to give up control of their government and then fight to gain control of the rest of the island.

An operation on this enormous scale would likely require several months of mobilization. China would move its ground, air, and missile forces toward its coast and move mobile missiles out of their garrisons. During this period, it might secretly mine Taiwan's ports. This mobilization would provide the United States with strategic warning—indications of China's intention to invade Taiwan. There is, however, the possibility that China would launch its attack following a shorter mobilization because this would enable it to reduce the time available for the United States to flow forces into the region. Either way, China might be able to achieve operational surprise (to be distinguished from strategic surprise), possibly through deception and normalization of higher-readiness activities.[7]

China would likely begin its invasion by attempting to destroy Taiwan's ability to attack naval forces crossing the Taiwan Strait.[8] China would employ ballistic and cruise missiles against Taiwan's air and missile bases, military and civilian logistics hubs, and command-and-control centers. China would also attack Taiwan's air defenses, which would enable attacks by China's crewed aircraft that would be used to attack mobile missiles, as well as other military targets, and to attack energy, communication, and economic infrastructure with the goal of demoralizing the civilian population.

China would have to decide whether to attack US forces based in East Asia at the outset of the war or instead to forgo these targets with the hope that the United States would not come to Taiwan's defense. China believes that the United States will come to Taiwan's defense, even though the US commitment remains ambiguous, which increases the probability of early attacks against US forces.[9] China's missiles can target US bases in Japan and reach still farther to US bases on Guam. If China does attack US bases at the outset, then it will also have to decide whether to attack Japanese bases. This choice is further complicated because there are some bases at which both Japanese and American forces are regularly deployed and because the countries would likely further mix their forces during a severe crisis or war. Japan has an ambiguous commitment about getting involved in a Taiwan conflict. Even if not attacked, Japan could provide logistical support to US military forces. If Japan's leaders believe China's attack poses a threat to Japan's survival, including but not limited to cases in which Japan is attacked, Japan could use its military forces in a combat role, under certain

---

7. Casey, "Firepower Strike, Blockade, Landing."
8. For a detailed description of the phases of the war summarized here, see Ian Easton, *The Chinese Invasion Threat: Taiwan's Defense and American Strategy in Asia* (Eastbridge Books, 2019), chap. 4.
9. Paul Heer, "The Inconvenient Truth About Taiwan's Place in the World," *The National Interest*, September 27, 2000, https://nationalinterest.org/feature/inconvenient-truth-about-taiwan's-place-world-169659.

conditions. However, even given these legal authorizations, "judgments about whether and under what authorities the Japan Self-Defense Forces (JSDF) could be mobilized specifically in a cross-strait crisis will inevitably hinge on legal interpretations and political decisions in Tokyo based on specific circumstances."[10] China might hope that not attacking Japanese bases and infrastructure would lead Japan to not support the US effort and, therefore, forgo these targets.

Since the beginning of the century, China has deployed forces that are highly capable of performing these missions. In 2022, it deployed well over one thousand ground-launch ballistic and cruise missiles that are sufficiently accurate to effectively target runways, the areas where aircraft are deployed, naval bases, and ammunition bunkers.[11] In addition, China has deployed the DF-26, an intermediate-range missile that can reach Guam; in 2024, China was reported to have deployed more than 250 DF-26 launchers and 500 missiles.[12] China has struggled to produce fifth-generation fighter aircraft (comparable to the United States F-35) but has deployed over one thousand fourth-generation aircraft that are capable of ground-attack and air-to-air combat. It is projected to have deployed over two thousand fourth- and fifth-generation combat aircraft by 2035. China has deployed a mix of nuclear and diesel attack submarines, but they will likely not pose the major threat to US attack submarines operating in the Taiwan Strait. Instead, it would be Chinese navy ships and patrol aircraft that possess the greatest antisubmarine warfare (ASW) capability, if US nuclear-powered attack submarines launch attacks that expose their location.[13]

Following attacks against Taiwan's antiship capabilities and air defenses, the next stage of China's campaign would involve transporting troops, equipment, and fuel to Taiwan and protecting them from attack. Given the large volumes that would need to be transported, the majority would cross the strait via ship. Although substantial, China's amphibious lift capability appears to be inadequate for the enormous transport that would be required by an invasion, given likely attrition. Chinese ships would make many trips across the strait, so China's overall ability to transport troops and materiel

---

10. Adam P. Liff, "The US-Japan Alliance and Taiwan," *Asia Policy* 17, no. 3 (July 2022): 125–60, quote at 148.

11. This paragraph draws heavily from Odell et al., *Active Denial*, 54–57.

12. US Department of Defense, *Military and Security Developments Involving the People's Republic of China*, 2024 Annual Report to Congress, 64–66, https://media.defense.gov/2024/Dec/18/2003615520/-1/-1/0/MILITARY-AND-SECURITY-DEVELOPMENTS-INVOLVING-THE-PEOPLES-REPUBLIC-OF-CHINA-2024.PDF. The DF-26 is a dual-capable missile.

13. Owen R. Cote, "One If By Invasion, Two If By Coercion: US Military Capability to Protect Taiwan from China," *Bulletin of the Atomic Scientists* 78, no. 2 (March 2022): 67, https://www.tandfonline.com/doi/full/10.1080/00963402.2022.2038782.

depends on how long it would take to get a given number of troops and amount of equipment across the strait, and its ability to do so as it suffers attrition. China will be able to supplement navy ships with Chinese Coast Guard forces and maritime militia forces, as well as with merchant ships. The adequacy of this overall capability will depend heavily on the ability of opposing forces to inflict losses.[14]

If the United States joins the conflict, China will face attacks by US antiship missiles that could be based on land and be carried by fighters, bombers, and surface ships. In addition, US submarines operating in the Taiwan Strait could attack with torpedoes.[15] China would employ a combination of submarines, undersea sensors, aircraft, and surface ships to try to attrite the US submarine threat.[16] It would rely on its missiles and ISR to keep US ships, especially aircraft carriers, distant from Chinese territory and to sink those that venture into range, and on its air defenses to intercept antiship missiles.

The final stage of China's invasion would involve China fighting to take control of the island. Once its ground troops land on Taiwan, China would need to continue to flow troops and supplies across the strait and capture ports and airfields. If Chinese forces land in the southern part of Taiwan, which is less heavily defended and therefore likely to be where China concentrates its landing, they would need to fight their way north to Taipei. This would be challenging because mountains run down the middle of Taiwan, which would confine China's advance to narrow coastal plains. China's airpower would play an important role in this phase of the invasion, both protecting landed troops and destroying bridges that would be used by Taiwan's troops to reach the landing area. To undermine this dimension of China's war plan, the United States would likely attempt to gain control of the air over Taiwan and the Taiwan Strait or at least deny control to China. Taiwan's ground troops would be critical in this phase of the war because, among other reasons, it would be difficult and risky for the United States to deploy its own troops to Taiwan once the war began. Experts have expressed serious

---

14. Conor M. Kennedy, "Getting There: Chinese Military and Civilian Sealift in a Cross-Strait Invasion," in *Crossing the Strait*. For a basic model of China's lift capabilities, see Eric Heginbotham et al., *The US-China Military Scorecard: Forces, Geography, and the Evolving Balance of Power 1996–2017* (RAND, 2015), chap. 6.

15. While highly effective and stealthy, submarines carry limited amounts of ammunition, which requires them to return to port to ream. Consequently, air-launched antiship missiles are more likely to pose the largest threat to China's ability to cross the strait. See Mark F. Cancian, Matthew Cancian, and Erik Heginbotham, *The First Battle of the Next War: Wargaming a Chinese Invasion of Taiwan* (Center for Strategic and International Studies, January 2023), 111, https://www.csis.org/analysis/first-battle-next-war-wargaming-chinese-invasion-taiwanSubmarines.

16. For a description of the basics and model of the battles, see Heginbotham et al., *The US-China Military Scorecard*, chap. 8

doubts about the quality and motivation of Taiwan's ground forces and have stressed the importance of improvements in the training and equipping of these forces.[17] Taiwan's extension of compulsory military service in 2024 to one year is designed both to enlarge its military and improve its training.[18]

US Strategy Options for Deterring China and Defending Taiwan

The United States has three broad strategy options for deterring a Chinese invasion of Taiwan and US allies more broadly. The most basic divide is between punishment strategies and denial strategies. Deterrence by punishment threatens to impose costs that exceed the potential benefits the adversary hopes to achieve. In contrast, deterrence by denial threatens to defeat an adversary's action, thereby denying it the benefit it hopes to achieve.[19] Recent discussion of US options has further divided denial strategies into two ideal types, which I term Offensive Denial and Defensive Denial.

Nuclear deterrence is usually based on the logic of punishment—deterrence is achieved by threatening costly nuclear retaliation against targets that the adversary values. Even the damage-limitation strategy discussed in chapter 6 is geared toward deterrence by punishment—by reducing the damage the United States would suffer, a damage-limitation capability increases the credibility of US threats to inflict massive damage. In contrast, conventional deterrence is most commonly based on the logic of denial: Deterrence is accomplished by promising to defeat an adversary's invasion. A standard requirement for deterrence by denial of conventional invasion is the ability to deny the adversary a quick victory.[20]

There are, however, exceptions for both nuclear and conventional deterrence. Threatening to use nuclear weapons to defeat a conventional invasion by destroying the adversary's forces would be a type of deterrence by denial. If, however, this tactical use was intended primarily, or even partially, as a means of threatening escalation to strategic nuclear war, then

---

17. Cancian, Cancian, and, Heginbotham, *The First Battle of the Next War*, esp. 3, 121–22.
18. Robert D. Eldridge, "Taiwan Extends Military Conscription, a System Japan Might Want to Consider," *Japan Times*, February 7, 2024.
19. The classic discussion is Glenn H. Snyder, *Deterrence and Defense: Toward a Theory of National Security* (Princeton University Press, 1961).
20. John J. Mearsheimer, *Conventional Deterrence* (Cornell University Press, 1983). Although the logic here at first appears to be denial, it includes an important element of punishment. If the adversary would be deterred by the costs of a long war, but not a quick one, then it is actually the costs of fighting the war, and its impact on the state's population, that are decisive. A long war may include elements of both punishment and denial; by creating uncertainty about the outcome, a long war promises some probability of defeat as well as costs. Karl. P. Mueller, "Conventional Deterrence Redux: Avoiding Great Power Conflict in the 21st Century," *Strategic Studies Quarterly* (winter 2018): 76–93.

even this use of tactical nuclear weapons would be partly a punishment strategy, not purely denial.[21] And conventional deterrence can be achieved by threats to impose costs; for example, by threatening to take the adversary's territory in response to an attack or to impose costs by destroying the adversary's military and disrupting its society.[22]

PUNISHMENT

The United States could implement a strategy of conventional deterrence by punishment in two broad ways. First, and most important, it could blockade China. China depends heavily on imports by sea, including energy, food, and advanced technologies. In a long war, a blockade could inflict extensive economic pain on China's citizens. The United States could blockade at a distance—including on the western side of the Strait of Malacca—that would be out of range of China's A2/AD capabilities, and it could complement this distant blockade with a close blockade.[23] A blockade could be reinforced by global sanctions designed to stop the flow of goods over land to China.

Distant blockade has a clear advantage—the United States might avoid attacking China's military forces and therefore should be less escalatory than other US options. Even if the blockade leads to military conflict, this conflict would be much less intense than a large conventional war over Taiwan, and the United States could avoid attacking the Chinese mainland, thereby avoiding a variety of escalatory pressures.[24]

There are major shortcomings of relying on blockade, however. It would not significantly reduce China's ability to invade Taiwan. Therefore, if China is willing to suffer the costs that would be imposed by a blockade, it would not be deterred from invading Taiwan. In other words, China might decide to invade Taiwan and then try to survive the blockade. This temptation might be reinforced by the slow speed with which a blockade would damage China's economy—it could take months to have a severe impact. Among other reasons, China has built up large petroleum reserves, which would give it a cushion against oil import cutoffs; in addition, energy imports will become less important as China transitions to renewable energy sources over

---

21. Thomas C. Schelling, *Arms and Influence* (Yale University Press, 1966), 181–84.

22. Samuel P. Huntington, "Conventional Deterrence and Conventional Retaliation in Europe," *International Security* 8, no. 3 (winter 1983/84): 32–56.

23. Sean Mirski, "Stranglehold: The Context, Conduct and Consequences of an American Naval Blockade of China," *Journal of Strategic Studies* 36, no. 3 (2013): 385–421; Fiona S. Cunningham, "The Maritime Rung on the Escalation Ladder: Naval Blockades in a US-China Conflict," *Security Studies* 29, no. 4 (2020): 730–68.

24. T. X. Hammes, "Offshore Control: A Proposed Strategy for an Unlikely Conflict," *Strategic Forum* 278, June 2012, National Defense University, https://ndupress.ndu.edu/Portals/68/Documents/stratforum/SF-278.pdf.

the coming decades. These concerns are consistent with the historical record: Conventional punishment strategies have rarely succeeded in compelling adversaries, reflecting states' willingness to suffer this scale of costs when vital interests are at stake, combined with their ability to adapt over time to economic damage and limited resources.[25]

The second punishment option, instead of or in addition to blockade, would be for the United States to threaten conventional attacks against China's civilian infrastructure. This approach would impose significant damage much more quickly than a blockade. It would still suffer the core problem of conventional punishment strategies, however: The costs would likely be insufficient to deter attack or to compel China to retreat once it controlled Taiwan.

Given these shortcomings, the United States should not base its defense of Taiwan on conventional punishment strategies.[26] Whether it should supplement a denial strategy with a blockade is a more complicated question. In a long war, the economic damage imposed by a blockade might contribute to reducing China's military capabilities, in addition to imposing large costs on China's society.[27]

OFFENSIVE DENIAL

Offensive Denial is an offensively oriented operational approach that is designed to protect the defender's country by winning a war quickly.[28] The

---

25. Robert A. Pape, *Bombing to Win: Air Power and Coercion in War* (Cornell University Press, 1996). There is the possibility, however, that China is uniquely vulnerable to an economic cutoff; see Stephen G. Brooks and Ben A. Vagle, "The Real China Trump Card: The Hawk's Case Against Decoupling," *Foreign Affairs* 104, no. 2 (March/April 2025), 76–89.

26. For disagreement based on the lower risks of a punishment strategy and the limited nature of US interests, see Melanie W. Sisson, "Taiwan and the Dangerous Illogic of Deterrence by Denial," Brookings Institution, May 2022, https://www.brookings.edu/wp-content/uploads/2022/05/FP_20220505_taiwan_strategy_sisson.pdf.

27. When evaluated as part of a denial strategy, an important consideration would be the diversion of US forces away from other demanding military missions; see Evan Braden Montgomery, "Considering a Naval Blockade: A Response to Mirski," *Journal of Strategic Studies* 36, no. 4 (2013): 615–23.

28. The descriptions and comparisons of Offensive Denial and Defensive Denial draw heavily on the work of Eric Heginbotham and his coauthors, including Eric Heginbotham and Jacob L. Heim, "Deterring Without Dominance: Discouraging Chinese Adventurism Under Austerity," *Washington Quarterly* 38, no. 1 (spring 2015): 185–99, Eric Heginbotham and Richard J. Samuels, "Active Denial: Redesigning Japan's Response to China's Military Challenge," *International Security* 42, no. 4 (spring 2018): 128–69, and Odell et al., *Active Denial*, esp. chap. 2. My synthesis, however, does not fully line up with this work. It also draws on Eugene Gholz, Benjamin Friedman, and Enea Gjoza, "Defensive Defense: A Better Way to Protect US Allies in Asia," *Washington Quarterly* 42, no. 4 (winter 2020): 171–89. Elbridge A. Colby, *The Strategy of Denial: American Defense in an Age of Great Power Conflict* (Yale University Press, 2021), prescribes a denial strategy that is close to Defensive Denial but appears to include elements of Offensive Denial as well.

key to accomplishing this is destroying the adversary's forces early in a conflict, which typically requires the defender to attack deep into the attacker's territory. Offensive Denial can have ambitious political aims—for example, regime change via the targeting of political leaders and their means of domestic political control—but need not. Its central goal is defense of the defender's territory. An offensive strategy can provide, or at least appear to provide, the defender with a clear path to victory because the defender plans to take control of the fight, define the path of the war, and eliminate uncertainties that inevitably arise in a prolonged conflict.[29] In addition, a relatively short war promises to be less costly for the defender, and its society, to fight.

In broad terms, Offensive Denial requires either forces that are much larger than the adversary's forces or technologies that favor offense over defense. If attacking the adversary's forces is difficult—because they are hard to find, well protected, and/or dispersed—defense will tend to have the advantage, so the defender will require forces that are much larger and/or more capable than its adversary's. Critical vulnerabilities in the adversary's overall system—possibly in its command, control, communications, and intelligence (C3I) systems or essential logistics—could ease the defender's task by alleviating the need to attack the full array of opposing forces. In contrast, if offense has the advantage, the defender may be able to launch efficient crippling attacks, enabling it to prevail without advantages in force size and the greater spending on military forces that this would entail. Offensive advantage will typically require that the adversary's forces are relatively easy to find and destroy, its forward defenses are vulnerable to quick penetration, and/or its air and missile defenses will be comparatively easy to spoof, cripple, or evade.

Because Offensive Denial is designed for early success, the strategy is typically envisioned as requiring the defender to deploy the necessary forces near the adversary's territory before the war begins. This could be especially demanding when protecting a distant ally, as the United States would be in East Asia. However, advances in long-range precision attack systems—including ballistic and cruise missiles—that can be carried by bombers and ships may be reducing the importance of the peacetime forward deployment of the defender's forces.

A Cold War example of Offensive Denial is the AirLand Battle concept that was adopted by the North Atlantic Treaty Organization (NATO) in the early 1980s. It stressed that, given NATO's inferior force size, maneuver and initiative were required for successful attacks. Deep attacks were intended

---

29. On why militaries tend to favor strategies with these features, see Barry R. Posen, *The Sources of Military Doctrine: France, Britain, and Germany Between the World Wars* (Cornell University Press, 1984).

CHAPTER 7

to gain advantages by destroying Warsaw Pact forces far from the immediate battle. The goal was "not to take or hold territory for the sake of doing so but is confined to operations that support the overall objective of the defense."[30]

The Air-Sea Battle concept, which the United States developed in the late 2000s, is a more recent example of an Offensive Denial strategy. Starting around the turn of the century, the United States faced a new challenge as China developed its A2/AD capabilities, which are designed to keep the United States away from China's territory and to restrict US freedom of movement near its territory, including Taiwan.[31] In response, the United States developed the Air-Sea Battle concept, which emphasizes maintaining the US ability to "confidently operate forward and project power throughout the world" and preserving the United States' freedom of action. It strives to preserve "the ability to defeat aggression and maintain escalation advantage despite the challenges posed by advance weapons systems."[32]

To achieve these objectives, the United States would launch a blinding attack against China's C2 and ISR systems at the beginning of a war. The attacks against ISR would include nonkinetic attacks against Chinese satellites, which are essential for identifying US ships in the theater and aircraft that have dispersed to remote bases. It would also launch early attacks against China's over-the-horizon radars, which are important for detecting ships and aircraft at greater distance—which would allow US forces to move closer to China's periphery—and against China's counterspace capabilities because protecting US space capabilities would be essential for the success of its attacks against mobile Chinese targets. The United States would attack Chinese air defenses, among other reasons, to enable stealthy aircraft and unmanned aerial vehicles to locate and attack mobile missile launchers, which is a key goal of Air-Sea Battle. Central to the concept's logic is Attack-in-Depth: "In traditional attrition models of warfare, forces attack the outer layer of an enemy's defenses and deliberately fight their way in. In contrast, under Air-Sea Battle, forces will attack adversary systems wherever needed to gain access to contested areas to achieve operational objectives."[33] To support its ASW campaign, the United States would attempt to destroy sensor arrays deployed on the seafloor. Because the war

30. Manfred R. Hamm, "The AirLand Battle Doctrine: NATO Strategy and Arms Control in Europe," *Comparative Strategy* 7, no. 3 (1988): 183–211, quote at 191.

31. Roger Cliff et al., *Entering the Dragon's Lair: Chinese Antiaccess Strategies and Their Implications for the United States* (RAND, 2007).

32. US Naval War College, "Air-Sea Battle: Service Collaboration to Address Anti-Access & Area Denial Challenges," 2013, *Current Strategy Forums*, 1, https://digital-commons.usnwc.edu/csf/1, 12, i.

33. Admiral Jonathan W. Greenert, USN & General Norman A. Schwartz, USAF, "Air-Sea Battle," *The American Interest*, February 20, 2012.

could last months or longer, the United States would establish a distant blockade of commerce, including energy imports, bound for China via the South China Sea. The primary purpose would be to weaken China's economy, not to directly coerce capitulation.[34]

DEFENSIVE DENIAL

Defensive Denial focuses more directly on defeating the missions that the adversary must accomplish to succeed, and less on destroying the adversary's military forces as an end in itself or a step toward military dominance. It essentially waits for the adversary's force to attack, then destroys invading forces. The defender may not need to dominate the entire battlefield but instead only the portion that is critical for defeating the adversary's invading forces. For example, in a Taiwan invasion scenario, Defensive Denial would emphasize destroying Chinese ships crossing the Taiwan Strait, while giving lower priority to destroying Chinese missiles that were attacking US and allied forces. Instead of trying to gain freedom of action over China's territory, it would attempt to deny China freedom of action in the Taiwan Strait. Similarly, for much of the Cold War, NATO doctrine for defending Western Europe was a type of Defensive Denial, designed to stop Warsaw Pact forces from breaking through NATO's forward defense and penetrating deep into NATO territory.[35]

By focusing on the adversary's attacking forces, Defensive Denial attempts to ensure that the adversary cannot win a quick victory, thereby promising a long and costly war. As noted above, denying one's adversary the ability to achieve a quick, and therefore relatively cheap, victory is considered a standard requirement for deterring a conventional war. The logic here is partly a punishment logic—the costs of fighting are imagined to exceed the benefits of conquest. At the same time, a long war creates uncertainty about the outcome, including the possibility of defeat, which fits the denial logic. Whether a very highly motivated attacker—as China would likely be regarding Taiwan—would be deterred by these costs can be questioned, but a long war and high costs are a reasonable minimum requirement. The likelihood of defeat would be a still better deterrent. The combination of high costs, even if not greater than the benefits, with a low probability of success could be sufficient to deter.

An essential feature of Defensive Denial is the ability of the defender's forces to survive early attacks; without this resilience, the defender is

---

34. Jan Van Tol et al., *AirSea Battle: A Point-of-Departure Operational Concept* (Center for Strategic and Budgetary Assessments, 2010), esp. 50–79.

35. Still more defensive approaches were proposed as alternatives to NATO's forward defense; forces would be lighter, more distributed, and deployed in depth from the border.

vulnerable to rapid defeat. Thus, proponents of Defensive Denial emphasize the necessity of hardening and actively defending bases, increasing the US ability to disperse its aircraft to a larger number of smaller bases, using camouflage and decoys to complicate the targeting challenges China would confront, and selectively using active air and missile defenses.[36] Air-Sea Battle also noted the importance of increased resilience, but it plays a less important and prominent role partly because early US strikes might be launched before US bases were attacked and partly because of its emphasis on offense operations.

In addition to generating high costs for the attacker, a long war could further support the defender under certain conditions. If the defender has substantial military capabilities deployed outside the theater of battle, a long war provides the opportunity to shift its forces into the region, thereby reducing this disadvantage of distance. The United States is clearly in this situation—only about 10 to 15 percent of US forces are regularly deployed in the Western Pacific.[37] The United States is likely to get months of strategic warning of China's preparation for an invasion, which could reduce the problems created by distance across the Pacific. However, the United States might not react quickly to this warning—possibly due to doubts about whether China would actually invade, to unresolved issues about whether the United States was willing to engage in a large conventional war with a nuclear power, or to concerns that US conventional mobilization might create a window that China would feel pressure to jump through. There is also the possibility that China would launch a war with shorter mobilization because, among other reasons, US troops were flooding into the region. Given these types of possibilities, a longer war would work to the US advantage.

A long war could also favor the state or alliance with the larger economy. A long war can require the production of new forces, the mobilization of additional troops, and the diversion of resources from the state's civilian economy and society. A larger economy can reduce the stress that this diversion places on the state. In addition, a state whose economy is less vulnerable to wartime disruption via blockade and/or reduced trade will fare better in a long war. A war over Taiwan would likely not last long enough for relative economic strength to matter, but it might. If it did, this feature would favor the United States and its allies—their combined economies are much larger than China's (and its potential allies), and they are less vulnerable to blockade.

A key factor that influences the feasibility and relative desirability of Defensive Denial is the offense-defense balance. When defense has the advantage, the defender can defeat the attacker at lower cost; smaller forces on

---

36. Odell et al., *Active Denial*, 87–89.
37. Odell et al., *Active Denial*, 80.

the defense have the potential to defeat larger forces fighting on the offense—that is, to prevent the offense from achieving its mission. The offense-defense balance can be influenced by a variety of factors, including geography and technology.[38] Distance typically favors defense because the attacker incurs the costs of transporting forces to forward positions and supplying them; in addition, movement toward to the front often increases the vulnerability of forces. However, when a defender is distant from its ally, this distance can favor an attacker that is closer to the ally. Separation by water favors defense against invasion because ships are expensive and exposed at sea, and invasion requires the transport of large quantities of soldiers and materiel. Firepower innovations, including precision, tend to favor defenders, as their effectiveness against exposed attackers is greater than against relatively more concealed defenders. Mines tend to favor the defender against an amphibious invasion because they can be deployed at a relatively low cost to make ports and beaches hard to access.

In a Chinese invasion of Taiwan, defense would enjoy important advantages. Most obviously, Taiwan and China are separated by the Taiwan Strait. Although not very wide—roughly one hundred miles—it nevertheless creates an imposing barrier to the vast quantities of men and materiel that China would need to transport across it. The United States' distance from Taiwan would, however, favor China, although, as discussed, warning provided by China's mobilization and by a long war would work to reduce this advantage.

In addition, key technologies favor the defense. In somewhat overly simplified terms, the key US and allied threat to China's invasion force will be antiship missiles—launched from ground, sea, and air.[39] The key threat to US forces deployed in East Asia and to allied forces would be China's missiles. China's missiles would pose a potent threat to stationary targets, including airbases, ships in port, and fixed missile launchers. However, mobile missiles based on land, including antiship missiles and air defense missiles, would be much harder to target than ships at sea or aircraft within missile range. This asymmetry results from the complex background provided by land, which makes mobile targets on land difficult to find compared to the much simpler background of the sea and sky, which leaves airborne and seaborne vehicles relatively easy to identify.[40] Consequently, mobile land-based antiship missiles should have a relatively good survival

---

38. Charles L. Glaser and Chaim Kaufman, "What Is the Offense-Defense Balance and Can We Measure It," *International Security* 22, no. 4 (spring 1998): 61–72.

39. As noted above, attack submarines would also pose a significant threat to China's invasion force.

40. Stephen Biddle and Ivan Oelrich, "Future Warfare in the Western Pacific: Chinese Antiaccess/Area Denial, US AirSea Battle, and Command of the Commons in East Asia," *International Security* 41, no. 1 (summer 2016): 7–48.

CHAPTER 7

rate against China's missile attacks and have the potential to be highly effective at sinking or disabling Chinese ships crossing the Taiwan Strait. Many of these ships are two or three orders of magnitude more expensive than the antiship missiles. The net result is an offense-defense balance that significantly favors defense.

However, most US antiship missiles are currently air-launched, not ground-launched. China's land-based ballistic and cruise missiles and its medium bombers and multirole aircraft pose a significant threat to US tactical aircraft while they are on the ground and to air bases—including runways and fuel storage—that are essential to the operation of the aircraft. There are diverse complementary options for defending ground-based air operations, including air defenses, hardening, camouflage, and dispersal of aircraft across multiple bases.[41] These efforts increase the cost of survivable air-launched antiship weapons, which reduces the advantage of defense relative to offense. Nevertheless, given the cost and vulnerability of Chinese ships, the offense-defense balance would continue to favor defense.[42]

The balance is less clear for aircraft based on aircraft carriers. If China were able to sink or disable a US aircraft carrier, the United States would lose the tens of tactical aircraft that carry antiship missiles, as well as other aircraft and the carrier itself. Given the costs of the carrier and its aircraft, and uncertainties about the vulnerability of carriers to Chinese missiles, estimating the cost ratio for destroying Chinese ships versus destroying US carrier-based antiship missiles (and their basing) requires complicated modeling.

Because it does not have territory of its own that is close to the Taiwan Strait, to fully benefit from the ground-based missile versus ship cost advantage, the United States would need its allies and partners to deploy large numbers of land-based antiship missiles or to allow the United States to deploy them on their soil. Taiwan is the most important option for obvious reasons: It is close to the Taiwan Strait, and it would be using the weapons to defend itself. There is an expert consensus that Taiwan should adopt an asymmetric strategy to defend against, and thereby deter, a Chinese invasion—the "porcupine strategy." The approach would be built on a "large number of small things"; the goal is to create a distributed system of mobile and affordable antiship and antiair defenses that is resistant to Chinese attack. In addition, Taiwan could deploy small fast

---

41. Miranda Priebe et al., *Distributed Operations in a Contested Environment: Implications for USAF Presentation* (RAND, 2019), 10–15.

42. The cost of the defense should also include the cost of US aircraft. However, because the United States uses these aircraft for other missions—for example, combat air patrol—allocating costs specifically to the antiship mission is quite complicated. Thanks to Eric Heginbotham for this insight.

missile boats, mine-layers and naval mines, and small drones for surveillance.[43] Taiwan has the potential, and increasingly the capability, to contribute significantly to its own defense. It is deploying an advanced version of its Hsiung Feng antiship missile and is planning to produce around two hundred per year; in addition, Taiwan is buying four hundred Harpoon antiship missiles from the United States.[44] Whether Taiwan could effectively deploy and operate this size force is another major question.[45] At a minimum, an important purpose of Taiwan's forces would be to prevent a Chinese victory until the United States is able to bring the full weight of its forces to the war.

The United States is acquiring mobile land-based antiship missiles that can be deployed on the territory of US treaty allies.[46] In April 2024, for the first time, the United States deployed mobile midrange ground-based missile launchers to the northern Philippines during an exercise, which can launch Tomahawk missiles. The Tomahawk has a range of more than one thousand miles, which would enable it to target the Taiwan Strait, as well as much of the Chinese coast, and it has an antiship capability. At the time of the exercise, the United States did not announce whether the missiles might be permanently deployed.[47] Japan is enhancing its own land-based antiship capabilities, which it is rushing to deployment in response to growing Chinese capabilities.[48]

---

43. James Timbie and Adm. James O. Ellis Jr., "A Large Number of Small Things: A Porcupine Strategy for Taiwan," *Texas National Security Review* 5, no. 1 (winter 2021/22): 83–93. For early assessments of this approach, see William S. Murray, "Revisiting Taiwan's Defense Strategy," *Naval War College Review* 61, no. 3 (summer 2008); for a somewhat different approach, see Jim Thomas, John Stillion, and Iskander Rehman, *HARD ROC 2.0: Taiwan and Deterrence Through Protraction* (Center for Strategic and Budgetary Assessments, 2014), https://csbaonline.org/research/publications/hard-roc-2-0-taiwan-and-deterrence-through-protraction.

44. The cost of these systems is reported to be approximately $1.2 billion; https://www.reuters.com/world/asia-pacific/taiwan-buy-400-us-anti-ship-missiles-face-china-threat-bloomberg-news-2023-04-17/. Especially with US support, much larger investments are certainly affordable.

45. On the logistical and personnel challenges, see Drew Thompson, "Winning the Fight Taiwan Cannot Afford to Lose," in *Crossing the Strait*.

46. Aaron-Matthew Lariosa, "Army Activates Latest Land-Based SM-6, Tomahawk Battery Based on Navy Tech," *USNI News*, January 18, 2024, https://news.usni.org/2024/01/18/army-activates-latest-land-based-sm-6-tomahawk-battery-based-on-navy-tech; Zach Abdi, "US Marines Stand Up First Tomahawk Battery," *Naval News*, July 26, 2023, https://www.navalnews.com/naval-news/2023/07/marines-stand-up-first-tomahawk-battery/.

47. Andrew Feickert, *The US Army's Typhon Mid-Range Fires (SMRF) System*, Congressional Research Service, April 16, 2024; Aaron-Matthew Lariosa, "US Army Deploys New Missile Launcher to the Philippines," *Naval News*, April 15, 2024; Jesse Johnson, "US Deploys Midrange Missile System in Indo-Pacific for First Time," *Japan Times*, April 16, 2024.

48. "Deployment of Longer-range Anti-Ship Missiles Eyed for Kyushu; Nearer Range to Be Covered by Hypersonic Missiles, Rockets," *Japan News*, July 22, 2024.

CHAPTER 7

In addition to these options for basing antiship missiles, the United States has others, including surface ships, submarines, and long-range bombers. Assessing the appropriate mix is well beyond the scope of this chapter; I briefly discuss some considerations later in this chapter.

CURRENT US STRATEGY

US strategy is shifting from Offensive Denial toward Defensive Denial. In 2016, the United States replaced the Air-Sea Battle (ASB) concept with the Joint Concept for Access and Maneuver in the Global Commons (JAM-GC). JAM-GC marks a significant change from ASB. Whereas the ASB concept was designed to counter emerging A2/AD challenges and hinged on a "disrupt, destroy, defeat" approach to specific adversary A2/AD capabilities, JAM-GC is focused on defeating an adversary's plan and intent, rather than concentrating on dismantling adversary A2/AD capabilities.

The change occurred because "A2/AD capabilities evolved more quickly than anticipated and could only be dismantled at high levels of risk." The focus on defeating the adversary's plan, which for our analysis is the invasion of Taiwan, makes JAM-GC essentially a form of Defensive Denial. In addition, JAM-GC includes key features that align with this approach. It calls for forces that are distributable, that is, that have "the ability to disperse, reposition, and use a variety of bases and operating locations, while retaining the ability to maneuver and concentrate combat power"; that are resilient, meaning they have "the ability to recover rapidly from adversity and setbacks, which usually come in the form of combat losses"; and that have staying power, which requires "logistics systems that provide redundancy and timely access to resources to withstand interruption, corruption, and attrition."[49]

However, two major caveats are required. First, there are elements of the JAM-GC that seem inconsistent with, or at least go beyond, its focus on the adversary's plan. The concept is said to acknowledge that "'access' to the global commons is vital to US national interests, both as an end in itself and as a means to projecting military force into hostile territory."[50] But defeating a Chinese invasion of Taiwan does not require access to the global commons—which includes the Taiwan Strait and the South China

---

49. Michael E. Hutchins et al., "Joint Concept for Access and Maneuver in the Global Commons: A New Joint Operational Concept," *Joint Force Quarterly* 84 (1st quarter, 2017): 136, https://ndupress.ndu.edu/Media/News/article/1038667/joint-concept-for-access-and-maneuver-in-the-global-commons-a-new-joint-operati/. See also Odell et al., *Active Denial*, 95–99.

50. Hutchins et al., "Joint Concept for Access and Maneuver in the Global Commons," 137; it also calls for planning to be able to use existing forces to "ensure access and freedom of maneuver."

Sea—unless access is understood narrowly to include simply penetrating with antiship missiles, submarines, and torpedoes but not with surface ships and aircraft. While the concept may intend a narrow interpretation of access, there seems to be broad room for interpretations that require more forward and offensive operations.

Second, the United States has not made many of the changes to its force acquisition policies that would follow from a full embrace of the focus on defeating the adversary's plan/mission.[51] Among possible examples are the large number of long-range land attack missiles that the United States is procuring compared to the much smaller number of long-range antiship missiles; the emphasis on deploying a stealthy penetrating bomber (B-21), when a larger standoff bomber would be better suited to launching large numbers of long-range antiship missiles from a substantial distance from China's coast; and the navy's continuing commitment to large-deck aircraft carriers.[52]

Escalation

When evaluating one's conventional strategy against an adversary that has nuclear weapons, the possible escalatory pressures the conventional strategy would create should be an especially important consideration. This section discusses various potential types of escalation and how Offensive Denial and Defensive Denial would influence them. It also considers pressures for escalation from a crisis to war. As explained in chapter 4, among the key arguments for ending the US commitment to Taiwan is the possibility of escalation to nuclear war. If instead the United States maintains its commitment, which is highly likely, understanding the escalatory pressures that conventional war could create is essential.[53]

WINNING AND LOSING

Although we typically think of escalation in terms of pressures and incentives to use forces that are created by the structure of the forces themselves, another set of incentives for escalation is driven by the political outcomes the warring states are trying to achieve. More concretely, a state that is losing a war might escalate to improve its prospects of winning.

---

51. Odell et al., *Active Denial*, 95–106, which identifies the Marine Corps as the exception among the US services.
52. For detailed analysis of these issues, see Odell et al., *Active Denial*, chap. 3.
53. On the variety of factors that can influence escalation, see Richard Smoke, *War: Controlling Escalation* (Harvard University Press, 1977).

CHAPTER 7

If losing the war over Taiwan, China could escalate to limited nuclear use to try to compel the United States to concede. The risks would be enormous, but there is some chance that China's leaders would be unwilling to lose the conventional war, maybe especially if they believed that the future of the Chinese Communist Party was at stake.[54] China's leaders might believe that they had the advantage in nuclear bargaining over Taiwan because their interests in Taiwan dwarfs the United States' interests, which would increase their willingness to escalate to limited nuclear attacks.

The United States would lack good options for reducing the probability of this type of escalation largely because it would result from American success in the conventional war. To deter China's compellent threat, the United States could take a variety of actions to further deepen and/or clarify the extent of its interests in defending Taiwan, including possibly deploying US troops to the island. None of these, however, seem likely to convince China that US interests are comparable to its own. Pursuing these options might nevertheless convince China that the risks of nuclear bargaining via escalation were too large. The other US option is to pursue a nuclear damage-limitation capability, which, if highly effective, could provide a bargaining advantage that would tend to offset China's interest-based advantage. However, as argued in chapter 6, the prospects of succeeding in this arms competition are too low and its risks are too large to make this a wise US policy.

The United States, too, might choose to escalate to nuclear war if it were losing the conventional war.[55] One rationale could be destroying Chinese naval forces if the US and Taiwanese conventional forces were proving unable to accomplish this mission. Another rationale could be to bargain with China, using nuclear weapons to demonstrate that the United States was willing to risk a larger nuclear war to prevail. The United States would be escalating in the face of the interest-based bargaining disadvantage discussed above. I find it is hard to see why US leaders would be willing to run the enormous risk entailed in nuclear escalation. If, however, US leaders were convinced that losing the war would jeopardize US alliances in Asia and possibly even across the globe, then they might risk rolling the nuclear dice. This would be a grave mistake, based upon a flawed assessment of how states evaluate US credibility for defending its interests. But we should not entirely discount this possibility because, as discussed in chapter 4, these credibility arguments are frequently used by influential proponents of defending Taiwan.

54. On a variety of nonrational factors that could make Chinese escalation more likely, see Joshua Rovner, "Two Kinds of Catastrophe: Nuclear Escalation and Protracted War in Asia," *Journal of Strategic Studies* 40, no. 5 (2017): 696–730.

55. Matthew Kroenig, *Deterring Chinese Strategic Attack: Grappling with the Implications of China's Strategic Forces Buildup*, Atlantic Council, November 2021, 17, https://www.atlanticcouncil.org/wp-content/uploads/2021/11/Deterring_Chinese_Strategic_Attack_Rpt_10312190.pdf.

CRISIS INSTABILITIES

Crisis instability occurs when two countries fear that the opposing state is going to escalate and each country believes that attacking first is better than being attacked first.[56] These arguments were extensively developed and applied to nuclear escalation, but they also apply to escalation from a crisis to conventional war. Related but different incentives for crisis escalation can occur when changes to the mobilization or readiness of the adversary's forces are reducing a state's ability to destroy them.[57]

Critics of Offensive Denial have argued that it reduces crisis stability by creating incentives for both sides to strike first. The danger results partly from the vulnerability of US forces to Chinese missile attacks, especially forces that have not dispersed from their bases. This danger is compounded by the increased size of US forces that would need to be deployed near China and the threat they pose to forces and command-and-control systems deployed deep inside China's territory. Defensive Denial would reduce these crisis pressures in three ways: giving priority to increasing the survivability and resilience of US forces deployed near China; reducing, or at least not increasing, the amount of US forces deployed in forward, vulnerable positions at the outset of a war; and, relatedly, reducing the US ability to strike quickly and massively deep into China's territory.[58]

Arguably, crisis stability at the conventional level should be less of a worry because the United States' central concern is a Chinese attack that China wants to launch, not one that it is driven into by crisis pressures. However, while this is the standard scenario, there are other important scenarios in which crisis instability could nevertheless be a serious danger. For example, China might impose a blockade without having decided to launch an invasion if the blockade fails; pressures for escalation could then lead to a larger war that might have been avoided. Alternatively, China might mobilize its invasion forces to pressure Taiwan to accept unification, but be bluffing or at least not have decided to attack if compellence failed. Crisis instability would again increase the probability of escalation to conventional war.

Chapter 6 explored a variety of possible crisis escalation pressures at the nuclear level. However, those pressures would be relatively insensitive to US conventional strategy. Those mobilization and window pressures would be driven primarily by the severe crisis and conventional war over Taiwan,

---

56. This is a bit of a simplification. Crisis stability does not require both states to hold this belief; for example, one state believing it and also believing the other believes it is sufficient. The classic type of crisis instability is Schelling's reciprocal fear of surprise attack; see Schelling, *Arms and Influence*, chap. 6.

57. On different types of window pressures, see Stephen Van Evera, *Causes of War: Power and the Roots of Conflict* (Cornell University Press, 1999), chap. 4.

58. Odell et al., *Active Denial*, esp. 80.

CHAPTER 7

not by how the United States was fighting the conventional war. The possible exceptions are inadvertent escalation and entanglement, which I discuss separately below.

ATTACKS AGAINST CHINA'S MAINLAND

Some experts believe that US attacks against China's mainland would increase the probability of Chinese escalation from conventional to nuclear war.[59] We can distinguish three potential causes of this escalation. The first results because Chinese leaders believe the US attacks indicate more ambitious US goals. US attacks against leadership and economic targets could convince China's leaders that the United States was trying to destabilize their government and achieve regime change. Targeting the full range of Chinese military forces, not only those directly engaged in the battle for Taiwan, combined with attacks against China's economy could convince China's leaders that the United States was attempting to so weaken China that it could not regain its regional and global standing. Attacks against communications could make negotiations difficult or impossible, leading China's leader to conclude that the United States was uninterested in a more limited war, thereby encouraging escalation.

The second reason that attacks against the Chinese mainland could fuel escalation is because the United States crossed a Chinese redline—China's belief its mainland should be a sanctuary in a limited war over Taiwan. The redline is not functional—that is, related to China's ability to fight or terminate the war—but is instead ideational.

The complexity and uncertainty surrounding territorial redlines are stark in the United States' evolving policy for the use of American weapons in the Ukraine war. The United States was slow to approve the sale of weapons that could reach far into Russia's territory and then restricted the range of these weapons, while banning Ukraine from using them against Russian soil. However, this provided Russia a sanctuary from which it could target Ukraine. Eventually, in spring 2024, the United States loosened this restriction, allowing Ukraine to target Russian forces in a specific Russian border region, while continuing to ban their use deeper into Russia; later that fall, the Biden administration allowed the use of US weapons for still deeper strikes.[60]

Some proponents of Defensive Denial suggest trying to navigate these escalatory mechanisms in a similar way—by limiting attacks against the

---

59. For discussion of opposing sides on this question, see Brian MacLean, "Reconsidering Attacks on Mainland China," *Journal of Indo-Pacific Affairs* 4, no. 2 (spring 2021): 216–27, https://original-ufdc.uflib.ufl.edu/AA00067831/00013.

60. David E. Sanger and Edward Wong, "Under Pressure, Biden Allows Ukraine to Use US Weapons to Strike Inside Russia," *New York Times*, May 30, 2024. On some of the conceptual issues, see Dan Altman, "The West Worries Too Much About Escalation in Ukraine," *Foreign Affairs*, July 12, 2022, https://www.foreignaffairs.com/authors/dan-altman.

Chinese mainland to high-value military fixed targets along China's periphery, including airbases and ports.[61] Destroying these targets would significantly improve the US prospects for defeating an invasion of Taiwan but would avoid generating Chinese fears of broader US goals. The United States would already be destroying Chinese forces at sea and in the air, so it would have already crossed the redline of killing Chinese military personnel. However, even this more limited military attack would cross China's mainland-sanctuary redline, if one exists.

Some analysts have warned that US leaders might not authorize strikes against China's due to fears of escalation.[62] To prepare for this possibility, they argue that while preparing operational plans for attacking these targets, the US military should also be prepared to defend Taiwan while withholding attacks against the Chinese mainland.

The third escalatory danger that could result from attacking the Chinese mainland results because the US attacks unintentionally damage China's nuclear capabilities. This is a form of inadvertent escalation, which I discuss in the following subsection.

INADVERTENT ESCALATION AND ENTANGLEMENT

As discussed briefly in chapter 6, incentives for inadvertent escalation are created when a country's conventional attacks unintentionally begin to reduce an adversary's nuclear retaliatory capability. This could occur in a variety of ways, including attacks intended to destroy an adversary's attack submarines that also destroy some of its nuclear ballistic submarines, attacks on air defenses that protect against strategic bombers as well as conventional aircraft, and attacks on radars that provide warning of a nuclear attack as well as a conventional attack. Its nuclear capabilities diminished and fearing that the state might be preparing to destroy its remaining nuclear capabilities, the adversary might escalate to nuclear use to destroy the state's damage-limitation capability, to destroy the conventional capabilities that are whittling down its nuclear forces, and/or to pressure the state to ends its conventional campaign.[63]

Experts have argued that US attacks against China's conventional forces could create these types of escalatory incentives. Thorough analysis in the mid-2010s showed that while US attacks would likely damage some of

---

61. Odell et al., *Active Denial*, 90–91.
62. John Speed Meyers, "The Real Problem with Strikes on Mainland China," *War on the Rocks*, August 4, 2015, https://warontherocks.com/2015/08/the-real-problem-with-strikes-on-mainland-china/.
63. Barry R. Posen, *Inadvertent Escalation: Conventional War and Nuclear Risks* (Cornell University Press, 1991).

CHAPTER 7

China's nuclear force—including nuclear missiles colocated with conventional missiles, ballistic missile submarines, and warning radars—China would likely retain a massive nuclear retaliatory capability. Based strictly on these military considerations, China's incentives for escalation should have been small. However, the fog of war—including flawed information about what is actually happening on the battlefield—could result in China's leaders exaggerating the extent of their incentives for escalation.[64] China's nuclear buildup since that time, as described in chapter 6, should have reduced and likely fully eliminated the military incentives for inadvertent escalation, which should in turn diminish the risks generated by flawed information. Thus, neither Offensive Denial nor Defensive Denial seems likely to create this type of escalatory danger. Nevertheless, there is some possibility that Offensive Denial would create inadvertent escalatory pressures because its massive attacks against China's territory, including its C2 and ISR, might deny China's leaders of accurate information.

A related, but partially distinct, set of escalatory incentives could result from entanglement—C3I systems that are used for both conventional and nuclear operations. There are a variety of possibilities, including some that involve Chinese attacks against US C3I systems. For example, if the United States relies on a constellation of satellites to locate both Chinese ships at sea and its conventional and nuclear mobile missiles on land, Chinese attacks against US satellites that were intended to protect Chinese ships at sea could begin to undermine US counternuclear capabilities. The United States would then have incentives to launch a damage-limitation attack before its capability was significantly diminished.[65] This possibility could add to the window pressures that could be created by a US damage-limitation strategy. Of course, the United States lacks a damage-limitation capability should greatly reduce or eliminate the basic incentives for escalation. However, as explained in chapter 6, the beliefs, perceptions and misperceptions that could be generated and sustained by a strategy that continues to be dedicated to achieving damage limitation could support pressures for a massive counterforce attack.

Although the incentive created by many forms of entanglement would not be influenced by whether the United States relies on an Offensive Denial or Defensive Denial strategy, there are some that could be. For exam-

---

64. Caitlin Talmadge, "Would China Go Nuclear? Assessing the Risk of Chinese Nuclear Escalation in a Conventional War with the United States," *International Security* 41, no. 4 (spring 2017): 50–92, provides citations to much of the relevant literature.

65. On entanglement in general and this possibility in particular, see James M. Acton, "Escalation Through Entanglement: How the Vulnerability of Command-and-Control Systems Raises the Risks of an Inadvertent Nuclear War," *International Security* 43, no. 1 (summer 2018): 56–99. On this damage-limitation window more generally, see chapter 6.

CONVENTIONAL STRATEGY

ple, to reduce China's ability to destroy US satellites, the United States might want to attack Chinese antisatellite (ASAT) weapons that were located deep inside China.[66] Offensive Denial might attack these targets early in the war and, in any event, would have attacked many targets deep within China. In contrast, Defensive Denial would have forgone these attacks. If, however, the United States adopted a Defensive Denial strategy but supplemented it with a limited number of deep strikes against key Chinese ISR assets, this could generate some of the escalatory pressures that the overall strategy was designed to avoid, thereby somewhat reducing the escalatory differences between the strategies.

CHOOSING BETWEEN THE DENIAL STRATEGY OPTIONS

Combining the analysis of the military effectiveness of Offensive and Defensive Denial with their implications for escalation, we are prepared to choose between these two approaches. Defensive Denial better fits the situation that the United States faces in East Asia—and specifically in a Taiwan scenario—than does Offensive Denial. Maybe most important, it benefits from defensive advantages that would favor the protection of Taiwan. Instead of giving priority to attacking China's land-based mobile missiles, Defensive Denial emphasizes reducing China's ability to destroy US antiship missiles, thereby preserving the US and allied ability to destroy China's amphibious invasion force. This works to the US advantage because mobility, dispersal, hardening, and decoys can be more effective than penetrating China's air defenses to find and target its mobile missiles. Also important, Defensive Denial can further protect the United States' antiship capabilities by planning to deploy the majority of them well beyond the range of China's A2/AD capabilities. In addition, Defensive Denial reduces the challenges created by the United States' distance from East Asia because it does not require the United States to have most of its forces in the theater at the beginning of the war. This provides a valuable hedge against a scenario in which the United States does not react quickly to the strategic warning of a Chinese attack.

In addition to these military advantages, Defensive Denial avoids some of the escalatory pressures that would be created by Offensive Denial.[67] Crisis pressures would be reduced because the United States would not be postured for massive strikes against China's mobile missiles and command-and-control early in a conflict. Not attacking the Chinese mainland would avoid crossing a

---

66. Acton, "Escalation Through Entanglement," 72.
67. A third advantage of Defensive Denial is that it would be less costly and less technologically risky than Defensive Denial. On costs, see Odell et al., *Active Denial*.

CHAPTER 7

potential redline and might enable the United States to signal that its goals were limited—restoring the status quo and preserving Taiwan's independence, but not overturning the Chinese regime or permanently weakening China.

That said, the escalatory differences between Offensive Denial and Defensive Denial may be smaller than is sometimes suggested. Key crisis incentives can be reduced by increasing the survivability and resilience of US and allied forward-deployed forces, which both strategies call for.[68] The military dangers of inadvertent escalation should have been greatly reduced or eliminated by the increasing size of China's survivable nuclear forces. And some versions of Defensive Denial do call for attacks against ports and airbases along China's periphery, which somewhat reduces the escalatory differences between the two strategies. Maybe most important, both strategies are designed to defeat China's invasion of Taiwan, which creates the most basic incentive for Chinese escalation to nuclear war.

Implementing Defensive Denial

While a strategy of Defensive Denial provides broad guidance for how the United States should plan to defend Taiwan against a Chinese invasion, a number of specific choices about how best to implement the strategy could significantly influence its shape. Proponents of Defensive Denial agree on some of the following issues, disagree on others, and have left still others largely unaddressed. My brief discussion highlights the key issues that should be addressed in a complete analysis.

OPERATIONAL RESILIENCE

Given the ability of China's missiles to destroy fixed targets, including airfields, throughout the first island chain, the United States, its allies, and its partners should give priority to increasing the survivability of their forces. This can be achieved by a combination of mobility, dispersal, hardening, and concealment. Missiles should be mobile, aircraft should be deployable to smaller bases, aircraft at major bases should be deployed in concrete shelters, and decoys and concealment should be used to further complicate China's targeting. Most of these measures are relatively inexpensive and therefore can further shift the cost-exchange ratio in favor of the defender. In addition to these passive measures, missile and air defenses, which are more expensive, might be efficient complements to these efforts to create resil-

---

68. However, the emphasis of Offensive Denial is on other features of the strategy, so survivability might be overlooked or done poorly in the competition for defense resources.

ience.⁶⁹ This set of recommendations is not controversial and is offered by proponents of Offensive Denial as well as Defensive Denial.

The US military has taken some important steps toward increasing resilience, including the Air Force's Agile Combat Employment concept, which emphasizes being able to disperse its aircraft rapidly between different types of airbases and requires reorganizing its personnel to support these bases.⁷⁰ However, some resilience measures continue to be neglected, including maybe most prominently the hardening of aircraft shelters.

FORCES

Exploring in detail which US force structure is best suited to implementing a Defensive Denial strategy is well beyond the scope of this chapter. Such an analysis requires evaluation of the capabilities of weapons systems across a wide range of options and complicated trade-offs among these systems.

That said, the nature of the challenges created by China's A2/AD capabilities and the United States' distance from Taiwan suggest a few important possibilities. Given the vulnerability of US forces deployed in East Asia, including forward-deployed aircraft carriers, the United States should give priority to deploying its forces outside of the range of China's missiles. Increasing the resilience of forward-deployed forces will enhance their overall effectiveness, but they will remain in a highly contested operating environment.

An important choice concerns which platforms, deployed outside the first island change, should carry US antiship missiles, which are key to defeating a Chinese invasion. The increasing range of air-launched antiship cruise missiles now makes it possible for bombers flying from Hawaii, Alaska, and Australia to launch their missiles from far beyond the range of China's air defenses.⁷¹ Bombers can carry large numbers of missiles—a B-52 can carry around twenty long-range cruise missiles, the United States' next-generation bomber, the B-21, is likely to be able to carry more than half that many. A mix of ten bombers could launch more than 100 long-range antiship cruise missiles in a single attack. In addition, bombers can reload quickly once they have returned to base and can soon be ready for another set of attacks. Even at a distance, bombers could face threats from Chinese

---

69. Odell et al., *Active Denial*, 87–89, 127–30. For a thorough analysis of the requirements for the air force, see Priebe et al., *Distributed Operations in a Contested Environment*.

70. US Air Force, *Agile Combat Employment*, Doctrine Note 1–21, August 23, 2022, https://www.doctrine.af.mil/Portals/61/documents/AFDN_1-21/AFDN%201-21%20ACE.pdf; Brian M. Killough, "The Complicated Combat Future of the US Air Force," *The National Interest*, February 9, 2020; Odell et al., *Active Denial*, 102–4.

71. Guam is frequently mentioned as a basing option and has the advantage of being significantly closer to Taiwan. However, Guam is increasingly vulnerable to Chinese missiles, which reduces its value.

fighters, so the United States would need to plan to protect its standoff bombers. Options include forward-based fighters that would intercept Chinese fighters as they left the Chinese mainland; ship-based air defenses deployed far from China; uncrewed aircraft that could accompany bombers and aid in its defense;[72] and relying on the stealth of the B-21.

An alternative/complement to bombers are naval strike fighters, which carry far fewer missiles than bombers. Although they can be deployed much closer to China, their contribution would be reduced by the need to keep US aircraft carriers largely outside the range of China's A2/AD capabilities. Attack submarines are another alternative and can launch torpedoes as well as antiship missiles. Although valuable, SSNs have important limitations—the rate at which they can prosecute attacks is low, they are expensive, and they become more vulnerable to Chinese ASW once they launch missile attacks.[73] Relying heavily on long-range bombers seems like the obvious choice, but striking the best balance will require detailed comparisons of these basing modes and the possible synergisms between them.

A second and related choice concerns US bombers themselves. The B-21 is a stealthy bomber, designed to penetrate China's air defense. Defensive Defense calls for not attacking targets deep inside China, which greatly reduces the value of a penetrating bomber, although there might be scenarios in which attacking targets along China's periphery would benefit from its stealth. A larger bomber, without the stealth features, that could carry more missiles appears in important ways to be better able to meet US requirements.

ATTACKING CHINA'S MAINLAND

If China launches an invasion of Taiwan, a major decision facing US leaders will be whether to attack the Chinese mainland. Defensive Denial forgoes attacks deep into China's interior for a variety of reasons, including that they are largely unnecessary, would be especially militarily demanding, and might suggest more ambitious US goals. However, attacks against Chinese airbases and ports that are relatively close to Taiwan would provide significant military benefits, including disrupting the amphibious transport of troops and materiel by destroying ports and naval bases, reducing China's ability to defend against antiship missiles, and weakening China's ability to control the airspace over Taiwan.

The problem, as discussed above, is that even these attacks would cross a possible Chinese redline. I am inclined to believe that China will not view

---

72. Mikayla Easley, "Air Force Designates CCA Drone as First Unmanned Fighter Aircraft," *DefenseScoop* (March 4, 2025), https://defensescoop.com/2025/03/04/air-force-collaborative-combat-aircraft-designation-anduril-general-atomics-cca/.

73. Odell et al., *Active Denial*, 141.

attacks against its military periphery as highly escalatory because the fighting at sea and in the air would already be quite intense. But there is no way to know for sure. Decisions about whether to launch these attacks should be informed by full analyses of their military benefits. The United States might be able to reduce the military penalty for forgoing these attacks by increasing its antiship capabilities, including ISR and missiles. In addition, improvements in Taiwan's land-based air defenses would contribute to reducing China's ability to control the air.

A set of potentially important targets that lie deeper in China are its over-the-horizon (OTH) radars. These radars can detect ships out to thousands of kilometers from the Chinese coastline. OTH radars cannot provide the precise location of ships, but using information from these radars to cue imaging satellites can greatly increase their effectiveness.[74] Because aircraft carriers play a key role in US plans for defeating an invasion, the United States would have significant incentives to destroy China's OTH radars, which it could do with cruise missiles.[75] Attacks against China's OTH radars could, however, generate two types of escalation dangers. First, because some are deep within China, these attacks might cross a Chinese redline. Compared to searching for and attacking China's mobile missiles, however, these attacks would be small and focused, which should reduce Chinese concerns about larger US ambitions. Second, there are entanglement dangers because these OTH radars provide China with early warning of a US nuclear attack, although the dangers should be limited, for the reason sketched above.[76]

ANTISATELLITE ATTACKS

The United States may have to decide whether to launch kinetic attacks against China's ISR satellites. If China is the first to launch ASAT attacks, then the United States will almost certainly respond in kind. But should the United States withhold its kinetic ASAT attacks with the hope that China will match its restraint? In other words, would the United States be better able to defeat a Chinese invasion of Taiwan if both countries' ISR satellites remained intact or, instead, if both had damaged and declining ISR capabilities?[77]

---

74. Heginbotham et al., *The US-China Military Scorecard*, 154–63.
75. Other options for undermining the effectiveness of these radars include jamming and avoidance, but these would be less reliable and verifiable than kinetic destruction; Heginbotham et al., *The US-China Military Scorecard*, 164–65.
76. Acton, "Escalation Through Entanglement," 78; Christopher P. Twomey, "Asia Complex Strategic Environment: Nuclear Multipolarity and Other Dangers," *Asia Policy* 11 (January 2011): 64.
77. By limiting the question to defeating China, the question excludes nonmilitary considerations, including the long-term implications of satellite debris in low-earth orbit (LEO), which could make certain portions of LEO unusable, and the economic costs of damage to civilian satellites.

CHAPTER 7

A full evaluation of this question is far beyond the scope of this chapter, but a few considerations suggest that the United States would do better if both countries launched kinetic ASAT attacks.[78] Degrading China's ocean surveillance satellites would enable US aircraft carriers to get closer to Taiwan at much reduced risk, thereby increasing the ability of carrier-based fighter aircraft to launch missiles against Chinese ships and to participate in the air war over Taiwan. Without these satellites, China would be unable to identify ships beyond somewhere between four hundred to six hundred kilometers from its mainland.[79] The United States would lose its ability to track China's mobile missiles that were deployed far from China's coasts, but this is quite difficult to do in any event and, more importantly, is unnecessary for implementing Defensive Denial.

A key question is how much the US ability to identify and target ships in the Taiwan Strait would be reduced by the loss of its ISR satellites. The United States has a variety of other options for locating targets. Maybe most promising, the United States might be able to deploy a network composed of a large number of inexpensive drones that could provide extensive sensor coverage of the Taiwan Strait.[80] Although individual drones would be vulnerable, the high density of the network and the ability to replace lost drones would be designed to provide substantial resilience. In addition, the United States and Taiwan could deploy sensors on a variety of other platforms, including fast patrol boats, submarines, sonobuoys, and undersea sensors.[81]

The potential effectiveness of these systems would be increased by the geographic limitations faced by China. Its amphibious ships would leave from a relatively small number of ports, and its invasion forces would have to be concentrated at one or two beaches on Taiwan. In contrast, to locate US aircraft carriers and other ships, China would have to search vast areas of the Pacific Ocean east of Taiwan. Consequently, its ability to regain the capabilities that its satellites had provided would be more limited.

The United States should deploy diversified and enhanced ISR capabilities even if it plans to forgo kinetic ASAT attacks, contingent on China's restraint, because China might initiate the war in space. But possession of these nonspace-based ISR capabilities would also put the United States into

---

78. For extensive analysis, see Zachary Burdette, "The U.S.-China Military Balance in Space: Implications for Future Warfare in the Pacific," *International Security* 49, no. 4 (Spring 2025): 71–118.

79. Biddle and Oelrich, "Future Warfare in the Western Pacific."

80. Thomas Hamilton and David Ochmanek, *Operating Low-Cost, Reusable Unmanned Aerial Vehicles in Contested Environments: Preliminary Evaluation and Operational Concepts* (RAND, 2020).

81. Burdette, "The U.S.-China Military Balance in Space"; David A. Ochmanek, *Determining the Military Capabilities Most Needed to Counter China and Russia: A Strategy-Driven Approach* (RAND, 2022).

a better position to start this dimension of the war. The US decision would need to incorporate a variety of factors beyond the technological feasibility of nonspace-based ISR capabilities, including when to launch such a campaign, how quickly China could disable a proliferated US satellite-based ISR capability, the entanglement/escalation dangers of an ASAT campaign, and the massive economic and societal damage that would result from the destruction of satellites in low earth orbit by the debris from large kinetic ASAT against military satellites.

A related consideration is how effectively the United States could defeat China's ISR with nonkinetic ASAT attacks, including cyberattacks. If sufficiently effective, the United States could forgo kinetic attacks, thereby avoiding extensive damage to satellites in low-earth orbit. The basic point made here is simply that the United States might benefit from the mutual degradation of space-based ISR.

DEPLOYING US TROOPS TO TAIWAN

An infrequently discussed possibility is whether the United States should plan to send ground forces to Taiwan to help defeat a Chinese invasion.[82] Starting in the early 2020s, the United States increased the number of troops it stationed on a rotational basis in Taiwan to train Taiwanese troops; these US troops were reported to number around two hundred. In 2024, there were reports that the United States had permanently deployed special operations forces to a couple of Taiwanese islands that are very close to China's mainland, where they would serve as trainers.[83] Committing US troops to defend Taiwan would be an entirely different undertaking. It would require much larger numbers of ground troops, large amounts of heavy equipment, and extensive coordination with Taiwan's military organizations.

Although Taiwan's military might be able to defeat Chinese troops that reach the island, there are uncertainties about the capability of Taiwan's ground troops, the resolve with which they would fight, and the capability of its air defense. The commitment of US ground troops would greatly reduce uncertainty about the outcome of the ground war and would thereby enhance deterrence. And using US ground troops might not, in and of itself, be escalatory because US plans for defending Taiwan already involve

---

82. Jacquelyn Schneider, "The Uncomfortable Reality of the US Army's Role in a War Over Taiwan," *War on the Rocks*, November 30, 2021, https://warontherocks.com/2021/11/the-uncomfortable-reality-of-the-u-s-armys-role-in-a-war-over-taiwan/.

83. This report was denied by the chief of Indo-Pacific Command a day after it was confirmed by Taiwan's Minister of Defense; Micha McCartney, "US Denies Reports of Troops on China's Doorstep," *Newsweek*, April 26, 2024.

directly fighting Chinese air and naval forces and would likely involve attacking some military targets on the Chinese mainland.

Despite these benefits, deploying US ground troops to Taiwan is a complicated issue for a variety of reasons. China would find peacetime deployment to be highly provocative. Some experts worry that US policies are already too provocative and could precipitate a war with China. US ground troops would be a move much further in this direction. Deploying US troops would only make sense if the United States had changed its ambiguous commitment to a certain one. The United States would be virtually certain to come to Taiwan's aid if its troops were attacked. However, this would make it impossible for the United States to make its commitment conditional—that is, to protect Taiwan only if China's attack is unprovoked by Taiwan's action. Consequently, the United States would lose most of its ability to constrain Taiwan. China would find this deeply troubling and would likely conclude that the United States was actively supporting Taiwan's independence, which could provoke a Chinese attack.

Waiting to deploy US forces until a severe crisis or during China's mobilization of its forces for an invasion would avoid these problems but create serious problems of its own. US deployment of troops would create a window that could create time pressure for China to launch its invasion, possibly when it had not decided whether to proceed. Waiting still longer, until the war had begun, would make getting US forces to the island much more difficult, if not impossible, because China would likely be able to target US ships and aircraft arriving at the island and would be able to significantly damage Taiwan's ports and airfields.[84]

In short, whether and when to deploy US ground troops to Taiwan is an important question about how best to implement the strategy of Defensive Denial. Both peacetime and wartime deployment would carry large risks. Peacetime deployment looks like a very bad idea. In contrast, analysis of the case for contributing US forces to a war that has already begun, including both the military and political dimensions, deserves careful analysis.

I argued in chapter 4 that the United States should end its commitment to using force to protect Taiwan. However, until the United States makes this major policy change—which seems unlikely any time soon, although the Trump administration makes this harder to judge—analyzing the United States' conventional strategy for defending Taiwan is essential. This chapter concludes that Defensive Denial is the United States' best option. It harnesses the defense advantages of regional geography and military technol-

---

84. Yet another concern is that a US commitment to use ground forces would reduce Taiwan's willingness to improve its own defenses.

ogy; relies on a theory of victory that benefits from the United States' ability to shift forces into the region during a long war; relies on the forces that Taiwan can deploy in its own defense, including mobile antiship missiles and air defenses, as well as heavy ground forces; and avoids some although not all of the escalatory pressures that would be generated by a strategy of Offensive Denial.

As sketched in the chapter's final section, the United States can implement Defensive Denial in a variety of ways. Many of the choices it faces require thorough military-technical analysis—for example, the distribution of platforms from which to launch antiship missiles and the military and escalation implications of launching kinetic attacks against China's ISR satellites. Some decisions would require significant changes that might challenge well-established interests; for example, giving priority for launching antiship missile attacks to the US Air Force instead of the US Navy. Other choices will require hard-to-calibrate judgments; for example, the escalatory risks of limited conventional attacks against Chinese military forces on China's territory.

There are two dangers that US conventional strategy cannot help the United States avoid. First, US policies for defending Taiwan generate Chinese insecurity and strain US-China relations. This is unavoidable because competition over Taiwan is not driven by a security dilemma but instead by a fundamental disagreement about the political status quo. Second, US success in a conventional war would create incentives for China to escalate to nuclear war. How the United States achieves this conventional-military success is unlikely to significantly influence China's nuclear decisions.

Conclusion

This book's starting premise is that a major shift in the balance of power—more specifically, China's greatly improved military capability in East Asia—requires the United States to revisit the most basic question about its foreign and military policy. The reason is obvious: China can now challenge the United States in ways that were beyond its means at the turn of the century. Important, and arguably vital, US interests are now more threatened. US policies designed to protect these interests are at once less feasible and riskier.

I focused on five issues that define the broad outlines of US foreign and security policy toward China:

- *Grand strategy*: What grand strategy can best achieve US security interests vis-à-vis China? Should the United States maintain its treaty alliances in East Asia?
- *Taiwan*: If retaining these alliances, should the United States also keep its ambiguous security commitment to Taiwan or instead end this commitment?
- *South China Sea*: How strenuously should the United States oppose China in the South China Sea?
- *Nuclear strategy*: What nuclear strategy can best protect US interests and its commitments in East Asia? More specifically, should the United States pursue a damage-limitation capability—the ability to reduce China's ability to inflict retaliatory nuclear damage?
- *Conventional strategy*: What conventional military strategy can best protect US interests and commitments in East Asia?

The vast majority of the US debate over China, explicitly or implicitly, assumes the answers to these questions and argues instead about more specific issues that are bounded by these answers. While important, analysis within these boundaries is insufficient—the international conditions the United States faces have changed so substantially that the established answers require reexamination.

To lay the foundation for this analysis, I started by identifying the range of broad options that may be available to a (relatively) declining state, which includes preventive war, intensified competition, partial retrenchment, and appeasement and full retrenchment. Options that involve cutting back on commitments—via retrenchment or appeasement—are generally considered flawed because they can encourage an aggressive adversary to pursue still larger territorial and political gains, and can increase the adversary's ability to achieve its goals. They are also often unpalatable because a declining state tends to see geopolitical retrenchment as clashing with its national identity and global purpose.

The next piece of the foundation is a theoretical analysis of the danger that China's rise poses to the United States. This is a necessary component of the policy analysis because the dangers and risks of US policies depend on the threat posed by China. I begin with defensive realism, which is a member of the structural realist family of theories. The application of defense realism shows that, if China is interested only in achieving security, it should be able to rise peacefully. Contrary to common arguments that focus on the pressures created by international structure and the danger of power transitions, defensive realism shows that both the United States and China can remain highly secure as China acquires power equal to or greater than the United States'. This mutual security reflects the advantage of defensive capabilities created by the distance and water of the Pacific Ocean and the deterrent potential of nuclear weapons. Mutual security is peace-creating because secure states tend to place less value on expansion and are more willing to accept the political status quo. In addition, defensive realism shows that international structure should not pressure China to pursue regional hegemony—China's security does not require it—nor should it fuel an intense arms competition. This is a surprisingly optimistic picture in light of the power struggle that realist theories frequently foresee and that commonsense intuition might reasonably anticipate.

The dangers created by China's rise turn out to flow from regional issues, which are far from the focus of structural theories. To explore these dangers, I applied motivational realism—which focuses on greedy states. China's growing power increases its potential to achieve regional goals that were previously beyond its reach. The most important is the unification of Taiwan with the mainland; increased control over the South China Sea is another. Experts on China disagree about how much further China's goals extend. While agreeing that China would prefer regional hegemony, which would require the withdrawal of the United States from East Asia, some judge that China is unwilling to run significant risks to achieve it, while others believe China is quite determined to push the United States out of the region. Experts also disagree about the extent of China's global ambitions, including over whether China is determined to spread its authoritarian model of governance. Given these uncertainties, US strategy needs to hedge against the possibility of a more expansionist China, while avoiding generating Chinese insecurity that could fuel more aggressive Chinese policies.

Unit-level theories—those that focus on features of specific states, such as national identity, international status, and regime type—complement motivational realism by providing explanations for the motives it posits. These theories also provide additional insights into the danger posed by China. Considering China's national identity provides a deeper appreciation of the great importance that China places on unification with Taiwan—overcoming past humiliations and achieving national rejuvenation require unification. Considering China's desire for status—which rising powers have typically wanted—helps to explain China's determination to dominate the South China Sea, as well as to unify with Taiwan. A rising power's drive for international status has also frequently fueled pursuit of a sphere of influence. A Chinese sphere of influence in East Asia would require the United States to withdraw from the region, radically changing US grand strategy. China appears to want a sphere of influence, but whether this is driven by its desire for status is difficult to separate from its desire for increased military capabilities that would be valuable for coercing Taiwan. A key question, then, is how much China would value a sphere of influence in East Asia if it had already achieved unification with Taiwan. Although necessarily speculative, little evidence suggests that China would have great determination—the value of Taiwan appears to dwarf the ideational value of a sphere of influence.

Working from this theoretical foundation, the book proceeds to answer the five policy questions listed above. Individual chapters present full analyses, including counterarguments and counter-counterarguments, and nuanced assessments of difficult trade-offs. Here I provide a brief summary that captures only the basics and my most controversial recommendations.

In broad terms, I argue that the United States should engage in partial retrenchment. It should maintain its treaty alliances in East Asia, most importantly with Japan and South Korea. However, the United States should end its ambiguous commitment to use force to come to Taiwan's defense. In addition, if China becomes more assertive in the South China Sea, the United States should reduce its level of resistance. I termed this revised US grand strategy *Deep Engagement Minus*.

The risks of maintaining the Taiwan commitment are too large, given the limited nature of US interests. China places great value on unification—reflecting, among other things, its history and national identity and desire for status; has an increasingly capable military; and faces decreasing prospects that Taiwan will agree peacefully to unification. A conventional war might escalate to nuclear war via a variety of intentional and unintentional paths. The lack of structural pressures pushing the United States and China into a major war, and for China to pursue regional hegemony, makes terminating the US commitment more attractive. If the United States and China were likely to get into a major war whether or not the United States defended Taiwan, then ending the commitment would yield smaller benefits. Fortunately, this is not the case. Ending the US commitment would be costly, most importantly to the well-being of

CONCLUSION

the people of Taiwan and also to the US goal of protecting democracy. Nevertheless, the hardheaded choice is to end the commitment.

The United States should still support Taiwan's efforts to defend itself. This would involve selling and giving Taiwan weapons systems and possibly providing training to Taiwanese forces. Although Taiwan would be unlikely to be able to defend itself, making a Chinese invasion more difficult and costly would contribute to deterrence. US support would, however, strain the US-China relationship, largely offsetting the potential political benefits of US partial retrenchment. Whether to provide military support to Taiwan is therefore a close call, and the United States should reevaluate it as the US-China relationship evolves.

The United States should retain its treaty alliances for a variety of reasons. If the United States withdraws from East Asia, it could get drawn back into a major war in East Asia. Its former allies would likely acquire (or try to acquire) nuclear weapons, and their transitions to adequate nuclear capabilities could be dangerous. In addition, the political dynamics of East Asia are sufficiently complex that US withdrawal could generate dangers that are difficult to foresee. Preserving US alliances is a prudent hedge against these dangers. If China's military modernization and expansion begins to jeopardize the ability of the US to deter a conventional Chinese attack against its treaty allies, then the United States should compete vigorously to maintain US conventional capabilities.

However, I judge that the dangers of the US commitment to Taiwan exceed the dangers of a complete US security withdrawal from the region. Consequently, if the United States' choice were between keeping all its current commitments, including Taiwan, and withdrawing from the region, I would recommend complete withdrawal; that is, adopting a Neoisolationist grand strategy.

The South China Sea presents the United States with a subtler set of trade-offs. The topic is itself complicated because the South China Sea involves a wide range of Chinese challenges, including to the territorial and maritime claims of US allies and partners, to international rules that clarify states' rights to resources, and to the principle of freedom of navigation. Far less is at stake than in Taiwan—US interests are quite limited. At the same time, the risks of a large war beginning in the South China Sea are much smaller than over Taiwan, even though a limited conflict might be more likely. I conclude that the United States should continue its current level of resistance to China's challenges, which includes ambiguity about whether it would use force to protect other states' claims and sending naval ships through the South China Sea during peacetime. These policies will help preserve US credibility with its allies and partners at reasonable risk because China can likely be deterred. If, however, China becomes significantly more assertive, then the United States should shift to partial South China Sea retrenchment, which would include rejecting the use of force to protect maritime features claimed by US allies and partners. Given the limited US interests, a greater risk of war would not be warranted.

Turning to military strategy, I explain that the United States' key nuclear-strategy decision is whether to pursue a damage-limitation capability—the ability to significantly reduce China's ability to damage the United States in a retaliatory attack. If highly effective, a damage-limitation capability would provide some benefits, most importantly, a reduction in the costs of an all-out war; it might also increase the credibility of US extended deterrence threats because the United States would be less vulnerable to Chinese retaliation. Nevertheless, I argue against a damage-limitation strategy. The first strike against pursuit of a damage-imitation capability is infeasibility. China's modernization and enlargement of its nuclear force, and its ability to respond to US counterforce programs, will almost certainly enable China to preserve its assured destruction capability. Moreover, the costs and risks of pursuing a damage-limitation capability are substantial. A damage-limitation strategy is highly competitive—the United States would be attempting to deny China capabilities it believes are necessary for deterrence and would add to strains to US-China relations. This would be especially true because the United States would be trying to acquire an offensive capability when defensive/retaliatory capabilities have the advantage, which signals especially negative information about US motives. In addition, a US damage-limitation capability would create incentives for escalation during a crisis or conventional war and would create time pressures that would increase the probability of accidental and unauthorized attacks. Even US efforts that failed to achieve a damage-limitation capability would generate many of these dangers. Instead of a damage-limitation strategy, the United States should adopt a strategy that emphasizes the ability of nuclear weapons to inflict damage—a countervalue strategy. This will minimize competition and reduce escalatory pressures in crises while providing the United States with a range of limited nuclear options that will support extended deterrence and crisis bargaining. Shifting to a countervalue strategy will require a major revision because US nuclear strategy has long emphasized counterforce targeting for both deterrence and damage-limitation.

The United States has a variety of conventional military missions it needs to be able to accomplish in East Asia, including defeating Chinese blockades and invasions of its allies and Taiwan. The most important and likely most challenging mission is preventing a Chinese invasion of Taiwan. In broad terms, the US choice is between an Offensive Denial strategy and a Defensive Denial strategy. The former emphasizes destroying China's forces early in a war, while the latter emphasizes destroying Chinese invasion forces as they cross the Taiwan Strait. Defensive Denial has a variety of strengths. Its focus on invading force benefits from the difficulty of crossing water and from technology that provides defense with an advantage in the fight between amphibious invasion forces and US and Taiwanese antiship missiles. It is

CONCLUSION

designed to ensure that China does not win quickly, which provides time for the United States to swing forces into East Asia. And it forgoes large early attacks against the Chinese mainland, thereby avoiding crossing redlines and a variety of escalatory pressures that could fuel escalation into an all-out war.

These policies will be challenging for the United States to successfully implement. Any retrenchment will lead the United States' treaty allies to fear that the United States may weaken its commitments to protect them. As I explained in the chapters on Taiwan and the South China Sea, the United States has available a range of policies for preserving its credibility with its allies, including increasing forces committed to their defense, increasing joint military exercises and consultations on the implementation of defense strategy, and continuing to increase US partnerships in the region, as it has with AUKUS. Nevertheless, US policy will need to be steady and consistent because allies will understandably be especially sensitive to any wobbling or inconsistency in US security policy toward East Asia.

This may be especially difficult given the growing number of Republican politicians who are leaning more toward isolationist positions or are at least reluctant to provide continuing support to Ukraine. Even more important, President Donald Trump's disregard for and hostility toward alliances, combined with his influence over the Republican Party, have intensified fears among US allies that the United States may not remain a reliable security partner.[1]

Having mentioned Trump, it is important to note again that my arguments for partial retrenchment share little to nothing with his sometimes isolationist leaning, which is often cast primarily in terms of the costs of the military capabilities required to meet these commitments. In contrast, I largely accept Deep Engagement's argument for maintaining America's alliances, including the significant value of deterring major-power wars in Asia that could draw in the United States and of preventing nuclear proliferation. I also see value in supporting democratic states, although rarely, if ever, through the use of US military force when democracy is the primary US interest at stake. My case for partial retrenchment emphasizes instead the risk side of the equation and focuses narrowly on the enormous risks surrounding Taiwan, given the limited extent of US security interests.

The United States is likely to avoid a major war with China even if it does not engage in partial retrenchment. In absolute terms, the probability of major-power war is not very high. This will tempt the United States to avoid making any concessions to China. But, given the potential and likely consequences, the probability of a large war is far too high. With reasonable luck, peace would prevail. However, given the stakes, US national security policy should rely on luck as little as possible.

1. See, for example, John Warrick, Michael Birnbaum, and Emily Rauhala, "Trump's NATO-Basing Comments Rile Allies, Rekindle European Fears," *Washington Post*, February 11, 2024.

Index

Acton, James, 251
Agile Combat Employment, 303
aircraft carriers, 292
AirLand Battle concept, 287–88, 290
air-launched ballistic missile (ALBM), 233
AirSea Battle concept, 53, 278, 288, 294
Albright, Madeleine, 77
allies
    and analysis of US policy toward South China Sea, 22
    and China's rise, 33
    and China's security-driven regional hegemony, 47
    and China's status interests in achieving influence in East Asia, 88–89
    and debates regarding US grand strategy, 18–19
    impact of Trump administration's hostility toward, 48n38, 66, 264, 316
    and potential costs and risks of territorial accommodation, 150
    preservation of US, 66, 138
    South China Sea and Chinese threats to US credibility with, 214–15
    and US damage-limitation capability, 273
    of US in East Asia, 89–90, 102, 138
    and US interests in South China Sea, 202–3
    and value of US damage-limitation capability for enhancing conventional deterrence, 262–63, 265–67
    See also grand strategy / strategies

antiaccess/area-denial (A2/AD) capabilities
    and AirSea Battle concept, 288
    and arms competition between US and China, 52, 53
    and change from AirSea Battle concept to Joint Concept for Access and Maneuver in the Global Commons, 294
    and China's growing presence in South China Sea, 191
    and Chinese military threats to US interests in South China Sea, 205
    and costs and risks of US accommodation on Taiwan, 172
    and ending US commitment to defend Taiwan, 153, 164, 175
    and Primacy, 129
    and US conventional strategy, 276
antisatellite attacks, 305–7
Anti-Secession Law (2005), 144
antiship missiles, 291–92, 293–94
antisubmarine warfare (ASW), 172, 173, 282
appeasement
    costs and risks of US accommodation on Taiwan, 165–74
    defined, 146
    potential benefits of, 147–48
    potential costs and risks of, 148–51
    and power transitions and preventive war, 43
    purposes of, 8
    versus retrenchment, 4–5
    See also territorial accommodation
Art, Robert J., 112n21

INDEX

ASEAN Regional Forum, 201
Asian powers, concert of, as alternative to ending US commitment to Taiwan, 179–80
Association of Southeast Asian Nations (ASEAN), 194–95, 215
Atlantic Council, 128
Attack-in-Depth, 288
attack submarines, 304
AUKUS, 5, 168, 182, 316
Australia, 101
autocracy, and competition between US and China, 133–34. *See also* regime type

B-21 bomber, 304
B-52 bomber, 303
Bacevich, Andrew, 61
ballistic missile defense (BMD), 251–54, 272
ballistic missile submarines (SSBNs), 190, 197, 210–11, 232–33, 246–49
bargaining theory, 49–51
bastion strategy, 247–49
Biden, Joe, 70, 71, 94, 133–34, 159n74
Blanchette, Jude, 96, 140n4
blockade, 153–54, 156, 206, 276, 285
bluffing, 160, 177–78, 218–19
Brands, Hal, 94
Brooks, Stephen, 114
Bundy, McGeorge, 238–39
Bush, George H. W., 125
Bush, George W., 126, 145
Bush, Richard C., 139n2, 167

Cambodia, 194
cartelization, 91, 95
century of humiliation, 78–79, 80
China
 analysis of US accommodation of, 142–43
 attacks against mainland, 298–99, 304–5
 blockade of, 285
 disagreement regarding growth of, 5
 economic interdependence with US, 69–72
 extent of ambitions of, 7–8
 implications of identity and status for competition with US, 89–90
 improvement of conventional forces, 227–28, 229, 275–76
 key US national security policy questions regarding, 11–15
 limited goals of, 49–51
 regime type of, 75–76, 93–96, 97, 159
 as revisionist state, 7
 status as driving policies of, 84–89
 as threat to United States, 62–63
 US nuclear policy toward, 23–24
China, rise of, 31–34, 72–73
 as cast in realist terms, 35

dangers of, 31–32, 34, 312
impact of, 31, 116
international structure and, 142
 See also grand strategy / strategies; unit-level / state-level theories
China Coast Guard (CCG), 191, 193
Chinese Communist Party (CCP), 79, 95–96
Chubb, Andrew, 79, 87
classical realism, 16n26, 32n3
Clinton, Bill, 145
Colby, Elbridge, 58–59, 169
Cold War, 69, 113, 125, 132, 235, 249, 287–88
command, control, communications, and intelligence (C3I) systems, 287, 300
"community of common destiny," 89
competition
 Biden on US-Chinese, 133–34
 and defensive realism, 16, 32
 and extended deterrence, 262
 military, between US and China, 129–30
 nuclear, 14
 rising powers and arms, 51–54
 and status and prestige, 83–84
 in US policy and foreign policy discourse, 2–3
concessions
 to greedy states, 55–56
 to limited-aims state, 55
 and power transitions and preventive war, 43–44
conventional deterrence, 284–85
conventional strategy, 25–26, 275–79, 308–9
 analysis of US, 11–12
 and China's Taiwan invasion requirements and challenges, 280–84
 and escalation, 295–302
 implementation of Defensive Denial, 302–8, 309
 options for deterring China and defending Taiwan, 284–95
 and Taiwan and generation of Chinese insecurity, 279–80
Copeland, Dale C., 67n86
Coté, Owen, 172
counterintimidation, 220–21
credibility
 damage-limitation capability and, of threats to escalate, 239
 and partial retrenchment, 10–11
 and potential costs and risks of territorial accommodation, 149–50
 preservation of US, 316
 South China Sea and Chinese threats to US, 211–15, 223
 Taiwan and assessments of US, 166–71, 181–82
 of US in defending allies, 263
crisis instability, 297

INDEX

Dai Bingguo, 80–81
damage limitation
  versus deterrence, 238–39
  infeasibility of, 254–57
  overview of concept, 234–39
  threshold for significant, 234–38
  See also damage-limitation capability
damage-limitation capability
  benefits of US, 23–24, 234, 257–67, 315
  costs of US, 267–72, 315
  feasibility of US, vis-à-vis China, 234–35, 240–54
  and state's deterrent, 239
  of US in surprise attack, 255n80
  US pursuit of, 228–29
  See also damage limitation
Davidson, Phillip, 155
declining power
  incentive to launch preventive war, 42–43
  and rising power's intensified pursuit of limited goals, 49
decoupling, 104, 117, 118, 185n185
Deep Engagement
  arguments for Offshore Balancing and, 124
  China and, 115–19
  and comparison of grand strategies, 135–36, 137
  defined, 19
  influence of China's rise on strength of argument concerning, 19–20
  and Liberal Hegemony, 132
  and Offshore Balancing, 103n8, 120–21, 122
  prosperity and, 113–14
  summary of, 112–15
  and US interests in South China Sea, 202
Deep Engagement Minus, 20, 106, 138, 276, 313
Defense Planning Guidance (1992), 125
Defensive Denial, 289–94
  and analysis of US conventional strategy for protecting interests in East Asia, 25–26
  choosing between Offensive Denial and, 301–2
  and escalation, 298–99, 300–301
  implementation of, 302–8, 309
  overview of concept, 278–79, 315–16
  shift toward, 294
defensive realism, 15–16
  and China's rise, 40–41, 44–45
  and dangers generated by rising power, 41–54, 312
  defined, 32, 74
  key assumptions and variables, 36–38
  and motivational realism, 33

  and power transitions and preventive war, 42–44
  and rising powers and arms competition, 51–54
  and rising power's intensified pursuit of limited goals, 49–51
  and rising power's security-driven pursuit of regional hegemony, 45–48
  and security dilemma, 38–40
democracy
  and competition between US and China, 133–34
  as US value, 166
  as value at stake in Taiwan, 134–35
  See also regime type
democratic peace theory, 91, 131
derisking, 70, 104, 111, 117, 118
deterrence
  against attack on US homeland as benefit of US damage-limitation capability, 259–60
  and China's security-driven regional hegemony, 48
  of Chinese invasion of Taiwan, 276–77
  damage limitation versus, 238–39
  dual deterrence, 218
  enhancing allies' confidence in US, as benefit of US damage-limitation capability, 265–67
  enhancing extended, as benefit of US damage-limitation capability, 260–65
  nuclear and conventional, 284–85
  by punishment, 278, 284, 285–86
  US conventional strategy options for, 284–95
  See also extended deterrence
deterrence model, 54–55, 64
deterrence theory, and rising power's intensified pursuit of limited goals, 49–51
DF-5A missiles, 241
DF-26 missile, 282
Doshi, Rush, 58, 60, 167
dual deterrence, 218

East Asia
  analysis of US conventional strategy for protecting interests in, 25–26
  and arms competition between US and China, 52–53
  China's rise and US security commitments in, 33
  China's status interests in achieving influence in, 87–89
  and debates over China's regional hegemonic ambitions, 57–60
  and implications of identity and status for US-China competition, 89–90

INDEX

East Asia *(continued)*
  and Neoisolation, 109
  Offshore Balancing and US commitments in, 123
  US alliances in, 89–90, 102
  US credibility and policies regarding, 168
  US withdrawal from, 314
East China Sea, 50–51
economic bloc, 58–59
economic interdependence
  as reducing probability of war, 34
  as source of peace, 66–72
Economy, Elizabeth, 59–60
entanglement, 299–301
escalatory pressures, 9–10
  trade-offs between enhancing deterrence and decreasing, 277
  and US conventional strategy, 278, 295–302
  and US damage-limitation capability, 267–71
  See also nuclear war
European Union (EU), 122
Exclusive Economic Zone (EEZ), 22, 86, 188–90, 192
expansion
  and China as threat to US, 62
  greed as motivation for, 54
  mixed-motive state's value of, 64
  and regime type and dangers posed by China's rise, 95–96
extended deterrence, 260–67, 273
Extended Deterrence Dialogue, 266–67

Fiery Cross Reef, 191, 195
fishing rights, 192, 193
Flournoy, Michèle, 155
Fravel, M. Taylor, 157n67
freedom of navigation operations (FONOPs), 185–86, 194, 212, 222–23
Freeman, Charles W. Jr., 141n11
"free to roam" argument, 124
French, Howard, 81, 86
Friedberg, Aaron, 93

Gallagher, Mike, 60–61
Glaser, Bonnie, 167, 169
global financial crisis (2008), 169
globalization, 67, 114
grand bargain, 21, 142, 178–79
grand strategy / strategies, 101–6
  comparison of, 135–37
  debates concerning, 18–19, 135–36
  Deep Engagement, 112–19
  Liberal Hegemony, 131–35
  Neoisolation, 106–11
  Offshore Balancing, 119–24

  policy question regarding, 12–13
  Primacy, 125–31
  and South China Sea, 184–85
  and US commitments as all-or-nothing choice, 137–38
  See also Deep Engagement; Liberal Hegemony; Neoisolation; Offshore Balancing; Primacy
greedy state(s)
  China as, 56–64, 65, 130–31
  China viewed as, by US, 33, 41
  and motivational realism, 16, 32–33, 54–66
  policy selection for, 38
Green, Brendan, 172–73
Ground-based Midcourse Defense (GMD) system, 251–54

Haas, Ryan, 140n4
Haines, Avril, 155
Harding, Harry, 63n81
Harpoon antiship missiles, 293
Hass, Ryan, 58
Hayton, Bill, 80
Heath, Timothy, 80
Heer, Paul, 57, 61
Heginbotham, Eric, 155n59
Hiim, Henrik Stalhane, 157n67
historical memory, 76, 84
Hong Kong, 79
Hsiung Feng antiship missile, 293
Hu Jintao, 80, 96
human rights, as value at stake in Taiwan, 134–35
humiliation, century of, 78–79, 80
hydrocarbon exploration and development, 192, 197

Indonesia, 192
Indo-Pacific Strategy, 183–84
intelligence, surveillance, and reconnaissance (ISR) capabilities, 275–76, 288
intercontinental ballistic missiles (ICBMs), 230, 232, 240–46, 252, 255–56, 273
international relations (IR) theory, 12, 26, 32, 56, 142, 146n29, 149–50
international system, 35, 36, 79, 94, 168
intimidation, in South China Sea, 193–94, 220–21
invasion of Taiwan
  as Chinese option for gaining control, 153, 154–57, 276
  US prospects for defeating Chinese, 181
  US response to, 178
  US strategy for deterring, 276–77, 315–16
Iraq, 132

Japan
 and arms competition between US and China, 52–53
 and China's security-driven regional hegemony, 47
 and China's status and desire for unification of Taiwan, 87–88
 and Deep Engagement and war between US and China over, 115–16
 factors favoring alliance with US, 263
 land-based antiship capabilities of, 293
 nationalist protests focused on, 81–82
 nuclear proliferation of, 110
 Offshore Balancing and US alliance with, 123–24
 protection from blockade, 109
 US commitment to Taiwan and assessment of US credibility, 169–70
 and US conventional strategy, 280
 and US defense of Taiwan, 281–82
 and US extended deterrence capabilities, 265–67
 US nuclear sharing agreements with, 229
Japan Self-Defense Forces (JSDF), 282
Jiang Zemin, 79, 80, 88
Jia Qingguo, 164n85
JL-3, 248
Johnston, Alastair Iain, 59n68, 61
Joint Air-to-Surface Standoff Missiles (JASSM), 208
Joint Concept for Access and Maneuver in the Global Commons (JAM-GC), 53n48, 278, 294–95

kill chains, missile, 173

Lai Ching-te, 158
land-based missiles, 232, 291–93
launch-on-warning (LOW) posture, 231, 249, 250–51, 268
Layne, Christopher, 120n41, 123
Li, Cheng, 88n61
Liberal Hegemony, 18, 19, 102–3, 105, 131–35, 136
liberal international order (LIO), 135
liberal-structural theory, 17, 66–68
Lieberthal, Kenneth, 163
Liff, Adam, 57
limited nuclear options (LNOs), 261–62, 296
Logan, David C., 233n12
long-range antiship missiles, 279, 295
long war
 and Defensive Denial, 289, 290
 impact of blockade in, 285, 286
 as including elements of punishment and denial, 284n20

Macclesfield Bank (Zhongsha), 187
Malaysia, 192, 193
Mao Zedong, 96
McNamara, Robert, 235, 236
Mearsheimer, John J., 37n12, 44–45, 121, 123, 124, 284n20
Medeiros, Evan, 63n82
military bases
 of China in South China Sea, 205, 206–8, 221–22
 and US interests in South China Sea, 204
military capabilities
 of China, 52, 152–53, 157
 and competition between US and China, 129–30
 and ending US commitment to defend Taiwan, 174–75
 improvement of conventional Chinese, 227–28, 229, 275–76
 and navigational rights of US in South China Sea, 222
 and state power, 37, 69
military personalist leaders, 92–93
Minuteman-III missiles, 240–41
Mischief Reef, 187, 191, 195
"Missile Defense Review" (2019), 251–52
"Missile Defense Review" (2022), 243–44
missile kill chains, 173
mixed-motive state(s), 17, 64–66, 130, 262
mobile missiles, 129–30, 241, 242–46, 255–56, 291–93
Montgomery, Evan Braden, 157
Morgenthau, Hans, 54n54
motivational realism, 16, 32–33, 35, 54–66, 312
mutual assured destruction (MAD), 230, 235

Nathan, Andrew, 57, 163
National Defense Strategy (2022), 57–58
national identity
 of China, 75, 78–82, 144, 152
 as factor motivating China's behavior in South China Sea, 198–200
 implications for US-China competition and conflict, 89–90
 and state-level theories, 76–82
 of United States, 77
nationalism
 and China's South China Sea policy, 200
 Chinese, 78
 and state-level theories, 76–82
national rejuvenation, 80, 144
National Security Strategy of the United States (2002), 58, 126
natural gas reserves, in South China Sea, 197–98
naval strike fighters, 304

INDEX

neoclassical realism, 16n26, 32n3
Neoisolation
 China and, 108–11
 and comparison of grand strategies, 135–36, 137
 conditions for reengagement, 120n41
 and divide among the security-focused grand strategies, 105
 influence of China's rise on strength of argument concerning, 19–20
 overview of concept, 18, 102
 summary of, 106–8
"new model of great power relations," 88n61
1992 Consensus, 158
no-first-use (NFU) doctrine, 161, 261n91
North Atlantic Treaty Organization (NATO), 19, 122, 262, 266, 287–88
nuclear command and control (NC2), 240, 249–51, 268–69
nuclear deterrence, 284–85
nuclear proliferation
 of China, 129–30, 227
 impact of China's rise on, 116
 Offshore Balancing's assessment of dangers of, 122–23
 Primacy as supporting nonproliferation, 126
nuclear revolution, theory of, 230
nuclear strategy, 227–31, 272–74, 315
 analysis of US, 11–12
 benefits of US damage-limitation capability, 257–67
 and concept of damage limitation, 234–39
 costs of US damage-limitation capability, 267–72
 debates concerning, 230
 feasibility of US damage-limitation capability vis-à-vis China, 240–54
 infeasibility of damage limitation, 254–57
 overview of China's nuclear forces and motivations, 232–34
nuclear war
 avoidance of, as benefit of ending US commitment to Taiwan, 160–62
 and US commitment to defend Taiwan, 6, 174
 See also escalatory pressures
nuclear weapons
 of China, 232–34
 and China's security-driven regional hegemony, 47
 and China's status, 85–86
 and Deep Engagement, 113, 117
 equivalent megatons of, 235n16
 and Neoisolation, 107, 109, 110
 and offense-defense balance, 37, 40–41
 and US defense, 106

Obama, Barack, 187
offense-defense balance
 factors influencing, 37
 and feasibility and relative desirability of Defensive Denial, 290–92
 and power transitions and preventive war, 42–43
 and rising power's security-driven pursuit of regional hegemony, 46
 and security dilemma, 39
 between US and China, 40, 44
offense-defense distinguishability, 38–39
Offensive Denial, 286–89
 and analysis of US conventional strategy for protecting interests in East Asia, 25
 choosing between Defensive Denial and, 301–2
 and crisis instability, 297
 and escalation, 300–301
 overview of concept, 278, 315
 shift from, 294
offensive realism, 45–46
Offshore Balancing, 18, 19, 102, 103n8, 119–24, 136–37
oil deposits, in South China Sea, 197–98
one-China policy, 158–59
over-the-horizon (OTH) radars, 305

Pacific Deterrence Initiative, 182
Paracel (Xisha) Islands, 187, 190, 199
partial retrenchment
 and credibility of US with treaty allies, 10–11
 recommended as US policy toward China, 5, 6–7, 316
 toward South China Sea, 185, 186, 216–17
Pelosi, Nancy, 140, 158
People's Armed Forces Maritime Militia, 191, 193
People's Liberation Army Navy (PLAN), 190, 191, 194, 216
personalist leaders, 92–93
Philippines, 101, 192, 193, 208, 214
 US treaty commitments to, in South China Sea, 218
 See also Scarborough Shoal
Philippine Sea, 172, 204
porcupine strategy, 176, 292–93
Posen, Barry, 103n7, 119n37, 123
Pottinger, Matt, 60–61
Powell, Robert, 42n25
power, state, and military capability, 37, 69
power transitions, and preventive war, 42–45
predelegated launch authority, 250
prestige, 82–90
preventive war, 5, 42–45, 49
Primacy, 18, 102, 105, 125–31, 132, 136

322

Pu, Xiaoyu, 84n43
punishment, deterrence by, 278, 284, 285–86

QUAD, 5, 168, 182

rational bargaining theory, 42n25
Ratner, Ely, 145n28, 184
realism, 34–35, 66–72. *See also* classical realism; defensive realism; motivational realism; neoclassical realism; structural realism
regime type, 75–76, 90–96, 97, 159
regional hegemony
  and China as greedy state, 56–60
  China's value of, 90, 169
  and Neoisolation, 107
  and Offshore Balancing, 119–22
  rising power's security-driven pursuit of, 45–48
  US commitment to Taiwan and China's value on, 165, 181
Reilly, James, 82n33
Restraint, 103
retrenchment
  versus appeasement, 4–5
  costs and risks of US accommodation on Taiwan, 165–74
  defined, 146
  implications of Trump administration for, 10–11
  potential benefits of, 147–48
  potential costs and risks of, 148–51
  and power transitions and preventive war, 44
  See also partial retrenchment; territorial accommodation
rising power(s)
  and arms competition, 51–54
  defensive realism and dangers created by, 41–54
  intensified pursuit of limited goals, 49–51
  security-driven pursuit of regional hegemony, 45–48
  and status, 83–84, 87, 200–201
rules-based international order, 22, 135, 203–4. *See also* liberal international order (LIO)
Russia, 298. *See also* Soviet Union

satellites, 244, 245–46, 300, 305–7
Saunders, Philip, 53, 233n12
Scarborough Shoal, 13, 183, 185, 187, 193, 194, 195, 200
Scobell, Andrew, 57, 163
sea lines of communication (SLOCs), 164, 182, 196–97, 206
Second Thomas Shoal, 193
security

and assumptions of defensive realism, 36
  as factor motivating China's behavior in South China Sea, 196–97
  methods for increasing adversary's, 39–40
  mutual, 312
  reduction of adversary's, 277
  See also grand strategy / strategies
security dilemma
  applicable to mixed-motive states, 64
  and defensive realism, 38–40
  defined, 9
  as primary cause of adversary's insecurity, 277
  regarding sea lines of communication (SLOCs), 164
  and unification of Taiwan, 146
security-seeking state
  policy selection for, 38
  and security dilemma, 39
Selective Engagement, 112n21. *See also* Deep Engagement
Shambaugh, David, 85
Shirk, Susan, 96
signals intelligence (SIGINT), 245–46
silo-based missiles, 240, 251, 255, 256, 273
Singapore, 101
South China Sea, 183–87, 223–24, 314–15
  analysis of US policy toward, 21–23
  China's behavior in, 190–96
  China's claims in, 187–90
  Chinese disputes in, 50–51
  Chinese military threats to US interests in, 205–11
  and Chinese national identity, 79
  and Chinese threats to UNCLOS and US credibility, 211–15
  factors motivating China's behavior in, 196–202
  and implications of identity and status for US-China competition, 89
  importance of, 184
  recommendation for US resistance in, 6, 215–23
  resources / resource rights in, 191–92, 197–98
  status and China's policies in, 86–87
  US interests in, 202–4
South Korea
  and arms competition between US and China, 53
  China as threat to, 109
  nuclear proliferation of, 110, 116
  prospects for defense against China, 263
  and US extended deterrence capabilities, 265, 266
  US nuclear sharing agreements with, 229
South Luconia Shoals, 193

INDEX

Soviet Union, 46, 68, 125, 235, 259, 262. *See also* Russia
space-based radars (SBRs), 230, 243–45, 272
spiral model, 38, 64
Spratly (Nansha) Islands, 13, 14, 22, 183, 187–88, 190–91, 193, 195, 198–99, 204–11, 222
stability-instability paradox, 270
state-level theories. *See* unit-level / state-level theories
status, 82–90
  as factor motivating China's behavior in South China Sea, 200–202
  implications for US-China competition and conflict, 89–90
  of rising powers, 83–84, 87
status dilemmas, 84
status immobility, 84
status quo
  disputed, 146n29
  preservation of, in US policy and foreign policy discourse, 2–3
  risks of maintaining, 7
straight baselines, 190, 195, 212, 222
strategic-choice theories, 17, 64, 74
Strategic Rocket Force, 85–86
structural realism, 32, 35, 48n37
Subi Reef, 191, 195
submarine-launched ballistic missiles (SLBMs), 232, 248, 273
submarines, attack, 304
Swaine, Michael, 61

Taiwan
  alternatives to ending US commitment to, 177–80
  and attacks against Chinese mainland, 304–5
  basic information on, 143–46
  benefits of ending US commitment to, 151–65
  and China as greedy state, 33, 56, 65
  China's invasion requirements and challenges, 280–84
  and China's limited goals, 50
  and China's security-driven regional hegemony, 47
  and Chinese insecurity, 34, 279–80
  and Chinese national identity, 79
  costs and risks of US accommodation on, 165–74, 181
  Deep Engagement and war between US and China over, 115–16
  Deep Engagement Minus, 20, 106, 138, 276, 313
  deployment of US troops to, 307–8
  ending US commitment to defending, 6, 11, 142, 174–77

  and factors motivating China's behavior in South China Sea, 196
  and implications of identity and status for US-China competition, 89
  Liberal Hegemony and US's key interests in, 134–35
  logics of territorial accommodation, 146–51
  and militarization of Spratly Islands and war with US, 207
  offense-defense balance in Chinese invasion of, 291
  and porcupine strategy, 292–93
  probability of war over, 7, 20, 134, 140–41, 151–52, 174
  status and China's desire for unification of, 87–88
  US arming of, 175–77, 181
  and US-China economic interdependence, 71–72
  US conventional strategy options for defending, 284–95
  and US pursuit of damage-limitation capability, 231
  as US security interest, 202–3
  US views on unification of, 56n58
  and value of US damage-limitation capability for enhancing conventional deterrence, 264–65
  See also invasion of Taiwan
Taiwan Enhanced Resilience Act (2022), 159, 176
Taiwan Relations Act (1979), 145
Talmadge, Caitlin, 172–73
tariffs, 185n185
Tellis, Ashley J., 127–28
Terminal High Altitude Area Defense (THAAD) missile defense system, 252
territorial accommodation, 146–51, 166. *See also* appeasement; retrenchment
territorial sea, 188
theater missile defense (TMD), 252
theory of the nuclear revolution, 230
Thitu Island, 193
thresholds, in war, 9–10
Thucydides's Trap, 35
Tomahawk missiles, 293
trade
  and Chinese military threats to US interests in South China Sea, 206–7
  and Neoisolation, 107–8
  as reducing probability of war, 67
  and US-China relations, 163
transporter-erectorlaunchers (TELs), 241, 242–43
Trident-II missiles, 240–41
Troan, Magnus Langset, 157n67
Trump, Donald

and decoupling, 104
impact of hostility toward US allies, 48n38, 66, 264, 316
implications for US retrenchment, 10–11
imposes high tariffs against China, 185n185
and need for reevaluation of US policy toward China, 3
and Neoisolation, 103n6
US-China economic interdependence under, 71
US-China relations under, 163
and US credibility, 168, 171, 182n127, 264
Tsai Ing-wen, 158
Tucker, Nancy, 167, 169

Ukraine, 298
United Nations Convention on the Law of the Sea (UNCLOS), 22, 185–86, 187–88, 203, 204, 211–15, 222–23
United States
analysis of accommodation of China, 142–43
China as threat to, 62–63
competition between China and, 133–34
deterrence of nuclear attack against homeland as damage-limitation capability benefit, 259–60
economic interdependence with China, 69–72
key national security policy questions facing, 11–15
military spending of, 129
national identity of, 77
need for policy reevaluation toward China, 2–11
See also conventional strategy; grand strategy / strategies; nuclear strategy
unit-level / state-level theories, 17–18, 74–76, 96–97, 313
and nationalism and national identity, 76–82
and regime type, 90–96
and status and prestige, 82–90
US Navy, 209
USS *Impeccable*, 191, 193

Vietnam, 192

Wachman, Alan, 87
Walt, Stephen, 121
Waltz, Kenneth, 35
Wang Jisi, 163
Wang Yi, 201
war

avoidance of, as benefit of ending US commitment to Taiwan, 151–62
Deep Engagement and major-power, 112–13, 114, 115–16
and democratic peace theory, 91
economic interdependence as reducing probability of, 34
Neoisolation and major-power, 107
Neoisolation and probability of, in Northeast Asia, 109–10
probability of, over Taiwan, 7, 20, 134, 140–41, 151–52, 174
reduced costs of nuclear, as damage-limitation capability benefit, 257–67
security dilemma and increased probability of, 9
trade as reducing probability of, 67
and US-China economic interdependence, 71–72
See also long war; preventive war
Washington Declaration (2023), 266
Weiss, Jessica Chen, 56n59, 61
White, Hugh, 179–80
Wohlforth, William, 114
Woody Island, 207
World Trade Organization (WTO), 127
World War II, China's national identity and evolving understanding of, 81

X-band radars, 254
Xi Jinping
call for new Asian security concept, 81
and China's regime type, 75–76, 96, 97
and China's status, 85–86
ideological turn under, 94
on national security, 88–89
"new model of great power relations," 88n61
on 1992 Consensus, 158
and South China Sea and Chinese national identity, 199
and urgency regarding unification of Taiwan, 13, 50, 139, 144, 152, 181, 228, 264
willingness to use force regarding unification of Taiwan, 152
Xu, Lucy, 88n61
Xu Hui, 163

Yang Jiechi, 201
Yan Xuetong, 85
Yong Den, 84n43
Yoshihara, Toshi, 157

Zheng Wang, 84–85
Zhou Enlai, 199

www.ingramcontent.com/pod-product-compliance
Lightning Source LLC
Chambersburg PA
CBHW020637230426
43665CB00008B/208